RHODE ISLAND

RHODE ISLAND

THE OCEAN STATE

An Illustrated History
George H. Kellner & J. Stanley Lemons

American Historical Press • Sun Valley, California

To Ellen, Nancy, and Linda

PAGE TWO: Upon dispatching the General Washington *in 1787, John Brown became the first Rhode Islander to enter the China trade. Pictured here is the second of his ships named after the first president of the United States, the* George Washington. *Brown's commitment to the national government was symbolized by his naming some of his ships after its leaders, such as the* President Washington *and the* John Jay. *Courtesy, RIHS (RHi x3 3085)*

Photos attributed to Religious Society of Bell Street Chapel
Courtesy, Bell Street Chapel
Page 58 A, RIHS (RHi x3 249)
Page 58 B, RIHS (RHi x3 2596)

Library of Congress Catalogue Card Number: 2004105458

ISBN: 1-892724-40-5

Bibliography: page 266
Includes Index

CONTENTS

PREFACE

Over 20 years have passed since the first edition of this history of Rhode Island was written, and so much has happened that it seems like many more years. We changed the subtitle of the book as we rethought our conception of the state's history. Back then, both of us, being transplants from the Midwest, were overly impressed by the independent, otherwise-mindedness of Rhode Islanders, so we opted to call the book *Rhode Island: The Independent State.* The original title page included a picture of the statue of "The Independent Man" which stands atop the State House. But, later we concluded that the validity of calling Rhode Island the "independent state" really ended in the 1790s. Rhode Islanders are still independent-minded, but from the 1790s to the present, the future and welfare of the state became increasingly dependent upon the rest of the United States. This dependence accelerated in the 20th century as a result of the governmental programs that poured money into the state. One need only think of the vast outpouring of money that built the interstate highways; supported the military presence and defense contracts; and paid Social Security pensions, research grants, and veterans' benefits. The rebuilding of Providence into the "Renaissance City" was done in large part (nearly 85 percent) with federal money. So, instead of "the independent state," we have turned to one element that has been present through Rhode Island's whole history: the ocean. The "Ocean State" is on the license plates, on buildings and in the names of organizations and on a new quarter.

While Native Americans had lived along the Narragansett Bay area for some thousands of years before European explorers and settlers arrived, we began our history with the coming of Roger Williams in 1636. He founded "Providence Plantations," and the followers of Anne Hutchinson, settling on Aquidneck Island in 1638, established what was named "Rhode Island." So, today's "Rhode Island and Providence Plantations" had its beginnings with those settlements of religious dissenters who created a place where true religious freedom was the rule. If Rhode Island had no other claim to primacy, being the birthplace of American religious liberty would be enough. However, it has other claims to fame and infamy.

Since we know how the story came out, it is easy to think that the survival and success of Rhode Island in its early years was inevitable. Actually, it is almost a miracle that Rhode Island survived to 1700. It, like Plymouth Plantations, could have been swallowed up. In fact, Rhode Island was extinguished as a separate colony during the period of the Dominion of New England. A constant factor in Rhode Island's history for the first century was the relentless efforts of the neighboring colonies to take over. That was

(continued on page 9)

The 1936 Tercentenary celebration was one of many such events held annually in historically conscious Rhode Island. Courtesy, Rhode Island Historical Society (RHi x5 44)

followed by growing pressure from the imperial government to rein in and control the colony, leading to Rhode Island's early participation in the movement for independence. While Rhode Island was not the first to declare independence (contrary to the "official history" of the state), it was quick to join and to provide soldiers and the Continental Navy's first ship. Later, when the American Civil War broke out, the First Rhode Island Regiment was the first fully-equipped Union regiment to arrive to defend Washington, D.C. In fact, Rhode Islanders have readily answered the call to military service in all of the wars.

While American participation in the African slave trade was minute when compared to Portugal, England and France, Rhode Islanders were the overwhelming leaders in the American part of that "iniquitous traffic." On the other hand, the graceful furniture made by the Townsend and Goddard families in Newport was arguably the finest created in colonial America. The American Industrial Revolution began in Pawtucket, and the growth of industry caused Rhode Island to become America's first urban, industrial and ethnic state. It would be the first state to have a majority Roman Catholic population. "Little Rhody" may have been a small place, but it was an industrial giant in the 19th century. It was also the "playground of New England" as its shores were lined with resorts, camps and amusement parks.

The surprising and shocking thing was that the state then experienced sharp "deindustrialization" in the 20th century.

With the decline of smokestack industries, the state saw a resurgence of concern about the physical environment, especially Narragansett Bay and the ocean. In addition to trying to build the new economy of high-tech, bio-tech and industrial technology, the arts, education and tourism have now become critical ingredients to a successful economy in the Ocean State.

We still recall the great support we received in creating the 1982 edition of this book, and we have added new debts to many people in creating a 2004 edition. Elizabeth Fitzgerald, Rhode Island Collections Librarian at the Providence Public Library, was an early and enthusiastic supporter of the idea of an updated version of Rhode Island's history. Scott MacKay, of the *Providence Journal*, was an excellent source of information, both from his reporting and from his willingness to extract additional details from the *Journal*'s archives for us. Various individuals have been helpful in locating visual materials including Robert Foley, preservation coordinator for the Newport Restoration Foundation; Mark Malkovich, IV, marketing director of the Newport Music Festival; Dan Aurelio, a photography enthusiast; and Peter Goldberg. We are grateful for the help and support of the staff of the American Historical Press for wanting to bring out a new edition of this history and producing the book.

George Kellner and J. Stanley Lemons

A shipping label decorated with the trademark for Hope Muslin, produced by the Lonsdale Company of the Blackstone Manufacturing Company, dates from the late 19th century. RIHS (RHi x5 33/William C. Gucfa photo)

Chapter One

THE HERETIC COLONY

THROUGH MOST OF THE colonial era Rhode Island* was condemned by many. A Dutch Reformed minister declared that it was "the receptacle of all sorts of riff-raff people, and is nothing else than the sewer of New England." A Congregational minister wrote that the colony was "a hive of hornets, and the sink into which all the rest of the colonies empty their heretics." Plymouth colony complained that Rhode Island was an "asylum to evildoers" and existed as an affront to all who tried to live an orderly life. In 1668 the Town of Stonington declared in a petition to the Connecticut General Assembly, "Our condition is truly deplorable to have persons of such corrupt principles and practices to live near us." Some denounced Rhode Island as "Rogues' Island."

Beginning as an unpromising collection of outcasts, malcontents, squatters, and dissenters, followed by a century and a half of internal dissension and external hostility, Rhode Island emerged as a special place. In a world of religious orthodoxy, conformity, and intolerance, it began and developed as an oasis of religious liberty. As a tiny and almost forgotten parcel of the British Empire, it governed itself with greater independence than any other North American colony. Its diminutive size, unfriendly neighbors, unique religious climate, and tradition of self-governance produced a people that were unusually sensitive to power and adept at securing an advantage. But in the beginning its founders were stiff-necked individualists, runaways, and exiled

Anne Hutchinson (1591-1643) was tried by the magistrates for "traducing the ministers" of Massachusetts. Convicted of this and heresy, she was banished to Rhode Island. From Scribner's Popular History of the United States, 1897. Courtesy, Pawtucket Public Library

heretics from religious and political authority, who agreed on little more than religious liberty for everyone.

By the late 1620s, the religious establishment in England had squelched most dissenters, and the Puritans resolved to create a society in the New World where they could set up a purified church and godly government. A thousand Puritans sailed to Massachusetts Bay in 1630 to found a colony. Roger Williams and his wife, Mary Barnard, arrived on the *Lyon* in February 1631. Boston welcomed the young man, as he was well known to the leading Puritans as a good preacher and devout Puritan. Invited to become the second minister in the Boston church, Williams confounded the Puritans by rejecting the offer because the church had not separated itself from the Church of England. As the purpose of the Massachusetts experiment was to create a purified Church of England, the Boston leaders found Williams to be unreasonable.

One problem that any highly charged movement faces when it comes to power is how to balance the drive of its zealous members with the need to govern ordinary people. Williams was one of several settlers who sought to maintain a higher, purer standard. He was the Puritan of Puritans and became the ultimate sectarian in his effort to cleanse the worship of God of all

*To avoid confusion, the name Rhode Island is used for the whole colony or state, while the original "Rhode Island" will be called by its prior and present designation "Aquidneck."

worldly corruptions. He believed that the compromises that the leaders of the Bay Colony had made in establishing a government actually polluted the worship of God. For him, logic led to separation of church and state in order to safeguard the purity of worship. Such a principle, however, would destroy the Holy Commonwealth that the Puritans were trying to build in Massachusetts.

Williams went first to Salem and then to Plymouth Colony, where he became assistant minister and supported himself through farming and trading with Indians. A born linguist, fluent in many languages, he quickly learned several Indian tongues and developed permanent friendships with Massasoit, sachem of the Wampanoags, and Canonicus, grand sachem of the Narragansetts, who came to view Williams almost as a son. These relationships were remarkable because the Wampanoags and Narragansetts were enemies, but Williams traveled freely around Narragansett Bay. Eventually finding the Plymouth church to be insufficiently separated from the Church of England, Williams returned to Salem and became the minister there in August 1634. His sweet, winning disposition swayed the congregation to his unorthodox ideas. He preached "Soul Liberty" which denied the right of town authorities to punish breaches of religious discipline, force religious beliefs, or compel church attendance. He condemned civil

interference in the church, saying it would render "the garden and spouse of Christ a filthy dunghill and whorehouse of rotten and stinking whores and hypocrites." Even worse in the magistrates' view was Williams' impugning the Christian character of the King and his charge that the King's charter was invalid in granting their land. As the charter was then under attack in England by the colony's enemies, they feared that news of Williams' unorthodoxy would be used to void it.

The magistrates remonstrated with Williams, browbeat his congregation into withdrawing support, and finally ordered him banished on October 9, 1635. Williams could remain until the following spring provided that he cease preaching seditious doctrines. But he would not be silenced; and learning that the order was to be carried out, he fled Salem in January 1636 to the camp of Massasoit at Sowams (present-day Warren, Rhode Island). There he spent the winter in the company of a few followers who had joined him. In April Williams led his little band to the bank of the Great Salt Cove and began the first of Rhode Island's four original towns. He wrote, "I, having made covenants of peaceable neighborhood with all the sachems and natives round about us, and having a sense of God's merciful providence unto me in my distress, called the place Providence; I desired it be for a shelter for persons distressed of conscience." Unfortunately, such was not the purpose of most of Williams' companions. Above all, they wanted land.

The settling of Providence is a fascinating study in the clash between the hopes of a God-intoxicated young man with no political or administrative experience and the individualism and land hunger of his "loving neighbors." Williams was only about 33 and had no plans to establish a colony. He was full of an uncompromising idealism that was untested by the reality of governance. He wanted to dwell in peace and harmony with the Indians, but lived to see Providence burned to the ground by them. He sought to create a place "for such as were destitute, especially for Conscience sake," but some took this to mean the end of all government or the right to grab as

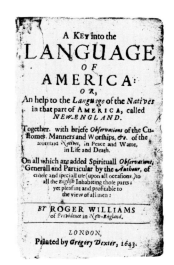

ABOVE: A Key into the Language of America *by Roger Williams was published in London in 1643 while Williams sought a charter for his colony. The printer, Gregory Dexter, returned with Williams and later became the pastor of the Baptist church. From the Imprint Collection, RIHS (RHi x3 774)*

LEFT: Though no actual likeness of Roger Williams (1603-1683) exists, C. Dodge in 1936 drew this study from the bust of Williams by McNeil in the Hall of Fame. Courtesy, First Baptist Church in America

much land as possible. He believed that "selfless benevolence" should prevail between neighbors, but he found bickering, litigation, and even brawling in the streets. He welcomed refugees from Massachusetts and made them coproprietors of the land that his Narragansett friends, Canonicus and Miantonomi, had given him, but some of these men betrayed him by summoning the authority of the Bay Colony. The resulting tangled land claims, lawsuits, and dissension jeopardized the independence of Providence Plantations.

Living as squatters beyond the jurisdiction of any colony, the settlers drew up a formal covenant in August 1637. The 13 who signed agreed to obey majority decisions of the heads of households "and all others whom they shall admit unto them only in civil things." This meant that religion was to be free of governmental interference. By 1638 enough of Williams' followers from Salem had joined him that they organized a church. Anne Hutchinson's sister, Catherine Scott, convinced Williams that only converted adults should be baptized; so when the church was gathered in late 1638, it rejected infant baptism and adopted baptism by total immersion. Having founded the first Baptist Church in America, Williams soon doubted this organization and resigned to become an unaffiliated preacher for the rest of his life. Only about a dozen of the 60 householders joined the only church in town, highlighting the individualism and religious anarchy that characterized the settlement.

"Rhode Island was purchased by love." This expressed Williams' relationship with the Indians, and no dispute ever arose between him and the Narragansetts who freely gave him land. But he had many problems with his fellow settlers. Chief among the land hungry was William Harris, whom one historian has described as "without doubt one of the most litigious of the early New England colonists." Harris had come destitute and Williams admitted him "out of Pity." Yet Harris eventually attempted to steal 300,000 acres from the Narragansetts by arguing that the original land grants, which were intended to be a few square miles, extended far inland.

When challenged by Williams, Harris began lawsuits which dragged on beyond his death in 1681. In the struggle with Connecticut over possession of the southern half of Rhode Island, Harris acted as Connecticut's agent. Likewise, William Arnold and other coproprietors demanded more land and received a special concession below the Pawtuxet River. When this group fell into dispute with their neighbors, they submitted themselves to the jurisdiction of Massachusetts, giving the Bay Colony grounds for asserting control over part of Providence Plantation. From 1642 to 1658 the Arnold group regarded itself as part of Massachusetts, and Arnold registered his land deeds there.

Arnold was wise because Williams' Indian purchases were invalid in English courts. The Crown and the other colonies

John Hutchins Cady drew this map in 1936 showing the 1636-1659 boundaries of Rhode Island. RIHS (RHi x3 855)

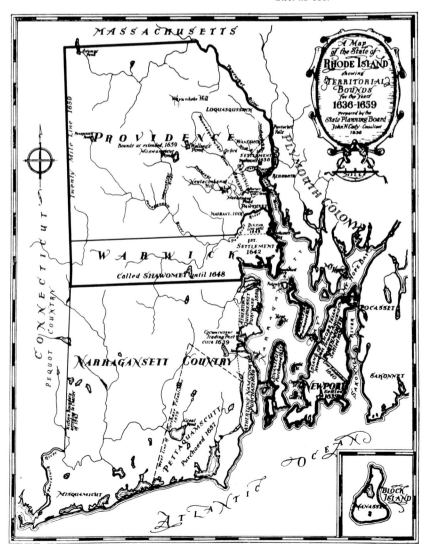

recognized land as being conveyed by royal charter, and buying land from the Indians without a charter's sanction was not valid. As Plymouth, Massachusetts, and Connecticut extended their claims over the Narragansett Bay, the Rhode Island towns were hard pressed to prevent them. In August 1642 the Massachusetts court summoned Miantonomi, sachem of the Narragansetts, to Boston to deny his sale of land to Roger Williams, to submit himself and his land to Massachusetts Bay jurisdiction, or to show what right he had to his lands! Miantonomi was deeply offended, as he considered his authority to be equal to any colonial government; and he rejected all demands. The court responded by forbidding him to sell land without its permission and ordered the Narragansetts to be disarmed. In the summer of 1643 war erupted between the Narragansetts and the Mohegans of Connecticut. When Miantonomi was treacherously murdered by the Mohegans with Puritan complicity, Rhode Island lost an important ally.

Williams had not meant to begin a colony, but his activities opened a door to a stream of refugees. He welcomed Anne Hutchinson and the Antinomians, who established Rhode Island's second town, Portsmouth. This group represented a far more serious threat to Massachusetts than Williams, and they became the strongest part of the heretic colony on Narragansett Bay. Williams had only a handful of followers in the outlying town of Salem;

the Antinomians constituted a large group in Boston. Antinomians were opposed to being ruled by other men, believing that God was the one true Ruler. The name, Antinomian, means "against the law." They were not truly anarchists, but they represented another of those purist challenges to Massachusetts Bay. The Puritans tried to balance the demands of external behavior and internal piety. The ministers and magistrates emphasized obedience to the laws of the church and state as a way of creating a well-ordered, well-regulated society ruled by visible saints. The tendency always existed for this to lead to empty form and ritual. Anne Hutchinson thought she detected such a tendency in Massachusetts; and she charged the ministers with preaching a "covenant of works," which emphasized right behavior. She preached a "covenant of grace" which

FACING PAGE: Roger Williams had exceptionally good relations with the Indians, and his Narragansett friends, Canonicus and Miantonomi, granted him the land for Providence Plantations. From Providence: The Southern Gateway to New England, Commemorating the 150th Anniversary of the Independence of the State of R.I., 1926. Courtesy, Providence Public Library

LEFT: The Narragansett sachem Miantonomi was captured by the Mohegans in 1643. He was later murdered by them with the approval of Puritan authorities. Engraved by F.O.C. Darley from History of the Indians of Connecticut by John W. DeForest. RIHS (RHi x3 634)

stressed the individual's direct apprehension of God's love and forgiveness. In fact, she was a mystic who believed that she received revelations directly from God. She preached a higher purity and declared that only two of the colony's ministers were truly saved. Her individualistic theology had particular appeal to certain leading Boston merchants, who felt confined by the corporate, communal nature of the colony. It also gave a sense of assurance to people who found no comfort in the stress upon pious behavior and practices.

William and Anne Hutchinson arrived in Boston in September 1634; and as Hutchinson was a successful merchant, the couple entered the highest levels of society. They built their house near the homes of Governor John Winthrop and William Coddington, the richest man in New England. An experienced nurse and midwife,

Anne's charisma won many friends among the women of Boston. She began holding meetings in her home with several women to discuss the ministers' sermons, but soon attracted so many men and women that she held two lecture days. As her ideas became known, her opponents called her an Antinomian.

In 1636 the Antinomians elected one of their group, Harry Vane, governor, defeating Winthrop. The church and town divided into factions. When the Antinomians refused to join the military expedition against the Pequot Indians in 1637 because the chaplain was not one of their men, the religious division took a dangerous turn. In May 1637 the towns outside Boston rallied to reelect Winthrop, and by November his forces had complete control and disarmed and disenfranchised the Antinomians. Defeated and facing exile,

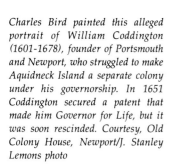

Charles Bird painted this alleged portrait of William Coddington (1601-1678), founder of Portsmouth and Newport, who struggled to make Aquidneck Island a separate colony under his governorship. In 1651 Coddington secured a patent that made him Governor for Life, but it was soon rescinded. Courtesy, Old Colony House, Newport/J. Stanley Lemons photo

William Coddington and other Antinomian leaders searched for another settlement. One of them, John Clarke, learned from Roger Williams that Aquidneck Island was available; and Williams arranged to buy the island from Canonicus and Miantonomi. The following spring the exiles began a town called Pocasset (later renamed Portsmouth). Anne Hutchinson joined them in 1638 after trials which banished and excommunicated her from Massachusetts. She was part of the turbulent history of Pocasset until her husband died, and she removed to Long Island in 1643. The next year she was massacred by Indians, an event which Puritan Massachusetts regarded as God's just punishment.

The leading figure at Pocasset was Coddington. He was by far the most important and powerful of the exiles from Massachusetts. He had been one of the original Assistants to Governor Winthrop in 1630 and later became treasurer. Winthrop sought to dissuade him from leaving when the Antinomian party collapsed. Nevertheless, Coddington took the lead in locating a new settlement and in organizing the exodus to Aquidneck. Since the wealthy exile supplied most of the purchase price, Roger Williams put the deed in his name.

Ironically, Coddington had been one of the judges who banished Williams from Massachusetts and would subsequently be a major obstacle to Williams' efforts to unify the Narragansett Bay towns. Coddington eventually connived with Plymouth, Massachusetts Bay, Connecticut, and the Dutch on Long Island to gain recognition of his separate and supreme authority on Aquidneck Island.

Exasperated by the machinations of Coddington, Williams wrote that he was "a worldly man, a selfish man, nothing for public, but all for himself and private." Coddington was actually a public-spirited man who devoted nearly 50 years to governance. However, he was deeply conservative and believed that deference was due him as a consequence of his wealth and social station. When the Antinomians signed a compact creating a government for their settlement, Coddington was elected "Judge." He expected to rule in Old Testament style over a Bible Commonwealth, but was thwarted and frustrated by the individualism and democratic tendencies prevailing in Rhode Island. He neither attained the order he wanted nor was he accorded the deference he expected. While he had the support of most of the "better sort," he was rebuffed by the ordinary people led by the Hutchinsons. When the chronic troublemaker, Samuel Gorton, appeared on the scene, Coddington lost control entirely and withdrew with some supporters to the southern end of Aquidneck. There in April 1639, he founded Rhode Island's third town, Newport. Those remaining at Pocasset adopted a new compact which restricted the magistrates to "civil things," required jury trials, and forbade a religious test for office. Finally they changed the town name to Portsmouth. However, by November, Coddington forced Portsmouth into a common government for Aquidneck by controlling the land titles.

The fourth of the original towns resulted from the gyrations of that cantankerous character, Samuel Gorton. He was so unorthodox and aggressive that he was driven successively from Boston, Plymouth, Portsmouth, and Providence before founding his own town at

Shawomet (soon to be renamed Warwick). Arriving in Boston in March 1637, he departed for Plymouth within two months, but the authorities there expelled him in December 1638. His bickering with Coddington's Aquidneck government led to his banishment after a public whipping in March 1641. Next he vexed Providence and Roger Williams, who wrote, "Master Gorton, having foully abused high and low at

The presence of the Gortonites and the argument with Roger Williams over the interpretation of the Indian deeds led the Arnolds, Harris, and others to appeal in September 1642 to Massachusetts for redress. Gorton thought it best to remove himself, so in October 1642 he purchased land (Shawomet) to the south from Miantonomi. But this came after Massachusetts had arbitrarily forbidden Miantonomi to

In the fall of 1643 Massachusetts dispatched soldiers to Shawomet (Warwick) to arrest Samuel Gorton. The Gortonites held off the soldiers for two days before surrendering and being marched away in chains to Massachusetts for trial. Engraving from Scribner's Popular History of the United States, *1897. Courtesy, Pawtucket Public Library*

Aquidneck, is now bewitching and bemaddening poor Providence both with his unclean and foul censures of all the ministers of this country ... and also denying all visible and external ordinances." Denied admission as freemen (voters) in Providence, Gorton and his followers purchased land but soon became embroiled with the Arnolds and William Harris over its possession.

sell his land. The Arnolds also wanted Shawomet, so they appealed to Massachusetts, which issued a summons to Gorton for trespassing on Massachusetts territory. Gorton ignored the summons. In October 1643 soldiers arrested him and took the Gortonites to Boston for trial. Gorton was sentenced to six months at hard labor in chains. When released and forbidden to return to Shawomet, he sailed to London and there, with the aid of the Earl of Warwick, secured a charter in 1646. The Gortonites returned, renamed the town in honor of their patron, created a government, and in May 1647 joined the other three towns as part of the "Province of Providence Plantations."

Roger Williams had labored seven years

to establish a community where no one could be persecuted for his religious beliefs, and he had built solid ties of trust with his Indian neighbors. But all was threatened by his greedy fellow settlers and by the formation of the United Colonies, a military alliance of the Puritan colonies of New Haven, Hartford, Plymouth, and Massachusetts (noticeably excluding the heretic towns on Narragansett Bay). Since the Puritans frequently asserted that the Rhode Islanders had no authority for civil government, Williams took a ship to England in June 1643 to secure a patent. He returned triumphantly to Providence in September 1644 with a patent establishing the "Province of Providence Plantations in Narragansett in New England." Undeterred, neighboring colonies continued their efforts to take the territory, basing their actions on treaties with Indians, submissions from both settlers and Indians in the area, fraudulent land claims and mortgages, arbitrary expansion of existing charter grants, and eventually by right of conquest in King Philip's War in 1675-1676.

William Coddington did not welcome the Charter of 1644 on Aquidneck Island. Portsmouth and Newport debated for two years as to whether to join Providence in a government under the Charter. When Plymouth suddenly asserted that Aquidneck Island belonged to it and threatened the inhabitants if they recognized Williams' Charter, Portsmouth broke with Coddington's Aquidneck government and cast its lot with Providence. Coddington was deeply opposed to federation and sought recognition from Plymouth or Massachusetts for a separate government on the island. Having been thwarted in America, Coddington sailed to England, secured his own patent, and returned in the summer of 1651 as Governor for Life over Aquidneck and Conanicut islands with virtual dictatorial authority.

The mainland towns rejected Coddington's patent and dispatched Roger Williams to England to confirm the Charter of 1644, and the freemen of Aquidneck sent John Clarke to seek revocation of Coddington's grant. Coddington, unable to govern, had to flee to Boston for safety. The

British Council of State rescinded Coddington's commission in 1652; however, the four towns did not reunite in a single government until 1654. Williams returned to be President for 1654-1657, while John Clarke remained in England as the colony's agent. At last Coddington ended his efforts to rule a separate colony and returned to Newport in 1656, apologized, was for-

Charles II, King of England from 1660-1685, granted the Charter of 1663, which created the English Colony of Rhode Island and Providence Plantations. His motives for permitting such independence and freedom of worship are not clear. RIHS (RHi x3 4247)

Depicted in this 1834 wood engraving is Metacomet, called King Philip, sachem of the Wampanaog Indians. He led the rising of his people against Plymouth Colony. The war spread to become the worst Indian war in New England history, 1675-1676. RIHS (RHi x3 771)

given, and served in various offices, including governor under the Charter of 1663, until he died in 1678.

The confirmation of the Charter of 1644 and the submission of Coddington to the unified government of Providence Plantations did not end the travail of the heretic colony. Its neighbors still behaved as though the Charter were invalid; and the

restoration of the monarchy in England in 1660, ending the Cromwellian Commonwealth, caused Rhode Islanders to question the Charter's legality. Charles II nullified all actions of Cromwell's government, making the validity of the Charter of 1644 doubtful. Just as Roger Williams had turned his personal acquaintance with Oliver Cromwell and Robert Rich, Earl of Warwick, into the Charter of 1644, so John Clarke found an advantage for Rhode Island in the new political situation in England in the 1660s. He secured a new charter in 1663 for "The English Colony of Rhode Island and Providence Plantations in New England in America."

The Charter of 1663 was amazing. It gave Rhode Island the freedom "to hold forth a lively experiment, that a flourishing and civil state may stand, yea and best be maintained ... with a full liberty in religious commitments." No person was to be "molested, punished, disquieted, or called into question, for any differences in opinion in matters of religion ... ." Rhode Island could elect its own governor and assembly and control its own military affairs. Essential power remained in the town meetings, which elected the General Assembly members and reviewed Assembly actions. This was a grant of freedom beyond that of any other colony and permitted it to become virtually self-governing.

No one knows why Charles II granted such a liberal charter as he was no advocate of dissenters and heretics. Perhaps he took some delight in twitting the noses of the neighboring Puritan colonies which grudgingly recognized his accession and which continued to harbor some of the regicide judges who had condemned his father in 1649. On the other hand, Rhode Island had been the first New England colony to proclaim its allegiance to the new monarch.

Unfortunately, the Charter did not end the United Colonies' efforts to seize most of Rhode Island. Their intrusions accelerated a land rush that had gathered momentum in the 1650s and pushed toward the catastrophe of the last great Indian war in southern New England, King Philip's War. Some Rhode Islanders joined the rush and

Benjamin Church (1639-1718) adopted Indian-style tactics to defeat Metacomet's warriors in King Philip's War. This questionable likeness was engraved by Paul Revere to accompany the publication of Church's account of King Philip's War. RIHS (RHi x3 559)

in 1657 bought claims to the Petta-quamscutt Purchase south of Wickford and by 1660 to the Misquamicut tract in the Westerly area. These acquisitions established a Rhode Island presence in territory that Connecticut and Massachusetts maintained was theirs by right of treaty, charter, and conquest.

The most notorious and fraudulent land grab was perpetrated by the Narragansett Proprietors, a group of businessmen and officials from Boston, Plymouth, and Connecticut. Ignoring Rhode Island laws against unauthorized purchases of Indian lands, they began buying land from the Indians in 1658. In 1660 the Narragansett Indians declared war against the Mohegans, but the United Colonies intervened and imposed a humiliating treaty and levied an impossible fine on the Narragansetts. The Indians were allowed four months to raise 2,000 fathoms of wampum on condition that they mortgage their lands to the New England Confederation as surety. The Confederation exchanged the mortgage for the fine with the Narragansett Proprietors. When the Indians failed to meet the payments, the Proprietors foreclosed in 1662 and claimed ownership of all Narragansett lands. The Proprietors felt secure because Connecticut's new charter of 1662 placed the eastern boundary of Connecticut on Narragansett Bay. On the other hand, Rhode Island's Charter of 1663 defined its western border as the Pawcatuck River. The conflicting charter claims of both colonies to all of southern Rhode Island went unsettled for 60 years as both sides tried to assert control, even to the point of absurdity. In one instance a homicide occurred and Connecticut officers arrived first, examined the corpse, and buried it without letting the Rhode Island representatives see it. After the Connecticut officers left, the Rhode Islanders dug up the body and conducted their own investigation. Some of Connecticut's strongest claims, however, grew out of King Philip's War on the grounds that it had conquered the Narragansett Indians.

King Philip's War brought to a bloody climax more than 50 years of English-Indian relations in New England and eliminated the Indians as a major factor in southern New England. One cannot read of the encroachment of the settlers upon the native population, the whittling away of their lands, dignity, and independence without a sense of sorrow; but it is difficult to see how it could have turned out differently. The Indians did not understand until too late that the straggling white settlements were the vanguard of a dynamic, expanding civilization. The settlers saw the natives as heathens and the land vacant for the taking. For their part, the Native Americans were not pawns of the settlers; and they had their own reasons for cooperation or hostility.

The English-Indian confrontation was, in reality, an English-Indian-Indian struggle. Each tribe used the settlers to gain an advantage over old adversaries, and the colonists seized this division to advance their interests. Massasoit made a treaty of mutual assistance with the Pilgrims at Plymouth because the Wampanoags wanted help against their traditional and more powerful foes, the Narragansetts. Historians have suggested that the Narragansetts welcomed Roger Williams in Providence and the Antinomians on Aquidneck to create a buffer zone between them and their enemies, the Wampanoags and Plymouth to the east. Canonicus and Miantonomi could then give more attention to the threat posed by the Pequots to the west. In the struggle to control trade with the Dutch and English, the Pequots had reduced most southern Connecticut tribes to tributaries. Their enemies accused the Pequots of cruelty and cannibalism, and they had defeated the Narragansetts in a fierce battle near Westerly in 1632. For their part, the English feared an Indian uprising. In 1622 supposedly friendly Indians suddenly massacred 347 colonists at Jamestown, Virginia; consequently the Virginia Company lost its charter and the Crown took over. Fear of such a massacre and the loss of their precious charters haunted the New England colonists throughout the 17th century. No weakness could be shown the natives; the colonists used force repeatedly to secure submission.

The Pequots sought to stop the advance of the English into Connecticut in 1637 and appealed to the Narragansetts to join them. They warned that if the English prevailed the Narragansetts would soon be subjugated. Massachusetts authorities now begged Roger Williams, banished under pain of death one year earlier, to prevent the alliance. He succeeded in this mission; and in the ensuing war the Narragansetts sided with the Bay Colony. The Pequots were defeated and most of the survivors sold either to the West Indies or given as slaves to the Narragansetts, Mohegans, and Niantics. Ironically, Massachusetts then used the victory to claim Rhode Island lands and moved to reduce Miantonomi to subordination.

When the Pilgrims arrived in 1620, the Wampanoag country extended from Narragansett Bay to Cape Cod, but by the time Massasoit died in 1661, the Indian lands had been reduced to Mount Hope Neck, Tiverton, and Sakonnet. The Puritans assumed after the Pequot War that Indians had to obey their laws. Violations were tried in Puritan courts, and the Indians often had to sell their lands to pay the fines. One of the principal grievances stated by Massasoit's son, Metacomet, was that the English "undertake to give law to the Indians and take from them their country." He declared at last, "I am determined not to live until I have no country." He would lose both his land and his life.

Massasoit, friend of Plymouth and Roger Williams, had kept the peace during the 40 years before his death; but his sons, Wamsutta and Metacomet (dubbed Alexander and Philip) burned with accumulated hatred and grievances that Wampanoags felt toward Plymouth. King Philip's War began in June 1675 in Swansea, spread to engulf most of New England, and 15 months later wound down to the Mount Hope Neck again. Plymouth failed to pin Philip at Mount Hope or in the Tiverton area, and he escaped to central Massachusetts where he gained the support of other tribes. The Narragansetts harbored Wampanoag refugees, giving the United Colonies an excuse to make a preemptive assault on the Narragansett stronghold. A 1,000-man army under Plymouth Governor Josiah Winslow invaded Rhode Island, and with the help of a traitor from within the tribe made a surprise attack upon the Narragansetts in the Great Swamp on December 19, 1675. Casualties were heavy on both sides, and many Indians died when fires destroyed their dwellings. After the battered colonial army withdrew, the Indians swept the mainland clean of settlers in the following months. All but 28 men fled from Providence; and on March 29, 1676, the Indians, despite entreaties from Roger Williams, burned the town, including Williams' house.

The Indian victories were temporary. Metacomet sought support as far west as New York, but the Mohawks drove him out and launched devastating attacks upon other Indians in western New England. One historian has said that the Mohawk attack "was the blow that lost the war for Philip." In the final phase, Philip and his remnant flitted through the woods and swamps near the place where it all began; and they were hunted by a force that included many Wampanoags commanded by Colonel Benjamin Church. At last in August 1676, one of Church's Wampanoags killed Philip.

The war broke Indian power in southern New England, and the tribes declined into dependency or disappeared entirely. The remnants of the once-powerful Narragansetts merged with the Niantics of southern Rhode Island, lost nearly all their land, and eventually settled on a small reservation in Charlestown. The destruction of the Narragansetts eliminated the only ally Rhode Island had had in its struggles with its neighbors, and Connecticut reasserted its claims to much of Rhode Island by right of conquest. During the war, Aquidneck became almost all that remained of the colony because by April 1676 not a single white family remained between Providence and Point Judith. Most of the population fled to the islands, as suggested by the Quaker-dominated General Assembly, which had refused to provide any military defense for the mainland towns. At war's end, people began drifting back, rebuilding, and staking out new claims in the interior. While Providence was rebuilding, Newport entered its period of dominance in the colony.

Chapter Two

THE ENGLISH COLONY OF RHODE ISLAND

WHAT WAS THE pivotal event in Rhode Island's struggle for survival in the 17th century? Some choose Roger Williams' patent of 1644, others pick John Clarke's Charter of 1663, and others single out King Philip's War of 1675-1676. One historian maintains that it was the first arrival of the Quakers in 1657. They assured the economic survival of Rhode Island by creating a commercial network within the British Empire which reduced Rhode Island's dependence upon its covetous neighbors. The Quaker majority on Aquidneck and their commerce helped Newport become the dominant town in the colony. However, these advances were made in the face of continuing threats to the independence of Rhode Island and even its temporary disappearance as a separate colony.

Other colonies thought that it was bad enough that Rhode Island had Baptists, Antinomians, Gortonites, Seekers, and other exotic religious groups, but admitting the Quakers was going too far. In 1656 Massachusetts treated roughly and then expelled the few Quakers who surfaced there. In 1658 the colony enacted a law that condemned to the gallows any Quaker who returned a third time after being banished twice. Under this harsh statute four Quakers were hanged in 1659 and 1660. Connecticut and Plymouth also enacted anti-Quaker laws; and the Commissioners of the United Colonies requested that Rhode Island banish its Quakers, threatening reprisals otherwise. The governor replied that there was no law

by which "men could be punished in Rhode Island for their opinions, and that the Quakers being unmolested, were becoming disgusted at their want of success." In fact, many leading Rhode Islanders, including William Coddington, John Coggeshall, Nicholas Easton, and William Harris, became Quakers in the 1660s. By 1690 Quakers were nearly half the people of the colony, and they dominated the government for years.

As neighboring colonies applied economic pressure, Rhode Island became more independent of them because the Quaker network provided connections in the British West Indies, Pennsylvania, Ireland, and England. Although the Quakers were a small minority in Britain's American possessions, they were dispersed more uniformly throughout the colonies than any other religious group. Fundamental to commercial success in the colonial era was a network of sound and trustworthy associates. What ties of family and friendship provided for some, religion supplied for others. Both the Quakers and later the Jews of Newport relied upon coreligionists to conduct their business in distant ports.

Aquidneck Island had developed a successful agricultural economy within a half-dozen years of its founding. Some pioneer families, such as the Coddingtons, Coggeshalls, Brentons, and Hutchinsons, were fairly wealthy; and moving from Massachusetts and Plymouth, they brought most of what they needed to get reestablished. Their agricultural land was among the best in southern New England, and the islands

Sir Edmund Andros (1637-1714) served as Governor of the Dominion of New England. Rhode Island was temporarily merged with the other New England colonies under the governorship of Andros. He was deposed in 1689 after the fall of King James II. From Scribner's Popular History of the United States, 1897. Courtesy, Pawtucket Public Library

"The Silver Fleece" was the first seal of the Town of Newport, 1696. The selection of a long-tailed sheep symbolized Aquidneck Island's commercial agriculture, the basis for Newport's prosperity. Courtesy, Newport Historical Society/John Hopf photo

were ideal for commercial livestock grazing. In addition, unlike Providence where Williams attempted to distribute land equally to inhabitants, Coddington and his friends created landed estates with tenant farmers, which soon produced agricultural surpluses for export. Newport had an excellent harbor, and a lively agricultural commerce was conducted with New Amsterdam, Salem, and Boston. The trade paid for a modest amount of imported British goods and provided capital to invest in mercantile activities. By the time the Quakers arrived, the colony was exporting hogs, cattle, sheep, and horses. The Quakers substantially improved the commercial opportunities. Rhode Island did so well that by the 1690s it probably had a favorable balance of trade, which was unique among the colonies because most imported more than they sold. The establishment of a thriving economic base for Newport in the 17th century allowed it to dominate the colony and to provide the leadership which preserved Rhode Island from threats to its charter privileges after 1663.

The greatest menace to the separate existence of Rhode Island came when it was reduced to a county within the Dominion of New England under Governor Edmund Andros. The Dominion was intended to embrace all the English possessions from New Jersey to Maine, and in 1686 King James II dispatched Andros to collect the charters of the New England colonies and begin the administration of the Dominion. The Crown hoped to rationalize the confused colonial administration and exert greater control. Rhode Island passively resisted the Dominion by ignoring directives and failing to carry out orders, and it and Connecticut hid their charters from Governor Andros. The Glorious Revolution of 1688 which drove James II from the throne also aborted the Dominion as armed citizens overthrew Andros in Boston in April 1689. The following month Rhode Island officials who had been in office in 1687 summoned a meeting of freemen in Newport, the charter was brought out of hiding, and the old government restored.

The reemergence of the colony brought a return to its independent ways and renewed attacks on the charter. Though this effort extended well into the 18th century, the period of greatest threat began in the 1690s and ended in 1707. Critics mounted an effort in England to revoke Rhode Island's charter privileges. The chief justice of New York wrote that Rhode Islanders "did in all things as if they were out of the dominion of the Crown." Newport in particular was accused of being "a place where Pirates are ordinarily too kindly entertained." In fact, pirates did vacation and refit their vessels there. Captain Thomas Paine, soldier, pirate, and privateer settled first in Newport in 1683 and then in Jamestown in 1688. His friend, the infamous Captain William Kidd, also received a friendly reception in Newport. In addition, Rhode Island was charged with issuing privateering commissions of dubious legality which cloaked some of the activities of piratical characters. Moreover, those endless boundary disputes with Connecticut and Massachusetts and the undying but fraudulent land claims of the Narragansett Proprietors surfaced repeatedly. Finally, some disgruntled Rhode Island royalists longed for the good old days of the Dominion of New England and its "proper" government; and they complained that the colony was governed by illiterates, incompetents, Quakers, and other sectaries. Nevertheless, all these charges came to naught in large part because of the shrewd and vigorous leadership of Governor Samuel Cranston.

Cranston began his long tenure as governor in 1698, just as the winds of criticism were rising to gale force. When he died in 1727, after serving 29 terms, Rhode Island had been transformed into a fairly secure colony. By cooperating where required while maintaining Rhode Island's independence, Cranston defused external critics; and the colony's internal affairs were reformed to promote commercial activities. In particular, the central government was strengthened at the expense of the towns, the General Assembly asserted its power to tax, the first paper money issues eased the credit and specie shortage, and Newport emerged as a booming commercial center.

Across Narragansett Bay from Newport there developed a society with large estates and slave labor that was more like the South than any other part of New England.

Because many of its principal landowners came from Aquidneck Island, this area was tied by family, economics, and politics to Newport. A number of families, the Hazards, Potters, Updikes, Robinsons, Gardiners, Champlins, and Marchants, acquired farms with thousands of acres. These "Narragansett Planters," as they were called, raised livestock and produced dairy products for export. One lucrative effort was the successful breeding of horses, especially the famous Narragansett Pacer. These activities supported Newport's dominant position in Rhode Island.

Newport would become the fifth largest town in the colonies before the American Revolution. At the end of the 17th century, however, it was little more than a single street (Thames Street) with various lanes running off to nearby farms. Pigs

Mary Dyer, one of Anne Hutchinson's closest friends, was among the first Americans to convert to Quakerism. On her fourth invasion of Massachusetts in 1660 to spread the Quaker gospel, she was hanged by the authorities. Engraving from Scribner's Popular History of the United States, 1897. Courtesy, Pawtucket Public Library

scavenged in the streets, and wolves were a problem in town. The merchant marine consisted of some small vessels and a few dozen sailors. In 1681 Governor Peleg Sanford reported that the town had "several men that deal in buying and selling," but none could "properly be called merchants." He said "that most of our Colony live comfortably by improving the wilderness." Although Rhode Island exported agricultural goods to other American colonies, it still had no direct trade with England. As late as 1708 it sent products to England by way of Boston. This would change by the 1720s as Newport surged forward when the imperial wars among the European powers provided oceans of opportunity.

King William's War (1689-1697) stimulated Newport by bringing in loot from privateering activities; for example, the Wanton brothers began their fortune by successful privateering in 1694. Queen Anne's War (1703-1713) produced even more vigorous privateering as well as the entry by the colony's traders into the French and Spanish West Indies. Rhode Island fitted out more privateers than any other northern colony during King George's War (1739-1748). Rhode Island vessels feasted on enemy shipping, taking 20 ships in 1745 alone. The privateering tradition carried through the French and Indian War (1754-1763), to the extent that in 1760 Governor Stephen Hopkins reported that Rhode Island had 50 privateers preying on French shipping. At the same time, it probably had more ships trading with the enemy: an interesting arrangement in which it destroyed enemy ships and replaced them with its own. British officials singled out Rhode Island as the most notorious violator of the prohibition against trading with the enemy. Some of this trade was done through neutral Dutch ports on Surinam and St. Eustatius or, during the French and Indian War, with the port of Monte Cristi on the Spanish half of Hispaniola. In another device, sailing under a "flag of truce," a ship carried enemy prisoners to an enemy port to be exchanged for British prisoners. Some ships carried only one or two prisoners with an entire cargo of goods to be traded. Some enterprising merchants took captives by privateering and then returned them to the enemy under a flag of truce.

These operations greatly accelerated commercial activities and shipbuilding. In 1708 Governor Cranston reported to the Board of Trade that the annual export to England was six times as high as 20 years earlier; and whereas Newport had had only four or five vessels in 1681, it now had nearly 30. By 1721 Newport's trade had doubled again, and by 1740 the colony had nearly 120 vessels trading with other American colonies, the West Indies, Africa, and England. By the end of the French and Indian War, Newport merchants alone owned 200 trading vessels, and Providence and Bristol were also putting increasing numbers of ships to sea. Still, it was Newport's Golden Age.

Politically, Newport dominated Rhode Island. Every governor from 1663 to 1743 was from Newport except Joseph Jencks of Providence (1727-1732), and the General Assembly insisted that he live in Newport during his terms. "The colonial leaders ... were Newport merchants who took it for granted that what was good for Newport was good for Rhode Island." The town's population rose from approximately 2,200 in 1708 to 9,200 in 1774, despite having Middletown separated from it in 1743. The entire colony increased from 7,000 to nearly 60,000 in the same time span. Some 5,000 people were added in 1747, when Britain ruled in favor of Rhode Island on a boundary dispute and Massachusetts had to cede the towns of Cumberland, Warren, Barrington, Bristol, Tiverton, and Little Compton. The number of towns jumped from nine to 30 between 1708 and the American Revolution. It did not escape the notice of some by mid-century that Providence County's population was actually increasing more rapidly than that of any other part of the colony, and this demographic fact was driven home by the economic and political challenge mounted by Providence to Newport's supremacy after 1750.

Part of Newport's Golden Age was its cultural flowering. Its culture was provincial in that it imitated the styles of London, but the town's population was the most

Sea Captains Carousing in Surinam *by John Greenwood, 1755, shows a number of prominent Rhode Island ship captains drinking in a tavern in the Dutch colony. The artist depicted himself vomiting in the doorway to the right, while at the table were Captain Nicholas Cooke of Newport (dressed in grey, wearing Quaker-type hat), Captain Esek Hopkins of Providence (glass in hand), his brother Stephen (asleep, head in hand), Joseph Wanton of Newport (sleeping bald man, about to be drenched with wine), and Captain Ambrose Page of Providence (vomiting into Wanton's pocket). Lord Loudon, British commander in America, wrote to Prime Minister William Pitt that Rhode Island traders were a "lawless set of smugglers." Courtesy, St. Louis Art Museum*

Aaron Lopez (1731-1782), a Portuguese Jew, arrived in Newport in 1752. Beginning with little, he busied himself in oceanic commerce, slave trading, and spermaceti candle manufacturing. By 1775 he had become the richest merchant in Newport. Courtesy, American Jewish Historical Society

diverse of New England. Religious freedom and the spirit of enterprise had attracted Quakers and Jews. Both groups had been made unwelcome in the English and Dutch colonies elsewhere, and the first of them arrived in Newport just a year apart. While the Quakers flourished and dominated Rhode Island, the original contingent of Jews dwindled until a new influx in the 1740s brought at least 15 families. Some would become leading merchants, and Aaron Lopez may have been the richest man in Newport on the eve of the Revolution. Newport was the home of America's first Jewish synagogue and of Rhode Island's first Anglican church, as well as a Congregational church established by missionaries from Massachusetts. The town's mild climate attracted people from many places, especially from the West Indies and the southern American colonies. So many planters from South Carolina came each summer to rest and repair their health that

by 1730 Newport was being called the "Carolina Hospital."

Growth and prosperity led the town's leaders to demand improved conditions and culture. A street committee worked to clear the streets and highways of garbage and filth, sought to control scavenging hogs and stray dogs, and had most streets paved by 1715. Newport opened the first poorhouse in Rhode Island in July 1723, thereby clearing the streets of cripples, beggars, and drunks.

Newport, both then and now, congratulated itself upon the visit in 1729 of the British philosopher and Anglican divine, George Berkeley. Discouraged by the skepticism, indifference, and immorality of Europe, he arrived in Newport on his way to Bermuda to found a college that he envisioned would promote education, religion, and morality in the New World. His entourage contained a number of literary men and artists, including the prominent portrait painter, John Smibert, who inspired Newport-born portraitist, Robert Feke.

Berkeley's dream never came true. He waited in vain for three years in Newport for Parliament to appropriate funds for the proposed college before returning to England in 1732. He never traveled to Bermuda; in fact, his experience in Newport so disillusioned him that he never traveled again. Charmed at first by the community's religious diversity and vigor, he came to feel that sectarianism was as damaging to faith and morality as the skepticism and atheism of Europe. In addition to Anglicans and Quakers, he was confronted by four Baptist churches, the result of splits of other Baptist congregations, and two Congregational churches, also the result of a split. Still, he found the ministers to be among the most learned and interesting persons in the town. The leading intellectuals in post-Berkeley Newport would be the two Congregationalist ministers, Ezra Stiles, pastor of the Second Congregational Church (1755-1778) and later president of Yale, and the pastor of the First Church, Samuel Hopkins, who was Jonathan Edwards' most brilliant disciple.

Berkeley's influence is difficult to measure because he did not take part in town affairs and lived in Middletown in Whitehall, the home he built. While he frequently preached at Trinity Church and entertained the local ministers and others, he took no direct part in the founding of the Society for the Promotion of Knowledge, which was Newport's equivalent to Benjamin Franklin's Philosophical Society in Philadelphia; and no evidence exists to indicate that he attended any meetings. His greatest impact was to bolster the small but growing and influential Anglican community in Newport. He donated an organ to Trinity Church after leaving Newport. He brought some 2,000 books with him and shared these with local merchants, some of whom also had impressive libraries. This eventually spawned the Redwood Library in 1747, endowed by Abraham Redwood with £500 sterling.

Rhode Island's first newspaper appeared in Newport in September 1732 when James Franklin, the brother of Benjamin Franklin, published a fortnightly called the *Rhode Island Gazette*. It disappeared shortly and Newport did not support a successful newspaper until the *Newport Mercury* appeared in 1758. (Providence acquired its first newspaper in October 1762 when William Goddard began the *Providence Gazette and Country Journal*.) Newport enjoyed other delights of civilization: a voice teacher could make a living there by 1732, French lessons were available, one could attend a class in psalmody, and Mary Cowley advertised a dancing school for "Gentlemen and Ladies of Family Character" in 1764. The first theatrical troupe ever to perform in New England came to Newport in June 1761. Having been well received, they made the mistake of trying Providence the next summer. The more puritanical Providence was so upset that it convinced the General Assembly to ban stage plays and theatricals in the whole colony.

Handsome homes and public buildings were built, and the first steepled church in Rhode Island, Trinity Church, was erected by the Anglicans. Such buildings provided opportunities for architects such as Richard Munday, who designed Trinity (1726) and the Colony House (1739); and Peter Harrison, who was responsible for the Redwood Library (1748), Touro Synagogue (1759), and the Brick Market (1760). For furnishings the merchants called upon talented silversmiths, interior decorators, and furniture makers, such as the Townsend and Goddard families, who crafted a distinctive Newport style. Except for the Brick Market, all of the major structures were completed by 1763. It was mostly a wooden town, but nearly all of the 1,000 buildings were painted, which was unusual for colonial America. All Newport lacked was a college. When the charter for a Baptist college was approved in 1764, it was assumed that the institution would be located there. But, when the contest had ended and Rhode Island College (as Brown University was then called) permanently located, the College Edifice rose on a hill in Providence.

In the first half of the 18th century,

Rhode Island's economy shifted from agriculture to commerce, but it had little of its own that anyone wanted. The raising of livestock, especially horses for export, remained a profitable enterprise through three quarters of the century; other products, such as pork, beef, wool and mutton, lumber, barrels and shingles, cheese, and dried fish came from local sources, but the colony would not get rich on its natural products. These were simply too limited. Because it had a tiny hinterland from which to draw raw materials or in which to sell products, its commercial prosperity was painfully and tenuously built on the reexport trade. Most of the industries which developed in the towns, such as making spermaceti candles, twine and cordage, and distilling rum, were linked to the reexport business. The remarkable thing about Rhode Island's prosperity in the 18th century was how well it did given the deficiency of local products. Rhode Island had to work harder than most for its prosperity, and this prosperity was precarious at best.

Of vital significance was the import of molasses (mostly from illegal sources) and the export of rum. The Rhode Island Remonstrance of 1764 indicated the significance when it stated that molasses "serves as an engine in the hands of the Merchant to effect the great purpose of paying for British manufactures." Nearly 500 vessels called Rhode Island home, and they transported nearly a million gallons of molasses annually. By 1769 Newport had 22 distilleries and Providence had 31, causing Stephen Hopkins to write that "distillery is the main hinge upon which the trade of the colony turns and many hundreds of persons depend immediately upon it for a subsistence." Half of the rum was drunk in Rhode Island itself, and about 10 percent went to the slave trade. Rum was the best product that merchants had for buying slaves in Africa. In the 30 years prior to 1764, Rhode Island annually sent out nine vessels to Africa carrying rum. However, "molasses to rum to slaves" was only part of the picture. Most of Rhode Island's shipping was not involved in the slave trade. Rum, however, was a staple item which merchants used in their indirect trade with

England. The refrain might as readily run "molasses to rum to bills of credit" because rum was exported to other colonies, the Caribbean, and South America for trade and sale.

The uncertain and difficult basis of the merchants' wealth drove Rhode Islanders in unsavory and illegal directions. After 1720 the slave trade became a significant enterprise of Newport merchants, some of whom piled up fortunes in this "iniquitous traffic." Also, they took advantage of the Anglo-French wars to enter a forbidden trade with the enemies of their Sovereign. One of the bitterest complaints against Rhode Island was this traitorous dealing with the enemy. Rhode Islanders argued that this commerce was positively good for the Empire because it secured products that allowed them to trade with England. Always short of specie, Rhode Islanders

The nine carved shells and rich mahogany of this desk and bookcase make it the grandest expression of the Newport block and shell style. The piece is believed to have been crafted sometime between 1760 and 1785 by John Goddard (1723-1785). Originally owned by Joseph Brown, it is now in the John Brown House Museum in Providence. RIHS (RHi x3 4328)

No. 65   **District and Port of Newport,** *August 28th* 1805

List of the names, places of birth and residence, and a description of the persons composing the company of the *Brig* called the *Hope* of *Newport* burthen *ninety seven* tons 84/ feet, whereof *Thomas White* is Master, bound for *Africa*

NAMES OF SEAMEN.	STATION.	Ages.	Height. Feet. Inches.	Complexion.	Residence.	PLACES OF BIRTH. States and Countries.	Towns.	Country of which they are respectively Citizens or Subjects.
William Spooner	1st mate	31	5 6⅞	light	Newport	R: Island	Newport	
William Johnson	2. mate	28	5 5⅞	light	ditto	Massachusetts	Salem	
George Washington Sanford	seaman	20	5 3⅞	light	ditto	Rhode Island	Newport	
Isaac Shene Jr.	seaman	16	5 6	light	ditto	Massachusetts	Taunton	United States of America apprentice to the Captain
Titus Sheffield	seaman	21	5 8⅝	black	ditto	Rhode Island	Shoreham	ditto
Stephen Gardner	seaman	22	5 9	black	S. Kingston	ditto	S. Kingston	
John Oxford	seaman	33	5 10	black	Boston	Massachusetts	Boston	
Ebenezer Underwood	Cook	20	5 6½	black	Newport	Massachusetts	Boston	Apprentice to the Captain

Thomas White

The complex nature of the slave trade was demonstrated by the voyage of the brig Hope on August 28, 1805: half of the crew was black. Newport's Free African Union Society (the first black organization in the United States) sought to discourage black participation by prohibiting membership or association with those "of the African Race that do or hereafter be the Means of bringing, from their Native Country, the Males, Females, Boys & Girls from Africa into Bondage." Free African Union Society, Proceedings, September 8, 1791. Courtesy, U.S. Customs House Records, Newport Historical Society/J. Stanley Lemons photo

got most of their gold and silver and good bills of credit in the Caribbean and South America, and these in turn paid the colony's bills owed to England for manufactured products and the comforts of civilization.

Slavery was slow to develop in Rhode Island; but once it became a commodity of commerce, the colony's involvement became sustained and deep. In 1652 the General Assembly sought to forbid black slavery, but Aquidneck, under Coddington's brief tenure as Governor for Life, refused to recognize the law. Rhode Island opposed Indian slavery, but King Phillip's War ended with the captives being parceled out to the towns as indentured servants or being handed over to Plymouth for export to the West Indies. The first recorded instance of a slave-trading vessel visiting Rhode Island was in 1696, when the *Seaflower*, out of Boston, brought a cargo of 47 slaves and sold 14 in Newport. In 1700 three vessels, fitted out in Newport but owned and commanded by Barbados merchants, sailed for Africa. Until the end of Queen Anne's War, Newport purchased its annual supply of 20 or 30 slaves from Barbados. After the war some of the town's merchants began investing in the growing slave trade.

Newport and later Bristol and Providence became major sources of the slavers, and by mid-century slaves sold in the Caribbean and in the southern colonies produced about £40,000 annually to merchants for remittance to England. Rhode Islanders participated in the African slave trade in a major way from 1725 to 1807. The peak year was 1805 despite the fact that Rhode Island law had forbidden its citizens to engage in the trade since 1787. Jay Coughtry's *Notorious Triangle* reports: "During that span of 75 years at least 934 vessels left Rhode Island ports for the west coast of Africa and carried away an estimated 106 thousand slaves." While it was a minor carrier compared with the British who transported 20 times as many slaves, "Rhode Island was the principal American carrier." Nearly every leading merchant of Newport, whether Anglican, Quaker, Jew, Baptist, or Congregationalist, engaged in the trade. The number of slaves in Rhode Island rose from 426 in 1708 to a peak of over 4,700 in 1758. By then it had the highest percentage of slaves of any New England colony, and Newport's population was 15 percent black. Nearly half of the colony's slaves worked on the great farms of the Narragansett Planters in South County.

The first slave ship from Providence was dispatched in 1736 by James Brown, the father of the four Brown brothers, Nicholas, John, Moses, and Joseph. The result was only marginally profitable and 23 years elapsed before another Brown ship sailed to the Guinea coast, but it never returned. The four brothers attempted a third voyage in 1764 and lost nearly $12,000; and all except John abandoned the trade. Moses became a Quaker, freed his 10 slaves, led the abolitionist movement in Rhode Island, and pushed the state to gradual emancipation in 1784 and a law passed in 1787 forbidding Rhode Islanders to engage in the slave trade. His Abolition Society brought the prosecution against brother John in 1797 in which the latter's ship was condemned, but John remained an advocate of the African slave trade until his death in 1803.

Merchants determined to engage in the slave trade did not permit Rhode Island laws to stop them any more than British navigation acts deterred them from trading with forbidden markets. When the post-Revolutionary depression pushed merchants back into old commercial patterns, all major ports reentered the slave trade. More than one third of all slaving voyages from Rhode Island occurred after the trade had been outlawed. Particularly notorious were James and George DeWolf of Bristol, who remained in the business until at least the 1820s. When South Carolina reopened her ports to the Guinea traffic from 1803 to 1807, slavers brought 38,775 slaves to Charleston. Despite Rhode Island's law, 7,958 of these were carried in 59 vessels from Rhode Island, half in DeWolf ships. The United State Congress outlawed the trade in 1808; and this, plus Moses Brown's antislavery crusade and the dogged enforcement of state and federal laws by William Ellery, United States Collector of Customs, ended the slave traffic by most Rhode Islanders.

However, the DeWolfs got around the law. James declared himself a Republican, and after Thomas Jefferson took office, was rewarded by the appointment of his brother-in-law, Charles Collins, as United States Collector for a newly created customs district—Bristol and Warren. This ended the scrutiny of Ellery at Newport, who protested while Collins closed his eyes as the DeWolfs outfitted one slaver after another. James left direct participation after 1808, turned to other business interests, and became a United States Sena-

George DeWolf (1779-1844), the most notorious practitioner of the illegal slave trade, profitted until his illicit empire crumbled with the failure of his Cuban sugar plantation in 1825. Bristol investors lost so much that the town did not recover for two decades. Oil painting by unknown artist. Courtesy, Linden Place/J. Stanley Lemons photo

tor in the 1820s. Cousin George continued smuggling slaves into the United States or dumped them on his sugar plantation in Cuba until the price was right. He also engaged in privateering along the South American coast when that region was torn with revolutions. His illicit but profitable empire collapsed with his sugar crop failure in 1825, and his London broker lost about $700,000. Uncle James lost the $250,000 he had invested, and Bristol took nearly two decades to recover. The United States Congress passed increasingly stringent laws to combat the African slave traffic, making slaving a capital crime in 1820. The only person executed under the statute was a captain from Portland, Maine in 1862.

Once Rhode Islanders found a profitable enterprise, regardless of its legality, they found it difficult to alter course. Their options were limited, and their reserves insecure; therefore, a change in conditions could mean success or failure. Just as earlier wars enticed Rhode Islanders to escape the confines of Narragansett Bay, the events of the French and Indian War and the new Imperial climate after 1763 offered new perils and opportunities. It brought hardship and disaster to Newport, but Providence gained a great advantage.

Chapter Three

THE INDEPENDENT STATE

This engraving entitled "Landing of the French Army... in R.I., July 1780" appeared in Historisch Genealogischer Calender, oder Jahrbuch, 1784. *In October 1779 the British had withdrawn from Newport in order to concentrate on the war in the South. In July 1780 a French army, commanded by Jean Baptiste Donatien de Vimeur, comte de Rochambeau, arrived to join the American cause. The following spring the army marched away to join George Washington to defeat the British at Yorktown, Virginia. RIHS (RHi x3 4317)*

The French and Indian War ushered in a period of difficulty for Rhode Island which emphasized its independent, otherwise-minded character. Problems of financing and taxation related to the war aggravated a growing political split in the colony, and the postwar revision of the British Imperial system moved the colony into early rebellion. Rhode Island resisted the regulations and reorganization which led to the American Revolution. In the event itself, it contributed heavily to the effort and suffered considerably. However, while the colony was first in war, it was last in peace. The fears that drove it into rebellion kept it out of the Union created by the Constitution.

As usual, Rhode Islanders rushed to take advantage of an Anglo-French war. More privateers sailed to prey on enemy shipping; more flag-of-truce voyages cloaked trading ventures with enemy ports; more blockade-runners attempted to evade British efforts to close French ports. Rhode Island was so notorious that Sir Francis Bernard, Royal Governor of Massachusetts, complained to the Board of Trade, "These practices will never be put an end to, till Rhode Island is reduced to the subjection of the British Empire." However, the price was high: Providence lost 65 vessels and Newport 150 to French privateers and British patrols, and Rhode Island's share of the war effort created heavy debts for the government. The colony had met previous financial pinches by issuing paper money, but this had been done so frequently and the volume had

risen so high that by 1750 the colony had £525,335 in depreciated paper floating around. Finally, in 1751 Parliament prohibited all issues of paper money; therefore, during the war Rhode Island footed its obligations by borrowing and issuing treasury bills redeemable in gold and silver. The royal treasury reimbursed part of the cost, but the rest had to be paid off by taxation. But who was to be taxed? Two strong political factions sought to place the burden upon each other.

Because of the Charter, Rhode Island had been virtually an independent, self-governing republic for a century. The Charter gave the General Assembly legislative, executive, and judicial powers, and authority to appoint all public officials not elected directly by the voters. As a consequence, political parties developed earlier in Rhode Island than in any other colony. These parties focused on their leaders, Samuel Ward of Westerly and Stephen Hopkins of Providence. In its simplest terms, however, the struggle was between Providence and Newport for ascendancy. Whoever controlled the General Assembly secured the spoils of office and determined how taxes would be apportioned. The election of Stephen Hopkins for the first of his nine terms in 1755 signaled that Providence was challenging Newport's political hegemony. While Hopkins got significant support from the Wanton faction of Newport, the base of his power was in the northern towns. Hopkins and Ward went head-to-head for the governorship for 10 straight years, and Hopkins won seven times. Because the elections were extremely close, vote buying became common.

The intense partisanship greatly distressed many in an age that considered factionalism to be contrary to good government. The vote buying, scramble for spoils, and blatant shifting of taxes to the towns of the losing party caused some to desire an end to Rhode Island's charter government. A group called the "Newport Junto," led by Martin Howard, Jr., favored greater British involvement in Rhode Island affairs and petitioned the King in 1764 to vacate the Charter.

The Ward-Hopkins feud ended in 1768 when the principals agreed not to run again, and the colony faced the newly aggressive enforcement of imperial regulations. Besides, the Hopkins faction clearly dominated now, electing Hopkins' former Deputy Governor, Joseph Wanton, annually from 1769 to 1775. One thing became apparent: in the end the issues which divided the colony were resolved in favor of Providence.

In 1763 Parliament transformed the wartime patrol along the Atlantic coast into an enforcement arm of the Navigation Acts. The Royal Navy was authorized to seize ships and goods under the British flag to check for compliance with the trade laws. Customs agents sent to America received one half of all ships and cargoes condemned as a result of seizures. Americans soon became thoroughly acquainted with "customs racketeering," the practice of selective enforcement of the laws to enrich the customs agents. Coercion arrived for Newport in the fall of 1763 in the form of H.M.S. *Squirrel*, followed by the schooner *St. John*. Within the year Britain announced the Sugar Act and the Stamp Act, and by that summer violence erupted between Newporters and the navy.

Enforcement of trade laws would mean ruin for Rhode Island merchants. The regulations had not been enforced for so long, and Rhode Islanders had created trade patterns that disregarded His Majesty's laws. With the announcement of the Sugar Act in 1763, the General Assembly responded with an official Remonstrance in 1764. They tried to demonstrate that the Empire was better off for

allowing them to trade where they could. Molasses was crucial; but of the annual import of 14,000 hogsheads, only 2,500 of it came from legal sources. If the Sugar Act were enforced and the new tax strictly collected, Rhode Island's trade would be devastated.

The *Squirrel* and the *St. John* not only began enforcement of the Sugar Act, they also recruited for the Royal Navy by impressing seamen coming to Newport. Local resentment of press-gang activities and the misdeeds of sailors led in July 1764 to an incident in which a crowd of townspeople stoned men of the *St. John* and the gunners of Fort George fired about 10 shots at the schooner. Despite promises

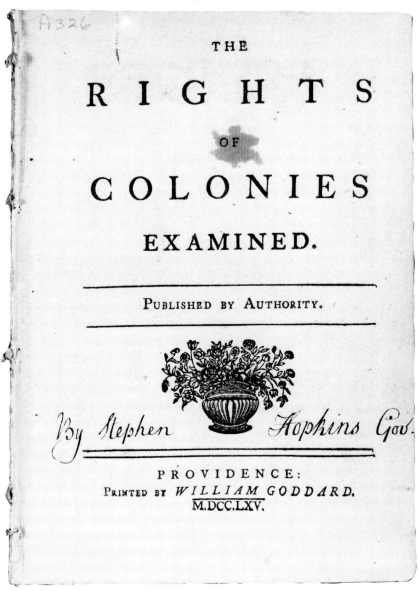

THE

R I G H T S

OF

C O L O N I E S

EXAMINED.

PUBLISHED BY AUTHORITY.

By Stephen Hopkins Gov.

PROVIDENCE:
PRINTED BY *WILLIAM GODDARD.*
M.DCC.LXV.

that no Newport resident or small boatman entering the harbor would be bothered, in the spring of 1765 the *Maidstone* actively pressed seamen from vessels outside the harbor and brought activity in the harbor to a standstill. Woodboats hauled no fuel, and fishermen refused to sail. When the *Maidstone* impressed the crew of a brig on June 4, a mob of 500 people seized one of *Maidstone*'s boats, hauled it to the public commons, and burned it.

When Britain announced in 1764 that it would impose the Stamp Act in 1765, Stephen Hopkins wrote a pamphlet, *The Rights of Colonies Examined*, in which he asserted that Parliament had no authority to levy an internal tax. He argued that the

rights of Englishmen required that there be no taxation without representation and that the colonies had their own legislatures. Martin Howard, Jr., wrote a blistering reply to Hopkins; but as he was known to be behind the 1764 petition to the King, he became a target of a Newport mob in the Stamp Act riots that followed in August 1765. In Providence the reaction was confined to burning an effigy, but in Newport mobs burned effigies of Stamp Master Augustus Johnston, and of Newport Junto figures. The following night rioters destroyed Howard's home and threatened the house of Customs Collector John Robinson. All had fled to safety aboard *Cygnet*, a British man-of-war in the harbor.

Howard caught the next boat to England to urge the King to revoke the Charter. Johnston resigned the next day, Robinson eventually departed, and his replacement found being Collector a dangerous occupation. He was continually harassed in his duties and even severely beaten and dragged through the streets in April 1771. His subordinates fared no better: in Providence one was tarred and feathered and a second nearly beaten to death.

The General Assembly met in September after the riots and adopted resolutions declaring that its citizens were "not bound to yield obedience to any law or ordinance designed to impose any internal taxation whatsoever upon them." They authorized officials to conduct business as usual without the stamps and sent two delegates to the Stamp Act Congress which met in New York in October. All colonial governors were to swear an oath to support the Stamp Act, but Governor Ward of Rhode Island alone refused. No stamps were distributed and the law was repealed the next year. By then the Sons (and Daughters) of Liberty had organized in Newport and Providence.

The Empire's need for revenue led next to the imposition of the Townshend duties of 1767, and Rhode Island's reaction displayed its contrariness. On the one hand, at the dedication of the Providence Liberty Tree on July 25, 1768, Silas Downer, secretary of the Providence Sons of Liberty, gave his *Discourse Delivered in Providence*. Downer denied the authority of Parliament over the colonies, and declared that "we cheerfully recognize our allegiance to our sovereign Lord, *George*, the third, *King of Great-Britain* ... but utterly deny any other dependence on the inhabitants of that island." He said, "I cannot be persuaded that the parliament of *Great-Britain* have any lawful right to make any laws *whatsoever* to bind us." One historian has said that Downer was the first person in America to declare this position publicly six years before anyone else. On the other hand, Rhode Island's lack of cooperation with other colonies weakened the non-importation agreements against British goods. Four months after the rest had agreed, Rhode Island had not joined the effort and would not until merchants in

FACING PAGE, TOP: Samuel Ward (1725-1776), member of the Stamp Act Congress, Continental Congress, and Governor in 1762, 1765, and 1767, was the leader of the Newport-South County faction that waged a bitter political war against Samuel Hopkins of Providence between 1755-1768. The controversy was characterized by intense partisanship and corruption. In 1762 the Ward-dominated Court denied naturalization to Aaron Lopez because Lopez favored Hopkins. From Rhode Island Portraits. *RIHS (RHi x3 628)*

BOTTOM: Britain's announcement of the Stamp Act prompted Stephen Hopkins to write The Rights of the Colonies Examined *in which he argued that Parliament did not have the right to tax the colonies by levying "internal taxes" because the colonies were not represented in Parliament. It was "no taxation without representation." RIHS (RHi x3 4291)*

THIS PAGE: Martin Howard, Jr., (d.1781) Rhode Island delegate to the 1754 Albany Convention, defended the Stamp Act. When a Newport mob destroyed his home in 1765, he fled to England. Appointed chief justice for North Carolina the following year, he was again driven into exile during the American Revolution. From a portrait by John Singleton Copley, 1767. Courtesy, Newport Historical Society

New York, Philadelphia, and Boston boycotted Rhode Island trade. However, with the repeal of the duties, except the tea tax, the nonimportation movement broke down everywhere by October 1770; and Rhode Island merchants bore considerable responsibility for the collapse.

Meanwhile, Newporters continued their violent clashes with the Royal Navy. In 1769 the British sloop *Liberty* seized a brig

Narragansett Bay in March of 1772 and stopped everything, even woodboats carrying fuel to Aquidneck. The *Gaspee*'s crew abused the boatmen, stole livestock from farms, and cut fruit trees for firewood. While pursuing the *Hannah* from Newport on June 9, 1772, the *Gaspee* went aground. Late that night, eight boatloads of men led by John Brown and Abraham Whipple of Providence attacked the *Gaspee*, shot and

RIGHT: This somewhat romanticized, 19th-century depiction of the burning of the Gaspee, Rhode Island's most famous incident of resistance to British efforts to enforce the trade regulations, shows several boatloads of Providence men capturing and burning the ship on the night of June 9, 1772. Steel engraving by J. Rogers after a painting by J. McNevin, published 1856. RIHS (RHi x3 119)

FACING PAGE, TOP: The Stamp Act of 1765 occasioned outrage in every colony in America. Protesters burned effigies of Stamp Act officials in Providence and Newport, and mobs destroyed the homes and possessions of the Newport Junto. Drawing from Henry Davenport, Pictorial History of the United States, 1901. Courtesy, Providence Public Library.

BOTTOM: Esek Hopkins (1718-1802) was commissioned by the Continental Congress to be the first commander-in-chief of the navy of the United Colonies from November 1775 to March 1777. Initially successful, Hopkins and the American navy became bottled up in Narragansett Bay when the British occupied Newport in December 1776, leading to Hopkins' dismissal from his command. Engraving by J.C. Buttre. RIHS (RHi x3 688)

off Block Island and brought it to Newport for condemnation. In port a scuffle broke out between crew members of the vessels, and the *Liberty* fired on the brig's men as they rowed to shore. An enraged mob scuttled the *Liberty* and the brig escaped.

The King's revenue cutters provoked the next outrage against the Crown's authority. The *Gaspee*, commanded by Lt. William Dudingston, took up station in

wounded Dudingston, and burned the schooner. The Crown appointed a commission with broad powers to investigate the incident and to transport to England for trial those responsible. Although a thousand people knew the culprits, only a deranged drunk and an unreliable indentured servant would testify; and nothing came of the investigation. Like every other incident, from the *St. John* in 1764 to the

Gaspee in 1772, no one was apprehended or punished for the offense. However, the intervention of the royal commission profoundly affected Rhode Islanders' perception of the threat to their independence, and they began to see the necessity of greater cooperation with the other colonies.

When the British enacted the Tea Act of 1773 to rescue the East India Company from bankruptcy, the colonies instituted another boycott and direct action against East India teas. The most famous incident was the Boston Tea Party of December 1773, which the British answered with the Coercive Acts in the spring of 1774. Rhode Island took the lead in giving aid to the distressed people in Massachusetts and in calling for a congress of the colonies. Before any other colony issued a call, the General Assembly urged that a congress be assembled and chose Stephen Hopkins and

Samuel Ward as delegates. The First Continental Congress met in Philadelphia that autumn and agreed to an embargo of all British products. This time Rhode Island heartily supported the embargo; and the Sons of Liberty, backed by mob violence and tar and feathers, enforced it. Towns sent donations and droves of sheep to Boston, and in October the General Assembly chartered the Newport Light Infantry,

Providence Grenadiers, Kentish Guards, Pawtuxet Rangers, and the Glocester Light Infantry. In December, four more militia companies received charters, and the cannons and ammunition at Fort George at Newport were removed to Providence.

The rebellion had begun. Extensive manufacture of firearms started, the Hope Furnace cast cannons, and enlistments in the militia proceeded rapidly. When Congress called for the suspension of the use of all tea, Providencians burned some 300 pounds in Market Square on March 2, 1775. Six weeks later came the battles of Lexington and Concord. When the General Assembly voted to send an "army of observation" of 1,500 men to Massachusetts, Governor Wanton refused to issue the commissions and was deposed. Within weeks the customs house in Newport was closed, and Rhode Island felt the oppressive weight of H.M.S. *Rose.* She harassed everything that sailed on the Bay, fired a few shots at Newport, cannonaded Bristol and Warren, and sent foraging parties ashore. The General Assembly authorized a small navy, commanded by Abraham Whipple; and it scored America's first sea victory when it captured a British vessel on June 15. The rebels built fortifications and observation points around the Bay and erected beacon towers. Defenders of British policy were arrested and roughly handled, and by the end of 1775 half of the population of Aquidneck had fled. John Brown's sloop *Katy* was sent to Philadelphia where she was rechristened *Providence,* becoming the first ship in the Continental navy. Stephen Hopkins had urged Congress to create a navy and secured the appointment of his brother Esek as first commander-in-chief. In 1776, the General Assembly commissioned 65 privateers, and before the British closed Narragansett Bay by occupying Newport in December 1776, privateers brought prizes worth £300,000 sterling into Providence.

It has become an article of state pride to maintain that Rhode Island was the first colony to declare its independence—on May 4, 1776—two months before the Declaration of Independence. But it is not true. The General Assembly repealed a test oath from 1765 which required government officers to swear allegiance to George III. Substituted for the King's name was "The Governor and Company of the English Colony of Rhode Island and Providence Plantations." Rhode Island still referred to itself as an *English* colony until July 18 when it ratified the Declaration of Independence. While Rhode Island had not declared its independence first, it was the first to renounce allegiance to the King. No public celebration accompanied the May 4th action; but when independence was proclaimed from the State House in Providence on July 25, jubilation reigned in the town. Most people readily supported the cause because they saw independence as a defense of their liberal charter privileges. They plunged into the fray, contributed proportionately more than nearly any other state, and suffered considerably.

The British occupied about a third of the state for more than three years and raided along the Bay. The great farms of the Narragansett Planters of South County were finished by the war. Already declining because of the British disruption of the West Indies trade, the Planters saw their markets disappear when the British occupied Newport and Conanicut Island and when British foragers killed their livestock, destroyed crops, and burned buildings. The British destroyed every house except one on Prudence Island, and at Jamestown they burned most of the houses in one raid in 1775. Then during the war, they cut down every tree for firewood, leaving Conanicut Island devastated and virtually depopulated.

Providence became the wartime capital

The effort to recapture Newport in August 1778 collapsed when the French fleet was crippled by a terrific storm, leaving the American troops stranded on Aquidneck. Though the British sought to capture the Americans as they withdrew, black soldiers in the First Rhode Island Battalion repulsed three assaults by Hessian mercenaries, allowing the Americans to make an orderly retreat. From Providence, The Southern Gateway to New England, *1926. Courtesy, Commonwealth Land Title Insurance Company*

and an armed camp. Fortifications were constructed at many points and a beacon tower perched on Prospect Hill. Although never attacked, Providence lived in continual fear during the British occupation of Newport. The town was disrupted by the presence of so many soldiers, whose principal leisure activity was drinking, but townsfolk made money off them. The number of taverns tripled between 1775 and 1778 so that Providence came to have one tavern or inn selling liquor for every 100 persons. Food shortages became critical in the winter of 1778-1779 with civilians and soldiers near starvation, causing two mutinies among the soldiers. University Hall was used as a hospital by the Americans and the French from 1776 to May 1782, and education was suspended at the college.

Rhode Island persistently urged the Continental Army to mount a major effort to expel the British, but always the attention was given elsewhere. The main attempt ended in the Battle of Rhode

38

Island, August 29, 1778. This battle was a rearguard action as the Americans extracted their troops from Aquidneck when French naval support failed to materialize because the fleet had been crippled by a hurricane. The most significant aspect of the engagement was the able fighting of the first black regiment ever employed in America.

While Providence escaped the ravages of war, Newport was severely damaged. Half of the population fled, many of its most enterprising merchants never returned, its wharfs and warehouses rotted and fell into ruin, and the British occupiers ripped down and burned 480 vacant homes and shops for firewood! When the war ended, Providence's population had declined slightly from 4,321 to 4,310, but Newport's had plummeted from 9,209 to 5,530. The contest between the towns was really settled, and by 1800 Providence counted 7,614 while Newport struggled behind at 6,739, considerably less than before the Revolution.

Because it rebelled to preserve its independence and because it felt slighted by the central government's lack of effort to dislodge the British from Newport, Rhode Island ended the war suspicious and hostile toward the new United States government. It blocked the attempt by Congress under the Articles of Confederation to strengthen the Union and then refused to ratify the Constitution. Rhode Islanders did not want to trade subjection to Parliament for subordination to Congress; consequently, it briefly became an independent republic.

When the Articles of Confederation were proposed, the General Assembly unanimously ratified it in 1778 because it created just the sort of central government they wanted, one with little or no power over the states. Rhode Island wanted to act without external restraint; but by behaving contrarily toward the Union, it helped to undermine the Confederation and produce the conditions that resulted in the Constitution, which reduced state independence. The Confederation government desperately needed revenue, but in 1781 and 1783 Rhode Island blocked the unanimous approval needed for an import tax. Instead it adopted a state import duty to pay the state debt. These actions caused other states to heap abuse on Rhode Island, and some sought to expel its representatives from Congress. One congressman declared that the "Cursed State ought to be erased out of the Confederation." Then when Rhode Island resorted to its favorite remedy for financial problems, another paper money issue, some states fairly roared with rage and denunciation. Rhode Island's self-absorption and the chorus of external abuse only served to weaken further its ties to the Union. By 1789 it would be outside the Union altogether.

The war debt had to be paid, but how? Because the commercial towns around the Bay had been occupied or had trade disrupted during the war, the burden of taxation had shifted to the rural towns. When the postwar commercial depression failed to generate much income from the state import duty, steep taxes were levied on real estate. These fell most heavily upon the farmers, who feared that they would be

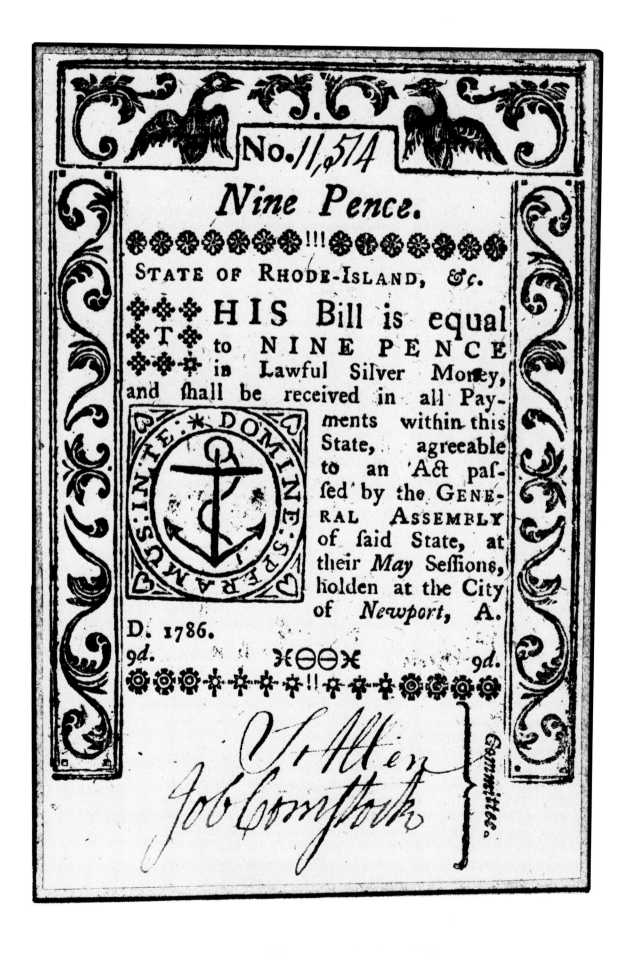

ruined unless relief were provided. They demanded the issuance of paper money based on land value. The Country party won on this issue in 1786 and held power until the state debt had been liquidated in 1790. Commercial interests bitterly opposed paper money, causing its value to depreciate rapidly. The Country party resorted to increasingly punitive measures to force creditors (some of whom fled the state to avoid accepting paper money for debts) to accept the money, including heavy fines for nonacceptance and trial without jury or appeal for violators. They even punished Newport. In 1784 Newport merchants had obtained a municipal charter, making it Rhode Island's first city. But the city council was anti paper money so, the General Assembly, under Country party control, revoked Newport's charter in March 1787.

The Country party opposed the Constitution and refused even to send a delegate to the Constitutional Convention in Philadelphia in 1787. Eleven times they rejected calls for a ratifying convention. Instead they presented the Constitution to a popular referendum, contrary to the recommendations of the convention delegates or Congress. James Madison said of Rhode Island: "Nothing can exceed the wickedness and folly which continue to rule there. All sense of character as well as of right have been obliterated." When the vote was cast in March 1788, Newport and Providence (pro-Constitution centers) boycotted the referendum, and the Constitution was smothered 2,708-237. The

rural towns were nearly unanimous in opposition: Foster voted 177-0, Coventry 180-0, Scituate 156-0, Glocester 228-9, and Smithfield 159-2 against ratification.

By late November 1789 only Rhode Island remained out of the Union, and the United States Congress began to move toward economic coercion. Meanwhile William Ellery of Newport, signer of the Declaration of Independence, was urging Congress to treat Rhode Island like a foreign country. In particular he urged them to levy duties on agricultural products so that the back-country farmers would "be compelled by a sense of interest to adopt the Constitution." Providence and Newport talked about seceding from the state! At last the General Assembly authorized a ratification convention, which in May 1790 approved the Constitution by two votes. The convention suggested 21 amendments to the Constitution; most would have weakened the central government. President George Washington made a special trip here in August 1790 to forgive and embrace the independent state.

Admission to the Union, however reluctantly accepted, closed one era. The state's economy had changed from agriculture to commerce in the 18th century and was on the verge of another transformation in the 19th. Rhode Island was on its way to becoming the nation's first urban, industrialized state.

FACING PAGE: Rhode Island turned to paper money to relieve the money crisis of 1784-1785, but this occasioned considerable resistance by local merchants and neighboring states. The Connecticut Wits denounced Rhode Island saying: "Hail! realm of rogues, renow'd for fraud and guile,/ All hail; ye knav'ries of yon little isle./There prowls the rascal, cloth'd with legal pow'r,/To snare the orphan, and the poor devour." RIHS (RHi x3 1056)

THIS PAGE, TOP: James Manning (1738-1791) was president of Rhode Island College (Brown University) from 1764 to 1791, pastor of the First Baptist Church of America from 1771 to 1791, and a leading opponent of slavery. An ardent patriot accused Manning of being a Baptist Tory, but after George Washington attended his church, Manning became a staunch nationalist and a member of the Confederation Congress. RIHS (RHi x3 4288)

BOTTOM: At the dedication of the Providence Liberty Tree in 1768, Silas Downer of the Providence Sons of Liberty declared that the British Parliament had no right to legislate for the colonies, RIHS (RHi x3 1251)

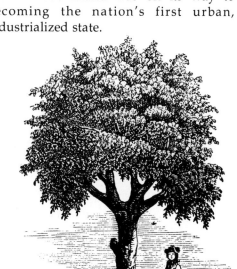

Chapter Four

REBELS, RIOTERS, AND PARTYMEN

Although Thomas W. Dorr (1806–1854) was born into wealth and power, he fought for liberal causes, including public schools and equal suffrage. He personally favored restoring the franchise to African Americans, but the Suffrage Association did not, and the otherwise progressive People's Constitution excluded black voters. Elected governor under the extra-legal People's Constitution in 1842, Dorr was forced to flee after a failed attempt to overthrow the legal government by force. Even though Dorr was imprisoned, the "Dorr Rebellion" resulted in the adoption of a new constitution for Rhode Island. Courtesy, RIHS (RHi X3 2013)

ADMISSION TO THE Union in 1790 brought Rhode Island into the fold of the states, but it did not settle its relationship with the United States. Its peculiar history and economic needs pushed the state toward secession a second time during the War of 1812. Just as its merchants in the 18th century had disregarded and then resisted the laws of the British government, so did the early 19th-century commercial interests contravene federal law. Meanwhile, the Charter of 1663, which had made Rhode Island the freest of the colonies, had now outlived its usefulness. The guarantees of religious freedom and democracy passed to the federal Constitution, but the old Charter was unsuited for an urban, industrial society. Rhode Island ran counter to the rest of the country: as most states became increasingly democratic, by the 1830s Rhode Island had become one of the least democratic. The result was an attempt to overthrow the state government by force. As Rhode Island modernized its constitution and developed as an industrial state, it turned from the freedom of the oceans to the ties of interstate commerce and the federal Union. Last among the original 13 states to ratify the Constitution, Rhode Island was first to pledge troops to defend it in 1861.

At the beginning of the 19th century, Rhode Island's economy depended upon oceanic commerce, so anything that disrupted it threatened the state's economic well-being. Still, the traders seemed to tolerate continued impressment by the British, hostile actions by warring European powers, and the perils of seizure and impoundment more easily than trade regulations of their own government. When the British warship *Leopard* fired upon the American frigate *Chesapeake* in mid-1807, killing three sailors, all America was outraged and clamored for war. Rhode Islanders flocked to large meetings and pledged their lives and fortunes to avenge this "flagrant insult upon our national honor." But instead of their lives, Jefferson asked for their fortunes. At his urging, Congress adopted the Embargo Act in December, which immediately cut trade and commerce. Exports from Rhode Island fell from $1.6 million in 1807 to $240,000 the next year. Experienced in disregarding or evading trade regulations, New Englanders tried to circumvent the Embargo; and the federal government, like the British before the Revolution, enacted increasingly punitive enforcement measures. The Rhode Island General Assembly protested in 1809, calling the Embargo and enforcement laws "unjust, tyrannical, and unconstitutional," and warning that a "dissolution of the union may be more surely, and as speedily, effected by the systematic oppression of the government as by the inconsiderate disobedience of the people." When Congress finally declared war on Great Britain in 1812, Rhode Island joined the condemnation of "Mr. Madison's War," refused to release its militia to federal service, and sent four delegates to the Hartford Convention in December 1814, where the

43

EMBARG

Office of the Newport

Embargo LAW.

the 2d day of March, 1799; and such penalties may be examined, mitigated or remitted, in like manner, and under like conditions, regulations and restrictions, as are prescribed, authorised and directed by the act, entitled "An Act to provide for mitigating or remitting the forfeitures, penalties and disabilities accruing in certain cases therein men-

des affaires at l papers mention Ships. *This ve* may appear, h. *War against Eng* that it is only by we can propitiat

unhappy New England states contemplated secession from the Union.

With nearly 400 miles of coast, Rhode Island felt exposed to the power of the British. It feared another occupation of Newport and the devastation of the Bay towns that had occurred in the Revolution. So, even while resisting the demands of the federal government, Rhode Island moved energetically to defend itself by constructing coastal fortifications and calling up the militia. The federal government expanded and strengthened Fort Adams at the same time. Rhode Islanders were probably relieved when the British chose instead to bombard Fort McHenry at Baltimore and to chase little "Jamie" Madison right out of Washington.

The state's honor was upheld by the 500 men who enlisted in the national army in 1812 and by Oliver Hazard Perry and the many Rhode Island seamen at the Battle of Lake Erie in September 1813. Oliver's younger brother Matthew, best remembered for opening Japan to western contact in 1853, also served in the navy and won a promotion to lieutenant at age 18 for his part in the first sea battle of the war. While some Rhode Islanders were sacrificing their lives on Lake Erie, others were earning their fortunes in a most traditional

manner—privateering. The state commissioned 31 vessels. Spearheaded by James DeWolf, Bristol became the principal privateering port. In July 1812 the *Yankee* began the first of six successful voyages which would seize 40 British vessels with property valued at $5 million, bringing DeWolf over one million dollars in profit.

The War of 1812 hastened the national trend toward greater democracy in state governments, but Rhode Island ran contrary to the tide. Of all the original states only Rhode Island and Connecticut had retained their colonial charters after the American Revolution. In 1818 Connecticut adopted a constitution, but it required nothing less than a civil insurrection to force Rhode Island to abandon its antiquated charter.

Complaints against the Charter of 1663 boiled down to two: malapportionment and disenfranchisement. The Charter fixed representation in the General Assembly, giving Newport six delegates, Providence, Portsmouth, and Warwick four each, and all subsequent towns two each. Although population growth shifted to the northern towns, representation remained fixed. By 1820 Providence had almost 12,000 people while Portsmouth had only 1,645, but both had four General Assembly representa-

& WAR !

Mercury, April 13, 1812.

he English
e of Eleven
strange as it
hurried our
s understood
mbargo that
ial Tyrant."

perhaps to ultimate defeat, if *they* may
be saved from shame and disgrace.

FREEMEN OF RHODE-ISLAND, do you
subscribe to *such* doctrines,—do you
approve of *such* measures, dictated by
such motives.—Are you ready to see
your country involved in all the horrors
and calamities of war, to save from
shame and disgrace the nice feelings

in order to ripen and bring it to perfec-
tion, we are pledged to assist in crushing the feeble exertions of Spain in de-
fence of her liberties.

In the name of Heaven, what has become of our Constitution ? The fram-
ers of that once-valued Charter endea-
voured to guard most securely the dangerous POWER OF MAKING WAR.—

tives. The rural-dominated legislature determined who could vote and how taxes were apportioned. It refused to remove the property qualification that disenfranchised the growing urban population. Consequently the expanding northern towns found themselves outvoted and overtaxed by the static, rural towns. Thus, as the state became more urbanized, its government became less democratic and more anachronistic.

Rhode Island was probably the most democratic state in 1780, as three-quarters of all adult, white males met the property qualification and were eligible to vote. As the state's urban population grew in the 1820s and 1830s, the percentage of eligible voters shrank. The requirement that a voter own $134 worth of real estate, or be the eldest son of a man who did, excluded the growing numbers of propertyless industrial workers. By 1840 the excluded equaled 40 percent in the state and probably 94 percent in Providence. Elsewhere the franchise was extended to nearly all white men in the 1820s, but Rhode Island resisted all efforts at constitutional reform. Consequently, it had the most conservative suffrage law in the nation.

The demands for constitutional revision arose in the 1790s over the issue of appor-

tionment as the growing towns in the northern part of the state resented the power of the static country towns. The town of Smithfield called for a constitutional convention in 1792, and Providence echoed this in 1796 after the General Assembly had quadrupled its taxes. George Burrill, an attorney, state legislator, and notary public for Providence County, argued that proponents of constitutional reform could bypass the General Assembly and go directly to the people to secure a

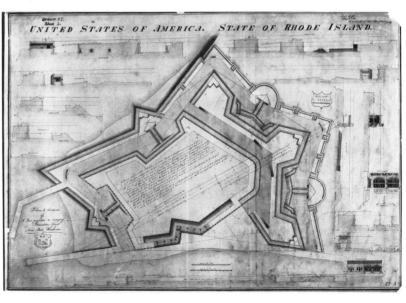

UNITED STATES OF AMERICA. STATE OF RHODE ISLAND.

A leading opponent of the suffrage movement, Henry B. Anthony (1815–1884) stirred nativist fears to defeat it. Later he was governor of Rhode Island (1849–1851) and U.S. Senator (1859–1884). As editor and joint owner of the Providence Journal, he elevated the paper to dominate the state and supported the Republican party and the economic transformation of Rhode Island. Courtesy, RIHS (RHi x3 1987)

constitution. While nothing came of his efforts in the 1790s, the Dorrites would follow this path in 1841 and 1842. Agitation subsided until 1811, when suffrage became a significant issue as a result of the political contests between the Federalists and Republicans for control of the state. A series of petitions followed from 1811 to 1823 which resulted in a proposed constitution in 1824.

The ferment was continued by a young journalist, James Davis Knowles of Providence, who declared that the people, sovereign and independent, could call their own constitutional convention if the General Assembly did not. About the time that Knowles surrendered political agitation for the Baptist ministry in 1820, the *Manufacturers and Farmers Journal* in Providence published articles attacking the state's constitutional system. The leading defender of the status quo was Benjamin Hazard, an attorney and General Assembly representative from Newport from 1809 to 1840. His 1829 attack, called *Hazard's Report*, dismissed the suffrage claims as demagoguery. He denounced the dis-

enfranchised as propertyless Rhode Islanders paupered by "their own improvidence, extravagence, or vices," as "improvident adventurers" from other states, and as "degraded" foreign-born. Hazard expressed the prevailing sentiment of the state's southern and western landowners who resisted every effort of the industrializing towns to revise either apportionment or the franchise.

The geographical split on the constitutional questions was clear. In an 1821 referendum on whether to call a convention, Providence cast its votes 598-2 in favor, while the static and declining towns to the south and west voted just the opposite. The referendum lost by 300 votes. In 1824, when a convention was held and a constitution submitted to the voters, it was crushed by a two-to-one margin. Again the towns that were not growing overwhelmingly rejected the change: Foster (242-2), Richmond (90-0), North Kingstown (207-6), and Newport (531-5).

The suffrage movement intensified in Providence after 1833. Seth Luther, a housewright, led workers and artisans in demanding the right to vote. He and Thomas Dorr, son of wealthy China-merchant and industrialist Sullivan Dorr, organized a suffrage convention in 1834 and launched the Constitutional party. The new party contended for offices in April 1834, but fared poorly, though Dorr was elected as one of Providence's four representatives to the General Assembly. By 1837 the Constitutional party had folded, but the agitation continued.

In the 1830s the Democrats dominated the state government because of malapportionment and a coalition with the anti-Masonic party. Their base was in the rural, downstate areas while the urban northern towns shifted to the Whig party. The Whigs favored reapportionment, but not expansion of the franchise. Eliminating the property qualification might mean enfranchising the landless and the foreign-born, in particular, the growing numbers of Irish. Not only did the franchise issue strike fear in the hearts of those who believed that only the propertied should vote, but the influx of Irish Catholics stirred the antipopery feelings of native

Americans. The number of unnaturalized, foreign-born residents in Providence increased from a mere 29 in 1820 to 1,005 in 1835. As the Irish tended to favor the Democratic party, the Whigs wanted to limit their influence. The Whiggish *Providence Daily Journal*, which had favored suffrage reform in the 1820s, opposed it in the 1830s, substantially on nativist grounds. With the rural-based Democratic party in Rhode Island wholly opposed to reform and the urban Whigs favoring only

reapportionment, the suffrage advocates turned to extralegal political action.

In 1840 a number of developments coincided to produce the final act in the suffrage agitation. In January the General Assembly passed a militia reorganization bill with a system of fines that fell heavily upon nonvoters who composed most of the militia. Second, Equal Rights Democrats from New York actively agitated in Rhode Island and published a brochure on how to call a constitutional convention by skirting the legislature and establishing another government. In March the Rhode Island Suffrage Association was formed and called for such a convention. That summer and fall Rhode Island witnessed the hoopla of the ''Log Cabin and Hard Cider'' campaign for President, which made those unable to vote more resentful. The Suffrage Association adopted some of the exciting presidential campaign devices, and the rallies for suffrage became bigger and noisier. Their great suffrage parade in Providence in April 1841 had two bands and more than 3,000 marchers. Thomas Dorr came under the influence of Equal Rights Democrats ideas and took the lead in 1841 in calling the People's Convention. The Convention wrote the People's Constitution, submitted it to a popular referendum of all voting-age men, and saw it approved 13,944-52 in December 1841.

Meanwhile the Whig-dominated state government summoned a Landowners

---

HURRAH
FOR THE
OLD CHARTER.

THE OLD CHARTER IS SAFE!

All who voted for the new Constitution prefer law and order under the Charter to an unquiet government under the Constitution! *One thousand men* who voted against the Constitution did so because they preferred the Charter. It can now be maintained! Suffrage men have cheated themselves, and the Charter is triumphant!!

Friends of the Charter, to the polls! Vote against the Constitution and the extension of suffrage, and secure the old Government!!

TOP: When the Charter government summoned a convention that drafted a constitution and submitted it to the legal voters, the latter rejected it by a 676-vote margin in March 1842. RIHS (RHi x3 4286)

BOTTOM: Exasperated with the old Charter government, Thomas Dorr attempted to overthrow it by force. On the night of May 18, 1842, the Dorrites tried to seize the state arsenal on Cranston Street in Providence; but the defenders, numbering some 200, protected the arsenal. The movement collapsed and Dorr fled the state. From ''Scenes in Rhode Island during the Rebellion. Upper Room of the Arsenal,'' Bouve's Lithographers, Boston. RIHS (RHi x3 4301)

Convention to draft another constitution, which went to the voters in March 1842. Dorr urged the suffragists to reject it, and the Landowners Constitution lost 8,689-8,013. The suffragists, declaring that the old Charter had been superseded by the People's Constitution, held elections on April 18, 1842, and elected Dorr governor. Two days later the regular state elections were held and Samuel Ward King of Johnston was reelected governor.

Because the People's government was locked out of the State House, it assembled on May 3 in a Providence foundry and inaugurated Dorr. The next day the Charter government convened in Newport and inaugurated King. Now Rhode Island had a popularly-elected, illegal government and a legal, unpopular government, one trying to govern from Providence, the other from Newport. Even at this moment, support for the People's government was waning. The Charter government had met in special session in April and outlawed the People's government and levied heavy penalties on those who accepted its offices. Furthermore, the Charter government received assurances from President John Tyler of federal support in case of an insurrection. Much of Dorr's support collapsed in the comic-opera attack upon the state arsenal on Cranston Street on May 18. Dorr led 234 men and two old cannons against the arsenal held by 200 loyal volunteers. The cannons would not fire and most of the men slipped away in the foggy night. Dorr fled to New York.

Anticipation and fear swept the state when word spread that Dorr was returning to reconvene the People's legislature in Chepachet on July 4. In the northern mill towns People's militia units with names like Dorr's Invincibles, Johnston Savages, Pascoag Ripguts, and Harmonious Reptiles formed, drilled, and nightly patrolled the highways. Dorr arrived and greeted about 1,000 supporters on June 25, and the Charter government began mobilizing 3,500 troops. Believing that Dorr was going to attack Providence, the state army assembled there and marched out to do battle at Chepachet on June 27. By then only about 225 of Dorr's followers remained, and none of the People's legislators had

appeared. He disbanded his forces and fled to sanctuary in New Hampshire. Still, the Charter army stormed Acote's Hill, where the Dorrites had erected some fortifications, and found it occupied by a cow. Frustrated, they searched Chepachet and the roads to neighboring towns and arrested about 100 suspected Dorrites. Under martial law, which continued until August, others, including Seth Luther, were arrested and jailed.

Dorr surrendered himself in October 1843. The government, determined to make an example of him, sentenced him to life imprisonment at hard labor in June 1844. A Liberation party, born of political backlash to this harsh punishment, won the elections of 1845 and freed the rebel leader. His health broken, Dorr died at age 48 in December 1854.

Although he lost the "war," his cause was partially achieved. Bending to the pressures, the Charter government, calling itself the Law and Order party, summoned another convention in September 1842. It produced a constitution which the voters approved 7,024-51 in a November referendum. Reapportionment gave northern industrial towns greater representation, although it was less than would be required in a "one-man-one-vote" system. Rural towns still controlled the state senate since every one of the 30 towns, no matter how tiny, had at least one vote. The franchise was extended to native-born men, increasing the electorate by 60 percent. However, the property qualification was retained for the foreign-born, leaving

them still second-class citizens.

Rhode Island's blacks were among the native-born who won the right to vote. This development, too, ran counter to the national trend. Constitutional revisions in most states after the War of 1812 extended the franchise to all whites but took it away from blacks. Rhode Island's blacks had lost the vote in 1822 as part of this trend, but they hoped that the political agitation of the 1830s and 1840s might restore their suffrage. They felt a particular need for any political leverage that their small numbers might provide because discrimination and violence continually afflicted them. By the 1820s half of Rhode Island's blacks lived in Providence and 50 percent of them owned their homes. However, their houses were crowded next to the dwellings of immigrant laborers in disorderly, poor neighborhoods. In 1824 the "Hard Scrabble" riot saw a mob ransack the black neighborhood as constables watched because they did not "think it proper or prudent to interfere." In 1831 the Olney Lane Riot, a three-day rampage against blacks, ended only when the Rhode Island Light Infantry fired on the white rioters, killing four of them. This was the first instance in America in which militia had been summoned to quell an urban riot, and it convinced Providence to adopt a city charter in 1832.

Regaining the vote was a case of taking advantage of cracks in the white political structure because no party wanted blacks to have the vote. The People's Constitution was a whites-only document; and leading

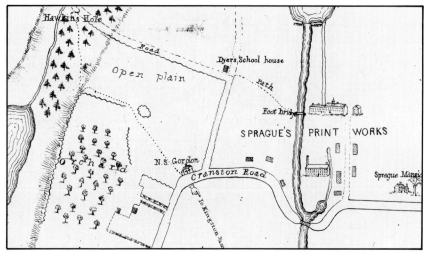

abolitionists, such as Frederick Douglass and Abby Kelley, campaigned against it for that reason. Rejected by the Dorrites, the black community supported the Law and Order party; and when the army marched to Chepachet, a volunteer force of 200 blacks patrolled Providence's streets to keep order. The Law and Order party rewarded them by including blacks in the expanded suffrage. As a result, Rhode Island's blacks generally voted for the conservative Whig party in the 1840s and 1850s.

While a Whig-Law and Order coalition dominated state politics in the 1840s, the period up to the Civil War was characterized by party instability, volatile alliances, shifting allegiances, and the rapid appearance and disappearance of parties. Some parties were temporary coalitions related to a state issue, such as the fleeting combination called the Liberation

ABOVE: A lithograph of A & W Sprague Print Works, 1844, shows the location of the Sprague Mansion and the home of John Gordon, who was convicted and hanged for the murder of Amasa Sprague. The affair triggered the crusade to abolish capital punishment in the state, but it was not until the Irish-supported Democratic party gained power in 1852 that it was abolished. When nativists and Whigs regained the governorship in 1858 they attempted unsuccessfully to repeal the statute. The area around the Print Works became the center of Irish settlers in Cranston. Lithograph by S.E. Cushing, from The Report on the Trial of John Gordon and William Gordon, 1844. RIHS (RHi x3 1039)

BELOW LEFT: The Law and Order army marched to the village of Chepachet and stormed Acote Hill searching for Dorrites on June 27, 1842. Lithograph by Thayer & Co., Boston, based on a drawing by H. Lord, probably an imprisoned Dorrite. RIHS (RHi x3 107)

The Providence City Guards

Blacks were winners in the Dorr War because they regained the vote. When the Law and Order army went out to face the Dorrites in Chepachet, a volunteer force of 200 blacks patrolled Providence to maintain order. A bitter Dorrite savagely attacked them in this 1842 broadside. From ''Governor King's Extra'' (Broadside, 1842). RIHS (RHi x3 4302)

party in 1845 which gained Thomas Dorr's release from prison. Others reflected some single issue: the Temperance, Liberty, and Free Soil parties. The Know-Nothings erupted in 1854, swept the state in 1855, and then faded rapidly under the names of the American party and the American Republicans. Not until the rise to power of the Republicans in the 1850s did Rhode Island achieve a stable, two-party system.

As the national Whig party crumbled over the issue of slavery, the Rhode Island Whig party declined in the early 1850s. The Democrats won in 1851, 1852, and 1853 only to be driven out by the whirlwind of Know-Nothingism. While in power, Democrats supported election reforms, including the secret ballot and expanded suffrage, labor reforms, and abolition of the death penalty. The latter had been agitated for since 1833, when Rhode Island became the first state to abolish public executions but retained one of the lengthiest lists of capital crimes in the nation. The controversy over the execution of John Gordon for the murder of Amasa Sprague in 1844 only

added to the crusade. In 1852 Rhode Island became the second state in the nation, the first in New England, to abolish the death penalty and held fast despite several efforts to reinstate it in the late 1850s.

The Know-Nothing movement in the United States developed in response to the tide of Irish immigration and the rise of anti-Catholic bigotry in the 1840s. A major element in the anti-Dorr argument had been its nativistic appeal. One opponent declared that if the foreign-born were given the vote, Rhode Island would ''become a province of Ireland: St. Patrick will take the place of Roger Williams, and the Shamrock will supersede the anchor and Hope.'' Such feelings developed as the Roman Catholic population, which was nearly all Irish, became more visible in the 1840s. Although nearly all foreign-born Catholics were excluded from voting, they favored the Democratic party. The triumph of political nativism meant the downfall of the Democrats in Rhode Island. Not until 1935 did Democrats regain control of both the governorship and the legislature.

The Know-Nothings worked in secret until they elected a candidate to the General Assembly in a special election in the fall of 1854. The following March they fielded a full slate for state offices. Governor William W. Hoppin, a Whig, was reelected with Know-Nothing backing, and they took all other state offices with nearly 70 percent of the votes. Yet, despite complete control, the Know-Nothings made no significant changes. In truth, most support for the Know-Nothing party came from voters dissatisfied with the failure of the Whigs or Democrats to take stands on the two major issues of antislavery and temperance, rather than from support for bigoted ideas. After winning nearly everything in 1855, the Know-Nothings faded rapidly in 1856 as the Republican party surged to power. Rhode Islanders gave the Republican candidate John C. Fremont 60 percent of their votes in the presidential election in 1856. A Republican legislature sent James F. Simmons to the United States Senate in 1857 and Henry B. Anthony there in 1858. The Senate voted to expel Simmons in 1862 for war-contract kickbacks, so he resigned; Anthony remained powerful in state politics until his death in 1884.

Despite the triumph of the antislavery Republican party, Rhode Island did not wish to aggravate the slaveholding South.

Too many ties of family, affection, and business existed between this state and the Cotton Kingdom. Newport had been a summer resort for southerners since the 1730s, and the state's number one industry, cotton textiles, depended upon the steady supply of cotton. While Rhode Island had been a leader in the antislavery movement in the days of Moses Brown, Samuel Hopkins, and James Manning, it had also been home port for some of the most notorious slavers. The abolitionist movement of the 1830s found greater sympathy in Providence than in Newport or South County. The Rhode Island Anti-Slavery Society was organized in 1836 in Providence, and abolitionist petitions to Congress emanated from there. By contrast, Newport's representatives in 1835 wanted the General Assembly to prohibit the publication of abolitionist newspapers in Rhode Island. The state denounced the Fugitive Slave Act of 1850, adopted a "personal liberty" law to thwart slave catchers, and voted for Fremont and Lincoln in 1856 and 1860. Still, when the Republicans nominated an abolitionist for governor in 1860, voters elected young William Sprague, a wealthy Democrat running under the Union party label. His coalition controlled the General Assembly and sought a compromise to the crisis of Southern secession. Rhode Island repealed the personal liberty law and sent five delegates to the Virginia Peace Conference that met in February 1861. At the same time it appropriated money for state military units in case of rebellion and Governor Sprague offered Rhode Island militia to President James Buchanan for the defense of Washington if it were threatened.

The compromise efforts failed. After the attack on Fort Sumter, Rhode Island immediately answered President Abraham Lincoln's call to arms, and the Rhode Island First Regiment was the first fully armed and equipped unit to arrive in Washington. Last to join the Union, Rhode Island was now first to defend it. Firmly in the Union, Rhode Island became increasingly aware that its economic life depended upon national markets for industrial products, a protective tariff, and a federal currency.

ABOVE: William W. Hoppin (1807-1880) won the governorship three times—1854, 1855, and 1856—by catching the winds of dissatisfaction and reform. Nominally a Whig, he came to power first with strong support from the temperance movement. He was reelected in 1855 when the Know-Nothings endorsed him; and he gained a third term with Know-Nothing and Republican support. After the Civil War he served as a Republican state senator. RIHS (RHi x3 4289)

BELOW LEFT: Anti-Irish, anti-Catholic nativism increased through the 1840s as the number of Irish in the state rose because of construction, industrialization, and the Irish potato famine. Nativism had a strong appeal to voters, and Governor Charles Jackson tried to refute the assertion that he favored expanding the franchise, which would allow naturalized citizens to vote. He lost the next election to the Whig candidate. (Broadside, 1846). RIHS (RHi x3 1266)

FRIENDS OF GOV. JACKSON, READ THIS!
IRISH VOTERS!!!

We have just been informed that the Country towns are flooded with *Infamous Handbills,* misrepresenting the views of GOV. JACKSON as to the *Qualification of Foreign Voters!*—It is well known that Gov. Jackson PROPOSED the *FREEHOLD QUALIFICATION* in the CONVENTION. The whole story that *Gov. Jackson* is in favor of ABOLISHING that qualification is *utterly* and *totally without foundation!* It is manufactured by SAMUEL CURREY, a *Naturalized Foreigner* from NOVA SCOTIA, who has been HIRED to *MISREPRESENT* the views of GOV. JACKSON and his friends.

People of *Rhode-Island* believe not these IN-FAMOUS LIES manufactured by this *HIRED TOOL* of the Providence ARISTOCRACY!—They are *INTENDED to DECEIVE you,* and thus prevent the election of GOV. JACKSON AND HIS PROX. They dared not *circulate* one of them in Providence, for they *knew* it would be refuted forthwith!

Friends of CHARLES JACKSON, are you willing to see *him* crushed by the FALSEHOODS and *MALIGNITY* of his bitterest enemies?—We know you are *NOT!*

Chapter Five

FROM OCEAN TO INDUSTRY

Calico printing, introduced from England in the 1820s, was an inexpensive alternative to pattern weaving. The delicate machinery required skilled operators and engravers. Wood engraving from the Memoir of Samuel Slater *by George S. White, 1836. RIHS (RHi x3 480)*

IN THE 17TH AND 18TH CEN-turies, Narragansett Bay and the oceans beyond provided Rhode Island with its main opportunities and means of economic development, but in the first half of the 19th century the state's energy and ingenuity turned to industry. Even while the outcome of the Revolution was in doubt, mercantile houses prepared to reenter oceanic enterprise. However, the depression of the 1780s, British trade restrictions, wars, revolutions, the Embargo of 1807, and the closing of the slave trade all dictated new patterns of commerce. Some merchants found lucrative new opportunities, others succeeded by disobeying the law, and still others were ruined. Newport never fully recovered from the exodus of capital and resourceful merchants. Bristol and Warren succeeded for a few decades by slaving, privateering, and whaling. Providence, the most aggressive commercial town after the Revolution, actively engaged in coastal trade, European and Caribbean commerce, and the newer traffic with South America, Australia, and the Orient. These enterprises were the state's last significant efforts in oceanic commerce.

After the Revolution, most Rhode Island merchants experienced difficulties reestablishing trade with Europe and the Caribbean. The British Order in Council of July 2, 1783, closed the British West Indies to American ships, and Great Britain imposed a heavy import duty on goods Americans traditionally shipped to England. The first action closed an important part of the triangular trade, and the second made the price of American goods prohibitively expensive in England. The turmoil of the French Revolution and Napoleonic wars, extending through the War of 1812, made trans-Atlantic commerce unusually difficult. Rhode Island merchants, however, persisted and took advantage of the European demand for American goods by diverting trade to Baltic, German, and Mediterranean ports. Trade with Europe peaked between 1800 and 1807, when the number of ships entering Providence nearly tripled and the duties collected more than doubled. Embargo and war suppressed the European trade until 1815, after which it showed renewed vitality, although the volume was below prewar levels. By the mid-1820s trade with Europe was in decline, and a decade later it had virtually ended.

The political troubles of Europe spilled into the Caribbean, the traditional market of the slave trade and Rhode Island merchants. With the slave trade prohibited in 1787 by the state and then in 1808 by the federal government, most Narragansett Bay merchants abandoned traffic in human beings. Legitimate trading operations shifted from one Caribbean port to another to sidestep wars, revolutions, pirating, and commercial restrictions and managed to keep trade and profits high for a time. Caribbean trade emerged strong in the 1790s when commerce with Europe was depressed; but after 1800 it gradually fell as the slave trade closed and Europe again became important to the merchants.

Trade with Europe and the Caribbean was unquestionably the mainstay of Rhode Island's business, but the opening of markets in the Orient, South America, and to a lesser extent Australia infused new life into the mercantile community. These routes were opened by Providence merchants who desperately sought new opportunities. Although the least damaged of the state's ports, Providence felt the depression of the 1780s. Its merchants believed that Americans hungered for Brit-

aggressive enterprise.

Nicholas Brown returned to rum distillation and traded with Surinam for molasses. A number of firms tried slaving; but when the trade proved only marginally profitable and then illegal, most withdrew. In one ill-fated venture, the Browns constructed 15 schooners for codfishing; but the family's confidence in recovery was apparent as John Brown invested heavily in constructing wharfs in Providence. Almost simultaneously, Providence's lead-

ish products; so in 1783, 10 leading firms formed a cartel to purchase British goods and sell them at a fixed, high price. The venture backfired. They overbought, the market was depressed and glutted, and the traditional goods for payment (whale oil, spermaceti candles, and spirits) were unsalable because of high British tariffs. The merchants fell deeply in debt. For example, the firm of Brown & Benson owed their London supplier £26,000 sterling. In addition, Rhode Island traders were plagued by a further reduction of exportable commodities: agricultural products peaked and pig iron declined, the Hope Furnace lost money, the whaling industry on Nantucket had nearly collapsed, and spermaceti chandlers stood in ruins. Even rum, one of the more intoxicatingly profitable industries of maritime trade, stumbled and staggered. As a result, Providence experienced a postwar "paralysis of commerce more catastrophic" than elsewhere. Nevertheless, the town's merchants weathered the depression by

ing mercantile family began exploring new economic avenues. Moses Brown immersed himself in textile manufacturing; and in 1785 Nicholas Brown became the first Rhode Islander to trade with Brazil. John Brown opened the China trade in 1787 with the dispatch of the *General Washington*, and in 1792 he began trading with Australia. In both markets he was the first Rhode Islander and the second American. Soon, Brown & Ives, Clark & Nightingale, Joseph and William Russell, Edward Carrington & Company, Welcome Arnold, and other Providence concerns as well as the DeWolfs of Bristol and syndicates in Newport and elsewhere were involved in the China trade.

They learned the China trade through trial and error and found that it required huge capital commitments. It was not a business for the fainthearted or the underfinanced, but profits could be enormous. Since Rhode Island had virtually nothing that anyone in China wanted, an elaborate network developed: goods were traded in the Canary Islands, the Baltic, Bremen and Hamburg, the Caribbean, Mediterranean ports, and India in order to obtain a cargo for the Chinese market. Most commonly, cotton from India was sold in Canton for tea, silk, lacquer ware, and china. Brown & Benson dispatched the *Rising Sun* in 1792 with a load of beef, candles, wheat, and fish and whale oil to India to trade for cotton. The beef violated Hindu religious beliefs and was unsalable, and the rest of the cargo was inferior to Indian products. The voyage was saved by a consignment of 36,000 Spanish silver dollars, and the firm earned a meager profit of $6,000. By the mid-1790s successful China traders had learned their lessons and carried salable goods and increasing amounts of silver, sometimes in excess of 100,000 Spanish dollars. The China ships were larger than most other commercial vessels, cargoes generally ran between $40,000 and $90,000, and voyages lasted 18 months. Profits regularly exceeded $100,000, but one Brown & Ives Indiaman brought $430,000 in Amsterdam. Only the larger houses commanded the capital to conduct the trade, although smaller merchants often bought shares in such undertakings.

Despite the China trade's profitability, losses were sometimes staggering. Brown & Ives lost *Ann and Hope* off Block Island in 1806 with a cargo valued at $500,000, and the following year the *John Jay* splintered on a reef off Java, wiping out an additional $115,000. Carrington was forced to sell other assets in the early 1830s to cover over $300,000 in China-trade debts. Losses might have been even greater had it not been for the new structures and relationships among traders. Overseas agents, commission houses, captains, supercargoes, and American consuls in China became important sources of trade information, credit, and skilled negotiators. The two American consuls at Canton between 1798 and 1811, Samuel Snow and Edward Carrington, were former employees of Providence firms.

By the 1830s the China trade was in decline, and ended for Providence in 1841 with the arrival of the *Lion*. Despite the glamor and fame of the China trade, during the peak years an average of only three

Edward Carrington (1775-1843), who served as U.S. Consul in Canton to 1811, was also a China trader, financier of internal improvements, promoter of the Blackstone Canal, and textile manufacturer. Carrington founded the firm of Edward Carrington & Company in 1815 and later owned 26 merchant ships. His career illustrates the transformation from ocean to industry and the accumulation of great wealth. RIHS (RHi x3 557)

ships returned to Rhode Island annually. Still, Providence was the third largest China-trade port in America, sizable fortunes were accumulated, and new trade routes were opened to the Pacific Northwest, Australia, and South America.

The Australian trade, supplying rum to quench the "unslackened thirst of the convict settlers," was over by 1812. The South American trade ran out of wind by 1831. The European and Caribbean commerce persisted but its volume was small. Customhouse duties fell from $400,000 in 1814 to $36,000 in 1860, while reexport trade declined from more than $1.5 million in 1805 to less than $10,000 by 1860. Brown & Ives sold their last ship, *Hanover*, in 1838, and joined other large mercantile houses in diversifying their economic activities. Oceanic commerce was nearly at an end.

Small merchants extended the maritime era by clinging tenaciously to a dying way of life. During the War of 1812 some Rhode Islanders, perhaps more greedy than patriotic, turned once more to privateering. After 1820, whaling rejuvenated shipbuilding, and both activities kept the towns of Bristol, Warren, and Newport in oceanic endeavors. But the whaling industry peaked in 1843, and by 1860 was finished. Freighting and coasting, the lifeblood of small traders, was strong in the 1840s and

Nantucket whalers supplied head matter for the spermaceti candle manufacturers of Massachusetts and Rhode Island until the industry collapsed in the 1770s and 1780s. Later, ships from Bristol went after the great whales, but the age of whaling was over for Rhode Island by the 1850s. Engraving from A System of School Geography *by S. Griswold Goodrich, 1837. RIHS (RHi x3 4278)*

remained fairly healthy until the Civil War. By this time, however, hauling coal and lumber from Canada, iron from Scotland and the Baltic, and cotton from the South had become a subsidiary part of Rhode Island's third economic phase — manufacturing.

Starting in the 1790s, some merchants began investing in industry and related enterprises. By the 1830s talent, capital, and power had shifted to manufacturing, especially textiles, metal trades and, to a lesser extent, jewelry. Merchants reoriented their interests and sought water rights, transportation facilities, banks, insurance companies, and a protective government. This economic transformation was nowhere more visible than in the northern towns of the state. There, Providence, Pawtucket, Woonsocket, and a host of mill villages gained supremacy and dictated the direction of the state for the next century.

Agriculture and maritime trade — Rhode Island's first two economic phases — had spawned lumber and gristmills, tanneries, slaughterhouses, cooperages, distilleries, iron shops, and forges. Mills appeared everywhere to harness waterpower; and where streams were unsuitable, as in Bristol, winds and tides were harnessed instead. By the 1790s the Providence Neck and the Moshassuck River were lined with

such enterprises and their discharge polluted the water. But it was shipbuilding and its relationship to the iron industry that proved significant to Rhode Island's industrial transformation.

In the 18th century iron ore deposits were mined in Glocester, Cranston, Cumberland, and at Mineral Springs in North Providence and processed at Hope Furnace and elsewhere. The demand for cannon, shot, and ships during the Revolution triggered the growth of ironworks and attracted skilled mechanics. Pawtucket, site of a waterfall, close to iron deposits and at the head of a navigable waterway, became a shipbuilding and ironworking town. There, Stephen Jenks, Sylvanus Brown, Oziel Wilkinson, and others manufactured muskets, nails, hoops, shovels, scythes, and marine hardware. The town's reputation extended to Halifax, Canada, whose merchants hired Sylvanus Brown and 50 Pawtucket mechanics to fabricate and install power systems for grist- and sawmills. It was not by accident that Moses Brown looked to Pawtucket for skilled wood- and ironworkers for his textile experiments.

In the throes of the post-Revolutionary depression, Moses Brown thought that textiles had the potential to help America become economically independent of Great Britain. At the same time he hoped to create employment for fellow Quakers, who were restricted in their choice of occupations, and possibly to help his two brothers out of debt. During 1787 and 1789 Moses learned what he could about the textile industry and attempted unsuccessfully to begin cotton manufacturing. In partnership with his son-in-law William Almy, he purchased from three Quaker craftsmen a crude spinning jenny and carding machine and installed them in the Market House in Providence. The machines failed but Moses' interest in textiles had not diminished. He wrote his Philadelphia Quaker friends for the names of newly arrived British mechanics.

The answer came unsolicited from New York in December 1780 from Samuel Slater who wrote that he could "give the greatest satisfaction, in making machinery, making good yarn...." Without awaiting Moses' reply, Slater headed for Providence. Almy & Brown hired him to build the machinery on the Arkwright system and to manage

their factory in Pawtucket. The firm agreed to provide raw cotton and to make the yarn. Slater built new machines, but relied upon Quaker craftsmen, especially woodworker Sylvanus Brown and ironworker Oziel Wilkinson. On December 20, 1790, Slater successfully spun cotton yarn on his water-powered machinery in an old fulling mill in Pawtucket. Rhode Island had given birth to cotton manufacturing in America.

By 1791, Slater was spinning yarn that exceeded local demand, so Almy & Brown pioneered market distribution and expanded their operation. First they convinced American weavers and merchants to use American-made yarn; then in 1803, they used their Quaker connections in New York, Philadelphia, and Baltimore to open up the West. Hard work, liberal credit, and subsidized merchants sustained the markets, and by 1819, 82 percent of their yarn was being sold to Philadelphia wholesale houses. Almy & Brown continued to expand and in 1807 constructed Warwick Manufacturing Company at Centerville, one of nine new cotton spinning mills opened in Rhode Island between 1805 and 1807. The Pawtucket operation became a model for the cotton industry as its craftsmen moved to other mills in Rhode Island and to New York and New Jersey. While Slater continued to manage Brown's mills, he built another plant in Pawtucket, Massachusetts, in 1799, became a partner in the Slatersville complex in 1806, and established a mill in Webster, Massachusetts, in 1811.

The Embargo of 1807 and the War of 1812 encouraged merchants, especially in Providence, to invest in manufacturing; and by the 1820s cotton processing displaced maritime commerce as the economic backbone of the state. Brown & Ives, who complained of their "increasing embarrassment" in commerce, spent huge sums in 1808 to establish the Blackstone Manufacturing Company. Edward Carrington had shares in eight mills and a host of other investments in nonmaritime enterprises. Throughout the war, expansion was virtually unchecked: 25 mills stood in nine Rhode Island towns in 1809; 100 mills operated in 21 towns in 1815. Prices for land and water rights increased dramatically as saw and gristmills along the Blackstone, Branch, Woonasquatucket, Pawtuxet, and Pawcatuck rivers gave way to new factories. New place names appeared yearly. Between 1807 and 1822 the Woonasquatucket River spawned the mill villages of Georgiaville, Greystone, Centerdale, Allenville (now Esmond), Allendale, and Lymansville. The process repeated itself throughout the river-rich northern half of the state, less so in the southern half, and virtually not at all east of the Bay.

ABOVE: Samuel Slater (1768-1835) built the first successful cotton-spinning machine in America in 1790. He served his apprenticeship with Jedediah Strutt, a partner of Richard Arkwright, the inventor of the power spinning frame, and emigrated to America carrying the design in his mind. Slater became a successful textile and cotton machine manufacturer and by 1827 was worth $700,000. Engraving by W.G. Jackson, D. Appleton & Company, New York. RIHS (RHi x3 2064)

LEFT: Philanthropist, industrialist, reformer, and leading antislavery figure in Rhode Island, Moses Brown (1738-1836) established important ties with the Quakers of Philadelphia during the American Revolution. The "Quaker connection" later proved significant in the distribution and marketing of the textile products of Almy & Brown. Oil painting on canvas, attributed to Henry E. Kinney, circa 1898. RIHS (RHi x3 3128)

ABOVE: Zachariah Allen (1795-1882) was an inventor, scientist, philosopher, and manufacturer. He pioneered the water reservoir idea in 1823, lightweight shafting, mutual fire insurance for mills, and patented a governor for steam engines. He was also known for his philanthropy, dry-season employment for his workers, and writings on solar energy. He also created a model mill village at Allendale (now part of North Providence) that included a Thomas Tefft-designed stone church and Sunday school. Oil on canvas painting by James Sullivan Lincoln, 1882. RIHS (RHi x3 3213)

BELOW: Saunders Pitman (1732-1804) fashioned this silver teapot about 1790. It is an exquisite example of jewelry items handcrafted in Rhode Island into the 1820s. Courtesy, Rhode Island Historical Society Museum

Rapid expansion during the war contributed to an equally rapid contraction after it. Capital flowed back into maritime efforts, British textiles flooded the market, and the 1819 depression destroyed demand. Although nearly two fifths of the mills closed, these problems only temporarily halted the industry's expansion. Depression removed weak investors, fostered innovation, and led to the consolidation of small operations. Some firms adopted steam power, installed Gilmore power looms, diversified their range of goods, and moved most operations to one site. Millowners secured favorable legislation from the state to impound water and won protective tariffs from the federal government. When oceanic commerce began its decline in the 1820s, the textile industry once again expanded, with larger mills and newer companies dominating the field. By the Civil War, Rhode Island's cotton industry ranked second in the nation with a total of 176 mills, 15,739 employees, and an annual production valued at $20 million. Slater's experiment had become an industrial empire.

The woolen industry experienced patterns of cyclical growth and development similar to those of cotton. Prior to the 1830s, the woolen industry was marked by small mills, low capitalization, and an average labor force of fewer than 10. In 1804 Rowland Hazard of Peace Dale built a mill for carding and dyeing, but he used local farmers for spinning and weaving. Realizing that the farmers were undepend-

able, Hazard cautiously expanded his mill, adding the first power looms in the American woolen industry in 1814, and bringing farmers to his mill to weave. Hazard's operation was the model for others, and Washington County emerged as the center of the woolen industry in the state.

The northern area was not outdone. In 1812, Sullivan Dorr, Samuel Arnold, and others built the Providence Woolen Company. Although it later failed, the company's introduction of steam power greatly benefited all textiles and stimulated others to expand. Zachariah Allen also contributed, first, by establishing the Allendale mill in 1822 and later through his innovations in power mechanics, mill construction, and mill fire insurance. The leader of the woolen industry both state- and nationwide before the Civil War was Edward Harris, a man with no formal education but a genius for organization. After working for several mills, he purchased a factory in 1832 in Woonsocket, and by the 1850s operated five woolen mills that produced cassimeres and other specialty items. Harris' success made him Woonsocket's first millionaire and primary booster of the town's early growth.

By the Civil War, Rhode Island's woolen industry was dominated by Providence, Woonsocket, and Burrillville. The state's 57 mills had an invested capital of $3 million, 4,200 employees, and more than $7 million in annual products. It was the second largest industry in the state and produced a range of specialty items greater than that of the cotton industry.

Closely related to textiles were two branches of the metals industry, one producing textile machinery and the other a diversity of metal products. While Slater could be called the father of American textile machinery, the sons of Oziel Wilkinson, the descendants of Stephen Jenks, and the many English and Quaker mechanics actually placed Rhode Island among the leaders in textile-machinery production. Some worked in maintenance shops attached to mills; others emerged as inventors and opened their own shops. Although slow to mature, the textile machinery business prospered as textiles expanded and managers exploited the

home market for the equipment. Soon, the state boasted of such establishments as James S. Brown of Pawtucket, Fales & Jenks of Central Falls, and the Providence Machine Company. Their power looms, ring spinning frames, and braiding machines were installed locally and as far away as Georgia, Louisiana, and even Scotland. Supplementary companies manufactured bobbins, spools, leather belts, and various items vital to the industry.

Related, but more diverse, and thus less prone to the business fluctuations of the textile market, was the metal-trades industry. Although slower in developing than textile-machinery manufacture, diversified metal shops emerged in the 1830s with the establishment of Brown & Sharpe, Eagle Screw Company, Barstow Stove Company, New England Butt Company, Builders Iron Foundry, and a host of smaller shops. The industry accelerated thereafter, and the addition of stationary steam engines launched George H. Corliss' career and gave Providence the distinction of making the finest steam engines in America. By the Civil War, Providence County had three fourths of the 142 metalworking firms in the state, and the American Screw works was the largest metals employer with over 600 employees. In the second half of the 19th century, four of the base-metal firms were among the "Five Industrial Wonders of the World." The fifth, Gorham Silverware, belonged to the jewelry industry.

The jewelry industry in Rhode Island did not benefit as directly as did textiles and base metals from the decline in oceanic commerce, and thus took much longer to mature. Without substantial capital or foreign competition, the production of jewelry remained primarily a handicraft industry. In the recessions that followed the War of 1812, jewelry makers turned to cheap items, such as gold-filled and gold-plated chains, necklaces, and rings, thereby expanding costume jewelry production. A notable exception occurred in 1813, when Seril Dodge entered into a partnership with Jabez Gorham and four other journeymen to produce fine silver items. In 1831 Gorham formed a partnership with a Boston silversmith, and in 1847 his son traveled extensively in Europe and brought English silversmiths to Providence and installed steam power to drive the machinery. Other jewelers soon moved into Providence textile complexes that had surplus steam power which the artisans used to run their operations. While Providence became the jewelry center of the state with 57 of the 86 establishments, the industry had only eight firms with more than 25 employees before the Civil War. Nevertheless, a foundation for one of the state's leading industries had been laid.

The concentration of industry and population in the northern part of the state might be construed as the result of geography, especially the availability of waterpower. However, men with vision and money made it happen. Recognizing that the limited hinterland was unsuitable for extensive trade and seeing the potential of manufacturing, Providence men worked to extend their domain. They embarked on internal improvement projects and simultaneously developed banks, insurance companies, and other service institutions. In the 1790s, the town rebuilt the Weybosset Bridge, John and Moses Brown constructed competing Central

ABOVE: The Blackstone Canal opened July 1, 1828, with chief investor and commissioner Edward Carrington traveling the length from Providence to Worcester in regal procession. Irish laborers built the canal, which was engineered by Holmes Hutchinson of Rhode Island, and established communities from Providence to Woonsocket and Worcester. From Providence Patriot and Columbian Phoenix, *November 11, 1829. RIHS (RHi x3 4305)*

BELOW: Designed by Thomas A. Tefft and opened in 1848, this elegant Romanesque train station dominated Exchange Place and the center of Providence for the next half century. (Photo, 1872) RIHS (RHi x3 379)

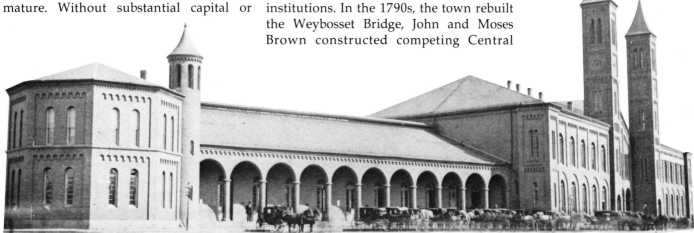

The H.L. Fairbrother & Company Leather Belting Manufactory, located in Pawtucket, is depicted here in 1819. It was an example of the secondary industries that grew up to supply a product to the new textile and machine tool industries. RIHS (RHi x3 1819)

(Red) and South (Washington) bridges, and merchants subscribed to the Providence-Norwich Turnpike, one of 46 such roads incorporated in the state by 1842. These turnpikes connected mill villages to each other, and turned Providence into the hub of an extensive transportation network.

Visions of draining commerce from western Massachusetts to Providence prompted John Brown in 1796 to apply for a charter to construct a canal from Providence to Worcester. Boston merchants opposed the idea; but in 1823 the Browns, Carrington, Dorr, and others renewed the plan, received charters from both states, and in 1828 opened the Blackstone Canal. The 45-mile canal was not an engineering marvel for it took barges all day to travel seven miles. Nevertheless, in its first few years it drained the hinterland and supplied mills with provisions and raw cotton. Competing water demands of mills, speedier overland freighting, and the opening of the Boston-Worcester Railroad in 1831 led to the canal's demise. The Blackstone Canal Company wanted to abandon operations as early as 1832, but millowners successfully fought the canal's closing until 1849. Although the waterway was a financial failure, it stimulated industrial growth in the Blackstone Valley and irreversibly tied that region to Providence.

Providence men turned to railroads at an early date and secured General Assembly support, but out-of-state companies were severely restricted. After several false starts and legislative restrictions which soured several Massachusetts companies on entering the city, the General Assembly granted Providence merchants a charter, without restrictions, to build a short line from a terminal at Fox Point across the Seekonk to connect with the Boston line. A horse-drawn car opened the Boston-Providence line in 1835, and two years later the Stonington Railroad terminated on the harbor in South Providence. In 1847 some of the merchants who had invested in the Blackstone Canal brought the Providence & Worcester Railroad to completion. Subsequent construction of the Providence, Warren & Bristol, and the Fall River, Warren & Providence railroads extended the city's hold on the eastern shores. Although Providence had only limited success in its attempts to expand its rail connections into upper New York and the West, the rail network made the city the undisputed transportation center of southern New England. To demonstrate its status Providence built the largest train station in America in 1848, and the Cove Basin was lined with stone and encircled by a fashionable, tree-lined promenade.

From slow beginnings, banking and insurance institutions soon became indispensable to the economic transformation of Rhode Island. As in other economic areas, the state's leading merchant family led the way: John Brown created the first bank in the state in 1791 with the Providence Bank, and in 1799 Brown & Ives founded the first insurance company with the Providence Insurance Company. The number of state banks in the first half of the 19th century fluctuated with business conditions and state regulation. Most bank directors were millowners; nevertheless, state banks generally followed sound practices, failures were few, and none occurred in the Panic of 1837. Part of this may be explained by the state regulatory policies. When in 1809 the Farmers Exchange Bank of Glocester became the first bank in America to fail, the General Assembly made bankers personally liable for losses. With the national rise of antibank sentiment in the 1830s, Rhode Island became the first state to enact a comprehensive banking statute. By 1860 Rhode Island had 91 banks and 21 savings institutions scattered in almost every mill village. Providence, however, had emerged as the financial center with two fifths of the banks and four fifths of the capital.

While banks provided an essential outlet for venture capital and financed economic growth, insurance companies protected the commercial community from loss. The Providence Insurance Company and the Newport Insurance Company, both started in 1799, met with competition when Richard Jackson organized the Washington Insurance Company in 1800. The Providence companies having survived the Providence fire of 1801, the flood of 1807, and the Great Gale of 1815, merged into the Providence Washington Insurance Company by 1820 and shifted from maritime to industrial insurance. Industrial fire insurance was expensive until Zachariah Allen established the Manufacturers Mutual Fire Insurance Company in 1835, organized specifically for mills. Within two years fire insurance rates fell 60 percent. By the Civil War, six underwriting companies operated in the state; and Providence, with four of them, nearly monopolized the business by issuing 92 percent of all fire insurance.

The economic transformation from maritime trade to manufacturing made Rhode Island the most industrialized state in the Union. In 1860, manufacturing engaged over 22,000, or 36 percent of all workers, while maritime trade employed less than 3 percent, and four fifths of the state's capital was invested in textiles and base metals. During the time the population of Rhode Island rose from 68,825 in 1790 to 174,619 in 1860, the industrialized northern towns had increased their share of that total from 30 to 66 percent. As chief contributors, Providence and the neighboring towns of North Providence, Smithfield, Cranston, and Warwick were also its principal benefactors. Between 1832 and 1861 Providence's population jumped from over 16,000 to 55,666 and her assessed valuation rose from $12 million to $61 million. Although hundreds of mill villages existed almost exclusively because of textiles, Providence had a more diversified economy; and it had emerged as the undisputed transportation, financial, and industrial capital of southern New England.

Banks proliferated all over the state of Rhode Island with each issuing its own paper currency which was supposed to be redeemable in gold or silver. The Farmers Exchange Bank of Glocester failed in 1809, and investigators found that it had $86.48 in specie in its vault against $500,000 in paper in circulation. The failure led to improved banking laws and closer supervision of banks in Rhode Island. RIHS (RHi x3 4308)

Chapter Six

INDUSTRIAL WONDERS OF THE WORLD

SOME HISTORIANS HAVE argued that Rhode Island's heavy concentration in a few industrial fields was the result of a pervasive economic conservatism within the business community and an unwillingness to take risks and diversify. Historians cite the top-heavy investment in textiles, the continued reliance on the labor of women and children, and the slow adoption of technological innovations such as the power loom. In fact, Rhode Island was a center of innovation in other textile machines, and some nontextile firms grew to become the largest of their kind in the world. The fundamental question is not why Rhode Island failed to diversify, but why did the state become the most industrialized state in the nation? While economic conservatism did emerge in the second half of the 19th century in contrast to the innovativeness of earlier industrialists, it rested not so much with business leaders as with conditions which the state's limited resources imposed. Most early manufacturers creatively juggled the limited assets at their disposal to develop the state's industries.

Rhode Island was an unlikely center for industry. It had no *good* deposits of iron, coal, or other minerals. It had a limited land mass for continued market and population growth. Except for the Providence & Worcester Railroad, the transportation system gave it access only to the coastal and competing centers of New York and Boston. Waterpower sites had to be developed, suffered through summer droughts and winter freezes, and were

owned by a large number of settlers. The labor force before the 1830s was the same Yankee stock that sailed the oceans, farmed the land, or built the mills. Rhode Island's investment capital could not compare with that of other states and came from surplus profits of oceanic commerce. To industrialize, Rhode Islanders had to import cotton, wool, iron, capital, and labor, and then ship most finished products through New York and Boston to regional and national markets that required cultivation. No wonder that in the early years most mills were small, had limited capitalization, experienced frequent changes in ownership, and employed the cheapest local labor available—women and children.

The types of investors affected the scope of industralization. From the outset three groups emerged: sea traders, farmers and merchants, and mechanics (especially the English or those trained in Samuel Slater's mills). Traders appeared more willing to invest their surplus capital in industry; but great sums were tied up in oceanic commerce. Their capital became available mainly during periods of trade contraction, such as the Embargo or War of 1812. Most merchants and farmers were underfunded, retained small mills longer, and were wedded to the mill village concept. Many succumbed to their competitors and sold out. Of the three, the English and the mechanics were the most conservative and traditional group. Samuel Slater, his brother John, and others established the early mills, introduced woman and child labor, and resisted mechanization.

This label for Perry Davis' Vegetable Pain Killer, a patent medicine containing alcohol and opium, dates from 1854. RIHS (RHi x3 4297)

William Sprague (1830-1915), shown here as the dashing "war governor" who accompanied the Rhode Island 1st Regiment to Bull Run, served as Governor (1860-1863) and U.S. Senator (1863-1875). He married Kate Chase, daughter of U.S. Supreme Court Justice Salmon P. Chase. An extravagant and flamboyant man, he pyramided the A. & W. Sprague empire toward bankruptcy in 1873. Lithograph by J.H. Bufford, 1861. RIHS (RHi x3 4304)

A major problem was finding workers in a small population already employed in agriculture. Alexander Hamilton suggested in his "Report on Manufacturers" (1791) that only "idle" women and children might be spared from farm work, and the early mills depended upon them. It is not surprising that Slater employed nine children to tend his first machines or that he recruited large families. The industry by 1820 employed more children than women and twice as many women as men. Millowners used the "Rhode Island" system which brought entire families into mill complexes and created a dependent labor pool. It also kept down production costs and facilitated gradual plant expansion until later immigration created a larger labor pool. The transition from artisan and agricultural pursuits to factory work occasioned friction even where the millowners were most paternalistic.

Slater recognized the inefficiency of the "putting out" system and installed looms in his mill to bring weavers to the factory, but in 1802 a number of disgruntled weavers protested against the new regimentation. Almy & Brown prevented Slater from installing a power loom until 1823; but when he and other Pawtucket millowners attempted to cut wages to weavers paid by the yard, the workers, led by women, walked out. The first textile strike in American history lasted a week, during which time arsonists set fire to one mill and workers demonstrated in the streets. Generally, however, most millowners were viewed as benefactors by the community; and labor problems were, on the whole, minor. The owners' paternalism gradually ended in the era of expansion and greater mechanization after the 1840s.

Rhode Island's slow adoption of the power loom has been most frequently cited as an example of economic conservatism. While it is true that the development of a power loom at the Waltham mill of Francis Lowell in 1815 thrust Massachusetts ahead of Rhode Island in cotton textile manufacturing, Rhode Island probably adopted the new loom as fast as it could. One must recognize that Rhode Island's economy was overextended by 1815. During the War of 1812, investors pumped money into mills, banks, and turnpikes, but during the postwar depression, mills collapsed at an alarming rate, markets disappeared, and the textile-machine industry was in disarray. The supply of adult workers had not appreciably increased since the 1790s, nor had labor shown a willingness to accept the regimentation of factory life. It should also be recognized that the Waltham power loom was a complicated machine that sold for $125. Consequently, most Rhode Islanders who were caught in the postwar financial squeeze had really no choice than to await better economic conditions. Most bought the Gilmore power loom, which was simpler and cost only $70. By 1826, one third of the mills had power looms, and in the 1830s nearly 90 percent engaged in power weaving. Considering the state's limited resources, it was not economic conservatism that allowed it to keep abreast of the bigger neighboring state; it was sound business practices, frugal methods, and calculated risk-taking and daring. These same traits thrust Rhode Island's industries into national dominance in the second half of the century.

One could scarcely accuse the Spragues of timidity as they piled up an empire worth $19.4 million. They began modestly enough when in 1808 William Sprague converted his gristmill on the Pocasset River into a small mill for carding and spinning cotton yarn; but the real founder of the fortune was his son William, Jr., who pioneered the use of power machinery. At the death of the first William Sprague in 1836, his sons William and Amasa formed

the 1860s and beyond financial safety by the 1870s. By then they owned a series of vertically integrated textile plants that covered all operations from the purchase of raw cotton to the manufacture of finished cloth. They owned timber in Maine, water-power sites for textile mills in South Carolina, land in Kansas and Texas, a street railway in Providence, a steamship line, five banks, an iron foundry, a mowing-machine factory, a horseshoe and horse-shoe-nail factory, as well as mills at Quidnick, Centreville, River Point, Crompton, and Arctic, and the Cranston Print Works. In the nearly self-contained mill villages their workers rented company-owned tenements and shopped at the company

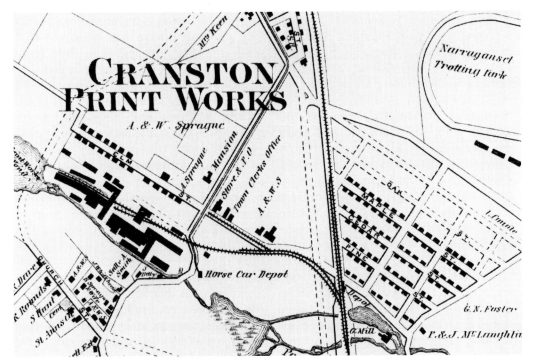

ABOVE: Robert Knight (1826-1912), top, and Benjamin B. Knight (1813-1893), BOTTOM, created the B.B. & R. Knight Company. At the Columbian Exposition of 1893 an enthusiastic description of their domain declared, "One corporation, the largest in the world, renders its dozen villages musical with the hum of 421,000 spindles and makes them beautiful by the happiness of more than 7,000 operatives." From Fruit of the Loom *(n.d.) RIHS (RHi x3 4294)*

LEFT: Beer's 1870 map of the Cranston Print Works of the A & W Sprague Manufacturing Company shows the layout of a mill village, complete with neat rows of company houses for workers, the company store and post office, church, and owners' homes. The Narragansett Trotting Park, another Sprague enterprise, was established in 1867. From Beer's Atlas, 1870. RIHS (RHi x3 4367)

the A. & W. Sprague Manufacturing Company and expanded the enterprise over the next 20 years. Not content with textiles, William was president of two banks and the Hartford, Providence & Fishkill Railroad. Economic power was translated into political power as he served as General Assemblyman, Congressman, Governor (1838-1839), and United States Senator (1842-1844). By the time William, Junior, died in 1856, the Spragues were the leading calico-printers in America.

Amasa's sons, also named William and Amasa, carried the company to its peak in

stores. Company farms raised cattle for slaughter for their stores and reared draft horses for their factories and street railway.

The Spragues used the political leverage of their 12,000 employees to dominate Providence politics, the state government, and even the Rhode Island Supreme Court. William III was elected Governor (1860-1863) and United States Senator (1863-1875). Despite his wealth, power, and ambition, William was unable to break the social and economic leadership of the Browns. When his speculation forced him to borrow from the banks, the Browns tried to stop his credit and encouraged his creditors to press him. The Panic of 1873 toppled the Spragues and forced their companies into bankruptcy.

By the end of the 19th century, cotton textiles in the state were dominated by four great combinations. Brown & Ives abandoned oceanic trade for textiles and owned the Blackstone Manufacturing Company, operating 300,000 spindles in Rhode Island and Massachusetts. The firm of B.B.&R. Knight, which was started in 1852, picked up portions of the crumbling Sprague empire, including six mills in Cranston in 1883 and the Cranston Print Works in 1888. Before World War I, B.B.&R. Knight owned 19 mills in Rhode Island and Massachusetts, including 15 mill villages in this state, and their trademark, "Fruit of the Loom," was world famous. The Lippitts, another great concentration, had begun in West Warwick in 1810. Each generation added to the company, but the greatest expansion came under Henry Lippitt, who took over in 1850. More the consolidator than the innovator, Lippitt acquired the Social, Harrison, and Globe mills in Woonsocket and the Manville Mill in Cumberland. He also acquired the Silver Springs Bleaching and Dyeing Company, and in 1865 he founded the Lippitt Woolen Company. Like the Spragues, the Lippitts entered politics. Henry Lippitt served as Governor (1875-1877) and his sons Charles and Henry F. were respectively Governor (1895-1897) and United States Senator (1911-1917).

Another giant, the W.F. & F.C. Sayles Company, dominated textile bleaching. Having started the company in 1847, William Sayles was joined by his brother Frederick in 1863 and together they owned the world's largest bleachery in Saylesville, the Moshassuck Railroad, the Lorraine Woolen Mills, and several other enterprises. Both attended to business, although Frederick became Pawtucket's first mayor in 1886, and William represented Pawtucket in the state senate for two years.

Although no one of them dominated textiles, the effect of these great concerns was to accelerate the consolidation of the industry. By 1900 the state had only half as many individual mills as in 1860, but they manufactured several times as much product with twice as many operatives employed in large plants. With the exception of the flurry caused by World War I, the era of the cotton textile industry had reached its zenith in Rhode Island and was passing. Investment and mill construction definitely slowed down and New England cotton textiles began to feel the competition from the South. In fact, a substantial part of the new investment in the second half of the 19th century was not in spinning and weaving but in bleaching, dyeing, and printing plants which processed increasing quantities of cotton cloth shipped for finishing from the South. More and more Rhode Island firms invested in southern mills. With capital going elsewhere, plants and equipment were not improved and modernized as needed. The *Providence Magazine*, voice of the Providence Board of Trade, warned in 1893: "Send all the surplus earnings away from our state for a decade, and you will have left general decay in business and bankruptcy staring you in the face."

As cotton declined and sent its capital to the South, the state's woolen industry matured and prospered with the infusion of foreign capital. By 1900 the value of woolen goods exceeded that of cotton. The industry was less prone to market fluctuations than cotton; and because it complemented rather than competed with cotton, it experienced growth during periods of cotton depression. For example, the industry leaped forward during the Civil War when the Wanskuck and Riverside mills were constructed, and boomed in the 1870s as the Atlantic and other large mill complexes turned the Providence Woolen Company into the state's leader. Providence became the center of the industry in Rhode Island and by 1900 was second in the nation in woolens and first in worsteds.

At the turn of the century, Aram Pothier encouraged French worsted manufacturers to invest in the state. Three French worsted mills were built in Woonsocket before World War I, and several more went up in the 1920s so that by the mid-1920s the so-called "French Mills" dominated Woonsocket. One of these, the Branch River

Wool Combing Company, was the largest of its kind in the world. Continuing investment in worsted mills meant that work remained there long after the last cotton mill had closed its doors. Other than jobs, however, these absentee French landlords contributed little to Woonsocket.

The future prosperity of the state depended on other forms of manufacturing and industry. Textiles arrived first and would continue to be Rhode Island's principal industry until the 1920s, but other enterprises grew alongside it. Most important were developments in base metals, jewelry, and rubber. Some companies became the largest of their kind, and by the 1890s Providence boasted of its "Five Industrial Wonders of the World." The city was the home of the largest tool factory (Brown & Sharpe), file factory (Nicholson File), steam engine factory (Corliss), screw factory (American Screw), and silverware factory (Gorham). The Hotchkiss Ordnance Company on Aborn Street manufactured the rapid-firing light cannon that massacred the Sioux at Wounded Knee in 1890; and later, local factories produced bicycles, automobiles, trucks, and airplane parts. Neighboring Pawtucket had a number of textile-related giants, including the

largest thread company (J. & P. Coats), hair cloth company, and wadding plant. Bristol and Woonsocket had big rubber factories, but an 1886 directory of Rhode Island's leading manufacturers and merchants did not list a single manufacturer in Newport.

Most of the large plants were in the metropolitan Providence area—where they were surrounded by a bewildering array of 1,500 other factories producing everything from buttons to blackboards, lightning rods to locomotives, hats to hydrants, and mirrors to monuments. At one time Providence ranked sixth among the nation's cities in her industrial production, and it was in the top 20 cities in population. It also had the highest per capita savings in the nation.

Most of the great businesses rested on some invention. The American Screw Company developed the first practical machine to make pointed screws in 1849 and, as a consolidated giant, nearly monopolized screw production in America. Brown & Sharpe grew from the 1833 partnership of David Brown and his son Joseph R. Brown making jewelry findings and repairing watches and clocks. Lucian Sharpe became a partner in 1853; and with a force of 14 employees, they manufactured

The C.B. Cottrell & Sons Company in Westerly, whose machines printed the nation's leading magazines in 1900—Scribner's, McClure's, Leslie's, Ladies Home Journal, and Saturday Evening Post—was the largest manufacturer of rotary printing presses. This engraving of an earlier plant of Cottrell & Babcock Works is by B. Bond of New York. RIHS (RHi x3 4361)

67

sewing machines, introducing mass production methods. The creation of accurate machines for standardizing parts led Joseph Brown to his invention of precision tools, including the Vernier Caliper (1851), the Tooth Rotary Milling Cutter (1864), and the Universal Grinding Machine (1874). Spurred by Brown's inventions and Sharpe's business acumen, by 1902 the company employed over 2,000 men in an enormous plant on Promenade Street.

William T. Nicholson transformed the file-making industry by inventing machinery in 1864 to mass-produce quality files. By 1900, the Nicholson File Company manufactured 60,000 files daily in 3,000 varieties and had begun to absorb its competitors. The company owned plants in seven states, marketed eight different

devised the first machine for making horseshoes in 1857 and prospered until electric trolleys and automobiles took over the streets. William Corliss invented a "burglar-proof" safe, and produced it for nearly 20 years before the Mosler Safe Company absorbed his business in 1895.

William's more famous brother was George Corliss, the inventor and manufacturer of the finest and most efficient steam engines. In 1849 he patented a new steam engine, and incorporated the Corliss Steam Engine Company in 1856. Using his inventions, he manufactured engines of the highest quality. By the Civil War the Corliss Company was the only factory capable of machining the turret washer and bearings for the revolutionary iron ship, the *Monitor*.

ABOVE: *Inventor and manufacturer George Corliss (1817-1888) came to Providence in 1844 hoping to produce his newly invented harness sewing machine. After designing a perfected steam engine, he began the Corliss Steam Engine Company in 1856 on Charles Street. He held 68 patents and pioneered ideas in standardization and mass production, but died before he could put them into full effect. From the* Life and Work of George H. Corliss, *1926. Courtesy, Providence Public Library*

LEFT: *Browne & Sharpe employees pose for the camera in front of the plant on South Main Street in Providence in 1872. Even though the metal trades required skilled workers, children (note those sitting on the curb in front) were employed as well. RIHS (RHi x3 4340)*

brands, and produced 80 percent of all files made in America.

Other innovators abounded. Frederick Grinnell invented a new automatic fire sprinkler in 1882, making his General Fire Extinguisher Company the leader in the field. Joseph Manton developed a ship's windlass in 1857, which became the standard for the United States Navy and most ships of American registry. Charles Perkins

His genius was limited only by a streak of inflexibility and the inability to delegate tasks to others. He was his own designer, architect, and builder; and he would not rely upon anyone to design his factories, machinery, or even his own home. His strong views about the Sabbath prevented the Centennial Exposition of 1876 from beginning on its scheduled Sunday opening date, despite President Grant's request for that day. Corliss had supplied the Exposition with a colossal steam engine. Symbolizing Rhode Island's industrial might, it was the center of attraction and the sole source of power for all of the 8,000 machines in Machinery Hall. So, he wrote, "Open these gates to desecrate the Sabbath and I will dismantle my engine and withdraw the power. You can do as you please with the Exhibition, but the engine will not run on Sunday."

Rhode Islanders used the popular international fairs and expositions to gain national recognition of the state's products. Corliss won the highest prize at the Paris Exposition of 1867, and Gorham silver was entered in every major exposition after 1879, winning top honors in all of them. For the Columbian Exposition of 1893, they cast a silver statue of Columbus, that fair's symbol, and won 47 awards. Caroline Hazard's poem for "Rhode Island Day" at the Exposition asked what Rhode Island's contribution might be:

Last of the thirteen, smallest of
   them all
What canst thou bring to this
   World's festival ... .
What can we bring? No outward
   show of gain,
No pomp of state; we bring the
   sons of men!

In fact, Rhode Island had plenty of gain to show: one hundred thirty exhibitors displayed products, causing one observer to say, "Scarcely another state in the Union furnished such a varied collection of interesting and important exhibits."

Energetic marketing and advertising advanced a number of products to national recognition: the underwear of "Fruit of the Loom," "Ban-Lon" sweaters, Clark and J.& P. Coats threads, Barstow stoves, Armington & Sims steam engines, C.B. Cottrell printing presses, and the streetcar bumper known as "Providence Fender." Rubber companies kept the nation's feet dry with the "Providence Shoe" and lessened laundry chores with the "Woonsocket Rubber Rollers" for washing machines. The nation's pain allegedly was relieved by "Yellow Dock," "Sarsaparilla," and Perry Davis' "Pain Killer," but the

The Corliss Steam Engine was the central attraction in Machinery Hall at the Centennial Exposition in Philadelphia in 1876. This gigantic machine supplied power to all the 8000 machines in Machinery Hall. Corliss' objections to the machine's running on Sunday forced the exposition to open on Wednesday, May 10, 1876, and his colossus was turned off every Sunday. Courtesy, Providence Public Library

medical and surgical supplies of Davol were a definite improvement. One could also bake a cake with Rumford Baking Powder, toss a salad with "Providence Salad Oil," fry up an egg from a "Rhode Island Red," delight in a Narragansett oyster or clam, and go sailing on a Herreshoff yacht. And if clothes and house needed whitening, one could always use Kendall's "Soapine" and Gutta Percha's "Barrelled Sunlight" paint.

Industrial diversity was a source of considerable pride to the state's boosters at the turn of the century; but more importantly, it allowed Rhode Island to survive the withdrawal of the textile industry in the 20th century. These things were especially true in the industrial heart in Providence. With the city's "Big Five" and its multitude of smaller establishments, its population, wealth, and influence grew significantly before World War I. One writer boasted, "Thus does Providence show an example which might well be emulated by the other cities of the country. With her glorious record in the past and her present assured, what may we not hope this city will have grown to be when her tricentennial comes around?" In fact, by the time of the tricentennial in 1936, one of the Big Five was gone, two more were slipping away, and the textile industry was rapidly disappearing. Two of the expanding industries that softened these blows were rubber and jewelry.

The manufacture of rubber goods had

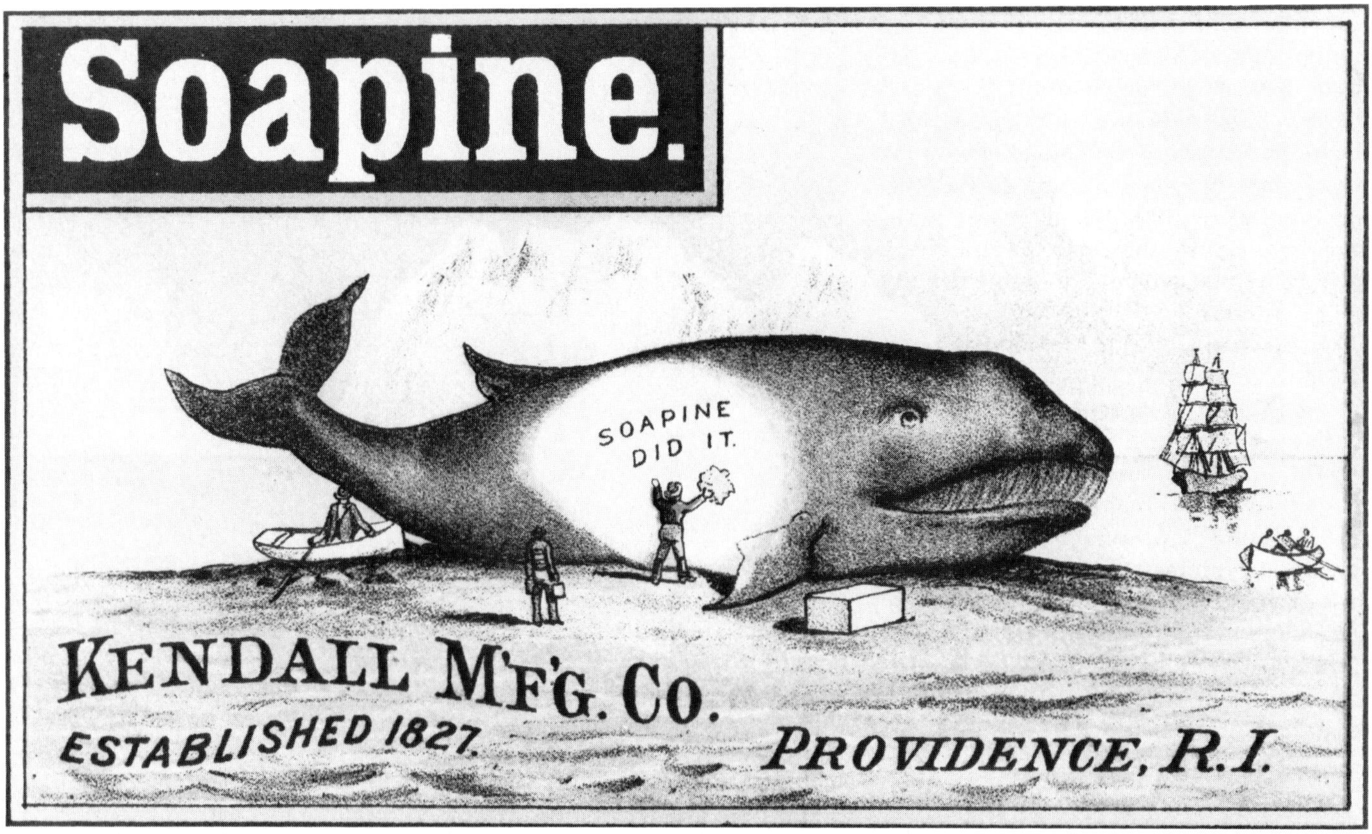

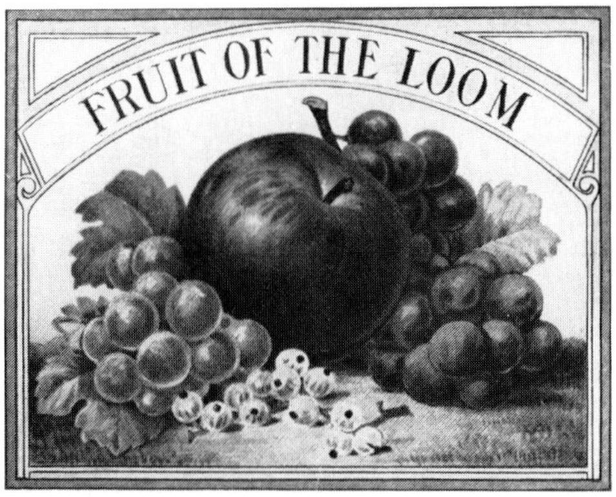

Reproduced here are the trademarks of B.B. & R. Knight Company's "Fruit of the Loom," (right), and the Kendall Manufacturing Company's "Soapine," (above), which was one of America's first soap powders. RIHS (RHi x3 4295, RHi x3 1744)

begun in Providence as early as the 1830s, and the "Providence rubber shoe" was being produced by 1837. The industry prospered, and a substantial number of companies appeared. In the 1870s and 1880s Joseph Banigan developed the Woonsocket Rubber Company into a large, prosperous concern, and by 1889 his Alice Mill was the largest rubber-shoe factory in the world. When the United States Rubber Company was formed, consolidating 15 independent firms, Banigan became its first president and general manager.

At least one Rhode Island governor, Augustus O. Bourn, was a wealthy rubber manufacturer. Founder of the National Rubber Company in 1864, Bourn entered politics as a state senator from Bristol in 1876. He served as governor from 1883 to 1885 and in 1888 authored the "Bourn Amendment" to the state constitution, which granted foreign-born citizens equal franchise rights in general elections. Other leading figures in the rubber industry were Joseph Davol, whose Davol Rubber Company specialized in medical and surgical wares, and Colonel Samuel P. Colt, whose National India Rubber Company in Bristol produced rubber boots, clothing, and wire insulation. Colt was also president of United States Rubber from 1901 to 1919.

With a few notable exceptions—including Ostby & Barton, Uncas, T.W. Foster & Brother, and of course Gorham—the jewelry industry was marked by small, labor-intensive shops. Starting in the pre-Civil War era, when even Brown & Sharpe made jewelry findings, the industry boomed with the increasing popularity of costume jewelry, innovations in plating and chain-making, and the evolution of jobbing shops which manufactured specialty items or performed one process, such as stone-setting or chain-linking. When the government demonetized silver in 1873, jewelry manufacturers took advantage of the drop in silver prices to produce novelty items such as silver toilet articles.

The undisputed giant was Gorham Silverware. Building on its pre-Civil War strengths, the company incorporated in 1865 and expanded to 450 employees by 1872 by securing a contract to manufacture all of Tiffany's silverware. After Tiffany opened its own factory, the new head of Gorham, Edward Holbrook, aggressively sought to make a world reputation for his firm. He entered its products in all world fairs and traveled each year to Europe to buy machines, recruit skilled craftsmen, and learn new techniques of manufacturing and sales. He built the world's largest bronze-casting plant, which turned out statues for the Columbian Exposition and numerous parks, gardens, and squares throughout the nation. In 1890 Gorham constructed the largest silverware factory in the world on Elmwood Avenue and began buying up its competitors in other states. By 1920 the company had 1,820 employees.

From 86 plants in 1860 the jewelry industry grew to over 300 by 1922 and employed 14,500 workers. Providence became the nation's jewelry capital, employing as many jewelry workers as New York, Philadelphia, and Newark combined. While the proliferation of small shops made the industry relatively flexible and able to adjust to fads and fashion's trends, salaries, benefits, and job security remained among the lowest in the state.

Government in Rhode Island was traditionally dominated by the prevailing economic interests of the day. Even in the 18th century when Rhode Island was the most democratic state, it had a "democracy of indifference" and deference. Generally few of the enfranchised voted and when they did, they nearly always voted for wealthy landowners and merchants. Before the American Revolution, Newport merchants dominated Rhode Island politics on behalf of the commercial interests because they believed that what was good for Newport

Irish immigrant Joseph Banigan (1839-1898) rose to become the first president of the United States Rubber Company. After resigning in 1896, he established the Joseph Banigan Rubber Company, erected the Banigan Building in Providence (the tallest structure in the city at the time), and lived in a mansion on Wayland Avenue. From Richard H. Bayles, History of Providence County, 1891. *RIHS (RHi x3 4226)*

was good for Rhode Island. When Providence became king of the Independent State in the 19th century, its merchants and industrialists felt that what was good for Providence was good for everyone. With a restricted franchise the sense of deference lasted until the end of the 19th century. Only with the rise of the ethnic Irish and the growth of the industrial working class was the democracy of deference seriously challenged. Until then, business and government had a close relationship, and the General Assembly created a friendly political and legal climate for industrial growth.

Businessmen and industrialists dominated all the high political offices for 90 years beginning with the election of William Sprague in 1838 and ending with the death of Aram Pothier in 1928. The 38 men who served as governor included 26 millowners, bankers, railroad owners, and manufacturers, 3 corporation lawyers, 2 physicians, and 2 newspaper publishers. A similar pattern was evident among Lieutenant Governors, United States Senators, and other important elected officials. Though city councils tended to be slightly more populist, the majority of their members came from the business community. The Providence Board of Trade, founded in 1868, exercised greater power than mayors

Marsden J. Perry (1850-1935), the "Utility King" of Rhode Island, came to Providence in 1871. He soon became a director of the Union Trust Company, owner of the Narragansett Electric Company, Providence's gas and water companies, and the Union Railway Company. Perry's downfall came shortly after the financial panic of 1907, which produced a run on the Union Trust Company and ruined his financial power base, but not his personal wealth. From Men of Providence in Cartoon, 1906. RIHS (RHi x3 4364)

and enjoyed a close working relationship with the Board of Aldermen and the General Assembly.

After the death of the powerful and popular Providence mayor, Thomas Doyle, the powers of that office were clipped, leaving the city council and a proliferation of commissions and boards to conduct the city's business. As in other American cities, corruption in the assessor's office, the public works department, and in virtually all urban service projects surfaced yearly. By 1880, Providence had exceeded its statutory limit of indebtedness by 200 percent and had abandoned the popular referendum as a means of securing voter approval of its servants' actions.

The state's legal system stood behind the industrial and commercial leadership. When railroad interests sought to erect a new terminal on Cove lands, citizens formed the Public Park Association and elected a whole slate of candidates to city and state offices. A fight among the association, the legislature, the city council, and the railroad interests pushed the matter

into the courts; but the railroads won. So, the Cove was filled, the terminal erected, and not a single claim of the city as to location and ownership was recognized.

As city councils desperately fought to retain local control, the higher stakes over corporate taxes and utility franchises between 1875 and 1910 shifted the center of power to the state legislature. In a series of moves which weakened the powers of city governments, the legislature passed laws exempting the stock of out-of-state corporations from local taxes, reducing the tax valuation on plant machinery by one half, and permitting cities to grant a 10-year tax exemption for new plants. Mature industrial cities, such as Providence and Pawtucket, lost as this "special" piece of legislation enticed Eugene Phillips from Providence to East Providence, where he developed the industrial town of Phillipsdale. But the greatest violation of local autonomy occurred over the franchising of transportation and utility companies.

Republican "Boss" Charles Brayton, United States Senator Nelson Aldrich, and Marsden J. Perry collaborated on a series of shrewd maneuvers that made Perry the utility king of Rhode Island. Perry became the veritable epitome of the rapacious traction magnate. He recognized electricity's potential and bought the small Fall River Lighting Company in 1882, the Narragansett Electric Lighting Company in 1884, and its only competitor, the R.I. Electric Company, in 1889. He also acquired waterworks, gas companies, and then the entire Union Railway Company. By 1890 Perry controlled 70 percent of the state's street railway lines and all electrical power in Providence. To electrify and extend his transportation holdings to all parts of the state, he needed money; and to overcome city control of utilities, he sought an exclusive franchise from the legislature. Aldrich secured the money from the Havemeyers, wealthy sugar barons of Philadelphia; and in 1891 Brayton manipulated the General Assembly to grant Perry "exclusive" franchises for 20 years for both his electric and streetcar systems. These franchises were made "perpetual" in 1895, cost Perry a meager 3 to 5 percent of his

TOP: *In 1881 Nelson W. Aldrich (1841-1915) succeeded Ambrose Burnside as United States Senator and eventually became so powerful that he was called the "General Manager of the United States." He was, in fact, well connected with the barons of railroads, industry, public utilities, and finance and served them in various capacities. In 1901 his only daughter married John D. Rockefeller, Jr., merging those two names and fortunes. His home on Benevolent Street in Providence is now the Museum of Rhode Island History at the Aldrich House. RIHS (RHi x3 789)*

ABOVE: *Brigadier General Charles Ray Brayton (1840-1910) was the "Blind Boss" of the Republican Party. Although never elected to office, Brayton controlled patronage, managed campaigns, and exercised a major influence within the Rhode Island Republican organization. Lincoln Steffens denounced the Aldrich-Perry-Brayton trinity in his 1905 expose: "Rhode Island has been a state for sale because the Rhode Islanders were a people for sale." RIHS (RHi x3 545)*

gross revenues, and, most importantly, rendered city government powerless to regulate the utilities.

The entire financial empire was incorporated in New Jersey as the United Traction and Electric Company: Aldrich was president, William Roelker, a state senator, was secretary and treasurer, Perry was a director, and Brayton acted as legal counsel for the railway company. Other companies, such as the Rhode Island Company, were also chartered by this group in New Jersey and their assets held by still more holding companies from whom various pieces of the empire were leased. Since Rhode Island did not tax corporate assets held outside the state, stockholders sheltered handsome profits and Perry emerged as one of the most powerful men in the state. As a symbol of his power, he bought the John Brown house on Power Street, present home of The Rhode Island Historical Society.

Perry also played a role in consolidating Rhode Island's railroads. Five years after the New Haven Railroad Company had negotiated an 89-year lease of the Providence & Worcester Railroad in 1889, Perry, acting as receiver, handed the bankrupt New York and New England Railroad over to the New Haven. Within New England, the New Haven faced only limited opposition, and within Rhode Island only Perry's interurban electric railroad offered short-haul freight competition. When the 1906-1907 depression left Perry's empire in financial difficulties, he was able to weather it by selling his interurban to the New Haven for four times its value. The New Haven now had complete control of all railroad and steamship transportation in Rhode Island.

Distressed by higher freight rates and monopolistic practices, the business community appealed to Governor Aram Pothier, who in turn enlisted the aid of Charles M. Hays, president of the Canadian Grand Trunk Railroad. Hays, previously prevented by J.P. Morgan from entering New York, planned to bring his line to Providence. This time the New Haven frustrated his plans by purchasing rights-of-way and short spur lines, driving up the cost. In 1912 Hays sailed to London

in pursuit of more capital. On his return trip aboard the *Titanic,* Hays and the Grand Trunk connection with Providence went down with the ship. Secret agreements with the New Haven made by the new president of the Grand Trunk so flagrantly violated the law that in 1914 federal authorities ruled that the Grand Trunk must resume its work. However, World War I and lack of money ended the scheme and attempts to revive it in the 1920s failed. Providence remained the largest city in America served by a single railroad, and Rhode Island industries were saddled with the highest freight rates of any city on the New Haven line.

Perry's power and arrogance provoked the 1902 streetcarmen's strike by his refusal to obey the 10-hour law passed by the legislature. Despite an occasional flash of militance, Rhode Island labor had traditionally been passive, weakly organized, and divided by the polyglot character of the population; but Perry's defiance of a popular law outraged the carmen's union. After a month-long strike Perry broke the union with the help of the Providence police, old-time carmen, strikebreakers from as far away as Philadelphia, and Governor Charles Kimball, who declared martial law and called out the militia for the first time since the Dorr War of 1842. When the state supreme court upheld the 10-hour law, Brayton and Kimball had it repealed in the legislature.

The friendly government-business alliance provoked opposition. Kimball was immediately succeeded in office by two reform governors, Lucius Garvin, a progressive Democrat and member of the Providence Radical Club, and George Utter, publisher of the *Westerly Daily Sun,* and by the first Roman Catholic Irish Democratic governor, James H. Higgins. As a result of the Brayton Bill of 1901, the office of governor had been reduced largely to a figurehead. Even so, the election of reformers and Irish Democrats symbolized the shifting of the political ground. The growing strength of the Democratic party, and the increasing power and militance of labor unions after World War I would end the cozy business-government relationship.

Chapter Seven

THE POLYGLOT STATE

Most turn-of-the-century immigrants arrived with skills unsuited for industrialized society. Many, such as this unidentified Italian laborer photographed around 1910, built up the cities, tended the textile machines, cast jewelry items, and fabricated metal products. Courtesy, Providence Journal Company

THE EXPANSION OF Rhode Island's economy was accompanied by an equally significant transformation of the state's population from native to immigrant. Although about 4 percent of its population in the 1820s was black, the Independent State's inhabitants were mainly white, native-born, English-speaking Protestants. The arrival of many different immigrant groups during the next 100 years changed this. These newcomers settled mostly in the industrial towns and mill villages; few found their way to the remote rural areas of western and southern Rhode Island. Immigrants swelled the industrial work force, strove to achieve economic security, and influenced the fabric and tone of organized labor. Some lived in mill housing, but the majority flocked to the urban tenements. Each group developed organizations and institutions that cushioned the shock of alienation and perpetuated Old World patterns of thought and behavior. This isolation from the mainstream of Rhode Island affairs deepened Yankee distrust of immigrants and kept the newcomers disenfranchised throughout much of the 19th century. The divisions and interethnic conflict that developed were more significant for the state's history in the 19th and 20th centuries than religious differences were for Roger Williams' time. Nevertheless, immigrants kept coming. By the 1920s Rhode Island had the highest percentage of immigrants in the nation, Catholics outnumbered Protestants, a cacophony of foreign tongues drowned out English, and

signs of ethnic diversity were everywhere. The "English Colony of Rhode Island and Providence Plantations" had become the "Polyglot State."

Before 1820, Rhode Island had well-defined black populations in Providence, Newport, and South County; some English and Scottish mechanics and weavers in mill communities; and a handful of French who had remained after the American Revolution. Over the years the number of blacks gradually increased and in 1980 stood at over 27,500. Despite this growth, blacks have declined to 3 percent of the total population while other ethnic groups have increased phenomenally. Rhode Island's economic transformation made the state attractive to immigrants. Textiles lured English weavers, loom-fixers, and skilled mechanics; and the expansion of the metal trades and the growth of fine-jewelry manufacturing brought many more. In 1865 the English accounted for 16 percent of the state's foreign-born inhabitants, and by 1905 more than 24,000 English lived here. So strong was this migration that only Irish, French-Canadians, and Italians outdistanced them in 1920.

In the 1820s and 1830s, work on the Blackstone Canal and railroads drew Irish immigrants to southern New England. Many also found work in the mills and on the waterfront. Their number, however, was small until the potato failure literally meant death for starving Irish peasants between 1845-1846. Nearly a million Irish fled from certain poverty to an uncertain future in America. Because most arrived penniless, many were trapped in coastal cities. Some fanned out into neighboring states in search of work and relatives, creating a chain that brought thousands of Irish to the state. By 1865, a whopping 68 percent of all immigrants in Rhode Island were Irish. Thereafter, Irish immigration remained steady, but their proportion of the total population slipped to 21 percent by 1905 because of other arrivals.

Although a few French-Canadians had immigrated to Rhode Island decades before the Civil War, they totaled only 3,687 by 1875. However, over the next 30 years they increased substantially, and by 1905 the percentage of foreign-born French-Canadians nearly equaled that of foreign-born Irish. Acute agricultural difficulties in the province of Quebec pushed about 700,000 to America; 500,000 of them settled in New England. In the early years of the migration, some French-Canadian males crossed the border to work in mills during winter and returned home for spring planting. Soon, entire families made the trek. When the agricultural depression deepened and the recruitment of these families by millowners was in full force, seasonal migrants became permanent settlers. By 1910, Rhode Island had 34,087 foreign-born French-Canadians, the third largest such community in New England. Although the Quebec government offered families free transportation, 100 acres of land, and grants up to $1,000 for clearing it if they returned to Canada, the vast majority preferred the meager rewards of mill work.

Between 1875 and World War I, as modernization of western Europe swept eastward, wars, economic crisis, land consolidation, political unrest, natural disasters, and the persecution of Jews by Russia and Armenians by Turkey sent millions of uprooted people seeking opportunity and sanctuary all over the world. Most came to America. In Rhode Island, the Italians outnumbered all the rest. Barely present in 1885, they began arriving in larger numbers in the 1890s; and by 1905 over 18,000 foreign-born Italians lived in the state. The peak years for Italian immigration were yet to follow. In 1911 a

RIGHT: In May 1911 the ship Madonna *of the Fabre Line opened direct connections between Providence and Mediterranean ports. By 1913 state officials had constructed adequate docking facilities and the arrival of the* Venezia *was used to dedicate the new State Pier. The Fabre Line continued to operate until it officially terminated service in 1934, but the flow of immigrants into the Port of Providence dwindled after 1921 and federal authorities removed Providence's official port-of-entry status. Photo by William Mills & Son, 1913. RIHS (RHi x3 4354)*

FACING PAGE: Italian immigrant women await immigration official inspection and documentation at the Providence Municipal Pier in July 1921. Problems with documentation at the Port and in the community prompted the creation of the Providence Legal Aid Society that same year. Immigrants suspected of carrying contagious diseases were detained aboard the ship Newark, *a makeshift quarantine station in the Providence harbor. Courtesy, Providence Journal Company*

French steamship company, the Fabre Line, established direct connections between Mediterranean ports and Providence. It brought thousands of Italians and smaller numbers of Portuguese, Greeks, Armenians, and Russian Jews. In 1914 over 18,000 immigrants disembarked at Providence, making the city the fifth largest port-of-entry in the United States. World War I halted the flow, but in 1919 it resumed with a rush as the Port of Providence welcomed more than 15,000 new arrivals. By 1920, of the state's 173,499 foreign-born residents, 19 percent were Italian. The federal immigration restriction legislation of 1921 brought the era of mass immigration to a close. The low quotas assigned to the Port of Providence forced the Fabre Line to suspend operation,

stripped Providence of its official port-of-entry status, and slowed the influx of newcomers for the next 40 years. Still, in 1950, as in 1920, Rhode Island ranked first in the nation in its percentage of foreign-born and native-born of foreign and mixed parentage.

In the past 30 years Rhode Island has lost that distinction but still attracts new immigrants. The majority of recent arrivals have come from the Orient and from Latin America. American involvement in Vietnam and that war's impact on surrounding countries left thousands homeless. With federal funding the International Institute of Rhode Island brought hundreds of Vietnamese, Cambodians, Laotians, and Hmongs to the state, raising the total Oriental population to over 10,000 by 1980. The largest number of recent arrivals, however, has come from Latin American countries. Some have been "freeway" or "spillover" immigrants from the huge Hispanic communities of New York City and New Jersey, others have been recruited by local textile firms, and still others have fled political turmoil or immigrated to join relatives. By 1980, preliminary federal census figures indicated 19,707 Hispanics lived here, although social agencies have estimated that their total might be 30,000.

Recent arrivals have state and federally funded social service agencies assisting them in finding work and housing, attending to legal matters, and in some cases providing job training. In education their children benefit from mandated bilingual and bicultural programs. Mutual self-help agencies, such as Acción Hispania, find themselves caught in the position of being a social protest group and of meeting the needs of an ethnically divided Hispanic community.

Nineteenth- and early-20th-century immigrants had little aid from such sources. Instead, they relied almost exclusively upon relatives, friends, religious and charitable institutions, and immigrant aid societies founded by the respective ethnic groups. Organized efforts invariably were handicapped by a lack of funds, insufficient knowledge of opportunities, and native resistance. Consequently, jobs, housing, legal services, and education tended to become a word-of-mouth experience. Occasionally, an enterprising immigrant would establish his own intelligence office or employment agency to place his countrymen, sometimes for a fee. Davide Senerchia went even further: he created his own immigration bureau and steamship company and brought hundreds of other Italians to the mill village of Natick from his hometown of Fornelli, Campobasso, Italy.

The opening of the Port of Providence in 1911 by the United States Immigration Bureau brought thousands each year and required better facilities. The city and state were slow in erecting a new pier, in heating it, in setting up satisfactory detention quarters, and in providing a quarantine station for those suspected of carrying a communicable disease. Local officials acted only after repeated threats by the Fabre Line to withdraw service and by the federal government to close the port. Perhaps the two most effective nonethnic relief organizations were the Immigrant Education Bureau and the Legal Aid Society. The Union of Christian Work established the

Bureau to relieve the "acute suffering of women and children" at the dock, in the home, and in the schools. This effort at Christian charity was soon tainted with the jingoism of the "Americanization Movement" which dominated the public and private institutions of the nation and Rhode Island during and after World War I.

Few immigrants who came to Rhode Island had a choice of settlement because employment opportunities, relatives, and friends acted as population distributors. Since industry concentrated most heavily in the northern section of the state, that area attracted a disproportionate share of the state's newcomers. The Irish concentrated in mill villages along the Blackstone and Pawtuxet rivers and along the waterfronts in Newport and Providence, in the latter at Fox Point, known as "Corky Hill." The least concentrated were the English and Scottish textile workers who flocked to Pawtucket, Central Falls, and Providence, although many others tended looms and carding machines in rural mill villages. Before the Civil War, blacks were

Jewish immigrants congregated in three areas of Providence. This photograph depicts the lower end of Charles Street in 1899, a part of the Charles-Orms section that included Poles, Armenians, Lithuanians, Greeks, Irish, and several other nationalities. Nearby stood the Sons of David synagogue. RIHS (RHi x3 4006)

A St. John the Baptist parade took place on Clinton Street in Woonsocket in 1906. Parades were popular forms of expression among all ethnic groups; and the various clubs, organizations, and institutions that ethnic communities generated added to both their vitality and their internal disunity. RIHS (RHi x3 4397)

found in Newport and Bristol and lived in two segregated areas of Providence, while a declining number lived in rural South County. This pattern of forced and voluntary segregation continued in the second half of the 19th century as industries expanded and new arrivals intensified the competition for housing. By 1910, the combined total foreign-born and native-born children of foreign or mixed parentage made up 80 percent of the population of Woonsocket and Central Falls: 70 percent in Providence, Pawtucket, and Cumberland; and more than 50 percent in Burrillville, Johnston, Cranston, Warwick, East Providence, Smithfield, North Smithfield, Bristol, Warren, Portsmouth, and Tiverton. These communities had become a microcosm of the world's nationalities, while the remote rural areas of western and southern Rhode Island had remained Yankee.

Some ethnic groups dominated specific neighborhoods and, occasionally, entire cities or towns. Warren, Bristol, and Portsmouth had heavy concentrations of Portuguese; and by 1930 over 5,500 Portuguese lived in East Providence, the largest concentration in the state. Central Falls retained its multiethnic mix, but shared most of Rhode Island's Poles with

the Olneyville section of Providence. French-Canadians turned Woonsocket into "French City" so that by 1920 nearly 75 percent of the population was of that nationality. It was said that natives were forced to learn French to survive. In northern Rhode Island the villages of Oakland, Mapleville, Harrisville, and others in the Pawtuxet Valley were also heavily French. The English were scattered, except for the mill village of Greystone in North Providence which was solidly English.

Within larger cities, ethnic neighborhoods often developed. For example, Cranston was once an ethnic mosaic: the Welsh settled around the pumping station in Pettaconett, Germans thrived by the breweries in Arlington, Swedes were isolated near Budlong Farms, Irish dominated the Cranston Print Works, and Italians occupied Knightsville. Within Providence, immigrants of all nationalities surrounded river valleys where mills and factories stood, while old-line Yankees preserved their domain on the East Side. By 1920, the 19,239 foreign-born Italians, the largest ethnic group in the city, had displaced the Irish on Federal Hill, taken up flats in the North End and Eagle Park, and congregated in Silver Lake. Jews clustered near Broad Street in South Providence, on

North Main Street, and in the Charles-Orms section, the most ethnically diverse neighborhood of the city. With the crowding from new arrivals and some degree of economic mobility, the Irish abandoned Fox Point in favor of suburban Cranston and Warwick, stayed in South Providence or moved to the middle-class Elmhurst section. The process was repeated with other groups: Italians left the Hill after World War II for garden plots in North Providence and Johnston.

Despite the exodus, Providence, Pawtucket, and Central Falls continue to be multiethnic, while East Providence, Bristol, and Warren became more Portuguese, and Woonsocket struggled to retain its French heritage. In 1980 Providence's residential segregation was largely confined to blacks, Jews, Italians, and Portuguese; and the vitality of ethnic neighborhoods such as Fox Point and Federal Hill depended heavily on federal funds for urban renewal and neighborhood rejuvenation. Hispanics and Orientals have congregated in cheap and low-income housing in South Providence, Pawtucket, Central Falls, and in various towns of the Blackstone Valley. While some have suggested that the presence of these new groups has driven population from the city, one could argue with greater persuasion that they have stabilized the housing market in blighted areas.

Throughout much of the 19th and first half of the 20th centuries, housing for immigrants was rarely adequate but generally sufficient for their pocketbooks. Although substandard by today's measures, mill villages and urban tenements were suitable housing for their time. Most Rhode Island immigrants, like the Irish, came from crofter cottages and shanties with earthen floors sometimes shared with farm animals. The majority were poor upon arrival, possessed little or no mechanical skills, and earned meager wages. Since 27 percent of all foreign-born were illiterate in 1880, Rhode Island ranked number one in New England in that category. These conditions created a captive, economically dependent population whose housing needs were met by millowners and tenement developers.

Nevertheless, adequate housing remained an acute problem. Immigrants managed to survive, however, by doubling up families, taking in boarders, and jamming as many people into the two- and three-deckers as was possible. Consequently, Rhode Island became the most urbanized, densely settled state in the nation.

Although Providence never experienced the crowding of New York City or Boston, immigrants and their descendants were slowed in their quest of the American dream of homeownership. For example, in 1920 more than 70 percent of all dwelling units in Providence, Central Falls, and Woonsocket were rentals; and by 1950 of the three, only Providence had dipped below this percentage. Today, second- and third-generation ethnic landlords live in their own suburban homes and rent their former tenement flats to blacks, Hispanics, and Orientals. Consequently, Rhode Island still has the lowest percentages of home-ownership in the nation.

Ethnically segregated neighborhoods preserved Old World customs and manners and nurtured a network of organizations, institutions, and businesses that catered almost exclusively to their own kind. Crowding brought out intraethnic tensions and conflicts which both divided and enriched immigrant communities. Northern Italians continued their long-standing feud with southern Italians, splitting them into separate churches, social clubs, fraternal, and benevolent associations. Portuguese remain divided by place of origin and color of skin among the mainlanders, Cape Verdeans, and Azoreans. Jews separated by nationality and then into Orthodox, Reform, and Conservative synagogues. Since the majority of immigrants were Roman Catholic, that religion most dictated the shape of institutional development and interethnic animosity.

The early arrival of the Irish made them the king of American Catholicism, and Rhode Island was no exception. Their pattern of establishing parishes and securing them with parochial schools, benevolent and mutual aid societies, and fraternal societies and clubs made the church indispensable for the retention of Irish

The three Santoro brothers, left to right: Giuseppe, Carmelo, and Sebastiano, and their families pose for their portrait in 1922, just prior to Carmelo's first visit to his native village. The brothers had immigrated in 1907, settled in the Italian North End of Providence, and together established a macaroni factory. They lived near each other, worked together, celebrated all holidays together, and their children grew up as brothers and sisters. Today Grazia Santoro (holding baby on the right) is the only one still living of that generation, but their offspring are still very close. Photo by J.M. Petrucci. Courtesy, Carmela Santoro

shaped most of their organizations. The resulting clubs, benevolent associations, and even their press, the *Italian Echo*, were more secular than religious, more particular than community-oriented, and generally weaker than those of other groups. Instead of establishing parochial schools, they sent their children to public schools. They failed to become a united political group, and some Italians converted to Protestantism. While 20th-century suburbanization has destroyed the old Irish neighborhoods, their suburban churches have perpetuated much of their institutional network. Suburban Italians, on the other hand, retain a deep loyalty to the old neighborhoods based on birthplace and family.

In contrast to the Italians, French-Canadians looked to their church for their institutional structure; and in contrast to the Irish, French *habitants* vested decision-making in a parish council which was headed by a *curé*, or pastor, instead of a bishop and church hierarchy. And while Irish clergy tried to overcome nativism by preaching assimilation, the French doggedly clung to *survivance*—the preservation of faith, language, and customs. From the outset, these two groups clashed over the establishment of national parishes, but by the 1870s four had been established and later 12 more were built in the state. Woonsocket was the center of this network. Here, parishes became neighborhood community centers; they erected parochial schools, built orphanages, supported clubs, generated social agencies, chartered insurance companies, and even sponsored their own athletic teams. In time, French-Canadian colonies all over New England were tied to each other and to the homeland by federations of these agencies and by frequent visits to nearby Quebec. The French-Canadian newspaper, *La Tribune*, became the organ of *survivance* when it editorialized that a woman's place was in the home, rearing and bearing children, and that young women should center their lives around the church and the home.

Survivance was reluctantly tolerated by Irish bishops until the "Sentinellist" controversy of the 1920s. The seeds of the crisis, however, were not exclusively

identity. In addition, Catholic high schools and colleges gave the Irish the educational institutions needed for upward economic mobility. But Polish, Italian, and French-Canadian Catholics had other loyalties and assigned different roles to their religion; thus, interethnic strife ensued.

Four Polish parishes left the Roman Catholic Church and affiliated with the Pennsylvania-based Polish National Catholic Church. Although the Irish church hierarchy under Bishop Matthew Harkins granted Italians the right to establish 12 national parishes, the appointment of northern Italian Scalabrini priests angered southern Italians. Southerners sought to oust the priests, stayed away from church services, and eventually created their own church in St. Ann on Federal Hill. Italian fidelity to family, place of birth, and social class rather than devotion to the church

religious as a combination of factors converged to trigger it. The French-Canadian community was hit hard by the postwar conditions: recession and the textile strike of 1922 put thousands out of work; the state's 1919 "Americanization Law" forced hundreds of adult immigrants into Americanization classes; the 1922 Peck Education Act mandated that English be the language of instruction in all nonpublic schools; and the authoritarian Bishop William A. Hickey, who wanted to centralize control of parish education in the diocese, announced in June 1922 a million-dollar high school fund drive with quotas for every parish. The Franco-American community's fear that the Bishop's assimilationist policy was designed to destroy *survivance* had come true.

Bishop Hickey had distributed "100 percent Americanism" pastoral letters, and he was a close friend of Democratic party leaders. Democrats could elect an Irish governor if the French-Canadians were alienated from the Republican party. The Bishop's assimilationist position and his friendship with Democrats led him to secretly work with the Republican-dominated Peck Commission. When the Act passed, French-Canadians blamed Republicans for attacking their schools, and William Flynn, a Democrat, was elected governor in 1922. The Republicans brought the popular French-Canadian, Aram Pothier, out of retirement in 1924 to regain the State House.

Initially, French-Canadians demonstrated widespread resistance to the fund drive and to Bishop Hickey. Militants unsuccessfully petitioned Pope Pius XI and brought suit in the state's courts. When the Pope excommunicated 63 petitioners in 1928, the movement had come to a bitter end. *Survivance* emerged scarred, but perhaps "more pliable" and moderate. Preservation of religion and some customs continued, but French instruction in their parochial schools began to decline; and by the late 1960s it was dead. While the Peck Act and the Sentinellist crisis played a role, the decline in French- Canadian immigration after 1930 stripped *survivance* of its traditional source of strength. Today, older Franco-Americans struggle to preserve a fading heritage among the young.

Ethnic communities were more than oases for religious, social, and cultural activities. In part, they became self-sufficient economic units. The larger and more densely settled groups, such as Italian, French-Canadians, and Portuguese, generated economic opportunities ranging from grocers to undertakers. Such enterprises advanced the economic worth and self-esteem of individuals, who often rose to leadership positions within their communities. The more resourceful were able to expand beyond exclusively ethnic patronage and local markets, thereby generating additional employment opportunities for their countrymen. In the 20th century Columbus National Bank, Gilbane Construction, Uncas Manufacturing, De Blois Oil, and Fain's Carpets have become important statewide enterprises.

For the vast majority of immigrants, from the Irish to the Hispanics, "American opportunity" meant working in textile mills, factories, jewelry shops, and on construction gangs. Most had no trade suitable for industrial Rhode Island and little or no education. They had, however, what the Yankee establishment wanted: hunger for work, muscle, pride of family, and respect for authority. As a consequence, unskilled factory work became their chief means of survival. In 1910, for example, 48 percent of the French-Canadian, 37 percent of the English, 32 percent of the Italian, 24 percent of the Irish, and 22 percent of the German industrial labor force worked in textiles. Most labored as machine operators under English and Scottish weavers and loom-fixers, who from the start had served as the "trained nurses of an infant industry." More striking was the concentration of immigrants in other unskilled categories: 64 percent of all Portuguese wage earners toiled as agricultural workers, domestics, laborers, and in transportation; 35 percent of the Italian workers were classified as agriculturalists, domestics, and laborers; and even among the Irish who had arrived much earlier, 20 percent earned a living as domestics and laborers, although the Irish tended to be fairly well distributed among a wider range of job classifications. The blacks of Providence on the other hand, were almost exclusively confined to laborer, servant, teamster, stevedore, and janitor. Only the English, Scots, and Germans demonstrated significant occupational diversity, but even they had fewer than 10 percent of their respective labor force in the professional and white-collar fields. These areas and the control of industry were with few exceptions in the hands of the Yankees. More than 70 percent of this elite had middle- and upper-class backgrounds and old-stock parents. A bastion of Protestantism, this elite had no Jews and only one Catholic. Over 90 percent had completed secondary school, and more than 90 percent belonged to the Republican Party. Rhode Island was a state of ''haves'' and ''have nots.''

The ''have nots'' toiled for low wages and found advancement to skilled positions slow. In the early years of industrialization, relatively uncongested communities and millowner paternalism, which provided mill housing, libraries, churches, and other amenities, partially offset the long working hours and low pay. However, rapid industrial expansion and mass immigration ended paternalism, and in its wake came housing congestion, an abundant supply of labor, and industrial poverty. For example, in the 1870s, Edward Harris' mills in Woonsocket paid workers $6.54 for a 12-hour, six-day work week. By 1919, despite wartime pay scales, the average take-home pay for all immigrant workers was just $14 per week, and 40 percent of the Italian work force received less than $10. In the 1980s some Hispanics and Portuguese work in jewelry shops that pay less than minimum wage and offer almost no benefits.

Such conditions confined the foreign-born to industrial poverty and led to an increase in the employment of women and children. Formerly, the Rhode Island System employed entire families; in later years, economic necessity and immigrant value systems sustained the practice. Millowners recruited French-Canadians because they supposedly were not averse to having the entire family employed and because they had greater respect for authority than the Irish. Some immigrant groups also placed more value on experiential learning and work than on formal education so that child labor was not a phenomenon alien to their culture. As a consequence, immigrant employment in industry reproduced the pattern of the Old World agrarian environment: entire families labored long hours at meager rewards. Understandably, in 1905 in Rhode Island 7,457 French-Canadians and 6,902 Italians over the age of 10 were illiterate, school attendance among most

ABOVE: Unlike most blacks throughout the 19th and much of the 20th centuries, restaurant or tavern owner Thomas Howland gained a little economic independence. Though he became the warden of the Third Ward in 1856, making him the first black elected to any office in Providence, the following year he emigrated to Liberia. From an oil on wood by John Blanchard, circa 1850-1857. RIHS (RHi x3 3106)

BELOW LEFT: Employees of Providence's Nicholson File Company tend file cutting machines around 1900. Dark, congested, and occupationally dangerous working conditions were a part of the industrial scene. Because on-the-job accidents increased as immigrants augmented native labor, to offset the language barrier many companies painted red those machine parts causing the most accidents. RIHS (RHi x3 2905)

foreign-born children was notoriously low, and 5.8 percent of the labor force consisted of children. The General Assembly enacted various laws to curb child labor, but work permits were readily granted.

Immigrant women played a significant role in the state's labor force. According to an 1892 directory, an estimated 21,000 were engaged in domestic service, but manufacturers employed significant numbers of them. Women comprised the majority of workers in 42 of 181 cotton and woolen mills, in 11 of 12 twine and thread factories, and in other textile-related plants. One of the largest employers of women was the Atlantic Mills with 1,037. Costume jewelry attracted many women, some as "homeworkers," but Ostby & Barton, with 53, was the largest employer of women in this industry. Although few metal firms hired women, those engaged in lighter and highly mechanized metal fabrication employed the most; for example, the American Screw Company had over 750 women in 1892. By 1908, observers noted a "significant increase" in female telephone operators, stenographers, typists, schoolteachers, bookkeepers, and clerks. Also recorded were 13 female dentists, 32 "physicians" (only one had an M.D.), 3 ministers, 1 advertising agent, 1 lawyer, 1 architect, 1 lighthouse keeper, 3 undertakers, and 51 hucksters and peddlers. The *Providence Magazine*'s claim that women had "apparently invaded every industrial class in Rhode Island" came close to truth, but trailblazing in nonindustrials was done by middle- and upper-class women of native stock who were also involved in social reform and women's rights. For a vast number of immigrant women and their daughters, the chief workplace was still the factory, so that by 1936 over 23,000 women operatives almost equaled the number of men.

The employment of large numbers of women and children and low wages were obstacles immigrants encountered in moving up the economic ladder. Those who did advance did so primarily outside of industry: the self-employed, the ethnic merchant, the construction worker turned contractor, and those who entered state and local government. Occupational suc-

With the introduction of the telephone, large department stores, expanded commercial offices, and other enterprises, the number of women in the work force increased substantially. These telephone operators monitored the Providence station and routed calls to all parts of the state. From Providence Magazine, *November 1921. RIHS (RHi x3 4349)*

cession, in which a new immigrant group pushes an earlier one into higher positions, seems to have worked badly throughout the 19th century. In the 20th, a mature economy, a rapid decline in the textile and textile-machinery industry, and the Great Depression wrecked the aspirations of many. Additionally, the slow rate of upward mobility was partially caused by the cultural baggage of some immigrant groups and the disenfranchisement of naturalized citizens with less than $134 worth of property.

Slowed in their advancement through legitimate means, some immigrants turned to marginal criminal activity. In time, gaming, black-marketing, and racketeering fell under Mafia control, and Rhode Island became the headquarters of organized crime in New England.

The French-Canadians' tenacious attachment to *survivance*, their respect for authority, and their large families imprisoned them in mill communities and hindered their geographic and occupational mobility. Italians, too, experienced problems because of their strong loyalty to family, their rootedness in neighborhood, and their commitment to experiential learning. Those groups which valued formal education, remained away from the mills, and encouraged their children to exceed their fathers' station tended to rise more rapidly. For example, Providence's Jews began as impoverished as any group, but by the 1950s they led all others in achievement: 90 percent had white-collar jobs and 40 percent had attended college, compared to 40 percent and 13 percent respectively for the population at large. While it is difficult to establish how many were economically hurt without the vote, the state's Irish were denied one avenue of upward mobility that they used with great skill elsewhere. Not until late in the 19th century could Irish politicians dispense patronage on the local level, and not until the 1930s could they do so on the state level. Once in control of the state government, Democrats secured economic advantages for the working class which organized labor had failed to achieve for a century.

Before then, organized labor in Rhode

Island was weak, split between rural and urban workers, factionalized by ethnic competition, troubled over tactics, and thus successfully opposed by management, the press, and even the general public. The major issues of the 19th century, the 10-hour day and effective child labor laws, were never resolved. Only among the skilled trades, such as carpenters, brewers, plasterers, weavers, loom-fixers, and mule-spinners, were small craft unions successful in improving conditions of work and in raising wages. These workers formed the Central Trades and Labor Union in 1884 and two years later affiliated with the American Federation of Labor. The textile portion of the A. F. of L. formed the United Textile Workers of America from a series of locals composed of skilled workers.

Despite this effort, by 1900 only about 10 percent of the state's textile workers were unionized. The first major attempt to include the unskilled operators occurred in 1882 when the Knights of Labor founded an assembly in Olneyville. Four years later, the Knights boasted a membership of 12,000 and issued a weekly paper, *The People.* By the early 1890s, however, only a few hundred belonged, and women ran the union. Elizabeth A. Hunt had become head of the Knights in the state, and the executive committee had at least seven women. The demise of the Knights resulted from its inability to enlist skilled craftsmen and because its membership was composed primarily of the curious, of politicians, and of laborers expecting miracles, revenge on the bosses, or continuous strikes. Another major drawback was its Irish leadership which alienated the French-Canadians and other ethnic groups.

Although carmen demonstrated some solidarity in 1902, organized labor was unable to gain statewide acceptance until the post-World War I years. Management could always rely on police and troops, immigrant strikebreakers, and disunity within labor. Radical labor organizations, such as the Industrial Workers of the World, had little success; workers in Pawtucket even asked city officials to throw the "radical and violent" IWW out of town. The city willingly complied. Labor

National Guard troops protect the property of the B.B. & R. Knight mill in Pawtucket in 1922. The United Textile Workers of America, composed of locals of skilled workers, called the strike with AF of L approval. It marked the first time that organized labor won any considerable public support after years of "yellow dog" contracts, blacklisting, labor spies, and strike breaking. Courtesy, Providence Journal Company

gained appreciable public support only after textile firms announced a 22.5 percent wage cut in 1921, followed by another 20 percent reduction in 1922. The United Textile Workers Union struck, millowners summoned the police, violence erupted on picket lines, and Governor Emery J. San Souci sent the National Guard. They failed to break the strike, which lasted through the summer; finally in September management agreed to withdraw the second pay cut and restore the former hours. Twenty thousand strikers had made their point: labor could win if it held out long enough. Unfortunately, while labor won some desperately needed benefits, the victory accelerated the destruction of a major source of its livelihood—the textile industry. Plagued by southern competition, unfavorable freight rates, and the failure to modernize, plants closed at an alarming rate in the 1920s and 1930s. The more organized labor succeeded, the fewer the mills remained in which labor could harvest the fruits of victory. When the bloody strike of 1934 erupted, one era ended and a new one began. Gone were most of the old-stock Yankee capitalists, their mills, and their Republican Party. Here were the Irish and other ethnic workers, the Great Depression, and their Democratic party. The alliance of labor and the Democratic party could not escape the past: it sought gratification, forged political machines, and struggled to dominate a polyglot population.

Chapter Eight

THE PLAYGROUND OF NEW ENGLAND

R HODE ISLAND HAS long been a place of recreation, rest, and sport; it could be called the "Playground of New England." Recreation became available for everyone from the super-rich to the urban middle class and the factory or mill operative. The ocean and Narragansett Bay have been permanent features even when the principal industries and the state's economy ignored them. In the 19th century, as oceanic commerce retreated, the Bay increasingly became a playground. Far more people fished or sailed for sport than for a living, and Presidents Chester Arthur and Grover Cleveland joined thousands in fishing Rhode Island's waters. In the last quarter of the 20th century, the state has reemphasized its connection with the sea and stressed its attractions by calling itself the "Ocean State."

Cleveland Amory, describing the decline and fall of the playgrounds and spas of the rich in *The Last Resorts*, included Newport as one of those last resorts. In truth, Newport was the first resort of America's wealthy. As early as the 1720s, health-seeking southerners came to escape the heat and disease of southern climes. First came planters from the British West Indies, then the stream widened to include the well-born from Georgia, the Carolinas, Virginia, and Philadelphia. In 1765 Robert Melville, Governor of Grenada, wrote: "The climate is the most salubrious of any port of his Majesty's possessions in America. ... It is made the resort every summer of numerous wealthy inhabitants of the Southern Colonies and the West Indies,

seeking health and pleasure." The *Newport Mercury* recorded 452 summer visitors between 1767 and 1775. The mixture of people made the seaport a lively, sophisticated place. Compared to Boston or Philadelphia, Newport was an open town that welcomed theatrical troupes and other entertainments and pleasures banned elsewhere.

The American Revolution interrupted the summer traffic, but it resumed in the 1780s with southerners from Savannah and Charleston. Even George Washington sent his nephew to Newport in 1783 for a rest cure. By the 1780s so many were coming that it became a business to provide for the annual increase in the town's population. The maritime and natural disasters of embargo, war, and hurricane between 1807 and 1815 set back Newport's recovery; but from 1815 to the 1840s its resort industry expanded rapidly. Formerly most vacationers stayed in rooms or rented houses, then a number of luxury hotels were erected, and a few visitors began to build summer homes. The famed Atlantic and Ocean houses were both raised in the 1840s on Bellevue Avenue. George Noble Jones of Savannah constructed "Kingscote" in 1839, and Ralph Izard, Henry Middleton, and the Balls of South Carolina built homes nearby. In the 1850s real-estate promoters Alfred Smith and Joseph Bailey developed the section along Bellevue Avenue and Ocean Drive. The right to build a bathhouse on Bailey's Beach went with the deed to each property.

After the appearance of grand hotels and as summer cottages were multiplying,

The beach at Narragansett Pier appears quite crowded in this 1890 photograph. While some aspects of Narragansett Pier rivaled the elegance and exclusiveness of Newport, many more middle-class people flocked to the hotels and summer cottages along the South County coast. Courtesy, Providence Public Library the *Newport Mercury* editorialized in 1850: "While we would throw no obstacles in the way of summer business ... we are firm in our belief, that the greatest calamity which has ever befallen Newport is making it a fashionable resort in the summer." If closing its doors to industry was a calamity, the editor was right; but Newport's future was as a watering place for High Society. It and the Navy kept the town from fading into just another Bay village. The *Mercury* soon joined the celebration and in 1864 began publishing annual "cottage lists" of

Julia Ward Howe (1819-1910), author of the "Battle Hymn of the Republic" and suffragist, summered in Newport with others of the intellectual and social elite. These included her husband Samuel Gridley Howe, philanthropist and abolitionist, Thomas Wentworth Higginson, author, abolitionist, and later commander of black soldiers in the Civil War, Henry Wadsworth Longfellow, both Henry James's, the historian George Bancroft, and artists John Singer Sargeant, John LaFarge, and William Morris Hunt. Courtesy, Newport Historical Society

owners and locations, including a rental list. These served the social purpose of announcing one's presence as well as the business intent of making property available.

In the two decades before the Civil War, some of Boston's Brahmins and an increasing number of New York and Philadelphia wealthy began summering in Newport and transforming it into a posh resort. Some were outspoken abolitionists who clashed with the slave-owning aristocrats. As a result, the Izards and other southerners ceased coming to Newport, and the Civil War left only northerners. Thereafter, the focus of the resort shifted from the hotels to the big houses and palaces, which the wealthy described as "cottages." As cottage construction accelerated Newport witnessed the lavish display of wealth.

America's dollar aristocracy con-

spicuously patterned themselves after the European nobility, built copies of chateaux, palaces, and castles, spent lavishly, and tried to snare a title or two. It is estimated that by 1909 more than 500 American heiresses had married titled Europeans with dowries totaling $220 million. The ninth Duke of Marlborough in 1895 married the beautiful but unwilling Consuelo Vanderbilt, who was forced into the union by her domineering, social-climbing mother, Mrs. William K. Vanderbilt. The dowry was $10 million. President Ulysses Grant frequently visited Newport in the 1870s, and his niece married the Russian Prince Michael Cantacuzene, Count Speransky at Newport in September 1899.

While being rich was a prerequisite, just having money was not enough to gain admission to High Society. One had to do the right things, go to the right places, and be accepted by the right people. New York's elite was compelled to summer in Newport because Mrs. William Backhouse Astor did. She was convinced by her confidant, Ward McAllister, that Newport was the place to go for summer. He drew up the list of the Four Hundred so Mrs. Astor could be certain to invite only the right people to her balls and parties. The competition to gain entrance into the Four Hundred became intense, and having a cottage in Newport was one test. Between 1890 and 1914 it was a Newport boast that "the eligible newcomer needed at least four seasons to get in." While money enabled Society figures to buy nearly anything, the social patterns were quite regimented. *Metropolitan Magazine* in 1897 observed: "Newport is a place where everyone does the same thing at the same time—like soldiers in a camp. ... The mess hall of this camp is called the Casino. Whenever a soldier gives a dinner, the fact is telegraphed all over the United States during the serving of the entrees."

When Mrs. Astor's reign ended, a mighty struggle for dominance ensued between Mrs. Hermann "Tessie" Oelrichs, Mrs. Stuyvesant "Mamie" Fish, and Mrs. O.H.P. "Alva" Belmont (formerly Mrs. William Vanderbilt, who scandalized High Society by being the first of that set to divorce). Society was a female-dominated sphere in which the drive and intellect that built industrial empires in the man's world found an outlet. Husbands tended to be weekend participants and bored bystanders in the whirl of Society, and they retreated to their New York offices or yachts as quickly as good manners would allow. Their reward was the prestige of being able to afford all of this costly ornamentation as a testimony to their wealth and success. And it cost a lot. In the depression days of the 1890s, America's worst economic crisis before the 20th century, some of the grand-

by shopping centers and apartment houses, others chopped into condominiums or occupied by schools and colleges. Mrs. Astor had received only the *right* people, but now her mansion is a tourist attraction and its ballroom used for wedding receptions.

All of this is not to suggest that Newport has been abandoned by the wealthy. Many of the cottages are still privately owned and occupied, and Bailey's Beach is still exclusive. The gaping crowd is no longer treated to grand carriage parades, osten-

Newport's Bellevue Avenue is depicted here in the 1870s. The correspondent for Harper's Weekly (August 1874) wrote: "The afternoon drive, usually down Bellevue to Ocean Avenue, and so back to town, is a superb pageant of carriages, handsome women, elegant men, and graceful children." Courtesy, J. Stanley Lemons

est cottages were built, including Ocher Court (1892), Marble House (1892), Belcourt Castle (1894), The Breakers (1893-1895), and Cross Ways (1899). Parties costing $200,000 gave little pause; and a banquet on horseback, a dinner party for dogs, or a party with diamonds and sapphires as favors only enlivened the round of balls, picnics, galas, and gatherings.

The opulent era ended in the 20th century because of new income and inheritance taxes, shifting sensibilities about the display of wealth, the disappearance of the servant class, and the ravages of death and depression. Some mark its end with the discontinuance of the Newport *Social Register* in 1936. One after another the great cottages have fallen, some replaced

tatious balls, and liveried butlers and footmen. Wealth abounds, but is displayed differently or discreetly. Newport is still a resort town with a substantial number of wealthy summer residents, but it also depends on the automobile tourist trade.

Newport was not the state's only recreational resort. No other was as lavish; but Jamestown, the West Island Club in Little Compton, Narragansett Pier and Casino, and Watch Hill in Westerly were worthy competitors. Surrounding these exclusive beaches, hotels, and clubs were more modest establishments which catered to the upper middle class. Along the upper Bay, between the 1840s and World War I, a series of beaches and amusement parks rivaled New York's Coney Island. Shore

resorts were developed at Oakland Beach, Buttonwood Beach, Mark Rock, Horn Spring, Rocky Point, Field's Point, Silver Spring, Golden Spring, Nayatt Point, Ocean Cottage, Boyden Heights, Bullock's Point, Crescent Park, Cedar Grove, Walnut Grove, Cherry Grove, Camp White, Kirwin's Beach, Pleasant Bluff, Hauterive, and Vanity Fair. The most popular were Rocky Point and Crescent Park, but Field's Point and Silver Spring gained international reputations for excellent clambakes and shore dinners.

Steamships and excursion boats were crucial to the development of shore resorts and parks. Even Newport depended upon the Fall River Line's daily runs between New York, Newport, and Fall River. The line's first overnight steamship sailed in 1847, and in the post-Civil War era it provided luxurious accommodations on magnificent vessels. Some of the beaches and resorts catering to the lesser folk also began in the 1840s, but their flowering awaited the excursion boats in the 1870s and 1880s. Many resorts maintained contracts with steamer companies to dock at their piers. In 1900 the excursion boats carried 1,250,000 passengers on the Bay, but they went into a decline after the building of the electric trolley lines to Crescent Park and Rocky Point. The automobile finished them off later. Even the mighty Fall River Line died in 1937, a victim of depression, labor difficulties, and dwindling passenger traffic.

Rocky Point had its beginnings in 1847 when Captain William Winslow of the *Argo* began taking Sunday School groups there. Winslow expanded slowly, then sold the park to Byron Sprague who spent

lavishly until he, too, sold out in 1869 to the American Steamboat Company. Under the expert management of Louis H. Humphreys, former proprietor of the City Hotel and then the luxurious Narragansett Hotel in Providence, Rocky Point became a major resort and excursion park. Humphreys hired his good friend, D.W. Reeves, leader of the famous American Band, to play for several seasons. Until Rocky Point passed into the hands of Colonel Randall A. Harrington in 1888, it had a genteel, Sunday School clientele. It was closed on Sundays and prohibited alcoholic beverages, dancing, and gambling, effectively excluding the typical mill-worker who labored six days a week. Harrington added a dance hall, opened on Sundays, and "made the place perhaps the best known shore resort in New England."

For a time Harrington was Rhode Island's amusement czar. He owned Rocky Point, its chief competitor, Crescent Park, and the amusement concession at Roger Williams Park. George Boyden had opened Crescent Park in 1886, then sold it to Harrington. In 1894 Harrington leased Cres-

cent Park to Charles I.D. Looff, a New York woodcarver who built the first steam-powered carousel for Coney Island. Looff moved to Riverside and established a factory to build merry-go-rounds. One of his most fabulous carousels, an elaborately carved 66-horse wonder, was installed at Crescent Park in 1895, and he developed the park into one of the finest in the East. The Filene Cooperative Association of Boston came by train for their annual company picnics. Their brochure touted it, say-

Servants of a Newport house pose in the late 19th century. At some "cottages" the servants were made up of many nationalities: the butlers and valets were often English; the housekeeper would be English, German, or Swedish; the maids, gardeners, groundskeepers, and groomsmen were usually Irish; and everyone wanted a French cook. Courtesy, Newport Historical Society

ing, "Crescent Park holds more opportunities for a good time for you and all your family and friends than any other place on the map."

When some Boston businessmen announced their plans for an expensive and elaborate amusement park in Rhode Island called Vanity Fair, the *Providence Magazine* was unrestrained in its praise: "You fill the mind with brightness and pleasure and you destroy at once much of the baser material composing it. Clean amusement is a positive antidote for crime and immorality, and the men who project such enterprises are public benefactors." Vanity Fair opened in May 1907, with the mayors of Providence, Woonsocket,

Pawtucket, and Fall River, accompanied by a throng of 25,000 people who came to see its boardwalk, water toboggan, roller coaster, Ferris wheel, Wild West show, Japanese village, circus and wild animals, children's theater, vaudeville, scenic railway, and midway. The most popular attraction was an act called "Fighting the Flames," in which fire fighters rescued pretty maidens from a burning five-story structure. The crowds loved it. Despite the brilliant opening, Vanity Fair did not pay enough, and it went into receivership at the end of its first season. An accidental fire in 1912 destroyed a substantial portion of

the park, and in 1915 Standard Oil bought the site for an oil tank farm.

Vanity Fair was a latecomer in a declining business, and its brief life warned of evil days for the Bay's amusement industry. Today, only Rocky Point is left. After Colonel Harrington died in 1918, it too entered three decades of decline and destruction. The Sprague Mansion House burned in 1919, and most of the park was leveled by the Hurricane of 1938. Before the site was rescued in the late 1940s and rebuilt in its present incarnation, it was eyed by real-estate developers and then by an oil company as a tank farm. Crescent Park died a lingering death, and the carousel closed in the late 1970s. The future use of the park grounds was a heated political issue in East Providence, and the beautiful carousel became the object of worry and vandalism.

The steamships, ferries, and trolley lines and the resorts they served all fell victim to changes in popular tastes. The "go-any-where vehicle"—the automobile—dispersed their customers, and pollution destroyed shellfishing and swimming in the upper Bay. The water flowing from the Providence and Seekonk rivers had been polluted since the 1790s, but Providence drank the water from the Pawtuxet River unfiltered until the early 20th century. However, the waste and sewage of a rapidly expanding population and industrialization soon made the river unfit for any living thing. Field's Point, despite its highly praised shore dinners and beach, fell to progress, pollution, and patriotism. In 1912 the Point was literally sliced away, the shoreline straightened for a seawall 3,000 feet long, and new piers for deepwater ships erected. Pollution made bathing unsafe, and the beach that remained became part of the Rheem shipyard in 1942 for the construction of "Liberty" ships.

One did not have to go to the Bay for sports and recreation because the cities provided such things all year round. In winter one had indoor recreation such as hockey and boxing, dancing at Rhodes-on-the-Pawtuxet or the Biltmore Ballroom, singing societies and recitals, and live theater and the movies. In summer, parks and gardens resounded with band music,

streets saw parades, and sports arenas filled with cheering crowds. By 1917 Providence had become an important theatrical city with 27 theaters. Over the years they presented minstrels, vaudeville, burlesque, stage plays, operas, musicals, symphonies, ballet, movies, and lectures. Minstrels and vaudeville became so popular that the larger amusement parks presented them to attract crowds. For example, Rocky Point had an outdoor theater called the Forest Circle which featured minstrels including the Forrest Amazons, the first troupe of female minstrels seen in New England.

Providence was once a major league city and home of championship teams. The Providence Grays won the National League pennant in baseball in 1879 and 1884, and the world championship in 1884. The National Football League, organized in 1916, was a struggling organization when the Providence Steam Rollers joined in 1925. They won the NFL championship in 1928, but financial hard times forced the owners to surrender the franchise in 1931. The Steam Rollers played in the Cyclodrome on North Main Street.

Cycling came to Rhode Island in the 1870s with the founding of the Providence Bicycle Club, and it got the bicycle officially classified as a vehicle with road rights. Similar clubs sprang up all over America. They converged on Newport in May 1880 for the first national meet of American bicyclists and formed the League of American Wheelmen. In 1886, as part of the state's 250th anniversary celebration, more than 1,500 league members wheeled in the bicycle parade. Inevitably, the bicycle craze led to the construction of the Cyclodrome for professional cycle racing. Eventually bicycling and the Cyclodrome were casualties to the automobile; and the structure was replaced by a drive-in movie theater in 1937. Bicycling has made a partial comeback today, and the Narragansett Bay Wheelmen regularly sponsor weekend excursions.

As professional sports have become truly national and heavily televised, Rhode Island has become part of the Boston market. Most Rhode Islanders consider the Boston Celtics, Red Sox, and Bruins, and the New England Patriots their home teams. The Rhode Island Reds hockey team folded in 1977 after 51 years and moved to Binghamton, New York, despite the opening of a larger arena, the Providence Civic Center. Various efforts at minor league basketball and soccer have all ended in failure. The principal local sporting attractions are now major college competition in basketball, hockey, and soccer.

In Rhode Island the "sport of kings" has disappeared or "gone to the dogs." Amasa Sprague established the fashionable Narragansett Trotting Park in Cranston in 1867. It hosted such notables as Cornelius Vanderbilt and J.P. Morgan and inspired William Sayles to buy and raise world-class horses. By 1925, the site was sold and platted. Thoroughbred racing began in 1934 at Narragansett Park, which the *Baltimore Sun* praised as "the showplace of the North, one of the finest tracks in the country." However, it, too, closed permanently in 1978 and the land is scheduled for industrial and residential development.

RIGHT: Matilda Sisseretta Joyner Jones (1869-1933), popularly known as Black Patti, sang as a soloist with various concert companies, the Levy and Gilmore bands, and other performing groups from 1888 until 1896. She sang at the Pittsburgh Exposition, the World's Columbian Exposition in Chicago in 1893, and all around the nation. From 1896 to 1916 she was the central figure in the Black Patti Troubadours. She retired to her home in Providence where she lived until 1933. Her funeral took place at the Congdon Street Baptist Church and she was buried in Grace Church Cemetery. Courtesy, Rhode Island Black Heritage Society

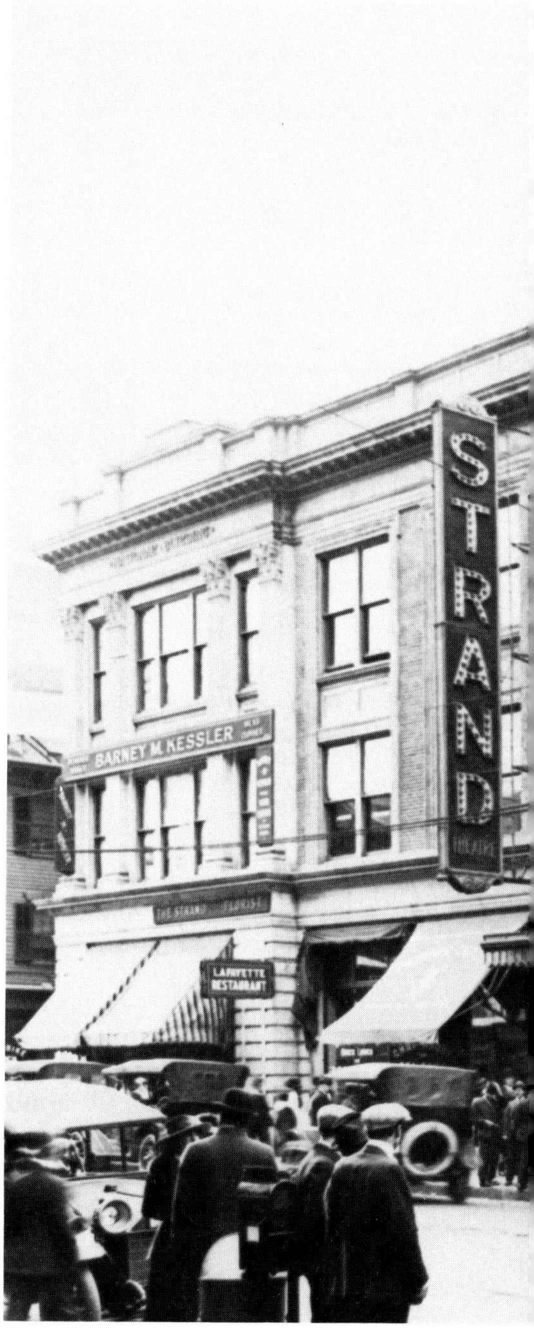

FAR RIGHT: The Strand Theater, shown here about 1919, was built in 1915 on Washington Street at Union Street in Providence. The Providence "theater district" had 17 theaters by 1920 that catered to nearly every level and taste in stage and screen entertainment. RIHS (RHi x3 2758)

The state's other track, Lincoln Downs, opened in 1947, but was converted to dog racing in 1977.

Newport has been home to several sports of the rich: polo, tennis, golf, and yachting. James Gordon Bennett, Jr., owner of the *New York Herald*, introduced polo to America in Newport in 1876 and frequently entertained leading polo players as guests. One such was an Englishman, Captain Candy, who rode his horse into the clubhouse of the exclusive Reading Room.

Candy was expelled and Bennett forced to resign. In retaliation, Bennett founded a rival club, the Casino, and in 1879 built his clubhouse, the famous Newport Casino. There, the United States Lawn Tennis Association held its first championship in 1881. From then until 1914, the Casino hosted the USLTA championships, and Tennis Week at the end of August became a highlight of the "Season." The USLTA moved to Forest Hills, New York, in 1917; but the National Tennis Hall of Fame

opened in the Casino in 1952 and is celebrated annually with a professional tournament. Rhode Island's first golf course was constructed in Newport, and the first amateur and open championships of the United States Golf Association were played there in 1895. Once golf and tennis were games of the rich, but today Rhode Island has nearly 50 golf courses, and almost everyone who can swing a racquet plays tennis.

Yachting still remains a sport of the con-siderably wealthy, and Newport is home to the most celebrated yachting competition, the America's Cup Race. The first race occurred off the Isle of Wight in England in 1851, and the trophy has remained in America since then. The New York Yacht Club, which sponsors the race, moved the competition to Rhode Island in 1930. The state had a reputation for having master builders of Cup racers, as the Herreshoffs of Bristol built every winner from 1893 to 1937. The biennial Bermuda Yacht Race

TRINITY SQUARE REPERTORY COMPANY

OF MICE
AND MEN
JOHN STEINBECK

13 weeks to see this spectacular production. In the 1890s the American Band played each evening to thousands during the season in Roger Williams Park. A rival venture, the Sans Souci Gardens of William E. White and the National Band, which also opened in the summer of 1878, staged operettas and featured band concerts and singers. One soloist in 1887 was Matilda Sisseretta Joyner, soon to become internationally famous as Black Patti. Although she was compared to the legendary Adelina Patti, Black Patti found her career shunted into singing in the Cakewalk Jubilee, musical variety shows, and the Black Patti Troubadours, which was essentially a minstrel show with an opera star.

The minstrel show was America's first mass entertainment form, and Providence became a major source of minstrel troupes and a thoroughly minstrel-mad city. In the 1870s and 1880s virtually every theater in Providence and Pawtucket featured minstrels, and shows often ran for 10 months. Ashcroft Street is named for Billy Ashcroft, leading endman in the late 19th century; he and Dick Sands, also of Rhode Island, shared the title of "Champion Clog Dancers of the World." The endmen were the stars. Jerry Cohan, father of George M. Cohan, was a minstrel endman as early as 1867. As minstrels declined, Cohan switched to vaudeville; and it was as part of the Four Cohans that George M. first appeared in the theater. The Four Cohans were featured at the grand opening of the Imperial Theater in 1902, and when the Albee Theater opened on April 21, 1919, George M. was the headliner. Born in Providence, he was a great favorite, even if he later declared that he hated the place. Vaudeville in turn faded before the movies, and Providence's largest theaters were built essentially to be movie palaces. The Strand opened in June 1915 and seated 2,500; the 3,000-seat Majestic began with movies and vaudeville in April 1917; and the 3,200-seat Loew's State was dedicated in October 1928. Nearly all theaters accommodated a variety of entertainments from girlie shows and Victor Herbert's operettas to the Boston Symphony Orchestra (since 1882), and legitimate theater.

New England's first theatrical perfor-

moved to Newport in 1936, and now the Transatlantic Yacht Race also sails out of the "Yachting Capital of the World." The newest ideas are a round-the-world yacht race beginning and ending in Newport, and an invitational "Hall of Fame" race for the top 20 yachtsmen.

For more ordinary folks, band concerts, parades, and theaters added gaiety to life. In the late 19th century Providence supported one of America's greatest wind bands, Reeves' American Band. Begun in 1837, the band came under the directorship of D.W. Reeves in 1866, and he expanded it into a full-time occupation. Nearly every significant occasion included the American Band. In June 1878 Reeves opened the Park Garden, near Roger Williams Park. The following summer he staged an awesome version of Gilbert and Sullivan's H.M.S. *Pinafore*, complete with a full-sized ship, a chorus of 100, and orchestra of 28. Audiences of over 4,000 came nightly for

mances occurred in Newport in the summer of 1761 when Hallam's Virginia Players appeared successfully. But when they played in Providence the next summer, over 400 citizens petitioned the General Assembly, saying that theatricals "not only occasion great and unnecessary expenses, and discourage industry and frugality, but likewise tend generally to increase immorality, impiety and contempt for religion." The General Assembly complied. Some determined opponents wanted to destroy the little theater on Meeting Street even before then, but John Brown and friends dragged a cannon from a nearby armory and threatened to fire on the mob. Theater returned to Providence in December 1792 when Joseph Harper's company played at the courthouse. A real theater was erected in 1795 on the present site of Grace Church with funds from that same John Brown and friends, and the statute against theatricals was repealed. As Providence grew to become New England's second largest city, it became a major stop on the touring circuit for minstrels, vaudeville, and individual performers such as Jenny Lind, whose triumphant appearance in 1850 was held in Howard Hall.

Over the years one could see nearly any sort of stage entertainment that the American theater industry provided. Occasionally the spirit of 1762 will arise and close a show. For example, Eugene O'Neill's Pulitzer prize-winning play, *Strange Interlude*, was banned in 1930 for being "too lewd"; and in 1940 the Providence police denied a license to present John Steinbeck's *Of Mice and Men*. But tastes change, and in 1981 the highly praised Trinity Square Repertory Company staged *Of Mice and Men* and took it on an international tour. Through the 1930s and 1940s the theaters of Providence and movie houses of any town could count on patronage for almost anything that Hollywood wanted to dish out. In the 1950s suburbanization and television radically transformed the theater business and the grand "temples of illusion" fell to wreckers and porno shows. The Majestic was rescued in 1971 by the Trinity Square Repertory Company; and Loew's State has been reprieved as the Ocean State Center for the Performing Arts.

Newport has sought to establish itself as a music and performing arts center during summer seasons. It began with the Jazz Festival in 1954, which occasioned "an uproar among the old guard that almost drowned out the music itself." But, the festival succeeded financially and featured many of America's famous jazz artists. Despite its great music, its troubled history forced the festival to close after the 1971 disorders. That year the billing included top performers, but the festival attracted thousands of the floating population of the youth culture. During Dionne Warwick's performance, a mob of young people, high on drugs and alcohol, abandoned their jugs of wine and tree-top hammocks and stormed the festival fence. In minutes they smashed the fence and rushed the stage. Audience and performers fled in fear, and the police had to restore order. For true jazz lovers, the evening was a sad occasion; jazz at Newport was abandoned in favor of New York City where it billed itself as the "Newport Jazz Festival in New York City." In 1981 festival promoter George Wein returned to Newport with a limited version held in old Fort Adams. Other efforts, such as the Folk Music Festival, the Newport Opera Festival, and a dance festival have all come and gone. The Newport Music Festival, the most elegant and elite, stages concerts in the mansions and has remained afloat with the support of wealthy patrons.

America's first resort and New England's playground are now fully committed to promoting their assets. The literal heart of enterprise in Newport is tourism and resort business. The city rebuilt most of its waterfront, added new hotels, and expanded moorings for pleasure craft. The state itself is contributing to these developments as officials promote Rhode Island nationally as the "biggest little state" with "something for everyone." The Bay teems with an estimated 30,000 vessels, and a true excursion boat returned in 1978 with the appearance of the *Bay Queen*. The opportunities for recreation are far more numerous than at any time, if not so spectacular as in the old days of the amusement parks.

FACING PAGE, TOP: Joe Williams sang with Count Basie and his band in the Newport Jazz Festival in the later 1950s. RIHS (RHi x3 4369)

BOTTOM: The Trinity Square Repertory Company presented Of Mice and Men *in 1981. Trinity Square Repertory Company, which began in 1964, was first housed in the Trinity United Methodist Church located at Trinity Square in Providence. In 1968 the company was the first American regional theater to perform at the Edinburgh Festival in Scotland. Artistic Director Adrian Hall led the company to national exposure on the Public Broadcasting Service's "Theater in America" in 1974, to a new home in the old Majestic Theater in 1973, and a Tony Award in 1981. Courtesy, Trinity Square Repertory Company*

1764   1914

150TH ANNIVERSARY
OF THE FOUNDING OF
BROWN UNIVERSITY
OCTOBER 11-15

Chapter Nine

THE STATE OF THE HEART, SOUL, AND MIND

RHODE ISLAND'S RICH religious and ethnic diversity has produced a varied and sometimes contradictory experience. The state takes pride in being first in America to conduct the "lively experiment" in religious freedom which has become part of the American system. The private, voluntary congregation became a model for other institutions as well. Private agencies generally preceded public ones, and a number of those that are publicly supported today had their beginnings as private or philanthropic endeavors. In time the increase in population and social complexity meant that private means were unable to accommodate all who needed services. Art and culture remain privately supported but social services have generally been assumed by the state.

To the horror and disgust of its neighbors, colonial Rhode Island admitted all the rejected consciences of New England and the New World, including, as Cotton Mather disapprovingly noted, "Antinomians, Familists, Anabaptists, Anti-sabbatarians, Arminians, Socinians, Quakers, Ranters, everything in the world but Roman Catholics and true Christians." In the beginning, religious toleration was almost the only thing that independent-minded Rhode Islanders could agree upon: and for them church and state were to be separate. Such principles have not, however, kept various religious majorities over the centuries from seeking to impose their morality upon everyone.

For Yankee Protestants, Sunday was a day of church-going and rest; but this clashed with the European notion that Sunday was a day of recreation. As a result, sabbatarianism produced "blue laws" which sought to limit Sunday activities. Various church groups fought the secularization of the Sabbath by trying to prevent Sunday baseball or the showing of movies. In recent years the Sunday sales laws crumbled in the face of the determination of the shopping malls and supermarkets to remain open. The crusade to prohibit alcoholic beverages became highly political, complete with party and officeseekers. The state's first temperance meeting was held at the First Baptist Meeting House in Providence in 1827, and the effort culminated in the statewide prohibition by 1852. While this law was repealed during the Civil War, prohibitionists' concern about the alleged affinity of the immigrants for ardent spirits drove them to amend the state constitution in 1886 to prohibit the manufacture and sale of alcoholic beverages. This, too, was repealed in 1889 in the first election after the Bourn Amendment had enfranchised naturalized citizens. So, by the time the national prohibition amendment arrived in 1919, Rhode Island refused to ratify it and unsuccessfully challenged its constitutionality in the United States Supreme Court.

Presently Rhode Island is the most Catholic state in the nation; Roman Catholics constitute nearly 70 percent of the population and 90 percent of the legislators. This Catholic majority, like its Protestant predecessors, uses its political power to legislate its morality, as for instance on the issues of

This postcard from 1914 announced the 150th anniversary of the founding of Brown University. RIHS (RHi x3 4330)

abortion or the survival of parochial schools.

Contrary to Roger Williams' principles, during most of the 18th century Roman Catholics were barred from the franchise when the colony's laws were first codified in 1719. No evidence exists to indicate that this prohibition was actually enacted before being slipped into the code; but, once in, it was not repealed until 1783. Rhode Island had only a few Catholics during the colonial period, but by the mid-1850s Providence alone had almost 10,000, and Rhode Island counted 19 Roman Catholic churches, 6 parochial schools, and an orphanage. With the creation of the Catholic parochial school system in the 1840s came an issue that has not been resolved to the present. Catholics made parochial schools a high priority; unfortunately, the drive to gain public funding for these schools began at the same time and has served to perpetuate the divisions between Catholics and Protestants.

The rise of parochial schools strengthened the effort to create a statewide public school system; and industrialization and immigration spurred educational reformers. In this respect, Rhode Island shared the national perception that the public school was the most effective, efficient instrument for bringing the children of immigrants into the mainstream of American life. Inasmuch as Rhode Island was America's first urban, industrial state, it is not surprising that she led the way in certain aspects of public education.

The impetus for a free public school system was led by John Howland of the Providence Association of Mechanics and Manufacturers, who asserted that "education is the common right of every child." As a result, in 1800 Rhode Island enacted America's first public school law to create a statewide system of free education. Unfortunately, except for Providence and Smithfield, the towns refused to implement the act, and it was repealed in 1803. Only Providence regularly maintained public schools for the next two decades, but even these educated only a fraction of the children because parents still had to pay for fuel and books. A new state law in 1828

established independent school committees and a permanent state fund for education. Thereafter, no town was without a school; but because many charged for books, the poor could not afford to attend. The wealthier people simply provided a private education for their children, as they always had.

One ignored problem was segregation of blacks. While the law did not mandate segregation, Providence, Newport, and Bristol, where most blacks lived, maintained segregated schools. In 1828 Providence had opened a school for black children, but the teacher was paid 20 percent less than teachers of whites. George T. Downing, a successful caterer and hotel proprietor in Providence and Newport, began his attack on school segregation in 1855, a campaign that lasted until his victory in 1866.

Thomas Dorr ought to be remembered for his educational reforms. As a member of the Providence school committee from 1838 to 1842, he helped to improve the schools substantially, and he was instrumental in Providence's appointing a superintendent in 1839, the first in the nation. He also sought to bring free public schools to the entire state through the People's Constitution, but it was defeated. However, the new Constitution of 1842 declared that "it shall be the duty of the General Assembly to promote public schools. ..." The legislature commissioned Henry Barnard to conduct a comprehensive survey of the schools, the first of its kind in the nation. Like similar investigations in Connecticut, Massachusetts, and New York, it revealed appalling conditions and provoked a general reorganization of education in the state. As a consequence of one recommendation, in 1854 the state began a teacher training school which by 1957 had evolved into Rhode Island College, a general-purpose institution of higher education.

Despite various reforms, the public schools were still poorly attended because of fees and textbook costs and because the Rhode Island System of hiring entire families for mill work kept large numbers of children away. The 1880 Census revealed that the illiteracy rate among

BELOW: *The driving force to abolish segregated schools in Rhode Island, George T. Downing (1819-1903), was the son of a successful New York caterer and oyster house owner. In 1846 George opened a summer branch of his father's restaurant in Newport. Four years later he started a catering business in Providence, and finally he built a luxury hotel in Newport called the Sea Girt House. He began his attack on segregated schools in 1855 and finally won in 1866. Courtesy, Rhode Island Black Heritage Society*

native-born whites (not to mention the foreign-born) was four times as great as neighboring Massachusetts, and that almost 22 percent of all school-aged children did not attend a single day of school. These shocking figures led to a free textbook law in 1893, higher requirements for attendance, a truancy law, and the lengthening of the school year.

Still, public education remained in a deplorable condition. It was underfunded and its curriculum unsuited to the ethnic and industrialized character of the state. The largest school district had only one truant officer until 1926, its administrators were Yankees, its teachers nearly all Irish, and its students polyglot. Manual training and commercial education were not introduced until late and were still unavailable in most places. In 1919 "Americanization" became a major thrust as a result of nativist fears, and a state measure forced public schools to assume the Americanization classes that had formerly been conducted by groups such as the YMCA.

Just as Yankee attitudes, financial restraints, and inadequate facilities sometimes alienated immigrant students, immigrant attitudes often precluded school success. Many ethnic groups did not identify with the public schools. The Irish and French preferred parochial schools, while a large number of children of the industrial working class left school at an early age. Woonsocket, with a population of 24,000 in 1890, graduated only 11 students from high school. In the first decades of the 20th century, Rhode Island had the lowest percentage of children attending any level of school in New England, and attendance after the age of 14 declined sharply since many obtained work permits. For example, in 1920 Providence handled 7,266 work certificates. Not surprisingly, juvenile delinquency rates were "higher than in any state in the Union except the District of Columbia and Delaware." With the exception of Nevada, Rhode Island had the highest illiteracy rate of all northern and western states. Only the South was worse off. The result of these factors was to create a weak educational system and a general state of mind which gave public education a lower priority. Even today, Rhode Island

ranks near the bottom in educational achievement as fewer than half of the adults have graduated from high school; and it is 34th in literacy, lowest in New England.

In sharp contrast, Rhode Island's wealthier classes have high educational achievement and schools to serve their aspirations. Upwardly mobile ethnics and professionals have created in their suburban communities, such as Barrington, Cumberland, and Lincoln, some of the best public schools in the state. Affluent Yankees send their children to Protestant academies or private schools. Such institutions antedate public schools as wealthier colonists educated their children with tutors, dame schools, Latin schools, and proprietary and private academies. Dr. James Manning, for instance, started a Latin preparatory school in connection with Rhode Island College (Brown) in 1764. The Quakers established a denominational school in 1784, today known as Moses Brown School. Over the years a host of academies and seminaries sprang up in every corner of the state.

The state's only institution of higher education until the mid-19th century was Brown University. While it was named for Nicholas Brown, Jr., in 1804, the name recognizes the crucial part played by the

ABOVE: Because of inadequate schools and direct costs to poor parents for the schooling of their children, the likelihood was that children such as these would grow up undereducated or virtually illiterate. This photo entitled "Along the Tracks: A Playground Badly Needed," probably by Lewis Hine, appeared in Child Welfare Conference and Exhibit, *January 6-12, 1913. Courtesy, Newport Historical Society*

FACING PAGE, BOTTOM: As a state legislator in Connecticut, lawyer, writer, and educator Henry Barnard (1811-1900) helped to establish a state board of education and served as its first secretary. He then became Rhode Island's first commissioner of education (1845-1849) before going on to become Connecticut State Superintendent of Education (1850-1854), chancellor of the University of Wisconsin (1858-1860), president of St. John's College, Annapolis, Maryland, (1866-1877), and the first U.S. Commissioner of Education (1867-1870). James Sullivan Lincoln painted this oil on canvas portrait of Barnard in 1857. RIHS (RHi x3 3110)

family, especially Moses, John, and Joseph, in the location and early development of the college. The family has continued its close association and benefactions over the years. Brown probably passed up a chance to become the state university because it did not wish to open an agricultural department after the General Assembly assigned to it the state's share of the federal land grant under the Morrill Act of 1862.

city." Brown could enrich its programs by "effecting a constantly widening affiliation with the cultural and scientific agencies of the state and of the metropolitan district." Subsequently, the university did institute several new programs, and in the 1970s developed the state's only medical school. Sometimes, however, the needs of the university brought it into conflict with local concerns. Brown's callous destruction

Woonsocket's Precious Blood Grammar School (left) and the rear of Precious Blood Church (right) on Hamlet Avenue, as they appeared around 1920. The French-Canadians, like the Irish, expanded their institutional network by building a parochial school system throughout their settlements. With the decline of new immigrants, coupled with gradual assimilation and rising costs, many of these institutions collapsed. The grammar school closed in the early 1970s. Courtesy, RIHS (RHi x3 2285)

Brown surrendered the aid; and in 1892 the legislature created Rhode Island College of Agricultural and Mechanic Arts, which in 1951 became the University of Rhode Island.

Under president Benjamin Andrews in the 1890s, Brown assembled a distinguished faculty, founded the Women's College (Pembroke), and began a limited graduate program. Although Brown was proud to maintain the atmosphere of a "typical New England college of arts and sciences," a 1930 external study criticized it for remaining aloof from the metropolitan context. They declared that Brown "has the possibility of a more distinguished service," but it would have to alter its "national state of mind" and accept that the university is "conditioned by a great

of several blocks of 18th- and 19th-century houses caused the historic preservation movement on College Hill to spring to life in the mid-1950s. Since then, Brown has been more careful that its internal needs are not destructive to the surrounding areas. While various local politicians continue to maintain that Brown ought to be wide open to local applicants, the school still sees itself as having a national constituency.

The Roman Catholic educational system reached maturity with the opening of Providence College in 1919. Founded by Matthew Harkins, Bishop of the Diocese of Providence, it has traditionally served the Irish and is the alma mater of a large number of the state's political leaders. A women's college, Salve Regina, began operation in 1947. The system underwent a transformation in the 1970s when Salve Regina expanded to a four-year institution, the unaccredited College of Mount St. Joseph closed, and Providence College went co-educational.

The late 1960s and early 1970s were flush times for higher education in the nation, and most of the state's colleges and universities expanded and developed. Rhode Island's public junior college, begun in 1964 with 250 students in temporary quarters in Providence, expanded by 1980 into the Community College of Rhode Island with 12,000 students on two permanent campuses in Warwick and Lincoln. Roger Williams College, founded in 1948, became a four-year institution and moved to a new campus in Bristol in 1969. Likewise, Bryant College, opened as a business college in 1863, moved to its new location in Smithfield in 1971. Into the vacuum created by the exodus of these colleges from Providence to the suburbs came Johnson & Wales, which has gone from a junior college in 1963 to offering graduate degrees by 1981. In the 1980s, with the rising costs of private education and the shrinking student pool, privately educated legislators have been seeking legislation to shore up their institutions. While this may guarantee the survival of Rhode Island's educational diversity, it comes, as it did with secondary education, at the expense of public higher education.

Just as private education predated the public school system, so did many other services begin in the private sphere; and many of the institutions that are now regarded as public had their origin in philanthropy. The earliest libraries, such as the Redwood Library in Newport and the Athenaeum in Providence, were private, or were philanthropic projects for the benefit of the public, as in the case of Edward Harris' establishment of a library and cultural center for Woonsocket in 1856. Dozens of private subscription libraries appeared and disappeared before a public system developed in the late 19th century. In 1875 the Free Library Act provided for matching state funds to any library that was free to the public. With this, library doors opened in virtually every town. The Pawtucket

Public Library illustrated the transformation. It began as a private subscription library in 1852 but was assumed by the town in 1876. It was the only Rhode Island library in the late 19th century wholly owned and supported by a municipality. However, it also benefited from philanthropy as Frederick Clark Sayles donated the land and building in 1899. A progressive institution, the Pawtucket Library was one of the first in the nation to adopt the open-shelf system, a Sunday reading room, a children's program, and a librarian to serve high-school students.

In the pre-Civil War years, the healing of the body was mostly a matter of luck because medical practices were premodern and health-care facilities were virtually nonexistent. From today's perspective, all of the competing medical theories of that age were quackery, whether it was the heroic medicine of the "regular" physicians or the unorthodox ideas of the homeopaths, hydropaths, heliopaths, mesmerists, phrenologists, or spiritualists. The era was one of great experimentation because it was clear that orthodox medical practice was simply dangerous to the patient. For example, Elizabeth Buffam Chace, a leader in abolitionism, women's rights, and poor relief, became deeply involved in spiritual healing, hydropathy, and "animal magnetism" after losing five children under the care of "regular" physicians. The *Providence Journal* supported dietary reform, specifically, the "Graham Cracker" crusade. Some local members of the Transcendentalist movement established a utopian community called Holly House near Providence in 1841 and sought to preserve their health by abolishing all coercion and private possessions and by abstaining from tobacco, alcohol, and sex.

Until the start of Butler Hospital for the Insane in 1847, Rhode Island had no hospitals. Butler resulted from the philanthropy of the Browns, Goddards, Hazards, and Cyrus Butler; and it was the state's only asylum until the public institutions were opened at Howard in 1870. Butler remains a private mental health facility, but Rhode Island Hospital became the first general hospital in 1868. It, too, had its beginnings in philanthropy with generous donations

Elizabeth Buffum Chace (1806-1899), an antislavery and suffrage leader, was reared a Quaker and an abolitionist by her father, who founded the New England Anti-Slavery Society. After her first five children died, Elizabeth devoted her life to the antislavery cause. Her husband was a successful industrialist who supported her reform activities. Though the couple had five more children, Elizabeth plunged into the suffrage crusade after the Civil War as well as working for penal reform, education, temperance, peace, and care of orphans. Portrait from Elizabeth Buffum Chace, Her Life & Its Environment, 1914. RIHS (RHi x3 2388)

from the Ives family. Although the hospital is publicly supported, the Goddards, Metcalfs, Sharpes, Chafees, Browns, and others have underwritten major development in the 20th century. Philanthropy launched Woonsocket's hospital in 1888, and Pawtucket Memorial Hospital (1910) resulted from nearly $500,000 in contributions from the Sayles and Goff families. Similarly, the Hazards were the principal founders of the South County Hospital in 1919. The Rhode Island School for the Deaf, started by Mrs. Henry Lippitt in 1876, assumed by the state in 1891, provided complete care and training for the children free of charge.

Rhode Island's parks reflect this same philanthropic impulse: Colt Park in Bristol, Goddard Park in East Greenwich, Wilcox Park in Westerly, Roger Williams, Metcalf, and Davis parks in Providence, and Jenks Park in Central Falls. The state park system grew out of a private organization, the Public Park Association. Begun in 1883, it labored to save the Providence Cove and Promenade from railroad development. While it failed in that, its petition to the General Assembly produced the Metropolitan Park Commission in 1904. The Commission developed a grand plan of parks, and began by opening Lincoln Woods in 1909. The Metropolitan Park Commission was absorbed in 1935 by the newly formed Department of Agriculture and Conservation, which in turn led to the Department of Environmental Management. The era of the magnificent donors is gone, and today most of the municipal and state parks, such as the new Bay Islands Park system, have to be purchased.

With the exception of prisons and poorhouses, most of the institutions in this state began as benefactions of the great industrialist families, and these same people pressed government to assume new responsibilities. The trend in the past has been to denounce such people as "robber barons"; but this ignores the many libraries, hospitals, asylums, boys clubs, museums, and parks that they gave. Whatever motivated these people, whether Christian stewardship, guilt, paternalism, or quest for recognition, it remains that they made a commitment to improve the

quality of life in their communities and state. They gave more to the general welfare than all other groups combined.

The role of philanthropy diminished and the reform impulse quickened as soaring populations pressed municipalities for far more services. However, getting government to accept changes and responsibilities was an arduous task. One major force for reform was the Rhode Island Council of Women, which coordinated the activities of women's clubs, charity organizations, and church groups that represented the growing activity of middle-class women. The council secured the appointment of a woman factory inspector in 1894 and made Rhode Island the first state to require every town to hire police matrons. It worked successfully from 1892 to 1910 to raise the minimum age for child labor from 10 to 14 years, but was totally rebuffed on prohibition. Its strong support for Charles V. Chapin, Providence's outstanding commissioner of public health, helped put the city in the forefront of public health. As the reform effort waned after World War I, cities and towns were unable to meet needs; consequently, general

Homeopathic medical practice put great store upon science and public health, with the result being that as medical science advanced, homeopathy converged with orthodox medical practice. In 1878 the Rhode Island Homeopathic Hospital opened and evolved into Roger Williams Hospital on Chalkstone Avenue in Providence in 1947. Pictured here is a nursing class at the Homeopathic Hospital in the 1920s. Courtesy, Roger Williams Hospital

Mary Ann Balch Lippitt (1823-1889), shown here at age 20, saw three of her children die and a fourth left deaf from an 1856 scarlet fever epidemic. Because no school for the deaf existed, she set about teaching her daughter to speak. This work led her to found the Clarke School for the Deaf in 1876. From a portrait owned by the Lippitt family. RIHS (RHI x3 4360)

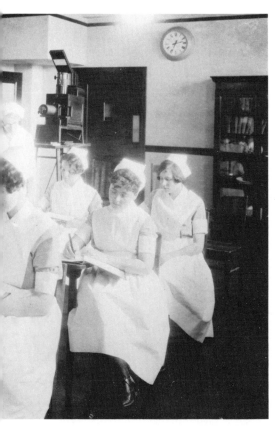

survive. The Providence Symphony Orchestra was first heard in 1890, was revived in 1911, and again in 1932, but succumbed to the Depression. The present Rhode Island Philharmonic Orchestra began in 1945 and has persisted only because of patrons and annual fund drives.

The state's artistic backwardness stemmed from at least two factors. Until the late 19th century Rhode Island lacked an urban middle class of sufficient size to support institutions of fine arts. In addition, the heavy presence of Quakers and Baptists had discouraged ornamentation and "impractical" arts. For example, the Newport Quakers remodeled their Meeting House to remove its interesting cupola because Philadelphia Quakers criticized it as being "too Popish." Half of the members of the Providence First Baptist Church seceded in 1771 because congregational singing had been introduced. It was not the poor musical quality that offended; music itself was a "desecration of the worship." Had they still been members, they would have strenuously opposed the form of the new building which was erected in 1774-1775. A radical departure from the plain meeting-house style, it was the first Baptist meeting house in New England to have a steeple and bell. But then, the leading figures in the Providence church were the Brown brothers, who were patrons of the arts and who dreamed of a greater Providence.

solicitations and religious charities tried to fill the gap. The *Providence Journal* started its Santa Fund in 1924, and the Community Chest (United Way) came to Rhode Island in 1926. Local and charitable resources failed in the Great Depression, but from the crisis came the urban-federal partnership which created a new dependency on the part of municipalities to maintain services.

Without philanthropic support, artistic institutions would have had little place in Rhode Island's life. Although artists had flocked to Newport in the 18th and 19th centuries seeking commissions from the rich, no art school or club appeared until after the Civil War. Newport had music teachers in its golden age, but the only long-lived musical organization in the state was the American Band, a military band. Eben Tourjee, born in Warwick, established a music conservatory in Providence in 1865, but found better opportunities in Boston, where he established the New England Conservatory of Music in 1867. The Boston Symphony Orchestra has regularly played in Providence since 1882, but local symphonies have struggled to

The Reverend Anna Garland Spencer (1851-1931) stands in the pulpit of the Bell Street Chapel, Providence, where she served as minister from 1891 to 1902. She led the Rhode Island Council of Women as president from 1896 to 1902 during its most reformist stage and served on the National Council of Women for years. She declined to accept the presidency of the National Council, but became a professor of sociology and ethics at Meadville Theological School in Pennsylvania, and then special lecturer in social science at Teachers College, Columbia, University. Courtesy, Religious Society of the Bell Street Chapel

Providence became Rhode Island's cultural center as it expanded in the next century. A growing city required buildings; and talented local architects, such as John Holden Greene, Thomas Tefft, and James Bucklin, created notable structures. In the late 19th century, the leading architectural firm was Stone, Carpenter and Willson which designed buildings in styles as diverse as the old Providence County Courthouse (1877), the Baker House on Hope Street (1883), and the Providence Public Library (1900). Still, when the state erected a new capitol building, the commission went to the New York firm of McKim, Mead, and White.

With the exception of an occasional portraitist, such as Gilbert Stuart, or the miniaturist Edward Greene Malbone (both of whom left Rhode Island to pursue their careers), the state could not boast of distinguished artists until the Gilded Age. The stimulus which led to an art school and the Art Club was the Centennial Exposition of 1876. Rhode Island's imagination, talent, and toil had largely gone into commerce and industry, and its industrial products compared favorably with those of other states at the Exposition; but it was obviously deficient in art. Rhode Island School of Design had its origins in this discovery.

The *Providence Magazine* declared: "To a few public-spirited, far-sighted women the city owes this ornament; one that will stand for ages as a monument to the Sex." Mrs. Jesse Metcalf and a small group of women, who had acted as a committee on the Rhode Island exhibit for the Exposition, began RISD in 1877. While its principal sources of support were philanthropic, the state began appropriations for scholarships in 1882. For many years RISD's principal role was to serve the textile and jewelry industries. Nevertheless, fine arts were taught, an art museum established, and cooperative arrangements made with Rhode Island Normal School for the training of art teachers.

Discussions in the spring of 1878 led to the founding of the Providence Art Club in 1880. Subsequently came Brown's first art professorship, the Water Color, Handicraft, and Ceramics clubs, and the Ann Mary Brown Memorial art museum. Providence became a regional center for professional artists, and RISD is now recognized as one of America's leading art schools. The state has a burgeoning artistic community which exhibits its work on many levels from the professional art schools to the local summer art festivals at Wickford, Burrillville, and Scituate.

ABOVE, LEFT: Thomas Robinson Hazard (1797-1886), "Shepard Tom," was one of five sons of the founder of the Peace Dale Woolen Mills. He sold his part of the property in 1838 and retired to a life of philanthropy, reform, and literary pursuits. From History of Washington and Kent Counties, R.I., 1889. Courtesy, Rhode Island College/Special Collections

ABOVE, RIGHT: Caroline Hazard (1856-1945) was the daughter of Rowland Hazard, superintendent of the Peace Dale Woolen Mills. She became Wellesley College's fifth president (1899-1910) and published 20 books of poetry, local and family history, and educational philosophy. RIHS (RHi x3 1678)

Similarly, creative literature was fairly rare until late in the century as most writers had been scribblers of little stories of limited interest or consequence. Even "Shepard Tom," Thomas Robinson Hazard, who is frequently cited as a major figure in the state's literary gallery of the last century, was a writer on local South County topics in books such as *The Jonny-Cake Papers* (1882). Shepard Tom was part of a prolific family noted for its industrialists, philanthropists, and literary figures. The first Rowland Hazard began the Peace Dale Woolen Mills and established a paternalistic mill village for his workers. His sons expanded the business, engaged in philanthropy and community improvement, and started a literary tradition that extended through several generations. The 20th century has seen a substantial increase in Rhode Island's literary output, including Pulitzer Prize winners Oliver LaFarge and Leonard Bacon, and the eccentric, misanthropic H.P. Lovecraft, one of the developers of the horror story and science fiction. However, Rhode Island still awaits the appearance of a school of literature or an author of the stature of a William Faulkner or Robert Frost.

The heart, soul, and mind of the state continues to reflect the independent nature of Rhode Islanders. A recurring theme of observers of its cultural scene has been that the varieties of cultures and the various artistic and intellectual interests have tended to act independently of each other. The elite cultural institutions have only a limited impact on the predominantly ethnic culture which is expressed in the fraternal societies, the saints' festivals, and the home. Rhode Island has several autonomous cultural centers. Newport tends to be a summer center with its music festivals (classics for the rich, jazz for the young), seaside activities, and night spots. A second area is in the rural region with its more traditional activities, such as May breakfasts, Grange, family reunions, and fairs. Metropolitan Providence, the third center, is home to most of the state's permanent cultural institutions. Although a small state, Rhode Island strives for cultural and intellectual excellence. It has the Trinity Square Repertory Company, which won a Tony Award in 1981, a professional symphony orchestra, two opera companies, a nationally recognized school of art with one of America's great small museums, a ballet company, a Shakespeare troupe, civic choruses, libraries, a zoo, and the rich cultural product of ethnic festivals, colleges, and universities.

ABOVE, LEFT: Leonard Bacon (1887-1954) was the son of industrialist Nathaniel Terry Bacon and Helen Hazard, a sister to Caroline Hazard. Reared in Peace Dale, he wrote 19 volumes of poetry, criticism, and essays, and won the Pulitzer Prize for poetry in 1940. Courtesy, Rhode Island College/Special Collections

ABOVE, RIGHT: Martha Bacon Ballinger (1917-1981), the daughter of Leonard Bacon, published nearly a dozen volumes of poetry, fiction, historical essays, and translations in addition to teaching English and literature at Rhode Island College. Her friend is Boz (1967-). Courtesy, Rhode Island College/Special Collections

Chapter Ten

THE PROVIDENCE CITY-STATE

I N THE MID-17TH CENTURY, a Newport man named the colony "Rhode Island and Providence Plantations," thereby relegating Providence to second place. Two hundred years later, the reverse had become true: Providence dominated Rhode Island and all of southern New England. The city was the focus of business and commerce, manufacturing and industry, education and culture, population and politics. While Newport still set the pace for High Society, Providence led everything else. In the years before the First World War, the city assumed a truly metropolitan character and its leaders' boosterism could hardly be contained. By the 1920s the city's hyperurbanization caught up with it and people began to seek a better quality of life in the outlying plantations.

After the Civil War, Providence's 5.4 square miles could no longer absorb industrial and residential growth. Mills and factories followed river valleys to the north and west, and platted residential settlements erupted to the south. Civic leaders could not readily accept this external growth; consequently, the city annexed eight separate adjacent areas between 1868 and 1919 for various reasons. For example, the Republicans engineered the 1868 annexation of the eastern half of Cranston so the party could retain the General Assembly seat from the town; and the industrialist George Corliss petitioned the legislature in 1873 for the annexation of the eastern half of North Providence. The industrialist-studded Assembly readily

Avery Lord took this aerial view of the downtown area of Providence about 1930. The construction of the 1910s and 1920s dramatically transformed the skyline. RIHS (RHi x3 4231)

obliged because the area was "simply a continuation of the compact part of the city of Providence. ... The needs, the activity, the course of trade, the intercourse of the population in matters of business are in and with the city." By 1919, when Providence annexed a portion of Johnston, the real-estate grabbing had come to an end. Through annexation Providence nearly tripled its area to 18.5 square miles and almost doubled its population. Expansion gave the city the potential for further growth, elevated it into the top 20 cities in the nation, and conditioned its leadership to think in terms of "Greater Metropolitan Providence."

As Providence increased its limits, it also expanded public services. Although slow to accept the new responsibilities, Providence later set the standard for southern New England in providing utilities and urban services. In the 1850s the city lacked nearly all essentials to attract additional population. Thomas A. Doyle, who was elected mayor 19 times between 1864 and 1888, vigorously attacked the lack of most urban services. Under his administration the police department went from a night watch to a professional force with expanded powers; the fire department improved dramatically and a modern system of electric fire alarms was installed; a municipal water system was built, and work began on adequate sewers. A new city hall went up in Exchange Place, and new streetcar lines extended from the city's center in all directions.

The need for an adequate water supply

led Providence in 1866 to draw it from the Pawtuxet River. The city embarked on a five-year, $5-million project that built dams and reservoirs, pumping stations, and water mains. On Thanksgiving Day 1871, an exhibition fountain ceremoniously shot a jet of water from the new system higher than the buildings in Exchange Place; unfortunately, it froze into icy sludge in the subzero winds and rained down on some spectators, nearly freezing them to death before it was shut off. The Pawtuxet system proved inadequate for the city's continued growth, so in 1910 Providence began acquiring land in Scituate for a new reservoir. Work started in 1915 and would cost $12 million before completion. A vast area was graded, and small towns

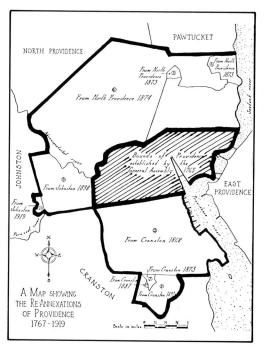

and factories were moved or demolished. The Scituate Reservoir, the "largest artificially created body of water in New England," was Providence's greatest public project. It became fully operational in 1928, and over the years other municipalities have tied into the system.

Unfortunately, no provision had been made for sewering the city so that the effluvia flowed into the Cove Basin, turning it into a big, open sewer. The "fearful odors" and "robust smell" of the Cove, especially in hot weather, and the periodic cholera outbreaks among people living along the Woonasquatucket and Moshassuck rivers so alarmed the public that the Cove was filled, sewers installed, and the Field's Point treatment plant constructed by 1900. As a result of the efforts of Commissioner of Health Charles V. Chapin, the city built a model secondary sewage treatment facility.

During his years in office, Chapin made many contributions to the city's health. Between 1856 and 1932, he and Edwin M. Snow placed Providence in the forefront of municipal health in America. Providence had the first medical examinations for the entire school population, first systematic medical care for the poor, and was first to abandon fumigation for the control of contagious disease. Providence City Hospital,

Providence traffic control policemen stand in front of the 1895 Fountain Street Station in the 1920s. Rapid growth and increased urban disturbances led cities to professionalize their police forces and assign them to ever more specialized duties, such as detective work, vice squads, and traffic control. Courtesy, Providence Public Library

opened in 1910, pioneered the use of aseptic nursing, and the city kept the most complete vital statistics of any municipality in the nation. Chapin even had the city post hundreds of signs against spitting on the sidewalks in an effort to combat the spread of tuberculosis.

Tuberculosis was so prevalent that it was called the White Plague; and as the city school system grew, "fresh air schools" were provided for tuberculosis-prone children. Rapid urban growth and the influx of immigrants forced Providence to build a large number of schools. Between the 1890s and 1920 the number of high schools went from one to four, and regular elementary schools rose to 96 plus five fresh air schools, one trade school, and 20 for "backward" (mostly non-English-speaking) children. The great influenza epidemic of 1919 left so many children with impairments that the city opened a special school for handicapped children and bused them to it.

By the 1920s school lighting had changed from gas to electricity, and all of the urban areas were linked by telephones. While Newport's Thames Street was the first American street illuminated by gas, Providence embarked on a large-scale lighting program before the Civil War. During the gaslight era, the Providence Gas Company supplied light, heat, and hot-flame fuel for towns, homes, and factories in three Rhode Island counties. The telephone and the telegraph emerged after the Civil War and in 1880 the Providence Telephone Company, born of the merger of two competing companies, began extending its lines to cover all of Rhode Island and parts of southeastern Massachusetts. With the telephone no longer a curio, by 1919 the company counted 60,594 subscribers in Providence alone.

As the technology of electricity advanced, the new industry began displacing gas companies. In 1884 Marsden Perry's Narragansett Electric Lighting Company was incorporated and received its first contract with Providence to replace 75 gaslights with electric streetlights. A generation later, when Exchange Place was lighted by modern arc lamps in August 1913, the *Providence Magazine* exulted: "As if by magic the great civic center and main business thoroughfares were transformed from inky darkness to brilliancy challenging almost the King of Day." Not everyone thought the new lights a good idea. When the city proposed to replace four old lights in Market Square with the new arc lights, one citizen protested that "if this were done it would make the square so brilliant at night that people would want lights burning all over the place."

Market Square and Exchange Place were the terminal points of the transportation network of the entire state. All roads, rails, and lines ran to Providence. By the 1880s, Thomas Tefft's elegant Romanesque railroad terminal was deemed insufficient and soon fell victim to progress and vandalism. The odorous Cove was filled and given to railroad expansion and the new Union Station erected on the site in 1894. The old station, where Abraham Lincoln had once spoken, conveniently burned one night in a fire of mysterious origin.

The street railway system and electric interurban lines radiated from this same center in all directions. Marsden Perry forged his monopoly in the 1890s and then extended the tendrils of the Rhode Island Company through the interurban trolleys west to Pascoag, north to Woonsocket, south to Cranston and Warwick, and east to East Providence, Barrington, Warren, and Bristol. The interurban lines became crucial to the economic health of shore resorts such as Rocky Point and Crescent Park.

The growth and prosperity of the streetcar company coincided with the heyday of Roger Williams Park. When Betsy Williams donated the land in 1871, the city accepted reluctantly because it was "so far out in the wilderness." Not until the late 1880s did the Providence park commissioners hire H.W.S. Cleveland to design and develop Roger Williams Park into one of the finest in New England. In the 1890s the park attracted throngs of people, and the trolley company subsidized the American Band to play nightly during the summer. The park commissioners reported in 1899 that 750,000 people attended the free band concerts, averaging 10,000 per night. Most people rode the trolleys to the park.

The Rhode Island Company had over 313 miles of track by 1909 and carried 80 million riders a year, but new competition had already begun. The city's streets not only echoed with the clang and roar of trolleys and the clatter of horse-drawn wagons and buggies, but also with the putt-putt and purr of horseless carriages. The *Providence Board of Trade Journal* in 1905 predicted, "The great number of automobiles now being used for pleasure only presages the use of trucks for business purposes in the near future; and the dray horse, in a few years, will be as uncommon a sight as is a horse car today."

In a few years automobiles and trucks added to the traffic congestion, and the streetcar company proposed in 1914 that the city build a subway system to solve the problem. In its grandest form, the subway would have connected with the interurban lines and extended from Taunton to Pascoag, Woonsocket to Bristol. However, the company was in no position to build it and the city was unwilling to risk such a venture. The Rhode Island Company, which had been operating at a heavy loss for several years, went into receivership in 1919. The United Electric Railways Company purchased the streetcar lines from the bankrupt company and began eliminating unprofitable services. From a peak of 138 million fares in 1923, ridership declined steeply so that by 1940 most of the electric trolleys were gone. Adopting the policy, "If you can't lick em, join em," the United Electric Railways Company put gasoline-powered buses on the streets and created a subsidiary which acquired 90 percent of the taxicabs in service.

Buses and automobiles had a tremendous advantage over electric trolleys in that they did not have to purchase rights-of-way or construct and repair their own tracks and roads. Streets and highways were built and maintained at the public expense. The paving of roads had begun as a result of demands from the bicycle interests in the 1890s and the state ordered the first sample macadam roads in 1895. The State Board of Public Roads was created in 1902 and highway construction advanced steadily thereafter, aided after 1916 by the federal government. At first

ABOVE: Dr. Charles V. Chapin (1856-1941), who served as superintendent of public health in Providence from 1884 to 1931, brought the city to the forefront of public health in America. While critics referred to him as a "harmless sanitary crank," he brought improvements in everything from clean milk to waste removal. His principal support in the period from the 1890s to the 1910s came from the Rhode Island Federation of Women's Clubs. He published extensively and lectured on public health throughout the nation. RIHS (RHi x3 1578)

RIGHT: This 1899 Providence scene shows the rear of tenement houses on lower Charles Street and the West River, a tributary of the Moshassuck River. Despite the installation of sewers, water pollution was a constant source of irritation for public health officials, with the outhouses on the banks of the river adding to their despair. RIHS (RHi x3 4345)

automobiles were toys of the rich, who showed them off and raced them; but assembly-line production soon brought the car to the masses. In 1904 Rhode Island had 767 automobiles; in 1921 it counted 43,662 automobiles, 64,118 licensed operators, 3,450 traffic accidents, and 98 highway fatalities. Throughout the 1920s the improvement of roads and highways brought every corner of the state within speedy reach of Providence, the focus of the system. However, the roads that led to Providence also ran the other way; and the movement to the suburbs was greatly increased by the "Go-Anywhere Vehicle."

This extensive transportation network terminated at Exchange Place, Providence's public square and outdoor community center. It also anchored a thriving downtown which contained the region's shopping, banking, commercial, entertainment, and cultural centers. But the hub of the city

Public concern about tuberculosis among schoolchildren caused Providence to open five "fresh air" schools by 1920. Children prone to tuberculosis attended these schools where the windows were kept open all the time, even during the New England winter. Though fresh air was supposed to control TB, one wonders about the incidence of pneumonia! From Providence Magazine, *April 1915. RIHS (RHi x3 4348)*

ABOVE: Trolley cars belonging to the Rhode Island Company are lined up on Westminster Street in the rain about 1905. Despite ridership in the millions, the Rhode Island Company was bankrupt by 1919 and was succeeded by the United Electric Railways Company. Peak ridership came in 1923 when the company collected 138 million fares; but even this was insufficient to save the trolley system. It soon gave way to buses and taxis. RIHS (RHi x3 1905)

RIGHT: The Crawford Street Bridge was heavily congested with traffic when this photo was made in 1927. Increases in the number of cars and trucks competed with pedestrians and trolleys. The Rhode Island Company paid $315,000 in accident claims in 1913, and it was reported "downright hazardous to be a pedestrian." Although some streets were repeatedly widened, the majority remained in their narrow colonial state, and traffic control devices were yet to be adopted. Consequently, during June and July 1923, 1,103 traffic accidents were recorded. Courtesy, Providence Journal Company

the state, western Connecticut, and southeastern Massachusetts came there to watch parades, participate in festivals, and welcome visiting dignitaries. They also came to shop, bank, and be entertained.

By the turn of the century, the shopping district and banking houses had abandoned North and South Main streets in favor of Westminster and Weybosset streets just south of Exchange Place. The area became a shoppers' paradise as the Boston Store, Diamond's, Gladding's, Shepard's, and the Outlet competed for trade. To accommodate mill workers, merchants stayed open until 11:30 on Saturday night. Diamond's advertised itself as "Rhode Island's Fastest Growing Store," and Gladding's held the distinction of being the oldest department store in New England, but the retailing showpiece was clearly Shepard's. It was the largest department store in New England, employed over 1,400, and contained 66 separate departments selling everything from groceries to furniture. In addition, the area's theater row, restaurants, and hotels attracted even more people.

Located nearby was the region's financial and commercial institutions. When Joseph Banigan erected the Banigan Building in 1896, the first steel-framed building in the city, he ushered in the era of highrise commercial architecture. Within two decades Providence's skyline had been dramatically altered as the Union Trust, Hospital Trust, and Turk's Head buildings all soared upward. The crowning achievement, however, was the construction of the 28-story Industrial National Bank building on the site of the old Butler Exchange on the south side of Exchange Place. When it opened in 1928, this building was the tallest in New England and symbolized the city's financial and commercial hold over the region. In addition to housing various banks, these buildings contained the greatest concentration of law offices, brokerage firms, insurance companies, and headquarters of factories and mills in all of southeastern New England.

Providence's leadership, not content with these gains, pressed private interests and municipal and state governments for additional civic improvements. The Cham-

had not always been west of the Providence River nor had Exchange Place been the showpiece of a booming city. Before the area was developed in the 1890s as the new train station and Exchange Place, it had been the Cove Basin. As the summer stinkpot, the Cove was bordered on the north by what the Providence Magazine described as the "grey, grim frowning State Prison, an ugly foundry, [and] a row of very disreputable tenement houses filled with undesirables. ..." But the businessmen's vision triumphed; instead of allowing the land to be used for "cheap restaurants, fishmarkets, and garages," they created what contemporaries called "a superb square and splendid garden, and a railroad entrance that is at present unsurpassed in America." People from all over

ber of Commerce spearheaded the fund raising for a new hotel; and when the Biltmore opened with the usual hoopla on the west end of Exchange Place in 1922, local enthusiasts dubbed it the "most luxurious hotel" between Boston and New York. The new hotel excited the Chamber, which immediately championed a convention center with an eye to hosting a national political convention. In 1926 the Rhode Island Auditorium opened, but instead of a national political convention it attracted the Providence Reds professional hockey team. The theater district was enhanced when lovers of the "silver screen" flocked to the lavishly appointed, 3,200-seat Loew's State Theater after it opened in 1928. The state government, too, augmented the city's domination over the plantations by centralizing formerly scattered state offices in the new State Office Building erected across from the capitol and by moving the judiciary into a new courthouse next to the financial district. In addition, state funds built the new Washington Bridge across the Seekonk River and created the first state-owned airport in America at Hillsgrove.

These decades of growth pulled all of Rhode Island under the domination of Providence. The city had annexed sizable chunks of the surrounding towns, making these communities into support towns for its reservoirs, prisons, reformatory, insane asylum, recreation facilities, and truck farms. It acquired a large part of Scituate and flooded it with water for the city, established a park system that extended into the towns of Lincoln, Cranston, and East Providence, and set the capitol on Smith Hill. It dominated the political, economic, educational, and cultural life of the entire state. All of Rhode Island's main roads terminated in or ran through the center of Providence; and most of the state received its telephone and electricity, gas and gasoline, coal and oil, and lumber and steel from the city. The state's first radio stations, beginning with WJAR in 1922, broadcast from Providence. Providence leadership tied the state together with highways, airways, trolleys, and transmission lines.

Little wonder then that city leaders both celebrated their achievements and looked for more progress. Combining boosterism with self-interest, they engaged in promotional activities and initiated plans for a better city. Central to these enterprises was the Providence Chamber of Commerce, which by 1914 called itself the Chamber of Commerce of Southern New England, and advertised Providence alternately as the "Gateway to Southern New England" and the "City of Fascination." After federal census officials assigned metropolitan status to Providence in 1920, the Greater Providence Chamber of Commerce was born, and within a year a promotional film on the city was distributed nationally.

Although these efforts were strictly promotional, civic leaders also pushed for urban planning and improvement in the quality of life. In 1909 they secured passage of a comprehensive building code, and in 1923 successfully lobbied for a citywide zoning ordinance. Another concern was the fouling of the Woonasquatucket and Moshassuck rivers and the polluted upper portions of Narragansett Bay. "If we are to act," warned the *Providence Magazine* in 1919, "we must act promptly." Two years later the General Assembly voted $1.5 million for water purification and sewer improvement.

One of the most noteworthy civic achievements was the creation of a City Plan Commission in 1914. Although other cities had adopted similar legislation earlier, Providence's commission, supported by business leaders and politicians and led throughout the 1920s by Henry Ames Barker, was lauded as one of the best in the nation. The commission spearheaded studies and surveys of the entire metropolitan region, including such areas for improvement as schools, traffic, public health, and industry; and it advanced a Plan for Greater Providence (1930). In addition, the commission proposed other projects, among them a plan to relocate the railroad terminal and remove the elevated tracks, called the "Chinese Wall." Although most of these plans were never realized, they document Providence's quest to improve itself and to dominate the surrounding communities. But underneath the boosterism and civic pride Providence

The business leadership of the Providence area worked to bind the entire southern New England region to Providence. This cartoon entitled "Pulling Together" is from the Providence Board of Trade Journal, March 1913. RIHS (RHi x3 4350)

was a mature and slowly weakening industrial city facing prosperous and assertive suburban communities.

Collectively, these 1920s studies painted a drab picture of Providence's situation and prospects. The Strayer School Report (1924) found the system glaringly understaffed and underfunded, and the schools mostly ungraded, overcrowded, badly equipped, lacking playgrounds, and unable to attract over 4,000 truants. The Public Health Survey (1928) noted that the city had lost its preeminence in the field with inadequate sanitary sewers, overcrowded housing, and expanding slums in the Wickenden, North Main, and South Main Street areas. Expenditure for public health was only one half that of comparable cities. The Whitten Thorofare Plan (1926) described the nightmare of traveling from one part of the metropolitan area to another because of narrow streets, lack of traffic control devices, and intersections with peculiar angles.

Most alarming, however, was the Metropolitan Providence Industrial Survey (1926-1928). Commissioned by the Chamber of Commerce of Providence and Pawtucket and conducted by a team of experts from the Massachusetts Institute of Technology, the report presented a grim story. Decaying plants, outmoded equipment, uneasy labor, high transportation costs, scarcity of liquid capital, and insuffi-

cient diversity placed the city in the backwater of industrial America. Despite an increase in white-collar employment and the rise of some new industries—electrical components, rubber goods, printing, and automobile-related enterprises—only 10 percent of the city's firms produced 63 percent of all goods and employed 51 percent of all workers. Equally disquieting was the finding that between 1900 and 1930, the city's population rose 31 percent, but the industrial work force increased by only 5 percent, the smallest gain of any American city. In addition, the survey concluded that Providence would have difficulty attracting new industries because, as the most densely settled of the nation's 29 metropolitan areas, Providence lacked adequate housing and had "no extensive areas ... for industrial development." Clearly, by 1925, Providence had reached its zenith of growth in population, industry, and land mass.

Nevertheless, the vision of a "Greater Providence" did not readily die. Most solutions to the problems, however, were handicapped by a steadily declining tax base, politics, divisiveness, and neighboring communities. The flurry of municipal projects before the First World War had saddled the city with one of the highest per capita rates of indebtedness in the nation. The state legislature, concerned about the fiscal solvency of all cities, imposed an indebtedness ceiling of 3 percent of assessed valuation in 1923. Providence's rate was already 4.7 percent, or over $30 million; and by the end of the decade it had risen to $41 million, nearly twice the debt of the entire state. Compounding the problem was a real decline in tax revenues despite an inflationary cycle throughout the decade. Between 1922 and 1926 tax revenues rose by $4 million, but this was only one fourth of the national increase. Providence was losing revenues as slum housing was abandoned, properties

city. Before World War I, the commission undertook appropriate projects and conducted its business with enthusiasm. By the 1920s, however, the annual reports chronicled its ineffectiveness. The commission's budget fluctuated between a meager $2,000 and $3,000; it had no monies to hire professional planners; its recommendations went unheeded by other municipal agencies; and it was forced to retreat to a survival philosophy that called for work only to "improve upon features already established, to correct mistakes due to earlier

ABOVE: This booster poster-stamp from the Providence Board of Trade Journal of February 1915 spoke more of hope than reality. Harbor improvement has been a continual desire at least from the time Mayor Doyle unveiled his grand harbor design in the 1880s down to the efforts of Mayor Vincent Cianci in the 1980s to make the Port of Providence the New England container cargo center. The reality has been that the port was mainly a place to land immigrants, fuel, and lumber. RIHS (RHi x3 4227)

LEFT: Following Boston's example, Providence business leaders sponsored Old Home Week. They decked the city with bunting, turned Exchange Place (now Kennedy Plaza) into a "Court of Honor," erected a triumphal arch on Weybosset Street, and threw a weeklong party. This view of Weybosset Street was made in the summer of 1907 during Old Home Week. RIHS (RHi x3 292)

depreciated, mills and factories closed, and central-city structures were demolished for parking lots. City officials, however, caught between the Republican and Democratic parties' fight for control of the city and the state governments, and wanting to keep both population and industry from fleeing the city, kept the tax rate at a relatively constant $23 per $1,000 valuation. Appropriations for public health, schools, police, fire, and other departments suffered accordingly.

The fate of the City Plan Commission and the Whitten Thorofare Plan show clearly the impact of these problems on the

lack of vision, and to make provision to better meet modern conditions." The commission had no impact on enforcing the zoning ordinance and variances were granted at "alarming rates." By 1928 the annual report declared that "this Commission has postponed active operations during the year," and would be of "little public usefulness until conditions existed for effective cooperation in a complete and comprehensive enterprise."

Part of the commission's inactivity stemmed from its difficulties in helping implement the Whitten Thorofare Plan. This scheme was intended to relieve traffic congestion in the entire metropolitan area. It called for two 140-foot-wide boulevards, one running east-west and the other north-south, a belt parkway circling the city, and radial arteries extending from downtown Providence to the beltway. In 1927 the plan had the endorsement of Democratic Mayor Joseph Gainer, the Republican Board of Aldermen, and the business community. But the following year the plan was killed by partisan politics. A Republican city council asked the state legislature to repeal the enabling statute that would have created a Providence Thorofare Plan Board to oversee between $40 million and $80 million in expenditures. The request was purely political. Mayor James E. Dunne, elected by a plurality of a mere 171 votes and lacking the education and business connections of his predecessor, selected four fellow Democrats for the proposed board. This was a clear challenge to Republicans who controlled the city council and the state legislature for the last time in this century. The General Assembly honored their fellow Republicans' request, effectively killing the thoroughfare plan. But Providence's business leadership was unwilling to abandon its dimming vision. Its new approach called for regional planning, regional industrial development, and a renewed interest in annexing the Edgewood section of Cranston.

With the endorsement of Mayor Gainer, the annexation forces had pushed ahead in 1926, but his successor, Mayor Dunne, strongly opposed the idea. Nevertheless, a Greater Providence Planning Committee that included representatives from North Providence, Cranston, East Providence, Johnston, and Pawtucket met on July 24, 1930, and heard the committee's chairman, Alderman Sol S. Bromson declare: "The small town is like the small business. It cannot have the conveniences and advantages of the larger communities. ... The word annexation ... is an unhappy one. ... What is proposed is rather a merger of interests to work under one central head of government." The suburban leaders disagreed. A *Cranston News* editorial on November 14, 1930, clearly presented that city's case. "Cranston is about to come into

Joseph Gainer (1878-1945) was mayor of Providence from 1913 to 1927. Despite being a Democrat, he worked closely with the Republican-controlled Board of Aldermen to advance a whole series of civic improvements. In 1918 the Republicans also nominated him for mayor, a distinction shared only with the legendary Thomas A. Doyle. During his term Providence created the City Planning Commission, adopted zoning, widened streets, and completed the Scituate Reservoir project. From Providence City Manual, 1915-1916. *RIHS (RHi x3 4336)*

its own," it proclaimed. "Manufacturing plants and new homes must be built here as Providence is overcrowded. Why give this plum to another city ... ?"

Cranston and other adjacent communities could well afford an independent attitude and thwart all further efforts at metropolitan cooperation. Suburbanization had become so pronounced by 1900 that Rhode Island was the most urbanized state in the Union. Although many communities gained in population, the most significant gains were scored in the industrialized northern section of the state. As Providence grew by 28 percent between 1900 and 1910, the surrounding towns expanded by nearly 40 percent. Between 1915 and 1925 Providence increased its population only 8.1 percent while East Providence gained 40.3 percent, North Providence 33 percent, Johnston 29.5 percent, and Cranston 27.9 percent. These communities grew even faster after this time as Providence stabilized and then rapidly declined, making Providence one of the first large American cities to experience a drop in population. Equally important as the automobile and new roads in bringing about the change was the contrast between the quality of housing in the city and in the suburbs.

Early real-estate developers in Providence built primarily for the exploding population of immigrants and industrial workers. Between 1883 and 1910, a total of 24,377 two- and three-decker tenements were constructed, and just before the First World War, 9 out of every 10 new dwellings were tenements. Consequently, by 1926 nearly 80 percent of all dwelling units in the city were tenements; by 1933, nearly 90 percent of all housing was over 20 years old; half of the houses were still heated with a wood or coal stove, and only 32 per-

had incorporated as cities, and their charters granted them sufficient home-rule provisions to embark on their own ambitious urban improvements. In the period between 1922 and 1927, Cranston more than doubled its budget, and worked diligently to provide all essential urban services without drastically increasing taxes. Despite the town's failure to hold the line, its taxes rose by only half of the national average. Cranston also took steps to preserve the quality of suburban life by adopting a zoning ordinance in 1924 and

When Lewis Hine photographed this Olneyville (Providence) tenement dwelling in 1912, he noted that it had "eight persons, three rooms." Nearly 20 percent of Providence's families lived in tenements of less than one room per person. Between 1915 and 1921 housing starts declined so that the city entered the 1920s with a substantial housing shortage. From Child Welfare Conference and Exhibit, January 6-12, 1913. *Courtesy, Newport Historical Society*

cent were owner occupied. In contrast, suburban communities contained predominantly single-family homes, with well over half of them owner occupied.

Besides giving their residents better housing, cleaner air, and a more agreeable life-style, some communities could offer other advantages. Because East Providence and Cranston had legislative authorization to exempt new businesses from taxes, both towns lured industrial companies out of Providence. For example, East Providence developed the industrial village of Phillipsdale and Cranston attracted United Wire & Supply Company and Universal Winding Company in 1914. While East Providence, North Providence, and Johnston retained the town-meeting form of government, Cranston and Pawtucket

by inaugurating city planning in 1934; North Providence enacted zoning laws and a building code in 1930.

Although these steps would not protect suburbanites from paying higher taxes in the years to come, they did create a favorable climate for continued growth. Between 1900 and 1930, the population of Cranston rose from 13,343 to 42,911, North Providence from 3,016 to 11,101, Johnston from 4,305 to 9,357, and East Providence from 12,138 to 29,995. Providence's plans for a "Greater Providence" metropolitan government had crumbled, and with the setback came a gradual erosion of her domination over the plantations. Having experienced the pains of growth, socialization, and accommodation, the city now faced the Great Depression.

Chapter Eleven

EIGHTY GRAVEDIGGERS AND ONE TAPDANCER

HE GREAT DEPRESSION shook Rhode Island's economic and political structure and forced it to depend increasingly upon a new federal-urban partnership. The national collapse exaggerated pre-Depression trends in Rhode Island because industrial growth was already declining in the 1920s. The Depression closed more factories and produced increased unemployment, but this, too, had been a common experience in Rhode Island. In 1935 the Democratic party capped its slow rise to power with the "Bloodless Revolution," ending nearly eight decades of Republican domination. State Democrats used New Deal programs to dispense jobs, construct public works, and hand out patronage. However, the resulting political corruption produced the "War of the Wild Irish Roses," handicapped relief efforts, and demanded reform. By the end of the 1930s state and municipal indebtedness had doubled, factories stood empty, and morale drooped. But the winds of nature and war soon halted the slide and cleared the way for revival.

The economic depression began for Rhode Island years before the Great Crash of 1929. Like other mature industrial centers, the state had gradually slid deeper into an economic crisis. Back in 1913 Brown University President William H. Faunce warned the business community: "We cannot browse upon the past and become fat. We cannot live on inherited wealth, inherited traditions, inherited memories when we should be getting together to create new wealth, to establish new traditions, and memories which posterity may cherish." Complacency, the First World War, and momentary prosperity blunted the message. Not even the crumbling of the state's textile empire in the 1920s created more than temporary efforts at relief.

War-inflated wages, falling prices for goods, transportation rates that were as much as 113 percent higher than other places on the New Haven Railroad line, and foreign cotton imports that rose from $10 million to $67 million crippled Rhode Island's industry. Some companies such as the huge B.B. & R. Knight "Fruit of the Loom" textile empire were sold at a loss. Other companies instituted steep wage cuts of 42 percent between 1921 and 1922, enforced work "speed-ups" and "stretchouts," and reduced their work force. Instead of modernizing plants or converting to synthetic fabrics, many owners continued investing in southern mills. These policies drove Rhode Island's generally docile textile workers to the brink of economic despair. They turned to labor organizations and the Democratic party for help. But the violent textile strikes of 1922 and 1924 benefited no one. The *Providence Magazine* in 1923 charged that the state's industries clung to outdated management and sales methods and failed to grasp the idea of the "new competition." Unfortunately, industry failed to heed the message and did not develop a collective course or follow the examples of other communities.

Some New England states and cities

Thousands of Rhode Islanders waited in lines throughout the Depression for food, fuel, medical aid, and jobs. This photo shows the unemployment line in front of the Cranston Street Armory, Providence, in January 1938. That year, despite massive public work projects, Rhode Island had the highest per capita unemployment rate in the nation with 121,394 people receiving some form of unemployment compensation. Although 1939 was slightly better, the state's economy did not improve until defense contracts stimulated production. Courtesy, Providence Journal Company

actively pursued new industrial development. They launched the New England Council of Economic Development, but Rhode Island tried an independent path, and by 1926 had assembled the Rhode Island Development Conference. As little came of it, the state decided to join the New England Council in 1929. However, one of Rhode Island's most illustrious and conservative industrialists, Henry D. Sharpe, president of Brown & Sharpe, cooled their interest. He asserted that 81.8 percent of all

"No Man's Land" during the September 1926 strike at the Jenckes Company mill in Manville. For the nation the 1920s was a period in which management and government cooperated to reverse gains made by labor during World War I; and Rhode Island was quick to employ force through local and state police and national guard troops to break strikes. Rhode Island's failing textile industry was hard hit by strikes as the formerly docile workers tried to prevent the repeated wage reductions. Courtesy, Providence Journal Company

new industries had come from within the state's industrial base and that it was a waste of time and money "seeking to induce industries to locate in Providence." The new competitors could be beaten by following the proven methods of the past. The industrial-credit fund of Lowell, Massachusetts, attracted 23 new industries with 3,200 new jobs in 1928; but Sharpe and other business leaders opposed a similar agency for Rhode Island as being too costly. By 1931 these same industrialists begged the state to create a publicly funded economic development commission with broad powers to extend low-interest credit to new industries locating in the state. Unfortunately, the state did not establish a professional economic development council until the 1950s. Instead, Rhode Island was preoccupied with the Great Depression.

Between 1923 and 1937 nearly 80 percent of the state's cotton mills closed and

the work force declined from 34,000 to about 12,000. In the first two years of the Great Depression all industries struggled to survive, and 40 percent of all textile workers, 47.1 percent of the jewelry workers, and 38 percent of the iron and steel workers lost their jobs. Those still employed worked from one-half to one-quarter time, and textile workers averaged less than $9 a week. By 1933 wages for all workers had fallen by 33.4 percent but those of industrial workers had fallen by 49 percent. Investment income dropped by more than one third, and building permits for new construction plummeted from $57 million in 1926 to $9 million in 1932. While all segments of the state were hit hard, urban areas felt the pain the most. Providence's retail stores lost more than 50 percent of their annual sales revenues, and over 20 percent of the stores closed. The city budget was reduced by $1.5 million, wages cut by 10 percent, and projects for civic improvement halted. In Woonsocket, French-Canadians looked longingly at their homeland, as 9 out of 10 cotton mills stood idle, including the gigantic Social Mills which had closed in 1927. The "French Mills," heralded only a few years earlier as saving the city, either operated at reduced capacity, converted from wool, or closed. In single-industry towns such as Harrisville, Greystone, and Slatersville, factory shutdowns meant near total collapse of the economic lifeline of the community. By 1932, from the beaches of South County to the hills of Cumberland, from the Connecticut border to Little Compton, 115,000 Rhode Islanders were out of work. Hard times and soup lines were here.

But as deep as the Depression cut into Rhode Island's economy, it did not affect all citizens alike. The old-line Yankees could afford to hold onto their mansions on the East Side of Providence, sail out of Squantum in summers, and winter at Palm Beach. In Newport, chauffeured limousines daily carried children enrolled in private schools. People along coastal waters lived on seafood, and one Jamestown resident remembered her grandmother eating so many lobsters during the Depression that she refused ever to eat another. In rural areas, such as Glocester,

where people had abandoned their farms for the factory in the 1920s, land was brought under the plow or sold. Perhaps some of the least affected during the Depression were municipal employees, especially teachers. In 1933 Providence tallied a record enrollment of 45,189 public school students. A substantial increase occurred in high schools, as youths who would normally drop out to work continued their education. Although teachers throughout the state experienced pay cuts and overcrowded classes, their employment was steady. Some, like Elmer C. Wilbur, chairman of the commercial department of Providence's Central High School, took their income and invested it in abandoned farms in northwestern Rhode Island. Industrial workers, however, depended on others for work or relief.

Care of the unemployed and revitalization of industry had been traditionally in the hands of private charities and business, but private relief soon proved to be inadequate and charity organizations were overburdened. Exhortations from citizens and from political officials generated some donations. With such help the Salvation Army provided 76,092 meals and rooms for over 22,000 in the first eight months of 1932. Neighborhood grocery stores extended credit, landlords postponed rents, and barter became a common way of doing business. Governor Norman Case and part of the business community subscribed to President Herbert Hoover's "trickle down" philosophy to pump new life into the economy, but they also called upon industries to employ more workers. Swan Point Cemetery responded by hiring 80 gravediggers in 1933, far above the normal number. The state's banking community was examined in 1930 and judged extremely secure with $328 million on deposit, fifth highest per capita savings in the nation. With so much money on deposit, People's Savings Bank called on people to save less and spend more to stimulate the economy. The state government, however, did little. Governor Case established a credit fund from which municipalities could borrow money to avoid bankruptcy, but critics accused him of being more concerned about his proposed bridge across Narragansett Bay. In the midst of personal and economic despair, Rhode Islanders did not resort to violence. Instead, they turned to the ballot box and elected Theodore Francis Green their Governor and Franklin Delano Roosevelt their President.

Throughout his campaign, Green promised that he would place "humanity first" and bridges last. On January 1, 1933, he announced a $6-million relief fund for the unemployed; and when the bill reached the General Assembly, over 700 of the jobless came to give their support. But Green's program needed more than the state could provide, so additional relief came from the federal government in the form of the New Deal. Green was the primary conduit for federal relief funds for Rhode Island. By the fall of 1933 Roosevelt's fireside talks and recovery programs had given hope to many Rhode Islanders, and they showed their approval by staging the state's largest parade in downtown Providence. On October 2, a procession of 70,000 marchers, ticker tape, flags, and a profusion of blue eagle emblems snaked through the streets of the city. Out in mill villages and towns, similar parades took place, and one had a float showing the slaying of "Old Man Depression." Unfortunately for Rhode Islanders, the entire 1933 relief effort removed only about 7,000 from the unemployment lines. This all changed with the subsequent New Deal relief and recovery measures which altered the physical, cultural, and economic contours of the state.

The Providence Housewife League (1912-1946) became the Providence Homemakers League and affiliated with American Homemakers Inc. after World War I. Among other activities, it operated a clothing salvage store at 136 North Main Street in Providence, pictured here about 1922. The store expanded its operations during the Depression; and in addition to those responsibilities, the organization labored to find work for the unemployed. Ida S. Harrington and Eleanor K. Dearborn even gave weekly radio talks in the 1930s on aspects of homemaking. RIHS (RHi x3 4351)

Although a host of agencies operated within Rhode Island, the work of the Civilian Conservation Corps (CCC), Works Progress Administration (WPA), and Public Works Administration (PWA) had the greatest impact on the unemployed and on the environment. Inner-city youths were packed off to the forests and parks throughout the state, where they prevented soil erosion, cleared paths, improved forest stands, and drained swamps. The CCC camps were phased out in 1942 when youths marched off to war and defense plants. The WPA gave work to over 60,000 before it was disbanded in 1943. In Providence, WPA funds paid for the labor to build a new police station and firehouse, a municipal dock, a sediment treatment facility at Field's Point, and Mt. Pleasant and Hope high schools. In East Providence they helped construct a new city hall, Pierce Memorial Field, and Arthur E. Platt Elementary School. In Newport, the Cliff Walk, sidewalks, and harbor improvements took shape. For the state, WPA cemented the runways, installed lights, built a hangar, and upgraded the weather station at the airport, developed Goddard Park in East Greenwich, and built the harbor at Point Judith and Scarborough Beach at Narragansett. Writers published *Ships Documents of Rhode Island* and *Rhode Island: A Guide to the Smallest State*, among others. Planners completed a careful lot-by-lot survey of the entire city of Providence between 1932 and 1934; and repeated it in

1935. Musicians played concerts before large audiences, actors staged plays, and artists painted murals in the State House cafeteria and in the Providence Public Library. And one unemployed tap dancer was hired to tap dance her way through the public playgrounds of Providence.

Housing conditions in the state's industrial centers were inadequate, and a variety of New Deal programs helped finance mortgages, guaranteed rents, and supported new housing construction. Blighted areas long scheduled for removal were razed and the first public housing projects, such as the Chad Brown and Roger Williams complexes in Providence, were constructed. The Federal Housing Administration produced hundreds of real-estate surveys for American cities, and Providence was no exception. There, the lot-surveys were employed to designate neighborhoods according to property value retention: desirable neighborhood, declining neighborhood, blighted neighborhood, and stable neighborhood were some of the designations. FHA officials used those plat maps in granting mortgage loan-guarantees, but most of the money went to the desirable areas. What started as a plan to stabilize urban housing (Providence had over 13,000 vacant units) turned out to favor new construction. As a consequence, thousands of people left the inner city for the undeveloped area of northwest Providence or moved to suburbs and built new homes. Inner-city housing gave way to parking lots, arson, and vandalism. As late as the 1970s, banks still used the 1930s neighborhood designations in granting mortgages and for red-lining. Instead of saving the cities, the New Deal urban programs inadvertently helped destroy them.

As municipal and state agencies sought to respond to the myriad federal programs and requirements, some misused the funds and others worked at cross-purposes. The federal government wanted to purchase the old fire station on Providence's Exchange Place and erect a new post office. The State Planning Commission, headed by John Nicholas Brown, gave its approval, but the city council delayed three years before selling the station. The first state WPA administrator took a very frugal

WPA workers are shown on Mineral Springs Avenue, North Providence, in March 1936. After nearly three years of debate and foot dragging, most communities had advanced public works projects for approval to the State Planning Board. WPA financed the labor costs for thousands of projects in the state, including the resurfacing or construction of over 500 miles of roads. Courtesy, Providence Journal Company

The Chad Brown Housing Project Between Brown and Berkshire streets in Providence is pictured under construction in November 1941. The removal of slum housing and the rehabilitation of structures was the chief responsibility of the City Housing Authority during the Depression and thereafter. By 1982 Chad Brown, Roger Williams, Admiral Terrace, and other public housing projects were nearly all abandoned, boarded up, and ready to be razed. Courtesy, Providence Journal Company

approach to spending the taxpayers' money, which made him expendable to the Democrats. After his resignation, his only public comment was, "I'm going fishing." Projects got started, nevertheless, and the WPA payrolls swelled shortly before election time. Conservatives, who saw the New Deal as being revolutionary, called these actions boondoggles and made them into great political capital.

Some of the greatest problems for Democratic leaders occurred when the state was faced with implementing NRA (National Recovery Administration) and PWA

requirements on wages and hours. In 1934, after the NRA proposed a $13 wage in the North and $12 in the South for a 40-hour week for textile workers, the United Textile Workers went on strike. The union demanded uniform wages throughout the country to keep northern textile firms from heading South. When the Saylesville Finishing and the Woonsocket Rayon companies continued to operate, violence broke out at Saylesville, rioters looted stores and set buildings on fire in Woonsocket, and Governor Green summoned the National Guard. In an exchange of gunfire, two strikers were killed and scores were wounded.

Although a truce was proclaimed, more than 19 separate strikes erupted in Rhode Island in 1935 over NRA codes. Not until 1939 did the state pass a 35 cent minimum wage for women and minors in the textile industry. Another costly program resulted from the establishment of an Unemployment Compensation Board in 1936, which paid out $9 million to over 121,000 unemployed workers in two years' time. Nevertheless, Rhode Island still had the highest per capita unemployment rate in the nation, a condition that even the adoption of food stamps in 1939 in Providence hardly relieved.

National Guard soldiers drive strikers away with tear gas at Saylesville. Eight thousand strikers, 51 state troopers, and 32 mill guards battled at Saylesville. In the fighting three strikers were shot and the state arrested a number of people accused of being "communist agitators." When the strike destroyed the Amalgamated Textile Union, in its stead rose the Independent Textile Union (later Industrial Trade Union, ITU) in the Woonsocket-Saylesville area. The ITU's slogan was "uniform wages within all mills." Courtesy, Providence Journal Company

Despite federal help throughout the 1930s, the various recovery and relief measures enacted and funded by the state and municipalities saddled them with heavy financial burdens. In 1939 the state debt stood at $33.5 million, but Providence's was $72.2 million, nearly four times that of 1920 when its debt was among the highest in the nation. An emergency bank loan of $2.5 million allowed Providence to fend off bankruptcy. The state debt was not as pressing but the Tax Study Board recommended to Governor Robert Quinn the enactment of a per-

Providence's Exchange Place was the location of this "Votes for Women" rally in May 1914. Suffragists toured the state in automobiles and made open-air speeches in their campaign to win the vote, but the conservative, Republican-dominated General Assembly refused to grant the franchise. Eventually Rhode Island ratified the federal suffrage amendment, but the legislature rejected the other progressive amendments: direct election of U.S. Senators, income tax, and Prohibition. Courtesy, Providence Journal Company

sonal property tax, a cigarette tax, and increased levies on corporations, public utilities, and pari-mutuel betting. Quinn, in political trouble, sidestepped the issues. By 1938 state voters were so demoralized that they rejected a slate of relief and capital-improvement bond issues totaling $28 million while approving a state holiday—Columbus Day.

The turbulence accompanying relief measure implementation reflected a half century of struggle which climaxed in the "Bloodless Revolution" of 1935. Democrats ended decades of Republican domination and initiated decades of Democratic domination. The Republican party had dug its own grave by refusing to reform and to broaden its rural, middle-class, Yankee base. The Democrats, on the other hand, tap-danced to power by seeking to lift the franchise restrictions and by backing causes favorable to labor, ethnics, and urban dwellers. The perception that the Democratic party was the "party of the people" was based on the reality that in 1910 over 50 percent of Democratic and only 7 percent of the Republican committee members were manual laborers.

To understand the struggle, one has to return to the 19th century. The Bourn Amendment (1888) had lifted the real-estate property requirement for voting for governor and mayor, but retained it in the city council elections and on financial questions. The office of mayor became largely ceremonial and was held by Democrats, while city councils, dominated by Republicans, had effective control, including appointments and patronage. When Republicans perceived that their grip on the governorship was becoming tenuous, they passed the so-called "Brayton Act" in 1901. It removed most of the powers of the office and vested them in the Republican-controlled Senate, made safe by the malapportionment of seats under the 1842 constitution. It was just in time, too, because a reform Democrat, Dr. Lucius F.C. Garvin, won the governorship in 1902 and 1903. Powerless to effect changes, he supplied muckraker Lincoln Steffens with information used in 1904 for the McClure's Magazine exposé of corruption in Rhode Island called "A State for Sale." The alliance of politicians and business interests under the leadership of "Boss" Charles Brayton, Nelson Aldrich, and Marsden J. Perry controlled state politics, patronage, and favors.

The Republican-dominated General Assembly was so conservative and contrary that Rhode Island was the only state to reject as many as three of the progressive era amendments to the United States Constitution. Only the Woman Suffrage Amendment gained Rhode Island's approval, and on it Republicans were too divided to resist. Besides, most suffrage leaders came from the Yankee upper classes upon whom the Republicans depended for support. Leading suffragists included Mrs. Marsden J. Perry, Mrs. John Carter Brown, and United States Senator LeBaron Colt's daughter-in-law; while the leading antisuffragists included Mrs. Rowland Gibson Hazard and Mrs. Charles

ABOVE: Robert E. Quinn (1894-1975), Lieutenant Governor (1933-1935), Governor (1937-1939), and member of the U.S. Court of Military Appeals (1951-1975), takes the oath of office as Governor of Rhode Island in his home in West Warwick on January 5, 1937. He passionately wanted to unite the various factions of the Democratic party, but his efforts to do so created more enemies than friends. His use of martial law in Pawtucket to destroy his chief competitors earned him the nickname of "Huey Long of Rhode Island" and cost him the 1938 gubernatorial election. Courtesy, Providence Journal Company

Warren Lippitt, wife of the former governor.

By the 1920s Democratic legislators in the General Assembly were numerous enough to keep the Republican majority from passing legislation or adopting a budget. In 1928 they used their power to force the Republicans to approve two constitutional amendments which helped end Republican rule. The first modestly reapportioned the state senate to increase urban representation, but every town, regardless of size, still retained one delegate. The second ended the property tax requirement for voters in city elections. The Democrats immediately captured the city councils in the 1930 election, although Republicans retained power in many of the unincorporated, rural areas—the "rotten boroughs."

Democratic victories in 1932 brought Theodore Francis Green to the governorship and Democratic control to the House. But Republicans still retained a 28-14 margin in the Senate; and "Boss" Brayton's successor as head of the Republican party, Frederick S. Peck, controlled the office of State Commissioner of Finance, which supervised the budget and all expenditures. This Republican lock on the fiscal management of the state precluded the Democrats from quickly taking advantage of New Deal programs. When the Republicans appeared to have narrowly retained a majority in the Senate in the 1934 election, Green and his party comrades, Robert E. Quinn, Thomas P. McCoy, and J. Howard McGrath engineered the "Bloodless Revolution" of 1935.

The election of two Republicans was challenged, leaving the Senate with a tie, which qave the deciding vote to Lieutenant Governor Quinn. A Democratic-appointed committee investigated the charges of fraudulent returns and awarded the seats to the Democrats. At last they controlled the General Assembly and the governorship, and they proceeded to break the Republicans. They replaced all five justices of the state supreme court, abolished the office of State Commissioner of Finance, flushed Republicans from the state administration, removed them from the Providence Safety Board, and returned local patronage to the city government. They

also reorganized the state government, eliminating devices Republicans had used to thwart and frustrate Democratic growth; and they created the various departments which have operated since then. This political revolution completed the takeover of Rhode Island by the Democratic party. While Republicans occasionally slipped into high office, Rhode Island became the most Democratic state in the Union by the 1970s.

The long denial of power to the Irish-led Democratic party by the Republicans through all manner of constitutional and administrative mechanisms had dammed a normal transition from one party to another. The dam broke, first in the city governments in 1930 and then in the state government in 1935, and led to such a scramble for power, position, and rewards within the Democratic party that it failed to deal with the fundamental problems of the state. After sweeping away Republican obstacles, Democrats turned to the politics of gratification. Instead of addressing the deteriorating industrial base, general shabbiness of the cities, inadequate transportation system, and the low skills and educational levels of the industrial workers, factions set upon each other, demanding rewards and scrambling for dominance within the party.

Thomas P. McCoy, "Prince of Pawtucket," challenged Governor Green for control of the state Democratic party and lost. As absolute boss of Pawtucket, McCoy controlled 10 seats in the General Assembly and had been appointed state budget director. Green ousted McCoy from the directorship. When Green was elected United States Senator in 1936 and Robert Quinn became governor, Quinn inherited the Green machine and its enemies. What followed has been variously called the "Narragansett Race Track War" and the "War of the Wild Irish Roses."

Walter J. O'Hara, a wealthy textile manufacturer, owner of the *Pawtucket Star-Tribune*, and founder and president of the Narragansett Race Track, was a McCoy ally, who first backed McCoy for governor and then sought it for himself. As the racetrack had become a focal point of extensive bookmaking, Governor Quinn

tried to discredit the McCoy-O'Hara faction by charging that the track was the haunt of thugs and gangsters. After failing in two attempts to use the courts against O'Hara, Quinn sued him for libel, decreed the racetrack area to be under criminal control, proclaimed martial law in October 1937, and occupied the track with National Guard troops. O'Hara was indicted by a grand jury for illegal contributions to political parties. While these charges were later quashed, O'Hara was forced to resign as president of the racetrack, his newspaper went into receivership, and he was finished in politics. McCoy continued to rule Pawtucket until his death in 1945; but Quinn's abuse of the courts and his use of military power in a Democratic party squabble resulted in his defeat in the next election by Republican William Vanderbilt by the largest margin since 1920. Democratic disarray and corruption led to the 1938 Republican sweep of the general offices and the General Assembly. However, this was an aberration; and the Democrats, led by J. Howard McGrath, won the following election, beginning nearly 20 years of Democratic rule.

The 1938 political winds also brought the first Republican mayor to Providence in 25 years and permitted the antiquated city charter to be revised to meet the needs of the 20th century. While the 1928 state constitutional amendment had allowed the Democrats to capture the city council at long last, the city's government was cumbersome and complicated by too many boards, commissions, and independent centers of power. All through the Depression the city's relief and recovery projects were severely hampered by the fact that the head of the Department of Public Works, the Harbor Master, and the City Treasurer were all elected separately and not accountable to the mayor or the city council. Too many individuals had a veto. Democratic Mayor James Dunne, a poorly educated political hack, had neither the imagination nor the power to change the situation during his tenure from 1927 to 1938. Mismanagement and growing corruption led to the victory of John F. Collins, a Republican running for the Independent Citizens for Good Government, promising

to clean up fraud and revise the city charter.

Republican State Attorney General Louis Jackvony began the prosecution of voting fraud that involved Democratic leaders and election officials. Unfortunately, the principal cases were lost when the key prosecution witness, Carmine Ruggiero, who had earlier identified the corrupt officials, suddenly "lost his memory" when he was put on the stand to testify. However, the charter revision was far more successful. A bipartisan City Charter Commission was appointed in May 1939. Democrats named former mayor Joseph Gainer, Dennis J. Roberts, and John O. Pastore; and the Republicans selected Jackvony, Walter Farrell, and J. Morton Ferrier. In September the commission filed its report, and Providence voters approved the charter revisions in a special election in November. While these won handily, Republican wards voted heavily against them because they would abolish the Board of Aldermen, the one remaining place where Republicans retained any power in city government.

The revisions provided for a strong mayor with increased administrative and appointive powers, a single-chamber city council of 26 members (two from each ward), the creation of new, streamlined departments and the abolition or consolidation of 26 old ones, a central purchasing department, specified fiscal and budgetary powers, and a civil service system. Collins, the reformer, was not the beneficiary of the new system; instead, Charter Commissioner Dennis J. Roberts swamped Collins in the next mayoralty election, ending the Republican interlude and ushering in another 34 years of Democratic mayors for Providence. Ironically, the Republican refusal for so many years to revise the old charter had saved Providence from Pawtucket-style political bossism. Once the charter revisions were implemented, little could be done by voters to prevent the formation of a Democratic city machine. In the hands of a visionary mayor, the machine could be an effective instrument in reviving a declining city, but it could be an engine of advancement for self-serving politicians, too.

Republican election upsets in 1938 have long since faded from the general memory; but the Hurricane of 1938 is not likely to be forgotten any time soon. It was the worst disaster in the state's history. The great storm, packing winds of 175 m.p.h., slammed into the southern New England coast around three-thirty in the afternoon of September 21, 1938, and within a half hour had done its greatest damage and killed most of its victims. Such was its power that brick factory walls collapsed in New London, Connecticut, and automobiles were sent cartwheeling in Stonington. A tidal wave 30 feet high washed ashore along the southern coast of Rhode Island and swept the beaches clean of human habitations at Napatree Point, Misquamicut, Quonochontaug, and Charlestown. It rolled on to deposit a moraine of shattered cottages and houses nearly a mile inland. More than 50 people died at Charlestown alone. Newport was pounded by raging winds and surf, and Ocean Drive crumbled into the sea along with the fancy beach pavilions of the rich at Bailey's Beach and the boardwalk at Easton's Beach. Towns all around the Bay found yachts and boats in the streets and yards, ferries crushed, and marinas stacked with wrecked vessels. The Rhode Island Yacht Club and the Bristol Yacht Club fell to the storm, as did church steeples all over the affected area. In Providence a tidal surge suddenly pushed water into the streets just about the time that people were heading home from work, drowning a number of them. At 4:16 all electric power and telephone service was lost in the city as the water rose to 13 feet above the mean high-water mark. In Woonsocket, the winds blew down the walls of textile mills and injured a policeman by lifting him from his feet and hurling him against a passing automobile. Even after the hurricane had passed, it caused more misery as the rivers in the region subsequently burst their banks from the torrents of water dumped on New England.

The WPA dispatched thousands of emergency workers to aid in the cleanup and help restore vital services. Rhode Island counted 317 dead and over $100 million in damages out of New England's 680 deaths and $400 million in losses. Nearly 2,000 houses of various sorts were destroyed in the state along with 2,000 barns and other buildings. Almost 900 boats were completely wrecked, including the entire fishing fleet on Block Island. Most of western Rhode Island was a scrapyard of fallen trees, and lumber companies rushed in to salvage millions of board-feet before the wood rotted.

In spite of all the terrible things the storm did, one is forced to recall the old saying, "It's an ill wind that blows nobody some good." Indeed, the Hurricane of 1938 was a cleansing force that swept the coast and upper Narragansett Bay almost clean of beachfront shanties, run-down docks, wharfs, and warehouses, decaying and abandoned amusement parks, waterfront whorehouses, slums, and ramshackle buildings of all sorts. While one might expect a severe economic dislocation from such a disaster, in fact, employment in the state increased. The lumber that was cut from the fallen trees created an enormous stockpile which was immediately available for the emergency defense construction needs that arose within a few years. Like the Great Chicago Fire which allowed that city to build anew and better, so, too, did the Hurricane of 1938 clear the way for new uses and development. Rhode Island was still battling the Great Depression when the hurricane wallopped it; and while most set to work picking up the pieces, many wondered if prosperity would ever return. But Adolf Hitler soon rescued Rhode Island from the Great Depression.

Chapter Twelve

THE PATRIOTIC STATE

ACH FOURTH OF JULY the little town of Bristol swells to a city's population of hundreds of thousands, and the quiet streets resound with the sounds of the nation's oldest Independence Day parade. The tree-shaded streets and warm hospitality of the local folks preserve an atmosphere of an old-fashioned, small-town parade; but this is *the* Fourth of July parade. It is a "must"event for local politicians and groups; some have fought and sued for the right to march. The sound and sight of the drum-and-bugle corps, the marching wind-bands, drill teams, horses, clowns, Knights of Columbus and Shriners, floats, and fire engines add verve and color. The real point of the day is brought home by the military units who march in uniforms that range from the American Revolution to the present. Thus does Rhode Island reaffirm an independent and patriotic heritage.

The Independent State's patriotic heritage grew gradually from seeds planted in the Revolutionary era and has been strengthened by economic, social, and strategic needs. While most Rhode Islanders wanted independence from Great Britain, only a minority favored a strong American union. Those early nationalists (who wanted closer relationships with the Union and ratification of the Constitution) came from the group engaged in oceanic commerce and trade. Although some flouted national trade regulations, they supported a strong navy and coastal fortifications like Fort Adams. When the state's economy shifted from ocean to

industry, industralists wanted protective tariffs, a national banking system, a strong defense, and federal support in securing overseas markets and raw materials. This economic nationalism was complemented by immigrants and their descendants who filled the ranks of the army and navy. Youth from lower socioeconomic orders found military service to be an avenue of opportunity; and the more veterans a family had, the more family pride was engaged. Homegrown veterans were joined by many who settled in Rhode Island after being stationed in the military installations that encircled Narragansett Bay. By 1982 Rhode Island had 152,000 veterans, nearly half of the adult male population. Their presence created a climate celebrating patriotism and traditional values.

The most independent and otherwise-minded colony in British North America had moved early toward concerted action to oppose the new Imperial order. The only way Rhode Island could preserve its independent ways was to surrender some of them to a united effort against the British. Local pride causes some to assert that the American Revolution "really began right here." They point to the cannons firing on H.M.S. *St. John* at Newport in 1764, the burning of a boat from H.M.S. *Maidstone* in 1765, the scuttling of H.M.S. *Liberty* in 1769, and the destruction of the *Gaspee* in 1772. Historians note that violence greeted British press-gangs and revenue agents in other colonies at the same times. Similarly, since 1909 Rhode Islanders have officially maintained that their state was the first to

The 1st Rhode Island Volunteers march down Westminster Street in April 1899 as part of the Welcome home parade for veterans of the Spanish-American War. The regiment, however, never left the country, and the greatest services were performed by the women of the Rhode Island Sanitary and Relief Association. Composed of 577 members, the association collected $21,496 and 18,076 garments for relief, and shipped jellies, mineral water, wine, and medicines to service hospitals. In Newport, Mrs. A. Livingston Mason gave one of her "cottages" to the Surgeon General of the Army as a convalescent home. The famous Casino was the organization's headquarters. Courtesy, Providence Public Library

ABOVE: Nathanael Greene (1742-1786), youngest general in the Continental Army, had no prior military experience before the American Revolution. Commissioned as brigadier general in June 1775, he served as quartermaster general (1778-1780) before taking command in the southern colonies in 1781. Engraved portrait by H. Gugeler. RIHS (RHi x3 582)

RIGHT: Oliver Hazard Perry (1785-1819) led his green-wood flotilla against the British on Lake Erie and won a decisive victory after a furious battle. His flagship, the Lawrence, was damaged so badly that Perry, shown here, transferred his command to another vessel. After the British surrendered, Perry reported, "We have met the enemy and they are ours." He died of yellow fever in 1819. RIHS (RHi x3 4298)

FACING PAGE: Ambrose E. Burnside (1824-1881) was Rhode Island's hero in the Civil War. His military disasters, however, led Ulysses S. Grant to say, "General Burnside was an officer who was generally liked and respected. He was not, however, fitted to command an army." Not only was Burnside a soldier, he was also an inventor, industrialist, and politician. RIHS (RHi x3 4344)

declare independence from Great Britain. This resulted from a misreading of the facts by a determined antiquarian in the 1880s who convinced school committees, the Colonial Dames, the Sons of the American Revolution, and finally the General Assembly of his view.

Still, there is no denying that Rhode Islanders threw themselves into the Revolution and suffered considerably in it. The state's greatest Revolutionary War hero, Nathanael Greene, was arguably the war's best general; and he and George Washington were the only generals in continuous service throughout the war. In his brilliant southern campaign of 1780-1781, Greene, the master of strategic retreats, lost every battle and yet won every objective. In the end the British withdrew from the interior of Georgia, North and South Carolina, and marched off to defeat at Yorktown, Virginia. Heaped with gratitude and land grants, Greene remained on his gift plantation in Georgia, died, and was buried there.

Bristol celebrated its first Independence Day parade in 1785; but coming as it did in the middle of Rhode Island's recession from the Union, the parade may well have reflected the state's attitude toward the Union. The Independent State would eventually submit to the Constitution, but its relationship to the United States was ambiguous until after the War of 1812. During that war, the official actions of Rhode Island were self-serving and obstructive to the national effort, but individual Rhode Islanders made significant contributions. Just as John Brown had given *Providence* to the Continental Navy in the Revolution, James DeWolf gave the United States Navy his *Chippewa* in the War of 1812. At the Battle of Lake Erie in September 1813, Oliver Hazard Perry commanded the American flotilla of 10 small vessels, and decisively defeated the British. One fourth of the Americans in this engagement were Rhode Islanders, five of the vessels had Rhode Island commanders, and 51 of 54 cannons were captained by its sons.

Between 1815 and the War of the Great Rebellion, the ambiguity of patriotism vanished. The state's principal interests were linked to the nation as oceanic commerce gave way to manufacturing for the United States market. Several months prior to the attack on Fort Sumter, Governor William Sprague offered troops to defend the nation's capital; and Rhode Island immediately answered President Lincoln's April 15 call for volunteers. On April 20, 1861, the Rhode Island First Regiment, commanded by Ambrose E. Burnside and accompanied by Governor Sprague, colorfully embarked with the American Brass Band from Providence. The state quivered with patriotic fervor. Within a month the banks and general public subscribed an extra half-million dollars to outfit Rhode Island troops. Little boys joined the Union Guard and Providence High School students formed the Ellsworth Phalanx to drill while men flocked to enlist in the real army. Women and girls sewed uniforms and trimmed hats, and inmates at the Reform School knitted socks for the troops.

Flags appeared everywhere, but the highest flew from the top of the 185-foot steeple of the First Baptist Meeting House in Providence.

The Rhode Island Second Regiment followed in June, and both units were heavily engaged in the battle of Bull Run on July 21. Governor Sprague served Burnside as a volunteer aide, and in the fighting his horse was shot from under him. While the Second Regiment fought bravely, the First performed badly and fled in panic. Rhode Island lost 167 men that day, and the American Brass Band lost its bass drum. Governor Sprague was so disgusted with the First Regiment's performance that it was disbanded. Nevertheless, honors followed for Burnside: Brown University gave him an honorary degree, and he rose to become the commander of the Army of the Potomac in 1862. However, he was blamed for two of the worst disasters suffered by the Union

Army: the slaughter at Fredericksburg (1862) and the fiasco at the Crater at Petersburg (1864). The latter resulted in Burnside's resignation, but he returned to a hero's reception. He became Governor (1866-1869), United States Senator (1875-1881), and president of the Providence Locomotive Works and two railroads.

As one of the industrial centers in America, Rhode Island secured a flood of war contracts. Builders Iron Foundry cast heavy 11- and 13-inch Dahlgren cannons and massive siege mortars. Mansfield & Lamb made bayonets, Corliss & Nightingale produced cannons, and another company manufactured the Burnside breech-loading rifle. Of course, the textile industry was a leading supplier of cloth for uniforms, blankets, and tents.

As the war ground on, inducements to volunteers were increased. The government offered bounties and improved the system of relief payments to dependents of soldiers and sailors. Total expenditures for bounties and relief in Providence alone amounted to $383,504. Immigrants enlisted in great numbers because service brought more acceptance from native Americans, and the bonuses and bounties provided immediate economic rewards. After the Emancipation Proclamation, blacks were recruited, and in June 1863 the Rhode Island Fourteenth Regiment began forming. One of its earliest duties was to patrol the streets of Providence, protecting military stores and guarding against draft resistance. Later, the Fourteenth spent most of its service in Louisiana, garrisoning captured territory. Before the end, the state contributed over 24,000 men, exceeding its quota by 5,000. The magnitude of that effort grows when one realizes that over 28,000 served in each of the two world wars when the state's population was four times as large.

For the next half century, the defense of the Union was recalled in the public ceremonies and remembrances. Rhode Island first celebrated Decoration Day on May 30, 1869, and in 1874 was the first state in the nation to make it an official holiday. This solemn day memorialized the 1,321 who died in the Civil War and those who joined them with the passing years.

Exchange Place in Providence sprouted several Civil War monuments and statues, and at least a dozen other towns also erected memorials. The General Assembly established the Rhode Island Soldiers' Home in Bristol in 1889; and beginning in 1902 schools celebrated Grand Army Flag Day each February 12, commemorating both the veterans and Abraham Lincoln. Since Rhode Island volunteers moved no nearer to the Spanish-American War than Columbia, South Carolina, only the First World War could begin to match the impact of the Civil War.

Rhode Island never got an accurate view of the conflict in Europe because the state's principal newspaper, the *Providence Journal*, was headed by a flamboyant liar who was determined to bring the United States into the war on the Allied side. Australian-born John Rathom (an assumed name) brought national attention to the *Journal* by filling its columns with exaggerated and often fabricated tales of German espionage, sabotage, and war atrocities. He annoyed the Germans to the point that their Ambassador protested to the United States Secretary of State. The reportage helped to generate a climate of patriotic fervor that spilled over into hysteria. One result was a mammoth Preparedness Day parade in 1916 which saw 54,542 men and women march in a six-hour procession that was cut short by a downpour. A similar parade in Boston the previous week marshaled only 38,000 marchers.

When America entered the conflict, Rhode Islanders enlisted in record numbers, bought war bonds far in excess of quotas, and joined the Red Cross, YMCA, and the Home Guard beyond all expectations. Over 12 percent of Brown & Sharpe employees entered the service, and those who remained behind subscribed $1.4 million in bonds and grew $40,000 worth of produce in the company war garden. War opponents were being arrested in the spring of 1917, and the *Providence Magazine* screamed when it heard of alleged food sabotage by German sympathizers: "The next man or woman caught in the act, or found guilty of destroying food supplies, should be summarily shot. Shoot first! Hold the inquiry afterwards."

The *Providence Journal* urged that Germans and Austrians be watched and suspicious activities reported. A campaign against German influences swept the state. The *Journal* charged that "disloyalty is being taught in American schools. Germanized teachers are everywhere. ... We must now purge our college faculties and public school staffs of every German propagandist." The State Board of Education imposed a loyalty oath on all teachers, and the teaching of the German language and literature disappeared from the schools. Rathom attacked Dr. Karl Muck, Bavarian-born conductor of the Boston Symphony Orchestra as "a man of notoriously pro-German affiliations" and demanded that the BSO play "The Star-Spangled Banner" at its five concerts in Providence. The Board of Police Commissioners refused to grant a license to the orchestra; and when other theaters threatened to cancel the season's concerts, the BSO caved in to the pressure. Dr. Muck resigned. This was patriotism running amok.

Although the war ended, the fear of subversion did not. On Grand Army Flag Day in 1919, the principal of English High School declared, "The Hun is defeated, but other dangers threaten us. The anarchist, the I.W.W., the Bolshevik menace us with loss of public order and security." The Providence City Council outlawed the carrying of the Red flag in any procession, and the Americanization effort was intensified among Rhode Island's foreign-born. As part of the nationwide sweep against foreign-born radicals in January 1920, local police arrested more than a dozen people. Nativist feelings persisted, and some Rhode Islanders enrolled in the Invisible Empire of the Ku Klux Klan in the 1920s. Especially shocking was the discovery in 1928 that the Klan was attempting to use enlistment forms for the Rhode Island First Light Infantry to recruit members for its own ranks. This ploy evaporated in the glare of an expose and legislative investigation.

The antiforeign, anti-Catholic aspects of this warped patriotism faded in Rhode Island in the 20th century. While the immigrant restriction movement had considerable power in Massachusetts and

Australian-born journalist John R. Rathom (1868?-1923) joined the Providence Journal *in 1906 and served as its editor and general manager from 1912 to 1922. He brought the newspaper to national influence during World War I with his daring and imaginative reporting of real and imaginary German threats, plots, sabotage, and atrocities. He promoted a climate of hysteria that led to political excesses in the postwar Red Scare. Courtesy, Providence Journal Company*

Connecticut, it had little support in Rhode Island; and Senator LeBaron Colt, chairman of the United States Senate Committee on Immigration, was able to block national immigration restriction legislation until his death in 1924. Besides, the coming to power of ethnic voters in the 1920s and 1930s in most urban areas of the state scattered the old nativists. What remained was antiradicalism, which appealed equally to Yankee and ethnic. The Yankee Governor Theodore Francis Green used the heavily ethnic National Guard to break the 1934 strike of ethnic textile workers by blaming the troubles on "outside Communist agitators," and by arresting 15 Communists. He lost little support from Rhode Island's ethnic working class because they shared his sense of patriotism. This patriotism carried Rhode Island headlong into World War II.

World War II converted Rhode Island into an armed camp. The deepwater harbor facilities in the Bay had attracted the Navy in the post-Civil War era; now those modest establishments expanded and were joined by a multitude of other bases and stations. The Naval Training Station at Newport had opened in 1883, but during the summer prior to Pearl Harbor a large portion of the Atlantic Fleet was at Newport and training of seamen accelerated. During the Second World War over 204,000 recruits trained there and additional thousands received instruction at the Anti-Aircraft Training Center and at

the Motor Torpedo Boat Squadrons Training Center. Two naval air bases opened at Westerly and Charlestown, and the Naval Air Station at Quonset Point became the largest in the East. Authorized in May 1939, nearly four months before Germany's attack on Poland, the base eventually covered 1,200 acres and housed

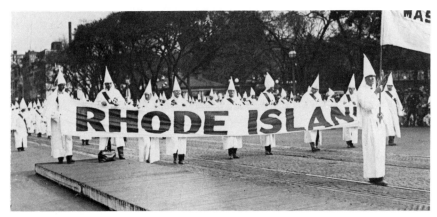

15,000 servicemen. Soon after Pearl Harbor, a training center for naval construction battalions opened at Davisville; and by war's end a total of 100,000 "Seabees" had been trained there. Across the Bay, Melville Fuel Depot had storage capacity for 13 million gallons of fuel in 1937, and this was expanded during the war. The Naval Net Depot at Melville, established in February 1941, trained men in harbor net defenses and constructed antisubmarine nets. The Naval Torpedo Station on Goat Island, established in 1869, expanded to become the nation's principal manufacturer of tor-

ABOVE: Members of Rhode Island's KKK march down Pennsylvania Avenue in Washington, D.C., on September 13, 1926, as part of the National Klonvocation. Klan activities in the state included a rally in Foster Center in June 1924 with an estimated 8,000 participants and a Klan wedding in Georgiaville in 1927 that attracted thousands. The Grand Dragon in the state, John W. Perry, was arrested and indicted for perjury but acquitted in 1929 as the Klan's visibility had disappeared. Courtesy, Providence Journal Company

LEFT: A "human flag" of 1500 schoolchildren and an honor guard of 200 Civil War veterans reviewed the massive parade on "Preparedness Day," June 3, 1916. The parade lasted so long that the children in the flag formation had to be replaced by fresh standbys at regular intervals. RIHS (RHi x3 2103)

pedoes. High-explosive storage facilities and a naval magazine were built on Gould and Prudence islands in 1942.

Other shipbuilding activities deepened Rhode Island's involvement in the war effort. The popular swimming beach at Field's Point became part of the Rheem shipyard in May 1942; and the first vessel, the *William Coddington*, was launched just after Thanksgiving. (It did not matter that Coddington had been an early convert to the Quakers in the 1660s; his Aquidneck Island was now thoroughly militarized and the Newport Naval Base surrounded Coddington Cove.) In February 1943 the Walsh-Kaiser Company took over the shipyard and continued production until July 1945 when the last of 64 vessels, the *Zenobia*, was launched.

Direct employment of citizens in military facilities was only one aspect of the boost to the state's economy. The artificial increase in population by a steady stream of thousands of service personnel afforded bountiful opportunities to all sorts of enterprises, not the least of which were the numerous "white cap" sailor bars and brothels along Thames Street in Newport. In addition, Rhode Island industries received millions of dollars in defense contracts and subcontracts. In the 18 months *before* Pearl Harbor, Rhode Island manufacturers were awarded more than $115 million in defense work, with nearly $75 million going to textiles and most of the rest to the metal trades. The textile industry, which had been in a steep decline since the 1920s, revived momentarily to produce all manner of cloth and uniforms. Belt and webbing manufacturers worked overtime to meet defense needs, and everything from machine guns to gas masks poured out of Rhode Island factories. Payroll disbursements in the state for 1942 reached $379 million, more than double that of 1939.

The war effort had a tremendous economic impact on the state. The Navy Department calculated that nearly $130 million was spent in erecting the Narragansett Bay defenses. Construction of the Quonset Point Naval Air Station commenced in mid-1940 and before completion cost $75 million to build. When the

United States entered the war, Quonset Point Station was still incomplete, so work was accelerated. Nearly 11,000 workers labored nonstop to finish the job, pumping a half-million-dollar weekly payroll into the state's economy and creating an acute housing shortage near the base. Nearly a million dollars were spent on the Wickford housing project, but the statewide housing shortage remained severe. In August 1940 the Newport Housing Authority received $1.1 million from the United States government for a "national defense" low-cost housing project. The old Perry Mill was converted into a dormitory for women workers. Employing more than 12,000 civilians, the Naval Torpedo Station became the "largest single industrial-type employer in the State of Rhode Island" by 1944. Two factories at Davisville, employing 3,000 workers, produced over 32,000 Quonset huts by the end of the war and shipped them around the world.

With such a concentration of military installations, Rhode Island's coast was proclaimed a military district in April 1942, the United States Army superseded civilian authority, and all lights visible from the sea were ordered blacked out. Fear of possible attack caused the Navy to mine the approaches to Narragansett Bay, and antisubmarine nets blocked the passages in the Bay. The antisubmarine devices were deemed necessary because prowling German U-boats sank nine merchant ships off New England's coasts in the first seven months of 1942. In the autumn Rhode Island was declared a "vital war zone" which brought tightened security against espionage and sabotage at military installations. On Chopmist Hill a top-secret, radio-monitoring station eavesdropped on enemy radio transmissions from as far away as Europe, Africa, and South America. The largest of a national network of 13 listening stations, the Chopmist Hill post was the most effective because of its location and atmospheric conditions. By mid-1943 the U-boats had been driven away and threat of attack had declined. Consequently, coastal defenses and artillery units were thinned or reassigned, and the antisubmarine nets in Narragansett Bay were removed in September 1944. Yet, the final battle of the Atlantic occurred in Rhode Island waters.

In early 1945 the Germans sent snorkel-equipped U-boats to the East Coast, but only three reached American waters. Two were destroyed in April, and on May 4 the German High Command recalled the other. The one remaining U-boat operating along the East Coast either failed to receive the message or disregarded it. The next day, the *Black Point,* a coal ship from New York, was torpedoed and sunk three miles off Point Judith, killing 12 crewmen, just 28 hours before Germany's unconditional surrender. The submarine-killer forces swung into action, hunted the U-boat, and destroyed her the following morning near Block Island. The *Black Point* was the last merchant ship sunk in the Atlantic war.

As *U-853* lurked outside the Bay, a few dozen German prisoners-of-war were in Rhode Island participating in a secret anti-Nazi indoctrination program and publishing a newspaper called *Der Ruf,* which circulated in the nearly 400 German POW camps in the country. During the war 370,000 German POWs were interned in the United States, and about 15 percent were clearly anti-Nazi. The government wanted to reeducate these to democratic forms and beliefs so they could assume leadership and police roles in postwar Germany. It started a program in the summer of 1944 at an old CCC camp in New York, but in March 1945 the operation moved to Rhode Island. In May a 60-day indoctrination course commenced at Fort Wetherill with the first class graduating on July 6. For the rest of the year Rhode Island was the "center of the most long-range and idealistic POW re-education efforts ever undertaken by the United States." When the press was allowed to know of the schools in September 1945, they dubbed it the "Barbed Wire College." Before they closed in December, the schools at Fort Getty and Fort Wetherill on Conanicut Island had graduated 1,166 POWs.

Rhode Islanders hailed the victory and the end of sacrifice. Nearly a thousand of her sons had been killed or wounded in combat. Unfortunately, the war-inflated economy began to shrink almost immediately with Japan's defeat in August 1945, causing employment problems for returning veterans and the swollen civilian work force. However, the Navy remained. This seemed only natural because Rhode Island had played a significant role in creating the Navy in the American Revolution, manning it over the years, and serving as a station for decades. Many came to assume that the Navy would always remain since it had invested so much in facilities and because of the state's proximity to the North Atlantic shipping lanes. Rhode Islanders believed that they had a natural affinity for the Navy. They recalled with pride that the first ship in the Continental Navy had been the sloop *Providence* and the first admiral had been Ezek Hopkins. They remembered the exploits of the Perry brothers in winning the Battle of Lake Erie in 1813 and in opening Japan in 1853. But most people forgot that the Navy had no base in Rhode Island until the Civil War.

During the undeclared naval war with France in 1799, the United States government sought a naval base in New England. Some advanced Newport as the site, but George Champlin, a leading merchant, argued that a base would produce too many "disagreeable circumstances." He recommended Fall River as a more suitable place, but the government abandoned the effort. The Navy came to stay during the Civil War when the United States Naval Academy was transferred from Annapolis, Maryland. "Old Ironsides," the U.S.S. *Constitution,* arrived on May 8, 1861, carrying the Academy's officers and professors. Although the Naval Academy returned to Annapolis in the summer of 1865, the Navy had become a part of Newport. Narragansett Bay was increasingly attractive after the war because of its natural facilities and because the social atmosphere of Newport suited the officers and gentlemen of the Navy. The captains of ships and the captains of industry shared many of the same backgrounds, attitudes, and pretensions. Consequently, the Navy established its experimental Torpedo Station (1869), Naval Training Station (1883), and Naval War College (1884) all in Newport. The War College was a postgraduate school "to prepare officers for high command." By

RIGHT: Seamen stand in formation during parade drills at the Newport Naval Training Station in August 1942. Shown in the background, the USS Constellation was used as a training vessel. The presence of thousands of seamen turned the town into a playground for sailors. Courtesy, Naval War College Historical Museum

BELOW: In the spring of 1942 the gun tube of a 16-inch seacoast cannon was hauled past the Stone Bridge Inn in Tiverton enroute to Fort Church at Little Compton. The tube was 68 feet long and weighed 150 tons. Two of these cannons composed "Battery Gray" and required gun crews of 42 men per cannon in addition to control officers, spotters, and security personnel. Courtesy, C.E. Hall & Sons Trucking Company

LEFT: *The SS* William Coddington *is shown here being launched in late November 1942 at the Rheem Shipyard, Field's Point, Providence. Among the 63 ships launched there was the SS* Nelson W. Aldrich. *Photo by U.S. Maritime Commission. Courtesy, Newport Historical Society*

BELOW: *The Naval Training Station in Newport provided the setting for this recruit parade around 1915. In the background, Navy ships lie at anchor in Narragansett Bay while the Naval War College looms in the center. On the top right is the Alfred T. Mahan Hall, once the Newport poorhouse. Courtesy, Naval War College Historical Museum*

1919 more than half of all flag officers and their staffs were graduates of the War College. Rear Admiral Alfred T. Mahan, twice president of the school, contributed to the college's curriculum; and his international reputation as an advocate of strong navies brought prestige to the institution.

By the time of the First World War, Newport viewed the Navy's presence as an economic necessity. During the war, the Torpedo Station employed some 3,800 civilians producing depth charges, mines, and torpedoes. Increased production of primers occurred in 1918 when women outproduced their male counterparts by six to one. Most of these jobs vanished with the return of peace, but the Newport Chamber of Commerce in the 1920s succeeded in having the Navy concentrate its torpedo manufacture and training operations there. Narragansett Bay was designated as one of two main bases on the Atlantic Coast, and the capacity of the Naval Fuel Depot at Melville was tripled in the 1920s. Of course, World War II greatly increased the Navy's presence at Newport as well as adding the Quonset Point-Davisville complex to the state's naval facilities.

For the state as a whole the Navy continued to be the leading employer through the 1950s, and the extent of Newport's dependency by 1960 was reflected in the fact that 73 percent of its employed residents were working directly for the federal government. As other economic elements in the state declined or stagnated, many regarded the Navy as a comfortable surety; but this proved to be a sand castle. The Navy began a major withdrawal of the North Atlantic Cruiser-Destroyer fleet in 1972, leaving behind the Naval War College and various scientific research facilities. However, many naval officers who had been stationed in Rhode Island retired here, adding to the substantial veterans' community and providing a climate favorable to patriotic sentiment.

Rhode Island welcomed the servicemen of World War II and discovered that its percentage gain in veterans was the highest in the nation. Providence gave Davis Park to the federal government for a Veterans Hospital, and the General Assembly adopted a $20-million Soldiers Bonus Act to pay each Rhode Island veteran a $200 bonus. Victory Day (V-J Day) became an official state holiday in 1948, and in the 1980s Rhode Island was the only state that still celebrated the end of World War II. The presence of so many veterans reinforced that uncomplex, general sense of patriotism so deeply felt in Rhode Island's ethnic, working-class population. The continuing presence of the Navy and the dependence of so many upon defense

industries has made Rhode Islanders supportive of patriotic appeals and military needs.

Many people identify various threats to the nation, cherished values, traditions, and institutions; and in the name of patriotism they have supported efforts to suppress alleged menaces. Sometimes this placed them on a collision course with organizations such as the American Civil Liberties Union, American Association of University Professors, and Americans United for Separation of Church and State, which have a different understanding of patriotism. Since the 1950s the state has had a steady diet of controversy over issues of academic freedom, censorship, free speech, public financing of parochial schools, municipally sponsored Nativity displays, antiwar protests, homosexuality, and abortion.

The most intense concern about Communist influences surfaced in the 1950s and early 1960s when being identified as a Communist would get one fired. A student class president at Bryant College was ousted when it was discovered that he was a Communist. When 87 Brown University professors signed a petition urging the abolition of the House Committee on Un-American Activities in 1961, the Rhode Island House of Representatives voted a resolution of support for HUAC, with only four dissenters, who included John Chafee of Warwick. The following year Thomas R. DiLuglio of Johnston introduced a bill to require all editorial writers to sign annual affidavits that they were not Communists. Following an appearance by a Communist speaker at the University of Rhode Island in 1963, a Cranston assemblyman demanded a legislative probe of the university; however, then-Governor Chafee opposed the move and the ACLU denounced it as a threat to free speech and academic freedom. The Vietnam War era brought new demands for intervention in campus disorders and efforts to command respect for the flag. The ACLU and similar organizations found themselves defending unpopular causes such as draft resistance, student rights, and the right of public protest.

A classic example of the clash of conceptions of patriotism occurred in 1964 over the issue of the Teacher Loyalty Oath. Since World War I, taking the oath had been a condition of teacher certification in the state, and at Rhode Island College it was administered to all student teachers in their final semester. Unexpectedly in February 1964, 20 seniors refused to sign the oath. The college's chapter of the American Association of University Professors, which had been privately considering the oath for some months, immediately supported the students. Dr. Kenneth Lewalski, chapter president, argued that the oath was vague and ambiguous, abridged academic freedom, and invaded personal privacy. Lieutenant Governor Edward Gallogly, soon to be the Democratic gubernatorial nominee, joined the issue in an address to a labor union gathering at the Naval Construction Battalion Center at Davisville. He declared that the nation faced a crisis when college professors teach that "the words loyalty and honor are vague and indefinite," when they assign pornographic literature such as *Fanny Hill* to students, and when students refuse to sign loyalty oaths. Governor Chafee, Gallogly's Republican opponent, observed at a press conference that the Teacher Loyalty Oath went far beyond the oaths that the governor or the legislators had to take and was unworkable. Subsequently, the State Board of Education, upon the recommendation of a special advisory committee headed by Associate Justice Florence Murray, revoked the oath on December 10.

In the early 1980s a similar clash occurred each Christmas season over municipally sponsored Nativity scenes. On the one hand were those who felt they were defending freedom of religious expression and the idea that America is a Christian nation. On the other hand were the ACLU and various religious leaders who maintained that the patriotic thing is separation of church and state and the preservation of Christian symbols from being reduced to secular objects equal to Rudolph the Red-Nosed Reindeer. Each side believed that the other was trampling on something that is holy. Roger Williams would have found it ironic that both sides invoked his name.

FACING PAGE, TOP: John H. Chaffee (1922–1999), governor (1963–1969), U.S. secretary of the navy (1969–1972), and U.S. senator (1967–1999), was the first Republican elected to the senate in 46 years. A nephew of Zechariah Chafee, Jr., the famous expert on the first amendment, John Chafee distinguished himself by his defense of civil liberties during the Cold War and as an environmentalist. From a 1966 campaign poster. RIHS (RHi x3 4320).

MIDDLE: Kenneth Lewalski, historian, veteran of World War II, and past president of the New England Historical Association, led the campaign against the 1918 Teacher Loyalty Oath. As an untenured assistant professor, he teamed with professors William McLoughlin of Brown University and Elton Rayack of the University of Rhode Island to successfully defend academic freedom and civil liberties. Courtesy, Rhode Island College News Bureau

BOTTOM: The Veterans Administration Hospital in Providence's Davis Park is shown here just after its completion in 1953. As the number of veterans in the state grew in the next three decades, the hospital expanded services and met the needs of a large outpatient population. Photo by J. David Lamontagne. Courtesy, Providence Journal Company

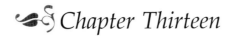

Chapter Thirteen

TRIBULATIONS AND TRIALS

In its nearly four centuries, Rhode Island has had four economies. Making a living in this small state has challenged the wits, ingenuity, and morality of its people. Agriculture was the essence of Rhode Island's 17th century economy; this laid the basis for the 18th century's oceanic commerce. "Fat mutton," cheese, horses, salted fish, shingles, and boards were a few of the products that led to the sea. However, the key to Rhode Island's maritime success was the re-export business, trading with slave-based economies and selling rum. The coastal towns, especially Newport, achieved some prosperity. However, by the 1790s Providence began to lead the way into an industrial economy. Manufacturing, beginning with textiles, grew and flourished in the 19th century, transforming Rhode Island into America's first urban, industrial state. What perplexed and vexed the state in the 20th century was the unexpected "deindustrialization" that began in earnest in the 1920s and which has lasted to the present. The challenge of the 20th century, and now the 21st, has been to create a new basis for prosperity. The economic tribulations of Rhode Island in the last quarter century were aggravated by a numbing litany of scandals involving public officials and agencies. The list of corrupt officials ran from the governor to city sidewalk engineers. There were so many crooked officials that people joked that the Adult Correctional Institution had a wing reserved for them. It seemed as if Rhode Island were "Rogue's Island."

World War II provided only a respite from a number of persistent problems that plagued Rhode Island. While the nation's economy escaped the Great Depression, Rhode Island's recovery was neither complete nor robust. The return of peace brought back many of the problems of the previous decades. Especially disturbing was the erosion of the industrial base. Some companies fell because of their dependence upon the war economy. For example, the Franklin Machine and Foundry Company, operating 100 percent on war contracts, went out of business when these were abruptly cancelled. The Walsh-Kaiser shipyard at Field's Point also closed.

The textile industry resumed its swoon. Cotton production for 1945 fell below that of 1935, as military orders ended and civilian demand was slow to materialize. Furthermore, unions struck nearly all of Rhode Island's textile mills during October and November, demanding a closed shop and retention of war-level wages. Within a year the mills were closing, and the jobs began disappearing. When the Harris Mill shut in 1953, it was the 15th concern to fold since 1946. In November 1953 the huge Guerin Mills in Woonsocket closed permanently after the company's 1,000 employees rejected a wage-cut request. A few months later the Lorraine Manufacturing Company of Pawtucket, which had employed 1,300 workers, closed. Between 1945 and 1982 the work force in textiles declined by 72 percent, shedding nearly 43,000 jobs. The proportion of the state's total work force engaged in manufacturing declined from 52 percent to 13 percent from 1945 to 2002.

For a time, the costume jewelry industry absorbed some of the lost textile jobs and by 1982 had the largest single industrial force. However, a 1981 exposé revealed that it was afflicted by many of the evils associated with turn-of-the-century sweatshops: health and safety problems; skimpy employee benefits; a largely unskilled workforce; exploitation of immigrants; illegal home work that used

Waterplace Park (foreground) and the renovated and reused 1893 railroad station (center) are examples of the city's revival. The tall buildings in the distance, Hospital Trust Company (left) and Fleet Bank (center and right), were all built by local banking and financial institutions. Courtesy, Dan Aurielo

The credit union scandal left one-third of the state's depositors without access to their bank accounts. Angry citizens packed the rotunda at the State House on January 26, 1991 to demand that Governor Bruce Sundlun reopen the banks. Courtesy, The Providence Journal

child labor and paid wages below minimum requirements; and little job security. The industry had 1,200 firms, many of which were small and subject to failure if forced to meet health and safety standards. The state's enforcement of these occupational safeguards had been slow and the larger, well-managed plants were reluctant to "blow the whistle" on their smaller subcontractors. By 1982 the novelty and costume jewelry industry was already in decline, having lost over 2,000 jobs in a year. As little as these jobs paid, they could not compete with Third World wage levels, and companies moved production off shore. Between 1992 and 2002 the jewelry industry declined by 43 percent.

At the turn of the 20th century, it was said that Providence had the largest tool factory (Brown and Sharpe), file factory (Nicholson File), engine factory (Corliss Steam Engine Company), screw factory (American Screw), and silverware factory (Gorham). Over the last century, Providence's Five Industrial Wonders of the World" have dwindled to just one. The Corliss Steam Engine Company was sold in 1900 to the International Power Company. In 1908 American Locomotive Company converted the plant to manufacture the ALCO, the finest automobile made in the United States, but that ended in 1913. Two more "Industrial Wonders" moved from

Rhode Island in the decade after the second World War. In early 1946 the American Screw Company decided to relocate to Willimantic, Connecticut. Most of its abandoned factory complex at Randall Square on Charles Street sat vacant until 1971, when six of the buildings were torched on July 9. In 1954 the Nicholson File Company, suffering a five-month strike from which it never fully recovered, moved its operations to plants in Indiana and Pennsylvania. In time Nicholson became a division of a large tool company and was consolidated to Georgia, employing only 400 people.

The last two "Industrial Wonders" lingered until 2002–2003. Gorham Manufacturing Company had once been the undisputed giant of the American silverware industry. Despite severe reversals during the Depression and changing lifestyles, it still had 2,400 employees in 1967 when it was purchased by Textron. Gorham soon experienced a major fall and was described as "a troubled company in a troubled, declining industry." In 1987 it abandoned its Adelaide Avenue site in Providence and moved to Smithfield. Gorham was then sold to Dansk which in 1991 was bought by Brown-Foreman, a Kentucky-based company best known as a whisky maker. In the end, the Smithfield facility had only 40 employees when the last

department was transferred to New Jersey in December 2002.

Now there is only one "wonder" left. Brown & Sharpe, now part of a Swedish company, still remains due to the fact that the state agreed to build the company a new $12 million facility at the Quonset Point-Davisville Industrial Park. When Brown & Sharpe was located in Providence, it had employed 1,600 workers in its Promenade Street complex (now called The Foundry). Cramped for space and needing a modern, single-level manufacturing facility, it moved to Precision Park in North Kingstown in 1964. Beginning in 1981, Brown & Sharpe suffered a bitter machinist strike that dragged on for four years, the longest-running strike in the nation. The company struggled financially and was purchased in 2001 by Hexagon AB of Stockholm, Sweden. The new plant at Quonset, promised for 2005, will keep the remaining 270 jobs in Rhode Island.

The most stunning blow to the state's economy since World War II was the sudden withdrawal of the Navy in 1973. As a result of President Richard Nixon's decision to con-solidate naval operations and personnel, most of the Newport-based Cruiser-Destroyer Force of the Atlantic Fleet and all of the Quonset-Davisville support operations were reassigned to southern stations. The number of active-duty personnel in Rhode Island fell from 25,881 to about 3,300, and more than 16,000 civilian jobs were eliminated. Eventually more than 30,000 people left in the Navy's wake, a $200 million payroll disappeared, real-estate values around the bases fell sharply, and local schools had to be closed. One consequence was that Rhode Island was one of only two states in the nation that suffered a population decline in the 1970s. In the 1990s the Navy presence modestly increased so that by 2001 it had about 15,000 active duty and civilian employees compared to 162,000 in 1944. However, the character and quality of the naval presence was significantly different. As Senator Claiborne Pell reportedly said, "We swapped the swabbies for the scientists." Instead of hordes of seamen, the Navy presence was generally represented by educators, researchers, and officers at the Naval War College and the underwater warfare research facilities. Periodically, vessels have been mothballed at Coddington Cove, and talk persists about the return of some active duty ships.

While a declining proportion of its workers relied upon Navy employment, Rhode Island remained significantly invested in defense and government contracts. In 1982 defense contracts for Rhode Island amounted to $336 million. In the early 1980s the state's largest defense contractor, Electric Boat, a division of General Dynamics, employed over 9,000 in its submarine-hull fabrication plants on former Navy land at Quonset. In Middletown, Raytheon Signal Division manufactured sonar and other electronic components. The Robert E. Derecktor Shipyard, located at the former Navy piers at Coddington Cove, won a contract in 1981 to build cutters for the United States Coast Guard. PF Industries, Inc., in Bristol was rescued from bankruptcy that same year to make military footwear, while the Imperial Knife Company, the largest manufacturer of cutlery in America, made bayonets and survival knives. A host of other companies making everything from service pins and

The submarine hull fabrication facility at General Dynamics' Electric Boat division, located at Quonset Point–Davisville Industrial Park, remains a major employer in Rhode Island. Since the 1970s the state has spent considerable energy trying to discover the proper direction for development of the former Navy base. Courtesy, Rhode Island Economic Development Corporation

insignias to screwdriver bits and gas masks held defense department contracts. The end of the Cold War in 1989 saw most of these contracts and companies swept away. With the sharp reduction in submarine construction, Electric Boat cut its Rhode Island work force to 1,450. The Derecktor shipyard went bankrupt. PF Industries closed and the Imperial Knife Company went out of business. By 1997 defense contracts had fallen to $257 million. Raytheon remained steady, in part because its work dovetailed with the Navy's own Undersea Warfare Center located in Newport. Still, the decline in defense contracts made New England "one of the hardest hit [regions] in the U.S.," and Rhode Island suffered accordingly.

In 1993 Governor Bruce Sundlun launched "R.I. Industry, 2000-Plus," a program to assist defense contractors weather the storm, plan and implement strategies to attract new industries, and retrain defense workers. In the following year 45 companies were accepting state and federal money to retrain their workers, and the state offered tax breaks and incentives to keep companies in Rhode Island. Nevertheless, Citizens for a Sound Economy, a group of business leaders, regarded these efforts as inconsequential and ranked Rhode Island as "dead last" in the nation in creating a favorable tax

climate for spurring business development. The conditions cited in 1991 by Nyman Manufacturing, maker of paper and plastic cups and plates, still prevailed. When Nyman expanded, it located its new facilities in Georgia because Rhode Island had 40 percent higher energy costs, 40 percent higher unemployment insurance rates, 42 percent higher property taxes, systemic political corruption, and each employee's annual worker's compensation was $800 higher. Later that year the *Providence Journal* published two lengthy articles entitled "Slow Death: Manufacturing in Rhode Island," calling existing conditions "deplorable." Although a few leading industrialists, such as John Hazen White, president of Taco, Inc., continued to argue that manufacturing was extremely important to the state as late as 2002, most business and government leaders diligently pushed in new directions.

Some of these initiatives to stimulate growth, such as Rhode Island's 1991 Enterprise Zone Program designed to attract businesses to decaying urban centers, only yielded limited success. The Minority Investment Development Corporation which granted loans, investments, and technical help to minority-owned businesses suffered from insufficient funding. The conversion of former Navy land in North Kingstown to industrial use brought about the huge Quonset Point-Davisville Industrial Park, one of three state-owned industrial parks. In the 1980s the state's aggressive promotion there created stormy relations with local town officials and environmentalists who feared that the park's inadequate sewer system would pollute Narragansett Bay and hurt the growing tourist industry. Despite these concerns, Governor Lincoln Almond in 1996 pressed for a new freight line and other improvements, believing that such additions would benefit the state "more than any other development." By 2001 Quonset Point-Davisville Industrial Park encompassed 115 firms employing over 6,000 workers. Some advocated creating a container port at Quonset, but this was such a controversial proposal that voters rejected a 2002 bond issue for needed infrastructure improvements even though these were unrelated to the container port.

Perhaps the most significant trend in Rhode Island's post-industrial era was a concerted movement toward the "new economy." The private, business-driven Economic Policy Council advanced a nine-part program in 1997 and lobbied heavily to push the state to invest in science and technology. The state's Economic Development Corporation created the Samuel Slater Technology Fund to provide matching grants to private money for fostering growth in emerging technology, especially in the area of biotechnology. This initiative created a partnership among the state's major universities and government.

Although sometimes criticized for its over-speculative expenditures, the Slater Fund had by 2002 invested in 23 biotech companies, and its supporters claimed it to be a success. In addition, the Economic Development Corporation in recent years has devoted its resources and talents to lure companies involved in information technology, financial services, and life sciences to Rhode Island. The corporation worked closely with the legislature to eliminate some of the drawbacks that Nyman Manufacturing described in 1991 and to enact business-friendly laws. These changes included a 10 percent tax credit on all new plants, machinery, and equipment; a 22 percent research and development tax break; the elimination of the inventory tax; and a sales tax abatement

for all expansion costs incurred by firms with more than 100 employees. In addition, job training and literacy classes necessitated by the state's sizeable immigrant population, were conducted on company premises and paid for by tax dollars and a company assessment per employee.

These improvements soon paid dividends. A significant success was the 1998 opening of a major facility in Smithfield by mutual-fund giant Fidelity Investments. Dow Chemical built an additional pharmaceutical manufacturing plant next to the Fidelity campus. Various incentives helped convince Amgen, which boasts of being "the world's largest independent biotechnology company," to build a $500 million facility in West Greenwich. The University of Rhode Island opened a new biomedical research lab in July 2003, financed by a $7.6 million grant from the National Institutes of Health. This lab was designed to be a central facility for researchers from seven Rhode Island colleges and universities. It was hoped that the lab's presence would generate spin-off companies and attract large concerns like Amgen, who want universities and professors that can do research for them. This part of the economy employs highly educated, trained, and skilled people. Rhode Island has a concentration of colleges and universities which can serve this specialized economy.

Higher education itself also became a major economic factor in Rhode Island, bringing in millions of dollars from students, attracting grant money in substantial amounts, and being an engine of innovation

Claiborne Pell (born 1918), U.S. Senator (1961-1997) and former chairman of the Senate foreign relations committee, is best known nationally for "Pell grants," which have allowed large numbers of students to attend college. Courtesy, Senator Claiborne Pell

Despite the efforts of firemen who charged into the burning building trying to rescue people, 100 died in The Station—the fourth most deadly nightclub fire in U.S. history. The tragedy resulted in statewide inspection of public facilities and triggered new fire-safety measures and codes across the nation. Courtesy, The Providence Journal

and ingenuity. One might even view the colleges and universities as continuing the re-exportation formula that was the basis for Rhode Island's 18th and 19th century wealth. In the 18th century sugar and molasses were imported and re-exported as rum. In the 19th century raw cotton and wool were imported and re-exported as textiles. The new version is the importation of students and the re-exportation of graduates. This is evidenced by the fact that colleges and universities produce more graduates than there are college-bound Rhode Island high school seniors. About 6,000 students graduate each year from Rhode Island high schools, half of these do not go to college and many others attend out of state. The colleges and universities in Rhode Island grant about 15,000 degrees each year, the vast majority to out-of-state students. Even the University of Rhode Island enrolls less than 50 percent of its students from the state, the consequence of having to recruit out-of-state students who pay higher tuition fees to make up for underfunding by the state. Only Rhode Island College and the Community College of Rhode Island draw the majority of their students from within the state. The growth of Johnson & Wales University and its conversion of vacant properties in Providence has also aided in the city's revitalization and recovery. In fact, Providence was reputed to have the highest per capita concentration of students of any city in the United States. Rhode Island graduates are meeting the employment demands of the new technology companies.

Health care has become "the fastest growing segment of the state's economy." Between 1987 and 1997 15,000 new jobs were added and health services accounted for 14.4 percent of the work force, the highest single sector of the economy. Rhode Island hospitals alone employed 23,000 people during this time and in 1999 Providence's ten hospitals, colleges, and universities generated $1.8 billion in revenues. First rate medical care was available in hospitals around the state. One of the principal engines of quality medical care was the Brown University Medical School, which graduated its first physicians in 1975. The medical school attracted outstanding physicians and surgeons to its faculty, who affiliated with the state's hospitals that became teaching hospitals and research centers. When The Station nightclub fire in February 2003 killed 100 people, all but 31 of the 227 injured were absorbed efficiently and treated in Rhode Island's hospitals.

Significant educational and scientific connections have developed in the state with respect to the ocean and environment. In 1971 the Graduate School of Oceanography at the University of Rhode Island was designated as one of the original, national Sea Grant colleges. In 1989 the National Oceanic and Atmospheric Administration (NOAA) named it as a Center of Excellence in coastal marine studies. One consequence that linked the state, the university, and private enterprise was a modest, but growing aquaculture industry. Located at Quonset-Davisville, several fish-farming companies were established as a result of the 2001 Rhode Island Aquaculture Initiative which was financed by a $1.5 million federal grant. In 2003 Brown University worked out an alliance with the Marine Biological Laboratory at Wood's Hole, Massachusetts for joint educational projects. These included research into the origins of life on earth, funded by a multi-million dollar grant from the National Aeronautics and Space Administration (NASA).

Unfortunately, the state also has a higher-than-average percentage of unskilled, under-educated workers. The overall educational achievements of Rhode Islanders are the lowest in New England. This is the result, in part, of the fact that the state has been and continues to be a lodestone to immigrants. For example in 2003 English was not the first

In 1972 Vincent "Buddy" Cianci first ran for mayor of Providence as "The Anti-Corruption Candidate." Ironically, he would be convicted of felonies that ended both of his terms in office. He presided over two corruption-riddled administrations. Courtesy, The Providence Journal

language of about 40 percent of Providence residents, and 85 percent of the Providence public school students were minorities. Providence was rated third-worst in the nation with respect to poverty among children. Many people were stuck at the other end of the service economy. They waited on and bussed tables in the restaurant industry; worked as aides in hospitals and nursing homes; drove trucks and delivered goods; stocked shelves in retail stores and groceries; and did grounds and custodial work at universities, financial institutions, hospitals, and public facilities. In an earlier time, immigrants performed manual labor and worked in factories. Now such folk are seen mopping floors, changing beds, serving food, and transporting patients inside of medical facilities.

The service industry in the state became the main employer, soaking up most of the losses from manufacturing. This sector included tourism and the restaurant industry, financial services, and health care. By the year 2000, tourism was said to be the second largest source of income for Rhode Island. While service employment tended not to pay as well as manufacturing jobs, the growth of the service sector was critical for the state. On the other hand, the growth of government employment saddled Rhode Island with a

higher-than-normal number of public employees. Government employment in Rhode Island grew more rapidly than any other sector of the economy between World War II and 1990, when it stabilized. By 2002 state and local governments employed 66,200 people, or 13.8 percent of the total work force. Many of these jobs resulted from the increasing role of government in providing social services through New Deal, New Frontier, and Great Society programs. However, many government jobs were patronage positions awarded through the "politics of gratification."

As the state struggled in the last 25 years to adapt to the new economic realities of deindustrialization, the public was constantly distracted by revelations of corruption. The scandals consumed public tax revenues, stunted economic development and growth, and brought shame to Rhode Island. No other state in the nation suffered the ignominy of seeing two consecutive chief justices of the state Supreme Court removed for corruption. Only a handful of states have sent a governor to jail. Embezzlement, fraud, extortion, bribery, perjury, and racketeering were all crimes committed by municipal and state officials. Illustrative of the morality of some public officials was the behavior of a top officer at the Department of Transportation who stooped to steal cookies from the scene of a semi-trailer rollover on I-95.

The scandals of the 1980s and 1990s overlapped each other like scales on a snake. Federal investigators began their "Providence Probe" in 1981. By the time they finished in 1988, 21 people had been convicted on various charges of municipal corruption, including several major figures in the first administration of Providence Mayor Vincent "Buddy" Cianci. In 1983 and 1984 federal and state investigations resulted in the indictment and conviction of the director of the Rhode Island Turnpike and Bridge Authority; the registrar, deputy registrar, and an inspector of the Registry of Motor Vehicles; and a field inspector and the chairman of the board of plumbing examiners. These events overlapped the end of the first coming of Cianci, as he was indicted on charges of extortion and kidnapping in May 1983. This led to his pleading no contest in March of 1984. Meanwhile several of his henchmen in the Providence Department of Public Works

W.L. "Bubba" Sayles and his wife Jane from College Station, Texas, were two of the thousands of people attending the national convention of the Fraternal Order of Police in August 2003. The "Renaissance City" used WaterFire and other attractions to promote conventions and tourism. Courtesy, The Providence Journal

were indicted and convicted of corruption in 1985. The extortion and kickback charges against Providence City Solicitor Ronald Glantz and Democratic City Chairman Anthony Bucci kept the corruption of the Cianci administration in the news, until their conviction and imprisonment in 1987.

On top of those events was the December 1984 spectacle of Chief Justice Joseph Bevilacqua, whose notorious associations with organized crime figures caused the Commission on Judicial Tenure and Discipline to appoint an investigating committee. The Bevilacqua issue dragged through 1985, when he was censured and forced to step down for four months by the judicial commission. In January 1986 he had to appear before the U.S. Presidential Commission on Organized Crime to explain relationships he had with criminals. A few days later the Rhode Island House of Representatives adopted a resolution to impeach Bevilacqua, the first impeachment ever under the 1842 state constitution. The hearings were seen on television in April and May, and one organized crime figure after another "took the Fifth" when called to testify. Bevilacqua resigned on May 28, halting the hearings.

Concurrent with the Bevilacque case was the scandal in the Rhode Island Housing Mortgage and Finance Corporation (RIHMFC) which ran from 1985 to 1987. RIHMFC had been established to provide low interest loans to low income, first-time home buyers. Instead, mortgages were secured for insid-

ers, friends, relatives, and "the powerful." The director, Ralph Pari, embezzled hundreds of thousands of dollars and lived a lavish lifestyle. Investigators found that he had 32 bank accounts, safe deposit boxes containing gold and diamonds, and a power boat. He pleaded no contest to 16 charges in November 1987. The attorney general recommended sentencing Pari to 10 years in prison and a $97,500 fine. Then Superior Court Judge John E. Orton, III provoked outrage when he gave Pari 16 months and an $8,000 fine, saying that Pari had "suffered enough." The U.S. Attorney did not agree and indicted Pari for income tax evasion in April 1988. He was convicted in mid-1989 and sent to federal prison for three years and fined $210,000.

At nearly the same moment as Pari's federal indictment, Congressman Ferdinand St. Germain was denying charges that he had violated House rules against accepting food and favors from financial industry lobbyists of the House Banking and Finance Committee which he chaired. By October of 1988 a U.S. Justice Department investigation found "substantial evidence of serious and sustained misconduct." These revelations led to St. Germain's defeat in the November elections by Ronald Machtley, ending 14 terms as U.S. Representative, the longest in Rhode Island's history. Machtley joined Claudine Schneider in the House, giving the Republicans both seats from Rhode Island for the first time since 1941.

Governor Edward DiPrete won a third term in November 1988, but charges of unethical behavior regarding a Cranston land deal surfaced during the campaign. The defeated challenger, Bruce Sundlun, sought to exploit the stories that DiPrete's fundraising activities bordered on extortion, but it was to no avail at the time. The allegations began to stick by the 1990 election, and ethics charges were filed against DiPrete. Sundlun won the election, and the criminal justice ordeal for DiPrete was about to begin. Although the Ethics Commission investigation cleared DiPrete of nine complaints in June 1991, including the Cranston land deal, in December the commission levied a fine of $30,000 on DiPrete for improperly steering state business to his campaign contributors.

In November 1990, in the waning weeks

of the DiPrete administration, state insurance regulators took control of the Heritage Loan & Investment Company after the books were found in such disarray that it could not be determined whether the bank was solvent. Two weeks later Heritage president Joseph Mollicone disappeared after being charged with embezzling at least $13 million. Thus began the collapse of the Rhode Island's private savings and loan system. The new governor, Bruce Sundlun, facing a major budgetary shortfall and a crumbling banking system, ordered the closure of the 45 credit unions and banks insured by the private Rhode Island Safe Deposit Insurance Corporation (RISDIC). A third of the state's bank depositors were blocked from their money. Angry citizens disrupted traffic on Interstate 95 to protest against what Brown University President Vartan Gregorian described as misdeeds caused by "an incestuous" political and financial system. The collapse of RISDIC left the savings and loan system in a shambles and exposed a corrupt alliance of politicians and bank officials.

About half of the closed banks were allowed to reopen within a week, but it would be the middle of 1992 before many depositors received their money. In the meantime the state created the Depositors Economic Protection Corporation (DEPCO) which took over the assets of the failed banks and pursued the money and property of those who corrupted the system. The investigation of the banking crisis revealed that Governor DiPrete had been warned five years earlier that RISDIC was liable to fail, but did nothing. Legislative allies of the credit union officials had prevented adequate regulation of the financial institutions, which allowed them to run wild. Insiders and their friends played a shell game with depositors' money, lending it back and forth in a fantastic orgy of real estate speculation.

In June 1991 a new scandal emerged in Pawtucket. Mayor Brian Sarault was arrested minutes after he received a final $1,750 payment from Robert Weygand, a landscape architect and state representative from East Providence. Sarault tried to extort $3,000 from Weygand who went to the FBI and wore a "wire" to catch Sarault. Within the next weeks eight more of Sarault's co-conspirators and allies were indicted, including his campaign finance chairman, the city's public works director, and a police captain. Sarault pleaded guilty and in January 1992 was sent to federal prison for five-and-a-half years. The rest received lesser sentences. Later in June 1992 it was revealed that Cranston Mayor Michael Traficante was the subject of a criminal investigation, and in November North Providence Mayor Salvatore Mancini was indicted by a federal grand jury for extortion. Mancini was found innocent the following year, but Traficante finally pleaded guilty in June 1994 to campaign reporting violations. The spectacle of three mayors being charged with criminal activities in the same year only increased the public sense of disgust with politicians. On the other hand, Weygand's reputation for integrity carried him to the lieutenant governorship in 1992 and a seat in the U.S. House of Representatives in 1996. Finally, he lost to another untarnished man, Lincoln Chafee, in the 2000 race for the U.S. Senate.

While the three mayoral cases ran their courses, Joseph Mollicone surrendered himself in April 1992 after being on the run since November 1990. He pleaded guilty to 47 counts, and in July 1993 he was sentenced to 40 years in prison and ordered to pay $12 million in restitution and a $420,000 fine. It was the harshest sentence ever imposed on a white collar criminal in Rhode Island.

Even before the banking crisis had resolved itself and Mollicone was sent off to prison, a new scandal unfolded which brought down another chief justice of the Rhode Island Supreme Court and his court administrator. Judicial corruption finally changed the way that judges in Rhode Island were chosen. The almost unbelievable spectacle of two successive chief justices of the state Supreme Court being forced to resign and the growing clamor against the system that elected such men caused the state to reform the system. Until 1994 the General Assembly had a nearly unfettered say over who was elevated to the bench, because it had the power to select all judges. The naked use of that power had been demonstrated in the "Bloodless Revolution" of 1935 when the General Assembly dismissed the entire Supreme Court, replacing them with judges that would uphold the legality of the "revolution." There was little question who had the

A state police surveillance photo showed Rhode Island Supreme Court Chief Justice Joseph A. Bevilacqua zipping up his pants as he was leaving the Alpine Motel after a noon-time assignation with a "Massachusetts woman" on June 9, 1983. The Alpine Motel was owned by an organized crime figure.

power to appoint judges, and appointments to the bench often went to former members of the General Assembly. Until the 1990s the General Assembly assembled its own list of court nominees and then decided who got the jobs.

With one exception in 1963 every person elevated to the Rhode Island State Supreme Court from 1958 to 1993 had served in the General Assembly. In addition, many of the judges on the superior, family, and district courts had been legislators. The most blatant example of the power occurred in 1976 when Speaker of the House Joseph A. Bevilacqua had himself elected as Chief Justice of the Supreme Court. Bevilacqua, a man with a long political career, replaced Thomas H. Roberts, who never served in the legislature but who brought a distinguished legal and judicial résumé to the court. Bevilacqua's term on the court ended in 1986 when he was forced to resign under impeachment for using court aides to work on his family farm; accepting free electrical work on his property in exchange for giving the contractor all the court's work; and committing adultery. However, the threat of impeachment was due in large part to the fact that he was seen in the company of mobsters so often that the state police had put him under surveillance by 1983. He once officiated at a mob wedding and earlier wrote to the parole board stating that Raymond Patriarca, head of New England's mafia, "was a man of good moral character."

Bevilacqua was replaced by Thomas Fay, a former legislator and chairman of the House Judiciary Committee who went directly from the House to family court in 1978. Fay was the favorite of then-Speaker of the House, Matthew Smith. When Smith left the House in 1988, he became the court administrator, working with his old friend Fay. These two abused the public trust, and their terms ended in disgrace. M. Charles Bakst, political columnist for the *Providence Journal*, said of them: "Like old-time political bosses, Fay and his pal, then-court administrator, Matthew Smith, presided over a court patronage empire." Fay used secretaries to do private real estate business, steered court work to business partners, and intervened on behalf of friends and relatives in traffic cases. He and Smith maintained a secret court bank account which was used to pay

for expensive meals, liquor, baskets of flowers, tuxedo rentals, and parties. From 1988 to 1993 at least $175,000 was spent from the secret fund, including auto repairs for Smith. Smith also helped State Auditor General Anthony Piccirilli cover up his son's embezzlement of $4,224 in court funds in 1989. In fact, it was the discovery of the embezzlement that triggered the investigation that led to Fay and Smith's secret fund. In 1993 Fay, like his predecessor Bevilacqua, was forced to resign under impeachment. He was convicted in 1994, given a five-year suspended prison sentence, and barred from legal practice. Smith, too, was convicted on two misdemeanor counts in 1994 and fined $1,000. However, with the felony charges dismissed, he was able to keep his $73,000 annual pension. Later in September, his former court secretary tried to burn down his house. She was sentenced to seven years on probation.

Just before the Fay-Smith debacle began to unfold Thomas Kelleher retired from the Supreme Court in July 1992, beginning the search for a replacement. By then the public was already clamoring for cleaner, more ethical government. A growing chorus which included Common Cause, the Rhode Island Bar Association, and a broad reform coalition called RIght Now! demanded a new selection process. Special attention was drawn to the judiciary branch because in 1992 a Superior Court judge was convicted of soliciting a $45,000 bribe from a lawyer, and a family court judge with a drinking and drug problem was convicted of bank fraud and for borrowing over $300,000 from lawyers who practiced in his court. Governor Bruce Sundlun had responded by setting up a commission on judicial appointments to assist him in nominating judges. But, the selection was actually in the hands of the General Assembly. By the time that the General Assembly got around to picking a new justice in April 1993, the scandal involving Smith and Fay was coming to light, and the legislature's selection was very controversial.

Kelleher's replacement provoked outrage because it went to another former legislator, Victoria Lederberg. She had never tried a case in court and her judicial experience consisted of being a part-time judge on the Providence Municipal Court from 1991 to 1993. Some Superior Court judges openly denounced

ABOVE: Reproduced here is lithographer Moses Swett's 1829 rendition of the Providence Arcade (1828), the first indoor shopping mall in America. W & J Pendleton, Boston, 1829. RIHS (RHi x5 35)/ William C. Gucfa photo

RIGHT: Touro Synagogue (1763), the interior of which is shown here, is the oldest synagogue in the United States. Courtesy, Rhode Island Department of Economic Development

FAR RIGHT: Historic Benefit Street, Providence, has many restored 18th-century houses. It is a part of the College Hill restoration project begun in the 1950s. Courtesy, Rhode Island Department of Economic Development/Chet Browning photo

PREVIOUS PAGE: Although an industrial state, Rhode Island takes pride in its annual town, county, and state fairs. This colorful poster was for the 1889 Rhode Island State Fair. RIHS (RHi x5 46)

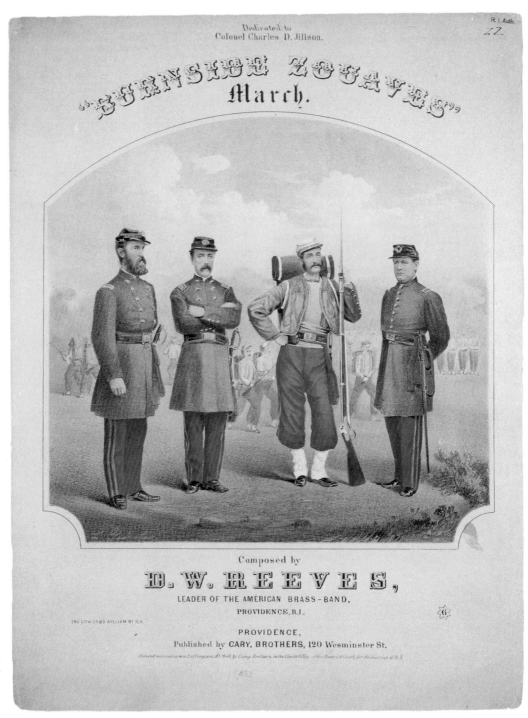

Davis W. Reeves, leader of the American Brass Band, composed the "Burnside Zouaves March" in 1868. RIHS (RHi x5 34)/William C. Gucfa photo

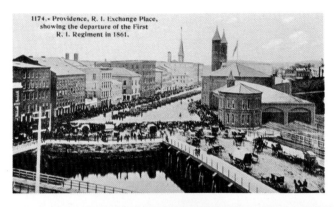

1174.- Providence, R. I. Exchange Place, showing the departure of the First R. I. Regiment in 1861.

FACING PAGE, TOP: The Household Sewing Machine Company distributed advertising cards such as this one. The machines were manufactured by the Providence Tool Company in the 1870s as part of its diversification efforts. RIHS (RHi x5 39)

THIS PAGE, TOP: The departure of the First R.I. Regiment from Exchange Place in April 1861 is shown on this color postcard. RIHS (RHi x5 38)

LEFT: Pawtucket, R.I., the birthplace of the Industrial Revolution in America, is seen from the south in this 1870s handcolored engraving by J.S. Lincoln, published by Terry, Pelton & Co. RIHS (RHi x5 37)

ABOVE: An autumn scene at the Arkwright Mill dam in Coventry. The old Arkwright Mill pond is part of the Greenway Project along the Pawtuxet River. It once was lined by textile mill villages including Quidnick, Anthony, Arkwright, Harris, Washington, Coventry Center, Summit, and Greene. Courtesy, Peter Goldberg

RIGHT: The Southeast Lighthouse, constructed in 1873, stands on Mohegan Bluffs on Block Island, overlooking the Atlantic Ocean. The lighthouse, the tallest in New England, was moved 360 feet back from the bluff in 1993 when erosion threatened to topple it into the sea. Courtesy, Malcolm Greenaway

One of America's architectural treasures, the Meeting House of the First Baptist Church in America was built in Providence in 1774–1775. The steeple was fully illuminated for the first time in 2002, complementing the revival of downtown. Courtesy, Dan Aurelio

BELOW: *At the turn of the century the* Mount Hope, *a Block Island-Newport ferryboat, steamed into Newport Harbor, which was filled with ships of the Atlantic Fleet— part of America's "Great White Fleet." Chromolithograph by Forbes, Boston. RIHS (RHi x5 42)*

Newport Harbor

RIGHT: *Narragansett Bay resorts did a thriving business in the 19th century as illustrated by this handcolored, photomechanical reproduction of the opening of the bathing season at Narragansett Pier in the 1890s. Drawing by Charles H. Provost from* Harper's Weekly. *RIHS (RHi x5 41)*

Crowds of people enjoy the Water-Fire spectacle on the Providence River, in front of the Rhode Island School of Design. Courtesy, Water-Fire/Providence. Photograph by Barnaby Evans

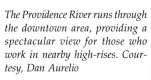

The Providence River runs through the downtown area, providing a spectacular view for those who work in nearby high-rises. Courtesy, Dan Aurelio

Providence Place Mall was opened in 1999 as a result of city, state, and private cooperative efforts to bring people back to downtown Providence. Straddling the Woonasquatucket River and the Amtrack rail lines, this eight-story, $450 million retail mall anchors the west side of the Capital Center development project. Courtesy, Dan Aurelio

Beachgoers enjoy the waves at Narragansett Town Beach, with a spectacular view of The Towers in the background. Courtesy, Peter Goldberg

ABOVE: *The Great Hall of Cornelius Vanderbilt's "The Breakers" was the setting for chamber music featuring the Swedish flutist Göran Marcusson (standing) and fellow Newport Music Festival musicians in July 2003. The festival presents over 60 concerts each season with artists from around the world. Courtesy, Newport Music Festival*

RIGHT: *Columbus Day Weekend Festival on Atwells Avenue, Federal Hill, Providence. Courtesy, Peter Goldberg*

A Revolutionary War fife-and-drum corps marched in the Ancients and Horribles 4th of July Parade in Chepachet. Unlike the more sedate July 4th parades, the Ancients and Horribles Parade is notable for its lampooning and sarcastic treatment of current events and politicians. Courtesy, Peter Goldberg

In summertime, Waterplace Park is the site for outdoor theatrical and musical shows. Courtesy, Peter Goldberg

On any sunny day, Brenton Point State Park in Newport is alive with colorful kites. Courtesy, Peter Goldberg

FACING PAGE, TOP: Arriving by ferry at Block Island. Courtesy, Peter Goldberg

FACING PAGE, BOTTOM: Sailboats on the Barrington River, looking from Barrington toward Warren. Courtesy, Peter Goldberg

Claiborne Pell Bridge to Newport at sunset. Originally called the Newport Bridge, it opened on June 28, 1969. Courtesy, Peter Goldberg

her nomination, but she was the favorite of Speaker of the House John Harwood. Lederberg proved to be extremely able on the Supreme Court, and her sudden death in late December 2002 was seen as a genuine loss to the judiciary. Even her severest critics changed their minds after seeing her work.

The uproar over the judges led to a major reform in the way jurists in Rhode Island would thereafter be chosen. Lederberg was the last Supreme Court justice chosen by the old system. In 1994, almost at the same time that Fay and Smith were being convicted, the General Assembly passed a bill to create the Judiciary Nominating Commission. The process allowed for the proper screening of candidates for judgeships and recommended that a list of five be sent to the governor, who then nominated one to the legislature for its approval. The new selection system did not eliminate politics from nominations, but it shifted the selection process from the legislature to the executive branch. The General Assembly could reject a name as it did with U.S. Attorney Margaret Curran, who was opposed by Speaker Harwood since she strongly favored separation of powers. It still helped to have legislative leaders support-

The elevation of Victoria Lederberg (1937–2002) to the state Supreme Court caused considerable controversy, which helped bring reform to the judicial selection process. She had been a professor of psychology at Rhode Island College and a state legislator before being appointed a municipal court judge. Courtesy, The Elect: Rhode Island's Women Legislators, 1922–1990

ing a nomination as was the case with Maureen McKenna Goldberg (1997), whose husband was the Senate Minority Leader, and Francis X. Flaherty (2003), whose brother was the chairman of the House Judiciary Committee. On the other hand, the new selection system made it possible for Robert G. Flanders, Jr., to be elevated to the Supreme Court in 1996 after being vetoed in 1993 by Speaker Harwood because he did not like Flanders' position on the issue of separation of powers. Significantly, none of the next six justices elevated to the Supreme Court after 1994 had served in the legislature. The selection of Paul Suttell in 2003 for the Supreme Court saw a return of the conventional résumé for judges: legal council to the House minority leader, state representative from 1983 to 1990 and appointment to the family court in 1990.

If a rotten banking system, a corrupt governor, crooked mayors, and venial judges were not enough to make one sick, the unsavory nature of the legislative pension game became utterly clear by 1991. The General Assembly had debated and argued about pay and pensions for years because the 1842 state constitution limited compensation to a mere $5 per day for a 90-day session. Most observers agreed that this was woefully inadequate. A way around the limitation was to grant pensions for service. However, reformers pressed for better pay, the abolition of the legislative pension system and four-year terms for state officers, and an improved ethics system. A state constitutional convention proposed all of those reforms in 1986, but the amendments were soundly rejected by the voters in November. In 1987 the General Assembly retaliated by voting to double their own pensions to $12,000 per year.

Worse, on the final day of the 1987 session a provision quietly advanced by the head of the National Education Association of Rhode Island was slipped into a bill, which was passed unread by most legislators in the last-minute crush. It enabled top teachers' union officials to purchase time toward state pensions for the years they had done full-time union work. Later most legislators learned what had transpired and, outraged, they repealed the provision in the 1988 session. However, a Superior Court judge ruled that the two dozen union officials who had

Edward DiPrete is shown here leaving the Superior Court building after pleading guilty to 18 counts of bribery, extortion, and racketeering. He was the first governor of Rhode Island to be convicted and sent to the penitentiary, where he became prisoner number 111056. Courtesy, The Providence Journal

applied for pensions before the repeal would be allowed to keep their lifetime benefits.

The issue became more heated in 1991–1992 when the pension records were pried opened, revealing the who and how of pensions. Later the IRS said that the legislative pensions violated the federal tax code, thereby jeopardizing the state's entire $2.8 billion pension fund for state employees and teachers. The records showed that legislators padded their state pensions by buying credit for time spent as a summer lifeguard as a teenager; for serving on town councils, boards and committees; for being a once-a-year town moderator or serving on local library boards; and even for serving as a House page. A state senator from Providence retired at age 52 and claimed public pensions of $106,000 by piling up 79 years worth of retirement credits. Perhaps the most outrageous case was the man who was allowed to buy three years of credit while working in a private warehouse, including the time he was there on work release from the state prison!

When Nancy Mayer became general treasurer in 1993, she denounced the enrollment of union officials in the state pension system as "the most egregious example of special legislation to ever pass the General Assembly." The *Providence Journal* pronounced it a "miracle" when in 1994 the legislature passed Mayer's bill to evict the union leaders. They sued to be reinstated. The dues of all ordinary teachers were spent in pursuit of court cases for the few privileged union leaders. Consequently a number of angry, local chapters of the National Education Association–Rhode Island (NEARI) withheld their dues in protest. The case went all the way to the U.S. Supreme Court which ruled in the state's favor in October 1999. Since the pension scandal was exposed not another special pension bill has passed. In November 1994 voters adopted a constitutional amendment which downsized the legislature and provided a salary for legislators, in lieu of pensions.

While the pension scandal unfolded, so did the undoing of former Governor DiPrete. The banking crisis led to him and his eventual imprisonment. After Joseph Mollicone became a fugitive, the special prosecutions unit of the attorney general's office began to investigate state dealings with Mollicone.

They learned that the department of employment security had been pressured by individuals close to Governor DiPrete to rent more space in the old Metcalf Building, which was owned by Mollicone. Henry W. Fazzano, chief of staff for DiPrete, and Rodney Brusini, a long-time friend and DiPrete fundraiser, were Mollicone's partners. Investigators uncovered many more instances of such pressure and learned that DiPrete required his personal approval of even minor contracts with the state. A state police investigation documented bribes, extortion, kick-backs, and fundraising violations. The governor shook down contractors and vendors who did business with the state, and they paid him in envelopes stuffed with money. In short, investigators found "a state for sale." Among the enduring images was the picture of the governor diving into the dumpster behind Walt's Roast Beef in Cranston to retrieve an envelope with $10,000 in cash—that he had mistakenly thrown there with the remains of his sandwich. The whole sordid mess was exposed and DiPrete was indicted in 1994. His case dragged on until he pleaded guilty in 1998 and became the state's first governor con-

Donald Carcieri, former CEO of Cookson America, was elected governor in 2002 with a promise to apply his skills to the economic problems of the state. His election, concurrent with that of the new mayor of Providence, David Cicilline, caused many to hope for a new order in Rhode Island politics. Courtesy, Governor Donald Carcieri. Photograph by Constance Brown

victed and sent to the Adult Correctional Institution. Ironically, one of DiPrete's legacies was the tough campaign finance law in 1992.

Philip West, executive director of Common Cause, said, "It was the excesses of DiPrete in so many areas of campaign finance chicanery that led directly to new laws that have made Rhode Island a national model for clean campaign financing laws, and such innovations as public financing of statewide elections for candidates who agree to campaign spending limits." Candidates could no longer use campaign money for personal use nor take political money in cash. Corporations could no longer make campaign contributions, and campaign financial disclosure laws were toughened considerably. In 1998 Darrell West, political science professor at Brown University, agreed that one consequence of the scandal was positive: "We actually now have the cleanest elected officials we've ever had, both in the (congressional) delegation and statewide."

Of course, reform came not just as a result of DiPrete's corruption; it stemmed from public disgust with the general sleaze and lack of ethics of so many politicians. Operation Clean Sweep, Operation Clean Government, and even the whimsically named Cool Moose party focused and reflected public anger. One of the most effective was RIght

Now! which was a statewide coalition of business corporations, civic and good government groups, and religious communities. One Sunday afternoon in January 1992 thousands of people proceeded from downtown churches and synagogues to rally at the State House, to demand tighter public ethics and campaign finance reform. They were part of the RIght Now! coalition. The Reverend James Miller, executive minister of the Rhode Island State Council of Churches, chuckled as he recalled the bewilderment of the politicians: "They didn't know what to do about all those preachers." RIght Now! was a loose cannon, completely beyond the control of the politicians, and could not be satisfied by the usual favors. The public outcry over pensions, RISDIC, and legislative corruption forced Speaker of the House Joseph DeAngelis and many tainted incumbents to abandon reelection in 1992. The new Speaker, John Harwood, presented himself as a reformer, but was not. He especially opposed separation of powers. A decade later, while fighting sexual harassment charges, he narrowly defeated a write-in opponent for his assembly seat. Two days later his party forced him to relinquish the Speaker's office.

Many of the reforms that advanced in the 1990s were aimed at the excesses of the General Assembly. The reforms did not end with tough campaign finance laws and an improved ethics commission. The voters approved four-year terms for the general officers while leaving legislators with two-year terms, which had the effect of increasing executive power. The General Assembly was downsized, and newly elected legislators salaried. A "revolving door" bill forbid legislators from taking any civil service position inside a year after leaving the legislature. Most significant was the struggle to correct constitutional defects in the governance of the state.

When the state adopted its first constitution in 1842, it retained the 1663 charter principle of legislative supremacy. With power concentrated in the General Assembly, the safeguards inherent in separation of powers and checks and balances were missing. In the late 20th century the Speaker of the House became the most powerful figure in the government. The problems caused by

FBI agents seized records in the tax collector's office in Providence City Hall on April 28, 1999 as part of "Operation Plunder Dome." Federal investigators played a key role in U.S. Attorney Margaret Curran's successful prosecution of the Cianci administration. Courtesy, The Providence Journal

this imbalance multiplied as the number of state boards and quasi-public agencies grew substantially after 1950. Many of them had legislators or legislative staff as voting members. Scandals arose in the state retirement system, Narragansett Bay Commission, Coastal Management Resource Council, Lottery Commission, Resource Recovery Commission, and the Unclassified Pay Plan Board. As the state grappled with banking, pension, and governmental corruption in 1992, Sheldon Whitehouse, executive counsel to Governor Sundlun, told reformers that they would "not cut the deep root of Rhode Island's corruption" until they addressed separation of powers. As other reforms were achieved, the clamor for separation of powers, which would eliminate legislators or their appointees from executive boards and commissions, grew louder through the 1990s. Not surprisingly legislative leaders were loathe to surrender power. However, in an advisory referenda in 2000 and 2002 the voters overwhelmingly endorsed separation of powers, and the General Assembly finally surrendered to voters' wishes and put a constitutional amendment on the ballot for November 2004.

With the structural problems in state government nearing solution, the focus of attention shifted to ethics. Within the first

months of 2004, two legislative leaders were forced out as a result of ethics violations. First, Senate President William Irons resigned after it was revealed that he had failed to disclose $70,000 in commissions he received from 2001–2003, as a broker for a health insurance policy for CVS employees. A Fortune 500 corporation and now the nation's largest drug store chain, the Woonsocket-based CVS had interests in various bills before the legislature. Then, John Celona, chairman of the Senate Commerce Committee, which handled all legislation dealing with the health care industry, was forced to resign. Celona had failed to disclose, as mandated by law, that CVS was paying him thousands of dollars a year to be a consultant. Additionally, he was a paid consultant to an ambulance company and a hospital that also came before his committee. These revelations intensified the efforts of Common Cause and other watchdog groups to strengthen and revitalize the state Ethics Commission.

Not even the disgracing of Supreme Court justices and the jailing of a former governor attracted as much national attention as the second fall of Providence Mayor Vincent "Buddy" Cianci. Despite court challenges to Cianci's eligibility to be mayor, Providence voters ushered in his second coming in November 1990. People around the nation

"The Towers" is the only surviving portion of the great Narragansett Pier Casino, designed by Sanford White and built between 1883–1886. The heart of an elegant gilded age resort complex, the huge hotel and casino were destroyed in a great fire in 1900. This view is from the Narragansett Town Beach. Courtesy, Peter Goldberg

were puzzled why Providence would reelect him in light of his first conviction and resignation. One answer came in the reply of a Federal Hill resident to an ABC-TV's *20/20* reporter who asked what she thought of the complaints of corruption against the mayor. She dismissed them, saying, "He never did anything to me." Witty, charismatic, and energetic, Cianci presided over the rise of Providence in the 1990s. He became a celebrity, trading quips and barbs with radio talk show hosts from New York. He had his own marinara sauce, and he tirelessly promoted the city. He even appeared as the mayor in an episode of NBC's popular TV series *Providence*. However, there was a dark side. He was a "coarse, petty, vindictive politician" who presided over a corrupt administration.

By late 1997 federal officers were back with "Operation Plunder Dome," investigating corruption in City Hall. In January 1998 the FBI recruited a Providence businessman who secretly recorded more than 100 conversations with corrupt city officials in the next year. Operation Plunder Dome became public in April 1999 when the FBI raided City Hall and arrested two tax officials. When the probes, indictments, and trials were finished by June 2002, the mayor, his top aide and campaign treasurer, the chairman and vice chairman of the Board of Tax Assessment Review, a tax collector, a deputy tax assessor, two lawyers, and a tow-truck operator had been convicted on various charges of racketeering and corruption. Cianci was forced to resign for a second time, and he entered a federal prison on December 6, 2002 to begin serving five-and-a-half years. The whole affair was worth a segment on CBS's *60 Minutes*. The Cianci saga rapidly became a cultural feast, retold in books, a documentary, a movie directed by Michael Corrente, a musical, and a production of the Ocean State Follies. Yet, beneath the sputtering conversion from manufacturing to the "new economy" and the seemingly systemic corruption in the state, Rhode Island entertained visions and pursued new directions.

The new series of U.S. quarters honoring all the states presents Rhode Island's image in 2001 as the "Ocean State." The coin features Narragansett Bay, the Claiborne Pell Bridge, and a 12-meter yacht. Courtesy, Dan Aurelio

Chapter Fourteen

REVIVAL AND VISIONS

Despite the ordeals of deindustrialization and rogues in government, recent decades have seen a substantial improvement in the quality of life in Rhode Island, leading to the state being nationally recognized as an attractive place. One reason why tourism increased so much was that Rhode Island became a destination for recreation, vacations, and conferences as the state capitalized on its historic, environmental, and recreational assets. The capital city went from being described as "a dump" to being toasted as "the best place to live in the East." Inspired by visionaries and funded with millions in urban redevelopment grants, Providence renovated and restored whole sections and established 30 historic districts in the city by 2003. Statewide, the Historic Preservation Commission listed at least 150 historic districts as most towns moved to protect historic structures. Freed of its dependence upon the Navy, Newport threw itself fully into tourism and became "The City by the Sea," one of America's top tourist destinations. A statewide effort to preserve open spaces and elevate the quality of life dovetailed neatly with the new image of Rhode Island as "The Ocean State."

The transformation was not easy. The problems and weaknesses that plagued the state's economy in general, deeply affected the older urban areas. The aging industrial areas were the centers of most of the decay. Cities that formerly boasted of their economic power and population growth had to cope with the reality of decline nearly every decade. On the other hand, suburban and rural portions of the state grew substantially, causing problems of sprawl and undesirable development. Except for the 1970s when the Navy pulled out, the state's population increased every decade; however, Providence, Woonsocket, Pawtucket, and Central

Falls all lost inhabitants. Providence had 248,674 people in 1950 but, despite having grown a bit in the 1990s, it counted 160,728 in the 2000 census—a 35 percent decline. The exodus in the 1950s was so great that the drop was the second highest among cities in the nation.

The heart of each city was filled with old factories, dilapidated tenements, and abandoned houses. Companies that remained in Rhode Island followed the interstate highways and, with state-supported industrial mortgages, headed for the newly created industrial parks. When Brown & Sharpe moved to the suburbs in 1964, Providence lost its second largest taxpayer. Likewise, upwardly-mobile ethnics and the new middle class headed for Johnston, Cranston, Warwick, Barrington, and other towns, leaving behind deteriorated housing around the closed factories and mills. Urban blight spread as the poor became increasingly concentrated in the central cities, and decaying neighborhoods fell to neglect, vandalism, and arson. Between 1966 and 1980, for example, more than 40 percent of the housing units in South Providence were destroyed and substantial demolition occurred in the neighborhoods of Smith Hill, Federal Hill, and Fox Point. At a time when thousands of new dwellings were being built in the state, the older cities suffered a net loss.

The older cities were ground down by the millstone of rising welfare and social costs and a falling revenue base. Empty factories and boarded-up tenements generated no revenue. The rootedness of the poor, the influx of immigrants, and the exodus of the middle-class compounded the problem. In the 1950s and 1960s the new interstate highway system cut swaths through both Pawtucket and Providence; and while decidedly necessary, taxable property disappeared in its path.

Rhode Island has one of the highest percentages of elderly in the nation, and veterans constitute an unusually large proportion of the population. Their political power, and a sense of generosity and appreciation for both the elderly and veterans, produced tax exemptions for them which, in turn, increased city revenue problems. For example, homestead exemptions constituted the largest segment of non-taxable property in Providence by the 1990s.

In 1982 Providence held about 17 percent of Rhode Island's total population; yet it had 35 percent of the welfare recipients in the entire state. Moreover, Providence had more than three-quarters of the state's minority welfare cases, while cities like Warwick and Cranston had less than one percent. A 1976 study of Central Falls, the tiniest, poorest, most densely populated city, concluded that its situation was almost hopeless. It recommended that Central Falls be merged with Pawtucket or Lincoln. But neither of these neighbors cared to shoulder such a burden. Central Falls became notorious for being the cocaine capital of southern New England. Because Central Falls lacked money, the state took complete financial control of its schools in 1992.

After World War II the suburbanization of the Providence metropolitan area produced a boom for the outlying towns. Garden City in Cranston, started in 1947, was the state's first planned suburban shopping center, and the nearby Dean Estates attracted professional and business people. Subsequent intensive commercial development on Bald Hill Road saw the opening of Midland (now Rhode Island) Mall in 1968 and Warwick Mall in 1970. These shopping areas and additional ones that sprang up in Lincoln and nearby Massachusetts sucked the retail life from Providence, and every department store in the city eventually closed. Providence, which in 1953 commanded 53 percent of the state's retail business, had less than 20 percent by 1980. The economic recession of 1990–1991 finished several die-hard retailers. Vacant stores lined the downtown streets, waiting for other uses or destruction. For example, the Outlet Store building was gutted in a spectacular fire in October 1986, but in 1992 Johnson & Wales University bought the site and built a

dormitory and the Gaebe Commons. J&W also took over a number of other properties including the vacant Gladding's department store and the WJAR-TV building. The Shepard's department store building became the Providence branch of the University of Rhode Island in 1995. While Providence shrank in the 1950s, 1960s, and 1970s, the suburbs and southern and western parts of the state grew appreciably. Newport County experienced continued growth despite the departure of the Navy fleet in the 1970s.

Revival required visions and hard work, and it took several decades of struggle. As far back as the 1940s Providence Mayor Dennis Roberts sought to initiate plans for a revitalized capital city. As a result of his efforts, a newly reorganized planning commission issued the city's first master plan in 1946. This was something that had been sought since 1914 when the commission was first created. Its appraisals were frank and its proposals generally modest, but little from this plan became reality because the city faced staggering financial troubles and a declining tax base. In 1960 a second master plan called for the relocation of the railroad tracks and terminal, a civic center for sports and entertainment, and a pedestrian mall in the shopping district. The relocation of the

Antoinette Downing (1904-2001), pictured here when she was chair of the Rhode Island Historical Preservation Commission, and Alfred Van Liew, president of the Heritage Foundation of Rhode Island, stand in the General Assembly room of the Old State House (built 1762) in Providence. This is where Rhode Island debated the issues of independence in 1776. The restored interior symbolizes the work of preservationists all over the state. Courtesy, Antoinette Downing

railroad was shelved at the time because of its prohibitive cost, and several blocks of Westminster Street were converted into a pedestrian mall with disastrous results to the businesses on the streets. In the early 1990s the street was reopened to vehicular traffic. The one great project to be completed successfully was the Providence Civic Center (now the Dunkin' Donuts Center). The opening of the civic center in 1973 was the first major public project in the revival of Providence.

These efforts paralleled significant developments in the attempt to preserve and restore some of the city's rich architectural heritage. Considerable credit for this accomplishment must be given to Antoinette Downing and the Providence Preservation Society. A native of New Mexico, Downing had made a name for herself with her extensive architectural study, *Early Homes in Rhode Island* (1937), and her work in a citywide historic survey of Newport. In 1952 she was asked to prepare a survey of Providence so historic houses could be saved from the interstate highway construction project that cut through the middle of the city. When she learned that many of the oldest houses on Benefit Street were scheduled for destruction in the name of urban renewal, she secured funds from federal housing authorities. With the backing of John Nicholas Brown, who was equally upset about the demolition of several blocks

of historic houses on College Hill by Brown University's expansion, they launched the Providence Preservation Society in 1956. Brown's president Henry Wriston had described his demolition efforts as "the greatest slum clearance since Sherman burned Atlanta." Downing's efforts and those of hundreds of volunteers saved the historic College Hill area and turned its houses into a showcase of Providence.

In 1963 Governor John Chafee selected Downing to organize the Rhode Island Historic Preservation Commission. Since then this agency has acted as a watchdog over the entire state, saved many buildings, encouraged private developers to renovate rather than raze, and published surveys of historic buildings for every town. In 1970 the College Hill Historic District became Rhode Island's first, and by 2004 all but four towns had at least one official historic district. Providence had 30. In addition, hundreds of individual buildings are registered even though they are not in historic districts, giving Rhode Island the highest percentage of buildings on the National Historic Register of any state. These efforts immeasurably improved the aesthetic quality of Rhode Island and lured thousands of tourists. The Providence Preservation Society's annual "Festival of Houses" gives residents and visitors alike a chance to inspect the benefits of historic preservation. In 1990 at age 85, Antoinette Downing retired from her commission, and she died in 2001 at 96 years old, a nationally-honored preservationist.

The 1970s were marked by such evidence that Providence was recovering that the *New York Times*, the *Christian Science Monitor*, and *Town & Country* ran feature stories on the city. A 1980 article in the *Times* declared that "poor, shabby Providence is blossoming." The city had suffered from economic decline for so long that it was usually described as "grubby." But the transformation had begun. The financial situation of the city had improved somewhat and the Great Society programs pumped huge sums of money into inner cities. Cianci, Providence's Republican mayor at the time, received a friendly reception from the Republican administration in Washington, DC, when applying for urban development grants. By the end of the 1970s, the city had cleared and redeveloped the Randall Square (now Moshassuck Square) area and most of the blighted sections of North Main Street. In 1981 the federal government completed the first phase of the development of the Roger Williams National Memorial on North Main Street. It was on land that had been donated to the city in 1928 by Judge Jerome J. Hahn in memory of his father, Isaac Hahn, who had been the state's first Jewish person elected to public office.

Along South Main Street, old warehouses were converted into attractive shops, offices, apartments, and fine restaurants. Just as they did in the 1920s, the banking and business communities proclaimed their faith in the city and erected the new Hospital Trust and 40 Westminster Tower skyscrapers in the financial district. The empty Loew's State Theater reopened as the Ocean State Theater (now the Providence Performing Arts Center). City Hall had been restored, the Biltmore Hotel reopened as a luxury hostelry, and Roger Williams Park Zoo, threatened with closure in 1971, was by 1982 rated as the best in New England.

In 1982 Fleet Bank revealed plans to build a $50 million office tower next to its headquarters facing Kennedy Plaza. The city also announced that federal officials had approved a $68 million Capital Center project. This grand project would lead to the most visible signs and examples of the Providence renaissance. When it was done, Providence had new office buildings, new hotels, a giant retail emporium in the Providence Place Mall, Waterplace Park, and a whole new waterfront.

With such visible evidence of revival and recognition by national media, it was particularly galling when the *Wall Street Journal* printed a sneering article about Rhode Island in 1983. The writer said that Rhode Island was a "dowdy neighbor" to the rest of New England and Providence was a "smudge beside the fast lane to Cape Cod." He referred to Governor Joseph Garrahy as "a former beer salesman" and said the state's old mills were filled with "dingy sweatshops around Providence, which turn out much of the country's trinket jewelry." The article noted that the New England Mafia was headquartered in Providence, the public schools were the worst in New England, oil tank farms marred the upper Narragansett Bay, and the Providence mayor had been indicted for kidnapping and extortion. It was all painfully true, but so one-sided. Nevertheless, the criticism acted as a further goad for changes that were already underway.

The state in general, and Providence in particular, had already begun to ascend. Well before the nasty *Wall Street Journal* article, much had been done and major plans were unfolding. In the 1970s Providencians agreed that downtown was dreary and nearly dead.

J. Joseph Garrahy, governor (1977–1985) and lieutenant governor (1969–1977), is the son of immigrants. He began his political career as a state senator from the Smith Hill area of Providence in 1962 and rose to deputy majority leader by 1967. He is particularly remembered for his leadership in the Great Blizzard of 1978, and his famous flannel shirt is now part of the collection at the Rhode Island Historical Society. Courtesy, Governor J. Joseph Garrahy

"resurrected" (*Adweek's Marketing*), had experienced a "renaissance" (*USA Today*), and was "the safest city in the U.S." (*Parade Magazine*), "the coolest city" (*Seventeen*), a "Hot City" (*Newsweek*), "an enlightened city" (*Utne Reader*), and in 2000 and 2001 the "best place to live in the East" (*Money Magazine*). It attracted ESPN's *Extreme Games* in 1995 and 1996 and NBC's *Gravity Games* in 1999, 2000, and 2001. The city basked in a postcard view of itself in the NBC series *Providence*, which ran from January 1999 through 2003.

While Mayor Cianci undoubtedly led the cheering, the renaissance was paid for by $1.5 billion in federal, state, and private money. The most visionary ideas came from architects like Connecticut-born William D. Warner, "the man who moves rivers," and artists like Californian Barnaby Evans, the creator of "WaterFire." Warner had already had a substantial impact on Providence with his preservation work in the Benefit Street/ College Hill district in the 1960s and the Orms Street/Moshassuck Square project in the 1970s. In 1981 Warner first suggested that the rivers be uncovered by demolishing the Crawford Street bridge ("the world's widest bridge") and removing "Suicide Circle" where the war memorial stood. This idea led to his design of Waterplace Park and the riverwalk. Completed in the summer of 1994, the beauty of Waterplace, the arched bridges, and

But, between 1980 and 1981 the city had pushed "Operation Clean-Up" and "Art in City Life," which spruced up the city and emphasized the role of arts and culture in revitalization. More importantly, the Capital Center project was launched in 1981–1982, which promised to transform a major section of the city. The railroad tracks that slashed through the heart of the city were relocated underground and a new station erected. As the project evolved it led to the uncovering and realigning of the Woonasquatucket and Moshassuck rivers and the creation of Waterplace Park and the riverwalk. The rebirth of the rivers led to the creation of WaterFire on December 31, 1994, to mark the 10th First Night celebration in Providence. By the late 1980s and 1990s, Providence was in the national spotlight as a city that was

the river walkway caused one longtime resident of Rhode Island to exclaim, "I can't believe this is Providence! This is so beautiful."

Even as the Capital Center site was being cleared, on New Year's Eve 1985, Providence artists staged First Night—a family-oriented, non-alcoholic festival copied from Boston. Thousands came year after year over the next decade to celebrate First Night, which was always crowned by a huge fireworks display over the State House. To mark the 10th anniversary of First Night the artist Barnaby Evans created WaterFire. He was inspired by the newly completed Waterplace Park to place a row of 11 fiery braziers in the river from the Waterplace basin to Steeple Street. The effect was so amazing that what was to be a one-time-only work of art was transformed into Providence's most attractive summer-night spectacle. Evans declared, "WaterFire is an attempt to create something that is open to the entire community, that will appeal to all ages." Over the next decade WaterFire grew in frequency and size (100 fires on three rivers), attracting thousands to the heart of the capital city and capturing international attention of art journals and tourist publications. When the economic recession caused the suspension of First Night for New Year's Eve 2003, the artistic community and the city of Providence kept the celebration alive by staging "Bright Night," complete with a special WaterFire show.

After *USA Today* profiled Providence in a 1996 series on America's "renaissance cities," Mayor Cianci seized upon the term and proclaimed Providence to be the "Renaissance City." To emphasize and capitalize on the idea, a connection and exchange was arranged with Florence, Italy, which resulted in the "Splendor of Florence," a display of the art and culture of Florence. Venetian gondolas plied the new Waterplace basin and rivers.

With the Rhode Island School of Design, the arts programs of other colleges and universities, and lower costs for lofts and studios, an increasing number of artists made Providence their home. The entire arts community experienced synergy. Providence created the Downcity Arts District and cleared the way for lofts in abandoned factories and downtown buildings. In 1987 the Providence Parks Department began sponsoring the Convergence Arts Festival in Roger Williams Park,

and by 1996 it became part of the summer activities in downtown Providence. This activity attracted the 16th International Sculpture Conference to Providence in June 1996.

Linked first to Rhode Island College and then to Brown University, Trinity Repertory Theater also expanded its operations. A number of small theater groups flourished, and the Providence Performing Arts Center hosted the touring companies of major Broadway shows, such as *Cats*, *Phantom of the Opera*, and *Les Miserables*. An improved Rhode Island Philharmonic played to large audiences, and Ann Danis, the state's only professional woman conductor, founded the Ocean State Chamber Orchestra in 1991.

Added to all of this was the artistry of Johnson & Wales University's College of Culinary Arts which helped make Providence into a gourmet's delight. The city was regarded as having better restaurants than Boston, and several were favorably reviewed by the *New York Times* food critics.

Providence cannot rest on its laurels because it requires continual effort to keep the forward momentum. In 2003 the new reform mayor, David Cicilline, moved immediately to confront the city's serious fiscal problems and reform the Providence Police Department, which had been rocked by scandals during the Cianci administration. And, the great effort to rebuild and improve the physical character of the city continues. Businesses that had shied away from Providence during the Cianci years because of endemic corruption began to look more favorably upon the city. Within the first five months of the Cicilline administration GTech, the world leader in the production of lottery systems, announced that it was relocating its headquarters to the Capital Center. In an effort to support the arts community and promote tourism, Mayor Cicilline announced the creation of a new cabinet-level department of art, culture, and tourism.

Even as this book was being written, two enormous public works projects estimated to cost a billion dollars were underway in Providence. One project is invisible to the eye but will help clean up Narragansett Bay; the other will physically transform part of the city. The one is an undertaking deep beneath the city that creates a massive system

Richard Bernier, the Narragansett Bay commission project engineer, inspects the start of the huge, three-mile tunnel being dug under Providence in June 2003. This monumental undertaking is intended to remedy the persistent problem of sewer overflows that pollute Narragansett Bay. Courtesy, The Providence Journal

to catch the overflow of sewage, and the other is the relocation of Interstate 195.

The sewage overflow project will cost $550 million. It has been designed to catch most of the 2.2 billion gallons of untreated sewage that overflows annually from the Providence metropolitan area into Narragansett Bay during major rain storms. A three-mile tunnel, 30-feet in diameter, runs from under The Foundry near downtown's Providence Place Mall to Field's Point wastewater treatment facility. The tunnel, several hundred feet underground, is connected to enormous storage pits and giant pumps which carry the sewage up to the water treatment plant. Phase I of the project is expected to be completed by 2007, but building the entire system will take nearly 20 years.

The I-195 plan is projected to cost $450 million with completion not until 2012. It will see the highway relocated to below the hurricane barrier, resulting in the reconnection of the jewelry district with downtown; the freeing of eight acres for redevelopment; the construction of 14 new bridges; and the addition of five miles of new city streets and 4,100 new feet to the riverfront walkway. The

riverwalk will connect with the existing waterfront walk that extends all the way to Waterplace Park and the Providence Place Mall. Not surprisingly, the architect for the proposed walkway is William Warner.

These great projects do not exhaust the plans that are being considered or proposed for the redevelopment of Providence. In 1999–2000 city planners unveiled a grand 20-year plan for Providence that was the equivalent to 10 Capital Center projects. They proposed a 120-acre harbor redevelopment plan of housing, restaurants, parks, offices, and marinas called "Narragansett Landing," that stretched from the Cranston line to Point Street. The relocation of I-195 began to clear the way for this project. However, many grand plans for development of the Providence Harbor have been advanced since the 1880s and none was ever carried through. Next, "Westminster Crossing" would create twelve new acres for development as I-95 from Atwells Avenue to Broad Street would be decked over and Westminster Street reconnected. Finally, the "Promenade," running from behind the Providence Place Mall to Olneyville Square, would encompass 200

The Newport Restoration Foundation, established by Doris Duke, saved a large number of colonial homes. In the foreground on Mill Street is the Beriah Brown House (circa 1709), beyond is the Billings Coggeshall House (circa 1784), and an old fire station (circa 1880s). Courtesy, Newport Restoration Foundation

acres for new housing, bike paths, and new buildings. None of these proposals is a small idea, but neither was the idea of moving the rivers or relocating I-195. As has been said of New York City many times, "This will be a great place when they finally get it built."

While Providence's "renaissance" was creating an aesthetic urban environment, Newport still generally excelled Providence as a tourist destination. However, Newport also experienced the stress of change. Keith Stokes, executive director of the Newport County Chamber of Commerce, suggested that the two individuals who had the most impact on Newport since World War II were Doris Duke and Ted Turner. While there was considerable truth in this assessment, it overlooked other long-term efforts and individuals, especially Katherine Urquhart Warren. In Newport, preservation and planning merged after World War II to create a tourist magnet. While the rest of the state pursued industrial development, planning in Newport heeded the advice of a 1926 report by a well-known New England planner, Arthur A. Schurtleff. "Industrial developments are incompatible with the enhancement of the city," he wrote, "and should be regarded as a liability." Eight additional planning reports up to 1962 expressed much the same view.

While industrial development took a backseat in Newport, plans for a better city never fully materialized. The rich and powerful secluded themselves on Ocean Drive

and Bellevue Avenue, the Navy occupied the upper harbor and surrounding land, and those who worked for and serviced both of these groups clustered in the town's run-down colonial castoffs. By 1947 the drastic reductions in war contracts and installations caused some Newporters to conclude that the city was at the "crossroads of destiny." Changing lifestyles and the Depression had turned many of the mansions into white elephants, so that some of the well-to-do summer people had departed. Others put their "cottages" up for sale, while others looked fearfully into the future. After seeing the construction of the "terrifyingly modern" high school across from her cottage, Idle Hour, Mrs. John Payson Adams (Muriel Vanderbilt) said that she feared that Bellevue Avenue "will inevitably succumb to subdividers who will finish the place." Indeed, a roofing contractor named Louis J. Chartier did buy some mansions on Ocean Drive and converted them into apartments that rented for $5,000 a year. The fact that some of the grand cottages were saved was a result of the effort and foresight of Katherine Urquhart Warren.

In 1945 Warren rescued the Hunter House from destruction, launched the Preservation Society of Newport County shortly thereafter, and in 1948 persuaded Countess Szechenyi (Gladys Vanderbilt) to open the family mansion, The Breakers, to the public. Soon several mansions, including Marble House and The Elms, came under the society's care and were opened to the public. By 1956 the *Wall Street Journal* carried an article on Newport entitled "Hometown, U.S.A.," and quoted Warren as saying, "All you need is leadership. Money is no object at all. I could raise $100,000 or $200,000 over the lunch table any day in the week. If we only had someone who could take charge." In fact, she herself took charge of the preservation movement. Over the years the Preservation Society came to own a growing collection of 11 properties, and these became a top tourist attraction. The Breakers alone is viewed by 400,000 visitors each year. While the Society concentrated most of its energy on mansions, tobacco heiress Doris Duke set out to save colonial structures. Founded in 1968, Duke's Newport Restoration Foundation saved and restored 83 colonial houses by the mid-1980s, giving Newport one of the nation's largest

The Polish pianist Piotr Anderszewski performed at "Marble House" in July 2001. The impresario Dr. Mark P. Malkovich, III, scours the international classical music scene to bring new talent annually to the "City by the Sea." Courtesy, Newport Music Festival

concentrations of 18th century houses. In addition, Doris Duke bankrolled the saving of Queen Anne Square from 1976 to 1978 which created a sweeping vista from the harbor up to Trinity Church. The restoration and preservation of so many architectural treasures, and the town's location on the ocean, continue to give Newport a charm and glamour that is hard to match.

Newport unquestionably had to make the transition from a home port to a tourist destination after the Navy withdrew the cruiser-destroyer fleet in 1973. The city planners recognized that the city was "adrift from the Navy pullout and tourism would be the life raft." Under the Newport Development Agency the entire wharf area was redeveloped with modern shops and restaurants in both the Brick Market and Bowen's Wharf. America's Cup Avenue was laid out, and nearby two new hotels and a marina were built. One of the most dramatic transformations occurred on Goat Island which was transferred to the Newport Redevelopment Agency around 1972 and went from being the location of the U.S. Torpedo Station to becoming the site for a luxury hotel, condominiums, restaurants, and a marina for pleasure craft. Critical to tourism was the

existence of the Newport-Pell Bridge, which had opened in June 1969. Meant to be part of a four-lane highway running from Interstate 95 to Cape Cod, the bridge was erected before the rest of the project was abandoned, but it proved to be a lifeline to Newport.

The city concentrated on tourism and took advantage of the elevated quality of the Navy presence on Aquidneck Island. The fleet left, taking with it the multitude of ordinary sailors who had made West Pelham Street into "Blood Alley." Instead, there was the Naval War College; various training institutes for officers and chaplains; and the Naval Undersea Warfare Center, the Navy's "premier research and engineering facility for submarines and underwater technology"—all high quality and much less intrusive. Thames Street was gentrified on both ends and filled with smart shops, antique stores, boutiques, and good eating places. It all fit nicely into the transformed harbor front. Newport enjoyed the reputation of having several premiere musical festivals, including the Newport Music Festival with its classical music in the mansions, described as one of the "Top 100 events in North America." In addition, on the grounds of the historic Fort Adams State Park, were the Newport Folk

Festival (returning in 1985 after an absence of 16 years) and the Newport Jazz Festival, which returned permanently in 1991 after fleeing in 1971 due to youthful disorder.

The notoriety of Ted Turner had significant consequences. Turner, founder of CNN and owner of WTBS and the Atlanta Braves, made the America's Cup fun. Sometimes called "Captain Courageous" or "Captain Outrageous," Turner captained his yacht to a successful defense of the America's Cup in 1977. Newport's society queen, Eileen Slocum, regarded Turner as "riff-raff," but he lifted the America's Cup from its stodgy yacht-club world and made the cover of *Sports Illustrated* and the nightly news, generating national interest in the races and Newport. Larger and larger crowds poured into Newport for the 1980 and 1983 cup races. When New Zealand won the America's Cup in 1983, 100,000 people converged on the city for the seventh race.

One effect of the attention was a tremendous real estate rush in Newport which overwhelmed the town in the 1980s. This resulted in the transformation of the waterfront from a traditional maritime harbor with boat builders, ship chandlers, and commercial fishing activity into a residential area with condominiums, timeshares, and "dockominiums"—docking slips and wharfs owned by condominiums. Virtually all of the traditional uses of the harbor were squeezed out and moved to the Melville Marina section of Portsmouth. Ocean Drive also felt the pressure, and in 1984 overdevelopment there resulted in a section being stripped of its designation as a National Historic Landmark. This marked the first time that the U.S. Department of the Interior had taken such an action.

Unquestionably Newport had replaced the old "solid summer economy" of high society and the rough-and-rowdy economy of the sailors with a "motoring tourist economy." While the tourists were the lifeblood, they were a mixed blessing. One Newporter described her hometown as a "zoo, and every year it gets worse." What had once been a close-knit black community in Newport was by 1982 described as totally disrupted and dispersed all over Newport County. A similar thing had happened in Providence as gentrification in the Fox Point area displaced the Cape Verdean community and squeezed out the Portuguese. In the Providence case, the financially-strapped city collaborated with restorers and developers to alter the character of the neighborhood in order to increase the tax base. The spread of historic district designation generally signaled the coming of gentrification as new funds and loans became available to people seeking to restore historic structures.

While the cities labored to save the architectural heritage of Rhode Island, those in the rural and scenic areas worked to save open spaces, farms, and forests. Foster and Glocester struggled to protect their rural heritage as city people sought to build homes in the quiet countryside. They coined the slogan "Keep Glocester Rural" and passed zoning ordinances calling for a minimum of five-acre building lots; however, opposition from smaller landowners and development-minded residents reduced it to three acres. In the 1980s and 1990s real estate prices skyrocketed to such an extent that even a three-acre parcel was beyond most middle-class families. In fact, "affordable housing" became a highly charged issue in the state, and the enlarged lot requirements in every town outside of Providence virtually excluded low-income families. In 2002 the General Assembly revised the 1991 Low and Moderate Income Housing Act, permitting private builders to erect more units than a town's zoning would allow, provided that 20 percent of the units would sell as affordable housing. It also called upon each town to provide 10 percent of its housing as affordable housing. The revision allowed developers to bypass the local ordinances and go to the housing appeals board for approval. Among the towns confronted by the effect of the new law in the first year were Bristol, Cumberland, Smithfield, Westerly, Charlestown, Lincoln, and Exeter. Because so many controversial proposals emerged within the first year, the General Assembly quickly enacted a moratorium in early 2004.

As a tourist destination Block Island was threatened with being overrun, and many sought to cash in on the invasion. Ferry boats full of day-trippers poured onto the island and moped and bicycle operators began to multiply. When Block Island tried to regulate the number of mopeds, the state said it

"2 Lanes: Safe and Sane." Expressing opposition to widening the highway to four lanes, Lester Stasey stands by one of the many signs dotting U.S. 44 through Glocester. Opponents feared that highway expansion would accelerate development and destroy the town's rural character. Courtesy, George H. Kellner

Keith Lewis sits on the bluffs above the ocean at Block Island, dubbed one of 12 "Great Places in the Western Hemisphere." He led the movement that fought over-development, and by 2001 resulted in the preservation of 40 percent of Block Island for open spaces. Courtesy, Malcolm Greenaway

could not be done. This so angered the town council that in May 1984 they called a meeting to consider seceding. Massachusetts, which in the 17th century had seriously sought to extend its jurisdiction over Rhode Island, graciously invited Block Island to join Massachusetts if it came to secession. It happened that a special session of the Rhode Island General Assembly was summoned to deal with repealing all of the legislation meant to implement the Greenhouse Compact. This highly touted, complex proposal to promote the economic growth of the state was overwhelmingly rejected by the voters in a June 12th referendum. Conveniently, the Block Island moped problem was added to the restricted agenda of the special session, and the legislature granted the island the power to regulate the mopeds. However, much more serious than tourists was the threat of real estate development.

The Nature Conservancy has described Block Island as "one of the 12 last great places in the western hemisphere." The fact that it remains a great place is a direct result of the dedicated, unrelenting efforts of people like Keith A. Lewis. A sixth-generation Block Islander, Lewis fought to keep the island from being utterly transformed by real estate development. The natural beauty and rustic charm of Block Island created such a demand that by the 1970s the land rush threatened to destroy the very reason why people wanted to visit or reside there.

The organized effort to slow down and arrest the rapid development of Block Island was begun by Captain John Robinson Lewis in 1972. He took the lead in founding the Block Island Conservancy, to save a 38-acre site called Rodman's Hollow. This organization was only the second land trust in Rhode Island. His son Keith, a merchant marine engineer, donned the mantle in 1984. He began a series of property donations and bargain land sales of his family farm to the Block Island Conservancy, which resulted in the preservation of a large tract adjacent to Rodman's Hollow. He could have received an estimated $6 million if he had sold his land to developers.

Lewis then spent the next two years lobbying the General Assembly to pass a bill that allowed Block Island to levy a real estate transfer fee to be used for the preservation of open spaces. He triumphed in the face of opposition from the Rhode Island Association of Realtors and the Rhode Island Builders Association. Block Island remains one of only two towns that has been empowered to levy this transfer fee. This bill led to the creation of the Block Island Land Trust, which used the collected fees to buy land. When Keith Lewis began only about 5 percent of Block Island had been preserved as open land, but by 2003 he and his dedicated band of preservationists had managed to save at least 40 percent of the island.

In the years since 1986, Block Island has been joined by many other Rhode Island towns that have established land trusts. Where only four land trusts existed in the state in 1980, by 2003 there were 47. Furthermore, the pace of creating land trusts to preserve open spaces accelerated in the 1990s. From 1990 to 1998, 10 land trusts formed, and by the end of 2002, 16 more had been established. Driving this movement was the rising concern over the disappearance of open spaces and also state bond issues that encouraged municipalities to create land trusts.

From 1986 to November 2000, Rhode Island voters overwhelmingly approved a series of bond issues amounting to $186 million for open spaces, historic preservation, recreation, bike paths, and farmland development rights. The formation of municipal land trusts quickened as seven more towns created a land trust in 2000 alone. Preserving open spaces especially accelerated in South County in the 1990s as that area began to experience rapid development. The state Department of Environmental Management (DEM) had the responsibility to oversee the granting of public money and to acquire ownership or rights to land. Since 1980 the state acquired nearly 25,000 acres, and DEM has a target of obtaining around 3,000 to 3,400 additional acres each year. In addition to state and federal funds for open spaces, a coalition of private organizations created partnerships to protect land. These included the Champlin Foundation (which granted $31.2 million between January 1, 1982 and December 31, 2002 to help to save over 17,000 acres), the Doris Duke Charitable Foundation, the Audubon Society of Rhode Island, and the Nature Conservancy. By the end of 2002 all of these efforts had resulted in 13 percent (or 93,000 acres) of Rhode Island being protected in various ways.

The historic building and land preservation movements, revitalization of Providence and Newport, and the growing artistic community had by the late 1980s made Rhode Island into an attractive setting for television and motion pictures. Although Little Compton rejected overtures to film part of *The Witches of Eastwick*, such movies as *Mr. North*, *Mystic Pizza* (1987), *Complex World* (1989), and *Reversal of Fortune* (1990) were filmed locally. With the emergence of director Michael Corrente and screen writers Peter and Bob Farrelly in the 1990s, "Little Rhody left a pretty large footprint in movies and TV," wrote the *Providence Journal.* The Farrelly brothers, born in Cumberland, relied on humor, film star Jim Carrey and Rhode Island's scenery for such box office hits as *Dumb and Dumber* and *There's Something About Mary*. Both films held their Hollywood-style premiers in their home state, the former in Warwick in 1994 and the latter at the Stadium Theater in Woonsocket in 1998. At the same time Corrente used the streets of Providence in his examination of Italian youth in *Federal Hill* (1994); a storefront in Pawtucket to shoot *American Buffalo* (1995), starring Dennis Franz and Dustin Hoffman; and the Cranston Street Armory as a film studio for his revealing coming-of-age movie, *Outside Providence* (1996). In addition another native son, James Woods, filmed *Killer: A Journal of Murder* (1994) at the state prison, and the BBC took over the Newport mansions for its production of *The Buccaneers* (1994) which aired on public television. Arnold Schwazenegger also filmed some action scenes for *True Lies* (1994) at a Newport mansion.

Rhode Island's Economic Development Corporation established a film and video office to promote and facilitate productions in the state. Its director, Rick Smith, said that filmmakers came when "we started to sell the state's remarkable architecture instead of its beaches." In 1997 alone directors and stars such as Steven Spielberg (*Amistad*), Anthony Hopkins and Brad Pitt (*Meet Joe Black*), Alec Baldwin, Carmeron Diaz, Morgan Freeman, Ben Stiller, Matthew McConaughey, and others came to practice their craft in Rhode Island. The movie companies recruited locals as extras and millions of dollars were added to the state's economy.

By the mid-1990s the Rhode Island International Film Festival, the Newport International Film Festival, and the New Latin American Film Festival brought stars and patrons from Providence to Newport. Lesser known filmmakers and filming equipment suppliers set up operations in Providence, and nearly a dozen film and documentary companies had emerged. The most successful of these was Gary Glassman's Providence Pictures Company. By 2000 this studio had produced or edited at least 15 productions for the Discovery Channel and PBS, including the acclaimed "Lost King of the Maya" for *Nova* on PBS. When film crews descended in the 1990s, a *Providence Journal* headline proclaimed, "Just Call Us Hollywood East," and amusingly suggested that Rhode Island "started to look like Universal City." While the rush had diminished by 2004, the star attraction, Rhode Island itself, had grown in stature in the nation.

Unquestionably, the credit belongs to the visions of dedicated individuals, planners, organizations, public officials, and spirited citizens. They laid the foundation for a post-industrial economy, reformed corruption, revitalized the cities and towns, and preserved the architectural heritage and natural environment of the state during the last quarter century. However, the reforms and visions are never-ending. If the voters approve separation of powers, the implementation of this reform will require diligent attention. The people will have to continue working to create the new economy and protect its cultural and physical environment. If the past is any indicator, Rhode Islanders will meet the challenges and overcome all adversity to build a better future. After all, the state's motto is "Hope."

WaterFire, created by the artist Barnaby Evans as a "fire-sculpture installation," evolved into a "civic ritual" attended by thousands each summer. WaterFire helped to transform downtown Providence. Courtesy, WaterFire/ Providence. Photograph by Barnaby Evans

Chapter Fifteen

CHRONICLES OF LEADERSHIP

The economic history of Rhode Island can be divided into four chronological periods: agriculture in the 17th century, oceanic commerce in the 18th century, the dominance of industry in the 19th century, and 20th century "deindustrialization," with diversification extending into the present century.

Until 1669 the only towns in Rhode Island were found around the edges of Narragansett Bay. Newport, situated on a protected harbor at the mouth of the inlet, developed into the premier town in the colony. Seated near almost all of the good farm land, Newport began to trade agricultural products with neighboring colonies.

The hospitality of Rhode Island for religious dissenters proved to be the key to Newport's entry into oceanic commerce by the end of the 17th century. The Jews and Quakers were free to practice their religion, and each brought connections that were at the heart of international trade. Newport raced ahead of the rest of the colony and by the middle of the 18th century it was a prosperous, sophisticated town—the fifth largest in Britain's North American colonies. Because Rhode Island had no raw materials or native products that were desired by others, the oceanic commerce was almost entirely based on transporting merchandise and the re-export of goods, such as rum.

Providence, on the other hand, was mostly a farming and fishing village which had a single dirt street until the 18th century. The first wharf for coastal trade was not built until 1680. Providence, like Bristol and other villages, began to follow Newport's path to the ocean, and by mid-18th century Providence was catching up.

The imperial wars damaged the sea trade, and the American Revolution left Newport in a devastated condition after three years of British occupation. Providence surged ahead and soon became the leading city in the state. Even before the Revolution, some of Providence's leading merchants had shifted from oceanic commerce to manufacturing. In the desperate search for economic opportunities, Providence merchants pioneered trade with China and sailed across the world. More significantly, they began the industrial revolution in America. Samuel Slater's power-driven spinning machine went to work in 1791 in Pawtucket. This led to the development of the textile trade, which was Rhode Island's leading industry until the 20th century. Oceanic commerce, including the China trade, helped merchants accumulate the necessary capital for industrialization. This turned Rhode Island into America's first urban, manufacturing state, and made Providence a powerhouse by the second half of the 19th century.

However, by the turn of this century, things had changed dramatically. The state's industrial base had melted away. Even the U.S. Navy, which had a large presence in the state since the 1880s, transferred most of its assets and personnel to other naval installations. Rhode Island worked to diversify its economy and create new industries and lines of endeavor.

As the state deindustrialized it turned to service industries, tourism, education, and health. Electronics and bio-tech enterprises were also encouraged and welcomed. Today, smokestack industries are being replaced by high-tech, bio-tech, information technology, and financial services. Rhode Island now can boast that it has a widely diversified economy. However, as a small state it still relies upon the ingenuity of its people to make a living.

Steamships docked at the wharves on the Providence River, 1907. Courtesy, Louis H. McGowan Rhode Island postcard collection

ALDEN YACHTS CORPORATION

Alden Yachts Corporation, located in Portsmouth, Rhode Island evolved from a division of the firm that exclusively built J.G. Alden design sailing yachts that were well-known for their structural endurance, classic design, and artistry. The company, which began building sailing yachts in 1976, has progressed into several divisions: Alden Yachts, Alden Yachts Brokerage of Rhode Island, Alden Yachts Charters, and Alden Yachts Service Yard. But the heart of the company still remains in the exquisite design and expert building of its boats. No one appreciates this more than David MacFarlane, president of Alden Yachts.

MacFarlane began working as general manager for the company in 1980. At that time, the company primarily built the J. G. Alden 44 Sailing Yacht. The company expanded its product line in 1983 with the addition of the Alden Yachts 50, 52, and 54 to the inventory. The boats were growing larger and so was the company.

In 1996 MacFarlane and a few other investors bought out TRCO, the rubber and chemical company that owned the enterprise, and became independent owners of the Alden Yachts Corporation. Expanding its four divisions, the company grew from 20 to over 60 employees.

Alden Yachts is known for superior custom composite construction.

David A. MacFarlane, president of Alden Yachts Corporation.

Diversification, while maintaining quality of service and expertise, has been paramount to the company's success. "We believe in providing a full plate of services at the highest professional level possible," says MacFarlane.

MacFarlane learned at an early age how to distinguish quality and elegance. His father was professional captain of the sailing schooner, *Mistress*. This beauty was the private pleasure yacht of Commodore George Roosevelt, nephew of President Theodore Roosevelt. When MacFarlane was only eight years old, he recalls successfully convincing his father to let him come aboard. "I pestered my dad until he let me go with him," admits MacFarlane. During school breaks, when the boat was in port, MacFarlane's father would let him tour

the vessel, taking in its majestic size and superior craftsmanship. "I liked what I saw. It was then that I fell in love with boats," remembers MacFarlane.

Later, as fate would have it, the 17-year-old MacFarlane was invited to join the crew of *Mistress*. One of the regular crew was badly injured leaving a shortage in the hands needed on deck. The new crew member had to be strong, willing, and ready to obey orders. "They needed someone who was young, strong, and able to keep their mouth shut. I could do that. I fit the bill," jokes MacFarlane. He completed the tour on *Mistress* under his father's guidance. His love and respect for sailing flourished and stayed with him well after he returned to his classes in the fall.

Throughout his high school years and on into college, MacFarlane spent his summers working around sailing yachts. During these summers MacFarlane discovered a new aspiration in the sailing world: racing. He was willing to sacrifice a paycheck just to be on the crew of a racing sailboat. He advanced to sailing longer passages and competed in such races as the Annapolis-Newport Race, Cape May-Newport Race, and the Marble Head-Halifax Race. His passion for racing grew with his level of expertise and he eventually competed in numerous Bermuda races, Trans-Atlantic races, and The America's Cup.

MacFarlane's experiences in racing and his innate love of sailing are immensely useful when working with clients who desire a custom-made sailing yacht. He understands that each new boat owner is unique, with his or her own requirements and specifications for a sailing yacht. MacFarlane and his team of engineers and craftsman are meticulous when carrying out their clients' desires.

The builders take their jobs to heart and often become attached to the sailing yacht they are building. One of the builders remarked to a buyer, "This is your boat now, but at some point you will wish to sell it. You will want something larger or something

Alden Yachts 54 Despedida *enroute to first class honors in Marion Bermuda race.*

repair, and winter storage. This division sees over 200 boats for maintenance or repair each year. Some are being prepared to move to Alden Yachts Brokerage department where the vessels are made available to potential buyers.

Alden Yachts also has a charter division for the adventure seeker not quite ready to purchase his own vessel. Vacations are planned and tailor-made to the individual, whether a short local excursion or a trans-Atlantic voyage. Trips range in price from $3,000 to $200,000 a week. Alden Yachts Charter division plans out and prepares the voyage to meet each traveler's individual wishes.

MacFarlane and his team of specialists provide boating enthusiasts with an array of choices, from a rented vessel to ownership of one's own yacht. MacFarlane's longevity in the business has produced a simple, straight forward philosophy: "We wish to create boats that are classic from conception. That's the goal." This is an accomplishment in which Alden Yachts succeeds time and time again.

new and you will sell it and it will no longer be your boat. But when we build it, it will always be our boat." There is a special tradition at the company. Once a boat is completed, the craftsmen insert a plaque in a secret place hidden in the boat. This commemorative inscription displays the names of every individual who took part in building that particular vessel. However, even the owner is unaware of its existence. At a new boat's launching not only are the new owner and his family present, but every craftsman and all of the family members are invited to the christening as well.

Because of the time allotted for excellence, only about five new custom yachts are built each year. Each yacht averages in size in the mid 50-foot range and the average cost is about $1.5 million. The materials used are hand-selected and tailored to each vessel. Not only is Alden Yachts known for its groundbreaking technology, the company is also set apart for its attention to fine detail. Unlike other boatyards where acetone and resin

are the prevailing aromas, the scent of raw or freshly varnished wood is what permeates the multi-building construction site. The wood interiors are finely finished with drawers in solid mahogany, all with dovetail joints. The cabin lockers are lined with real cedar.

Alden Yachts Service Yard is a continuation of dedication to craftsmanship in the area of maintenance. Fifteen employees work in this division offering refurbishing, general

Alden Yachts 44, second in class finisher in Newport Bermuda classic.

191

AMERICA TRAVEL, INC.

America Travel, Inc. is located in East Providence, a city of 60,000 inhabitants just outside of its bigger namesake, Providence. America Travel celebrated its 30th year in business in 2003 and continues to flourish. Two Portuguese immigrants, Joe Serodio and John Botelho, started the company in 1973 with a $30,000 investment. Two-thirds of that was invested by Serodio, who had wanted to have a travel business since he was a child.

Joe Serodio came to America in 1961 with his parents from the Azores, a group of Portuguese Islands in the Eastern Atlantic. From an early age it had been Serodio's dream to start his own business in the states. The child of a poor farming family, America was the land of opportunity and the place where Serodio believed his dreams could be realized. Serodio got his first taste for business when he opened a successful driving school, the East Providence Driving Academy, which he ran for 20 years. But his goals didn't stop there. He had always loved travel, and set his sights on opening a travel agency, one that would serve the inhabitants of East

Joe Serodio, president of America Travel, Inc.

Providence, especially its sizable Portuguese community. At a church function he was introduced to John Botelho, a travel agent and—like Serodio—a Portuguese immigrant from the Azores, who had also hoped to one day own a piece of the travel business.

In 1973 the two men founded America Travel, Inc. in rented office space on Warren Avenue, one of the main streets of East Providence. Since Serodio was just learning the ins and outs of the travel trade, it was decided that he would concentrate on marketing and sales while Botelho, with his considerable experience as a travel agent, would see to the actual bookings and arrangements of vacation packages. The pair also saw that there was a need for group and wholesale travel services, and they quickly filled the void. In the same year that the company was founded, the men put together two major charters. In July of 1973, for their first group excursion, they chartered TWA for a trip to the Azores. In October of the same year, they put together a Pan Am charter to Málaga and Costa del Sol in Spain for the Amway Corporation.

America Travel continued to grow throughout the 1970s. It became the agency of choice for the Portuguese community in the Providence, East Providence, and southern Massachusetts areas. Serodio believes that their success is a direct result of their advertising and marketing campaigns, which have been a mainstay of the company's strategy since its founding. When they first started the company Serodio went on foot to various social and church events, handing out brochures and leaflets, and as the business grew he expanded into newspaper, radio, and television advertising.

The tremendous success the company had with its group travel business brought about the establishment of Festive Tours in 1980. Where America Travel handles both individual clients as well as groups, Festive Tours was dedicated exclusively to group travel.

As the company continued to grow, Serodio and Botelho decided to purchase a permanent home for the agency. They found a property on Warren Avenue that was up for sale, located on a prominent corner lot just two blocks from

Joe, Inês, and Eugenio Serodio in East Providence, 1965.

America Travel's office in East Providence.

and Liberians. Many of the group tours that Festive puts together are religious pilgrimages to places such as Fatima, Portugal, Lourdes, France, Santiago de Compostela, Spain, the Holy Land, Athens, Cairo, and Rome.

The company has also gone to great lengths to create travel and cultural experiences for members of the Portuguese American community to help them learn more about their Portuguese ancestors who settled in Brazil during the 1940s and 1950s. To that end, Serodio has taken exploratory trips to Brazil to plan customized journeys for his Portuguese American clients. One such area in Brazil is the state capitol of Florianopolis in Santa Catarina, an island just off the coast of Brazil. Travelers also visit areas in and around Rio de Janeiro and São Paulo which was settled by the Portuguese and make stops at churches and shrines, like the Shrine of Our Lady of Aparecida, the Patron Saint of Brazil. Visiting these Portuguese settlements in Brazil gives America Travel clients the opportunity to not only experience their culture in a new environment, but also to do genealogical research on family members who settled in Brazil. Serodio takes great pleasure in helping his clients discover their family heritage, which they may never have known if not for his efforts.

Serodio, who is now 58, still loves to travel and immensely enjoys the fact that he can share his passion with his clients. The journey has now come full circle for him. He came to this country with the dream of owning a travel business. Today this successful enterprise brings him back to the Azores frequently where he shares its beauty with new generations of Portuguese Americans, helping them to see the land of their forefathers for the first time.

where their business first began. Serodio purchased the property on sight, demolished the existing structure, and built a new one-story brick building in its place. The lot also holds several parking spaces, making a trip to their office convenient and more accommodating for their clientele. The 3,000-square-foot office space is tastefully decorated and was designed with customers in mind.

By 1985 the company expanded once again, founding Azores Express, which put together travel itineraries for groups from Providence and Boston, who were traveling to the Azores. The company was owned in partnership with the regional government of the Azores, which was also the major stockholder. In 1988 America Travel sold its shares to its partner, and the company still exists today.

The travel business has changed dramatically since Serodio and Botelho first started in 1973. The company has weathered many local and world events that have had a tremendous impact on travel including the Rhode Island credit union crisis, the Gulf War, and most recently the tragedies of September 11, 2001. In addition, the explosion of the Internet has also drastically changed how people travel. Today many people book their travel online from their home or office and no longer use travel agents. Because of these changes, many travel agencies have closed their doors permanently, but America Travel and Festive Tours have survived. Serodio believes there are a number of reasons for their good fortune. The fact that they have been in business for 30 years and have invested wisely over those years, has enabled them to weather the storms. Their retail service has also always been much more personalized to the point where they are now seeing third generations of families coming to them to book their vacations, honeymoons, and group packages.

America Travel has also fine-tuned some of their offerings to specific ethnic communities such as the Portuguese, immigrant Africans, Cabe Verdeans,

ARDEN ENGINEERING CONSTRUCTORS, LLC

Arden Engineering Constructors, LLC, (originally called Arden Engineering Company, Inc.) was founded in Providence in 1954 by Irwin Arden. Today, the company remains family-owned. Under the capable leadership of Robert M. Bolton, it is a highly respected full-service mechanical and electrical contractor that can handle the installation and maintenance of all critical functions in both newly constructed and renovated buildings. Now located in Pawtucket, Arden's philosophy is the same today as it was back in 1954: *All work performed is based on the concept that creativity and innovation must always be linked to technical know-how.* This underlying principle continues to serve as Arden Engineering Constructors' key to success.

Under the initial leadership of Irwin Arden, the company operated as both a mechanical and general contractor. In the early 1960s two individuals joined the company who would play significant roles in its future. Andrew (Andy) Port, Arden's son-in-law, joined the company working in the accounting

Boiler/chiller room pumping system at T.F. Green Airport in Providence.

Robert M. Bolton, present owner of Arden Engineering Constructors, LLC.

department and would eventually go on to oversee all of its financial aspects. At approximately the same time, Robert H. Bolton joined Arden working as a union pipe fitter. By 1964 he had become a junior project manager on a major construction project at Thule Air Force Base in Greenland. Throughout the '60s and '70s Arden aggressively increased its presence beyond the New England states by developing additional construction projects in Greenland, Newfoundland, and the Caribbean. With the success of the Thule project, Bolton continued as a project manager, overseeing many of the company's international projects, including those in Puerto Rico.

During the mid-1960s, Arden's son Peter also joined the company after returning from military service as an officer in the United States Navy Air Corp. When Irwin Arden died unexpectedly in 1969, Peter, also a talented engineer, became company president. Andy Port was named vice president and Robert H. Bolton was appointed general manager. Over the next 15 years, Peter focused the company toward mechanical construction. Although computers were still in their infancy during the 1970s, Peter decided to invest in this exciting new world of technology. A Burroughs™

mainframe computer was purchased to streamline job costs, accounting, and estimating procedures. Punch cards and 12" tape drives were everywhere.

As the company continued to grow and prosper during the late 1970s, Peter Arden was named chairman, Andy Port became president, and Robert H. Bolton became vice president. In 1980 Bolton was promoted to executive vice president, while appointing Carmine J. Puniello, Steven Arden, and Michael Sweeney as vice presidents.

Puniello, who joined the company in the mid-1960s, brought to Arden his strong engineering background in the areas of Power Piping and Process Systems, which allowed the company to pursue new projects in these fields. Over time, he would create Arden's Quality Assurance program that eventually led to the company's ASME certifications. John Puniello, Carmine's son, also joined the Arden team after graduating from Rhode Island's Roger Williams College, and has steadily worked his way up through the ranks to become a project manager.

In 1985 Peter Arden offered Robert H. Bolton a well-deserved opportunity to purchase certain assets of the company.

Robert H. Bolton (center) and Carmine J. Puniello (right) purchased Arden Engineering Constructors, Inc. from Peter Arden. Robert M. Bolton, vice president (left).

On January 1, 1986 Bolton partnered with Puniello to form Arden Engineering Constructors, Inc. This newly reorganized company then continued to focus its core competencies in three main sectors: HVAC, industrial/power, and environmental applications.

By the early 1990s Bolton's son, Robert M. (Bob) Bolton, who had been working at Arden since he was a teenager, was named vice president. The younger Bolton, who received his mechanical engineering degree from Roger Williams College, immediately moved the company into a new line of business. He created the innovative on-site building services and maintenance division that is offered to all Arden clients. Bolton's vision of a building maintenance division has proven to be a sound business decision, as it has become one of the company's more successful divisions in just a few short years. Michael Sullivan, who has been with Arden since 1998, is vice president of building services.

On January 1, 1999 Arden was sold to PSEG Energy Technologies, Inc., a business unit of Public Service Enterprise Group of New Jersey. However, this acquisition proved to be a short-lived chapter in Arden's history. During the second half of 2002, PSEG decided to exit the mechanical construc-

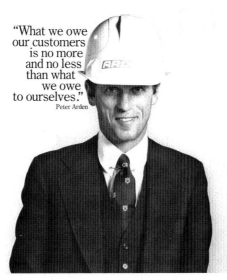

"What we owe our customers is no more and no less than what we owe to ourselves."
Peter Arden

Peter Arden ran the company after his father, Irwin.

tion market. On April 18, 2003, Bob Bolton purchased the company back from PSEG. The newly invigorated business operates under the banner of Arden Engineering Constructors, LLC—and is stronger than ever.

Throughout Arden's history, many factors have contributed to its continuing growth and success as an industry leader in its field.

Prefabrication: many of the piping assemblies built by Arden for its wide range of projects are prefabricated at the company's Pawtucket plant. Arden has learned that the higher quality control achieved in the fab shop has drastically reduced the incidence of faulty parts that can later cause system failures. By creating assemblies that are manufactured to the highest standards of reliability in every instance, Arden ensures greater cost efficiency and a more cost-effective operation. Prefabrication has also proved to be a time saver, as well as affording greater safety on the construction site because more of the work is completed in a controlled environment.

A worker welds stainless fabrication for an industrial client.

Advanced computer systems: an integral part of Arden's services has revolved around the development and implementation of these. Arden is equipped with the newest 3-dimensional visualization Computer Aided Design (CAD) systems, which greatly reduce drawing and rendering time. Arden also uses state-of-the-art software to generate project estimates. Other sophisticated programs developed by Arden allow it to remotely monitor building operations. Locating potential problems within the system allows Arden to respond quickly, sending out the appropriate technician. This monitoring service has proven to be an invaluable cost saving tool for the company's clients.

Quality control: evident in all aspects of Arden Engineering's operations, it is especially significant within project management. Beginning with the company's highly-experienced estimating department, add to this Arden's 50 years of knowledge and expertise in overseeing the purchase of all project equipment, clients are always assured that all project components meet or exceed their intended and specific uses. All building systems are installed by highly-trained field personnel to ensure that all equipment and system components are set per the engineers' design and specifications, as well as remaining in accordance with manufacturers' recommendations. Start-up crews are present on all projects and are supervised by highly-experienced project managers, such as Kenneth Demers, Arden's vice president of construction operations, who brings 20 years of experience to his position. These managers monitor all aspects of the work to ensure that piping and fixtures are installed properly and the correct ductwork is installed. Parts are always double-checked for size and specification. Once the construction crews have completed their work, Arden's Testing, Balancing, and Commissioning Group carefully inspects to verify that all the installed systems operate and perform in accordance with the design criteria.

Safety: another issue of paramount

An Arden technician uses digital equipment to monitor a precision clean room application.

importance to Arden Engineering and an area in which the company prides itself. The creation of Arden's safety committee wherein management and field personnel meet monthly, as well as a company-wide safety incentive program, are major contributing factors to the firm's 50-year success story. Arden's safety program requires that all employees—from the secretaries to the construction crews to management—participate in a 10-hour Occupational Safety and Health Administration (OSHA) training course. Union workers from the five major trades—plumbers, pipe fitters, sheet metal workers, electricians, and sprinkler fitters—are also given additional safety training beyond the extensive programs already provided by their unions. The company's safety record is especially impressive considering that on any given project up to several hundred construction workers could be present on a job site—many doing high-risk work. Arden stresses the fact that there is a direct correlation between the company's continued success and the tremendous focus on safety training it

requires of all of its full-time and project-specific employees.

Arden is also considered at the forefront of pioneering new approaches. Traditional plumbing and heating contractors generally offer services only within those two specific areas, but Bob Bolton recognized an area of tremendous potential growth that was a sure fit within those two disciplines. Expanding Arden's services to include fire protection and electrical work has helped make the company a true full-service contractor for today's multi-faceted marketplace. Adding electricians to the Arden team was another way of streamlining the company's projects. Arden technicians and engineers no longer need to rely on outsourcing to problem-solve or plan a project more effectively. Additionally, Arden is developing the use of more energy-efficient and environmentally-friendly systems for its future design/building projects.

Arden Engineering Constructors, LLC, is currently completing projects in the pharmaceutical, biotech, microelectronics, and health care industries and the company has recently signed maintenance contracts with several financial institutions. Arden has 45 full-time office employees and on any given day employs 125 to 225 union craft personnel. Its Pawtucket headquarters contains more

An Arden service technician completing start up at Rhode Island Hospital 50,000#/hour boiler installation

Arden founder, Irwin Arden.

than 25,000 square feet, including both the company's executive offices and physical plant. Arden is a member of the New England Mechanical Contractors Association (NEMCA) and the Mechanical Contractors Association of America (MCAA).

Arden President Bob Bolton recognizes that much of Arden's success over the years comes as a result of its employees. Bob believes in giving them the space and ability to be creative. He does this by offering himself as coach and advisor and by instilling confidence through training and understanding. He makes a point of offering Arden employees the opportunity to reach beyond their limits, while always honoring the company's code of ethics and respect for fellow workers. Bolton, who served as president of the National Environmental Balancing Bureau (NEBB), the Rhode Island chapter of the American Society of Heating, Refrigerating, and Air Conditioning Engineers (ASHRAE) and the Providence Engineering Society (PES), knows the importance of strong leadership and has successfully applied this, as well as many other talents, to running Arden Engineering Constructors, LLC. At Arden, the future is very exciting. The strength, commitment and dedication consistently shown by its employees will ensure its continuing growth and success as the company moves confidently into the 21st century.

BROWN UNIVERSITY

The Colony of Rhode Island and Providence Plantations was well into its second century before it finally acquired a college of its own. James Manning, an emissary of the Philadelphia Baptists, came to Rhode Island in July 1763 with a plan for an institution that would be grounded in interdenominational cooperation, a proposal that was readily endorsed by the colony's leading citizens. The College's charter specified that its mission would be to prepare "a Succession of Men duly qualify'd for discharging the Offices of Life with usefulness and reputation." Brown was unique in its declaration that "Sectarian differences of opinions shall not make any Part of the Public and Classical Instruction." The College was formally established in 1764, making it the third college in New England and the seventh in America.

Today Brown University is a leading Ivy League institution with a distinctive undergraduate academic program, a world-class faculty, outstanding graduate and medical students, and a

At the heart of Brown's campus is the College Green, a showpiece of architectural treasures dating from 1770.

Wayland Arch was named after Brown's fourth president, Francis Wayland, who led the University from 1827 to 1855.

tradition of innovative and rigorous multidisciplinary study. The main campus covers nearly 140 acres on a historic residential hill overlooking downtown Providence. True to its nonsectarian roots, the University has maintained a strong commitment to diversity and intellectual freedom.

Brown's unique undergraduate curriculum provides bright, self-motivated students the opportunity to become architects of their educational experience. Ninety-one percent of recently accepted students were in the top 10 percent of their graduating high school class. Of those, 30 percent were valedictorians and 29 percent were salutatorians.

Brown's faculty is known for its multidisciplinary scholarship and singular dedication to teaching; virtually all faculty teach undergraduate courses.

In 2002 the University launched an exciting program of initiatives for academic enrichment that will enlarge the faculty by 100 members, improve support for graduate students, and invest in libraries, information technology, and academic space.

Brown Medical School, the only school of medicine in Rhode Island, is renowned for innovation in medical education. A central feature of its curriculum is integrating medical studies and the liberal arts. A unique eight-year continuum combines undergraduate study in any concentration area with professional studies in medicine, producing broadly educated physicians.

The Graduate School is a national leader in the creation and dissemination of knowledge. It offers 40 master's-level programs and 35 Ph.D. programs. Recently established Ph.D. programs expected to achieve national stature include those in brain sciences, theater studies, and modern culture and media.

Carrying on an intercollegiate athletic tradition more than 100 years old, the Brown Bears compete against the seven other Ivy League schools and against other universities at the NCAA Division I level. Brown has one of the nation's broadest arrays of varsity teams—37 in all, 20 for women and 17 for men.

Brown's mission today takes a page from its historic charter, vowing "to serve the community, the nation, and the world by educating and preparing students to discharge the offices of life with usefulness and reputation, through a partnership of students and teachers in a unified community known as a university-college."

AUSTRIAN MACHINE CORPORATION

At Austrian Machine Corporation, precision is the standard. Since 1971 when 29-year-old Walter Josef Kern founded the company, Austrian Machine Corporation (AMC) has provided innovative and reliable solutions to the rotogravure industry. AMC is a custom engineering and manufacturing facility as well as one of the largest replacement parts suppliers to the publication gravure industry. Walter Kern's vision is directly responsible for modifications to existing presses, reels (unwinders) and folders that have dramatically improved the performance of existing gravure printing equipment on an industry-wide basis. Today AMC is the only company of its kind in the United States.

Born in Hall, Austria on October 30, 1942, Walter Kern was an excellent skier and member of the Austrian Olympic development team, who entered technical school and earned a machinist degree. He became a technical representative for a Swiss company that manufactured post-press equipment and was soon put in charge of exploring international opportunities. In 1968, Walter traveled to America for the

Walter J. Kern, 1942–2001. Founder of Austrian Machine Corporation.

company's first installation overseas. That success led to a second installation at the Providence Gravure in Rhode Island.

It was a challenging assignment for a young Austrian technician, especially one that could not speak English. However Walter quickly picked up the

language and adapted to the culture. During the installation in Providence, Walter's co-workers introduced him to a young woman named Marjorie. On their first date, he told Marjorie that they would be married.

"Of course my mother thought he was crazy," recalls Kurt Kern, Walter and Marjorie's son and the current vice-president of marketing at Austrian Machine Corporation. "Thankfully he was not. Shortly thereafter he left his employer to stay in Rhode Island and marry my mom; he was ready and willing to accept the family of three young girls she already had."

With his technical background and strong work ethic, Walter Kern overcame all obstacles. He accepted a position at Providence Gravure as a maintenance machinist on the night shift and in his spare time earned his U.S. citizenship. During the day, Walter mounted and tuned skis for a popular local ski shop. After a few years of working day and night for himself and Providence Gravure, Walter decided it was time to take control. He wanted to work for himself and started Austrian Ski and Machine in 1971. Ultimately he phased out the ski portion of the company as custom design and manufacturing for the gravure industry expanded.

In the 30 years that Walter served as president of the corporation, he led the engineering of many one-of-a-kind press, folder and reel conversions. Walter Kern also earned two U.S. patents. One was in the area of ski design and the other for the AMC 2000 Variable Print Unit Conversion, a gravure press conversion system that is unmatched in the industry.

Though he passed away in 2001, Walter Kern's legacy of hard work and technical innovation lives on at Austrian Machine Corporation. AMC is a leader in the design and manufacturing of new pressroom equipment and modifications for reels, presses, and folders. In addition to many installations of the AMC 2000 Variable Print Unit Conversion, multiple press and folder overhauls and installations,

Austrian Machine Corporation's assembly facility.

AMC has become the primary pressroom and bindery replacement parts supplier of many gravure facilities all across North America.

AMC's expertise and service increases its client's productivity while reducing their expenses. Over 5,000 detailed drawings on electronic file, continued refinement of the original design, large inventory, and custom design availability serve as distinct advantages for the company. They allow AMC to provide clients with cutting-edge designs, exemplary customer service, and the highest quality manufacturing standards. With satisfaction guaranteed, AMC is not simply an alternative but rather the preferred choice of some of the largest printing facilities in North America.

Thirty-two years of profitability is perhaps the best indication of AMC's ability to meet any customer need on time and on budget. By focusing on press and folder modifications and replacement parts, Austrian machine has established a proven track record of project delivery and completion unmatched in the industry. AMC has built bonds of trust with its clients and subcontractors, who continue to

Austrian Machine Corporation's manufacturing facility.

The company's office at 25 Stamp Farm Road in Cranston, Rhode Island.

demand and receive the highest quality of service.

The secret to AMC's success has been its people. "Walter Kern felt each person who worked for him was an extension of him and his company," explains his son, Kurt Kern. "Together Walter and Marjorie developed a family company that anyone would be proud and happy to work for."

David Machado, Walter's son-in-law, has been with AMC for 27 years and is currently the general manager and part owner. Thomas Costa began working hand in hand with Walter in engineering and project management and has been with the company for 23 years. William

Welch began his career at AMC 19 years ago as a machinist and has been the manufacturing manager for the last 15 years. Another 19-year veteran, Michael Hurley, started at AMC in shipping and has become AMC's replacement parts salesman. With the addition of Darryl Huckaby in 1996 as project manager, AMC and its invaluable employees have the experience, craftsmanship and pride to continue Walter's vision.

Kurt Kern, Walter and Marjorie's son, earned a BS in Finance at Providence College in 1992 and tried being a stockbroker. "I hated it!" Kurt confesses. "My dad offered me a job in assembly in October 1992. I worked in the assembly shop for a few long years and then in the engineering department and eventually hand in hand with my father. He was old school and it paid off. He was the hardest person to work for, the most demanding and at the same time he offered the most rewarding employment experience I have ever experienced."

Today Kurt Kern and the other employees at Austrian Machine Corporation continue to demand excellence as they provide the gravure printing industry with a unique level of service. An American company with a world of experience, AMC understands the importance of precise execution and delivery. After all, precision is the standard at AMC.

CARBONE FLORAL DISTRIBUTORS

There is a popular phrase in the floral industry, "If you get a little soil under your fingernails, you get hooked for life." Robert J. Carbone, founder of Carbone Floral Distributors, knows firsthand the truth behind that statement. For half a century, the Cranston wholesaler has gradually transformed the company from a two-person operation to one of the most respected floral distributors in the country.

Bob Carbone started out pedaling buckets of gladiolas in his car in 1952. A family friend was raising the flowers as a hobby and Carbone saw an opportunity to sell them to local flower shops. He was 21 years old, married, and had an infant son. The side job was merely a way to supplement his full-time employment at a retail flower shop.

"I was making $65 a week at my regular job," says Carbone. "I was soon earning more selling gladiolas than working for $10 a day in a florist shop."

The venture became a family project. His wife Elaine, with baby Thomas beside her, delivered the buckets of gladiolas while Carbone was at work. They enjoyed enough success in the first summer that the following year he decided to go into business for himself. He had $400 and a 1946 Mercury car. Carbone traded in the car and paid $200 for a Dodge panel truck.

In those early years, Carbone peddled his flowers from shop to shop

The company's first location in 1957, a former grocery store in Meshanticut Park, Cranston, Rhode Island.

The founder and president of Carbone Floral Distributors, Robert Carbone.

working to establish a customer base and a reputation for handling quality products. "We used to have to buy and sell flowers on the same day," says Carbone. "These were perishable products and it wasn't good not to have refrigeration. It was a pretty humble beginning."

In 1957 the R. J. Carbone Company Wholesale Florist opened its first location, a vacant grocery store within a residential neighborhood in Cranston. The store's old meat cooler was precisely what Carbone needed to take his business to the next level. Later Carbone added more refrigeration equipment to the store. By 1968 the business had prospered so much that it outgrew the building. He moved his operation to a facility he built on Jefferson Boulevard in Warwick. After constructing two additions to that location the company, renamed Carbone Floral Distributors, returned to Cranston in 1991 where they had constructed an 80,000-square-foot building in the Howard Industrial Park.

Today as a full-service wholesaler, Carbone Floral Distributors is comprised of three main departments—fresh flowers, greenhouse plants, and floral supplies. The latter department alone contains nearly 8,000 items, ranging from silk flowers and baskets to ribbon, glassware, pottery, and home

decor. The company has blossomed into a thriving multi-faceted enterprise that showcases 250 varieties of fresh flowers and cut greens brought in from four continents. Its plant department sells about 50 varieties of seasonal flowering and foliage plants throughout the year, some of which are grown in Carbone's own greenhouses in Cranston and Scituate, Rhode Island. In addition, the floral supply department offers an assortment of other goods for every season. The company sells products to florists, garden centers, gift shops, and supermarkets throughout the Northeast.

As the descendant of Italian immigrants, Carbone fully appreciates the value of hard work and sacrifice in achieving the American dream. He inherited his entrepreneurial spirit from his grandfather and father, whose work ethics have indelibly shaped his life.

Luigi Carbone, his grandfather, emigrated to the Federal Hill section of Rhode Island in 1903 from the small mountain village of San Carlo, south of Rome. Coming from a rural, agricultural background he gravitated towards the produce market and soon was in business for himself.

"My grandfather sold fruits and vegetables from a pushcart," Carbone says. "He would also take the train to New York to buy a carload of walnuts and other products and had them shipped to the rail yard in Providence. There he would wholesale them to other pushcart vendors."

Bob's father Joseph left school in the eighth grade to work in the construction industry. At age 21, after serving an apprenticeship in home construction, Joseph decided to go into business for himself. However he faced an unexpected, uncontrollable setback. When the stock market crashed, the bank repossessed Joseph's houses and he had to find another source of income.

Making cemetery baskets at Christmas time was one of Joseph's many efforts to support his family during the depression. He would gather twigs, moss and evergreens from nearby woods to make these decorations.

Joseph did not earn much money from the endeavor, but the fruits of his labor proved to be far more significant than he could have imagined. When his son Bob was in his early teens, Joseph taught him how to make the Christmas decorations. Soon Bob was earning spending money making his own baskets, wreaths, and centerpieces. His career path was taking shape.

After graduating from Cranston High School in 1949, Bob attended a floral design school in Boston. He landed a job working six-and-a-half days a week at a combination greenhouse/florist shop. His responsibilities at the shop ranged from changing soil in flowerbeds and glazing greenhouses to designing arrangements for weddings and funerals.

Then, in the summer of 1953, the Carbone entrepreneurial spirit kicked in and Bob started his own business pursuits. With his wife working alongside, he proceeded to establish a small family business that today has more than exceeded his expectations.

From the very beginning, Carbone sought out the highest quality and freshest flowers. "The source was equally as important as the customer in those early days," explains Carbone. "Today you have an overproduction in the market, but in those days it wasn't

Construction of a second level begins in 1984 on the Jefferson Boulevard building in Warwick, Rhode Island.

Bob, Tom, and Steve Carbone inspecting the poinsettia crop grown in their Scituate, Rhode Island greenhouses.

like that. There was very seasonal production with limited availability. When I walked into a customer's shop, I needed to offer the best product or there would be no sale." Throughout his career, Carbone has worked to align himself with producers of superior products and to establish strategic alliances and enduring business relationships.

Dramatic changes have occurred in the floral industry worldwide since Carbone staked his claim in the business 50 years ago. United States floral production has been replaced by imported products, with 60 to 70 percent coming from offshore into Miami. His company, always receptive to new and innovative opportunities, was one of the first U.S. wholesalers to import flowers from South America.

By 1977 U.S. wholesalers were faced with petitions from domestic growers calling for the Federal Trade Commission to stave the flood of floral imports from other countries. But Carbone believed it was in the best interests of U.S. wholesalers to forge relationships with overseas growers, such as those in the South American country of Colombia. He led the charge later that same year, taking 72 industry leaders on an orientation tour to Bogota where they visited

the new flower farms and witnessed the beginning of one of the greatest changes in the history of American floriculture.

Because of the global economy, consumers no longer are limited to the more traditional flowers, such as carnations, gladiolas, and chrysanthemums. Today there are hundreds of different varieties from which to choose. The Netherlands, in particular, has been instrumental in introducing new varieties to the United States. In 1976 Carbone served as chairman of a wholesalers' delegation to Europe that broke barriers and helped to introduce the Dutch market.

The influx of Dutch novelty products, however, soon became a threat to California growers. To combat this, producers in California began raising many of the new varieties themselves. In 1989 Carbone, who was then president of the Wholesale Florists and Florist Suppliers of America, decided to hold the organization's annual convention close to the California growing areas. The event, held in nearby Monterey, broke attendance records and "was instrumental in reawakening the California market," says Carbone.

Tom, Bob, Elaine, Joseph, and Steve Carbone at the 1988 groundbreaking ceremony for the construction of their 80,000-square-foot building in the Howard Industrial Park in Cranston.

It gave the growers in California the showcase they were looking for and gave wholesalers the awareness that California product could be equal to Dutch product. Today California is a very important source of novelty and specialty floral crops.

Roses, once the pride of American floristry, have also been lost to overseas competition. For the past decade, Ecuador's roses have been considered the finest in the world. To keep up with the constant changes in the industry, Carbone says he has to "heed the demand and roll with the punches."

"It is really important to be on the cutting edge and willing to make changes and grow with the industry," he says. "We have to focus on added value to try to maintain our market share. We have established high standards of customer service by developing a most proficient and knowledgeable sales team. Selling is a people business. Our success is due to the commitment and expertise of a dedicated staff. Through their efforts we have been able to establish a loyal customer base."

The company currently employs about 100 workers at its headquarters in Cranston. Another 50 employees work in three additional locations, including sales space in the Boston Flower Exchange, a distribution center in Bedford, New Hampshire, and a small cross dock operation in Middlebury, Vermont.

The truck loading area at the rear of Carbone's current Cranston facility.

Bob's two sons, Tom and Steve, currently serve as vice presidents of the corporation. Tom says he always knew his career would be in the family business. When he began full-time employment with the company after graduating from college in 1974, the spirit of his forefathers kicked in. Wanting an accomplishment of his own, separate from his father's, Tom took the company's fledging floral supply department and developed it into one the largest of its kind in the Northeast.

Bob's other son Steve, who joined the company in 1978, is responsible for the operation of the fresh flower departments at all locations, as well as serving as information systems manager. Daughter Patricia works part-time overseeing the accounts payable and human resources departments. Another daughter, Linda, also worked for a time in the business. Bob's wife Elaine, who he says has "been side by side with me for 50 years," is currently involved as a part-time administrator. As the company celebrates its 50th anniversary Carbone hopes at least one of his 12 grandchildren will someday assume a leadership role in the company.

Through the years Bob has been active in local and national trade associations. He has served on the Board of Directors of the Northeastern Florist Association and the Rhode Island Florist Association. He held various positions in the Wholesale Florists and Florist Suppliers of America for a period of 13 years, serving as director, treasurer, and president. During the past nine years, he has served as a trustee of the American Floral Endowment, culmi-

Steve Carbone checks out the fresh floral products on the sales floor of the Cranston facility.

nating with the position of chairman in 2002. This national organization provides nearly $800,000 each year in funding for biological research projects by land grant universities, for market research, and for student internships in horticulture. In 1974 Carbone was elected into the prestigious American Academy of Florists. He was inducted into the Cranston Hall of Fame in 1991.

The standard of excellence and commitment established during the past 50 years has positioned the company to build on its' success. While the Carbone family looks to the future, they remain proud of the past and thankful to those who have contributed to their success.

CAVANAGH COMPANY

The Cavanagh Company of Greenville evolved from a meeting with a Jesuit retreat master 60 years ago. In 1943 local priests invited John F. Cavanagh Sr. and his son John to meet with the retreat master, Reverend Peter Dolan, to discuss a problem in his parish. Father Dolan said the equipment used by the nuns for the baking of altar breads, the wafer distributed during Holy Communion in the Catholic Church, was antiquated and sadly in need of repair. John Cavanagh Sr., then in his 60s and an inventor of some merit, took up the challenge. He readily converted waffle irons, humidifiers, mixers, and cutters into tools for the baking and cutting of the unleavened Communion offering. Cavanagh's kindness, skill and ingenuity led to the creation of a company that now spans four generations, and represents the largest supplier of altar bread in the country.

John Sr.'s sons, John Jr. and Paul, eventually became part of the new operation. Both were fine artists and portrait painters who would apply their considerable talents to the growing company. In 1946 the brothers formed a partnership to produce the machines that their father had designed, and kept him on to advise them.

The need for better equipment among convent bakers became even more pronounced during the post-World War II boom in the population, when returning servicemen married and raised families. Many of these households practiced within the Catholic faith, and churches filled with the new communicants. Nuns baking in convents could no longer keep up with demand. The Cavanagh Company petitioned Bishop McVinney of the Diocese of Providence for the special permission needed to become bakers of the symbolic breads. By the mid-1950s, volume dictated the purchase of a 10,000-square-foot plant on Putnam Pike in Greenville. Symbols engraved by the two brothers stamped

TOP: The Cavanagh Company's current offices in Greenville.

RIGHT: Wafer baker produced by Cavanagh Company during the early '40s and '50s. Many are still in operation throughout the world.

BOTTOM: First automatic altar bread cutter produced by founder Paul Cavanagh.

Sheet of bread coming out of the oven, just before being dampened and cut.

the first wafers distributed by the Cavanagh Company. Distribution during the early 1950s still passed through the convents, with the sisters packaging Cavanagh's breads for distribution to churches. Two hundred and fifty convents continued to bake and supply altar breads at this time.

The Second Vatican Council in 1962 "really changed everything," according to Brian Cavanagh, Paul's son and current head of management, sales and marketing for the company. The Catholic Church, like so much of society during that decade, reevaluated its symbols. The Church's Council of Trent, which convened during the mid-16th century to codify Catholic dogma, reaffirmed the significance of the seven celebrated sacraments. Communion wafers at that time became ethereal both in symbol and in substance. The wafers were one thirty-thousandth of an inch thick, shiny, "white like milk glass," and baked to dissolve on the tongue. These rarefied wafers fell out of favor during Vatican II, with an impetus toward celebrating the sacrament of the Eucharist with wafers that more closely resembled bread.

The Catholic Church's modern philosophical stand presented the Cavanagh Company with a real engineering dilemma—how to make an unleavened product seem like food. Wafer baking ovens provided the solution enabling the company to produce wafers that were two times as thick, with a sealed edge to prevent crumbs. John Jr. and Paul again applied their talents, this time to the development and subsequent patenting of a certain cutting technique for the new wafers.

The Cavanagh Company moved into its third generation in 1970, when Paul's son Brian joined the firm. An English major, Brian brought his own new ideas to the bread-making business. Using extruder equipment "like they use for cheese puffs," he produced the "Grainfield Biscuit," using only organic grains and sea salt. Ten national distributors moved 1,000 cases of biscuits a week, until the price of organic grains doubled, ending Brian's venture into the health food industry. He then turned to the family altar bread business, focusing on promoting and marketing his father and uncle's highly respected products. He learned the business from the ground up, working in the firm's machine shop, bakery, and shipping and marketing departments.

A decrease in vocations among religious orders, dating from the late 1950s, led to fewer nuns as bakers for altar breads and a larger demand for Cavanagh Company products. By the early 1970s, the firm was producing 6 to 7 million Communion wafers per week. "Convents that had 12 nuns doing the baking now had five," notes Brian Cavanagh. Rules for fasting also relaxed, allowing more Catholics to receive Communion on a regular basis.

George Farrelly joined the firm during this time, a period of intense growth for the company. Farrelly and Brian Cavanagh knew each other from high school days, when they played basketball and football together. In 1974 Farrelly moved into sales, joining Brian on sales trips to convents and religious orders around the country and overseas. At that time the Cavanagh Company held 60 percent of the Catholic market for altar bread.

Paul's other son, Peter, came to work at the family business in 1974, apprenticing in all of the firm's departments as his brother Brian had. Peter, a liberal arts major, brought his grandfather's love of invention to his new situation. His grandfather, who loved experimenting

Altar bread being sifted for packaging.

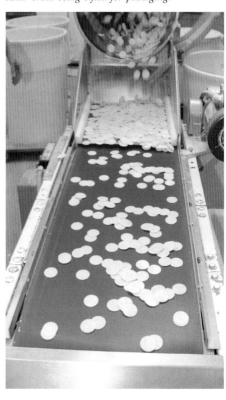

making chased vessels from "flat-stock silver" and donating gifts in the form of presidential medals and crucifixes to many universities. A 14-foot bronze sculpture created by Paul, who worked in bronze, wood and stained glass, now graces Salve Regina University.

In 1990 the firm expanded its operations to overseas, acquiring F.A. Dumont in Kent, England, on the Dover coast. The Cavanagh's brother-in-law, Steve Gilson, oversaw the acquisition of the British firm, which serves as a distributor both of altar breads and an extensive line of candles, vestments, clerical garments, chalices, and liturgical accessories.

Peter also established Episcopalian and Lutheran churches as clients, when he developed a packaging machine designed to those denominations' specifications. Company personnel still operate three of the machines, designed to produce rolls of 100 breads per second. Over time, the firm also added Southern Baptist churches to its client list.

All the breads currently produced by the company pass through ovens that have been researched and fine-tuned by

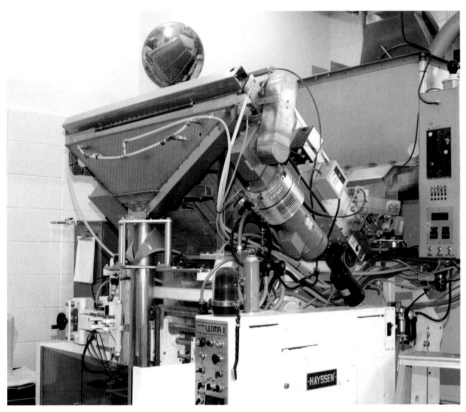

High-speed automatic bagging machine, built by Peter Cavanagh.

with gadgets, had a list of about 120 patents to his name, including a mechanical stapler, a roofing hammer, and the "bar switch" that can be found on lamps in many homes today. During the 1950s, long before the advent of fiber optics and sophisticated technological innovations, John Cavanagh Sr. spent hours perfecting a page turning machine for paraplegics. Cavanagh's inspiration for the device, operated with the blink of an eye, came from a chance encounter with a hospital patient. Peter also branched out in unexpected ways, inventing both a tennis ball machine called the "Cannon" and a retrieval system for tennis balls. Today Peter serves as head of research and development for the firm.

John Cavanagh Jr. withdrew from the company in 1980, selling his interest to his brother Paul. Paul remained active in the business even after his retirement, coming in to the plant every day until illness intervened. A full art studio on company premises serves to remember its founders' talents and abilities. Upon discovering that artwork-for-profit yielded little gain, John and Paul Cavanagh both employed their gifts as liturgical artists by donating their efforts to numerous Catholic institutions. John worked primarily in silver,

Cartons of altar bread ready for shipping to convents and dealers worldwide.

From left to right: Steve Gilson, Peter Cavanagh, Dan Cavanagh, George Farrelly, Andy Cavanagh, Kerri Cavanagh Freeza, and Brian Cavanagh.

Peter Cavanagh. As their predecessors did, Peter and Brian use baking methods established by historical liturgical guidelines, combining only flour and water for the process. The mixture is then spread between flat, rectangular plates that compress it as the plates move through a gas-fired oven. These ovens produce rectangular sheets of wafer-thin bread, which are then passed through a humidifier for dampening, enabling the bread to be cut into circles without crumbling. As the bread is cut it passes under a turning drum of dies that incise the wafers with religious symbols, such as a cross or a lamb, which are used as a symbol of Christ.

The practicalities of producing and packaging altar breads present difficulties not encountered by other bakers. Unlike ordinary wafers and biscuits, altar breads require special dampening techniques to prevent the breads from crumbling. Peter is "constantly making improvements" to existing equipment, notes George Farrelly, who is now general manager for Cavanagh. Due to the uniqueness of the product, demands on company designers are particularly intense. Machines used for commercial baking must be modified to accommodate the bread's special characteristics.

The Cavanagh Company also offers its customers Christmas wafers during the holiday season, incised with depictions of the manger scene; the Madonna and Child; and the Holy Family. Company literature notes that "the spiritual lesson in this age-old custom is unity of the family." The breaking of this bread by family members serves as a sign of "charity, unity, and friendship," with a simple prayer of grace said for all members of the family, present and absent. The baking and sharing of these wafers seems a particularly fitting tradition for a company based on a long history of mutual interests, loyalty, and bonds that go well beyond those of most businesses.

The company now runs round-the-clock shifts to produce 20 million Communion wafers weekly, representing 85 percent of the U.S. and Canadian markets for the product and 50 percent of the market in the United Kingdom. Even requests for large volume orders, as during papal visits, are routinely handled.

As successful as the company is today, Brian Cavanagh says he will always remember the early days—especially the relationship shared by his father, Paul, and his uncle John. "I can't ever remember them having an argument," he says, noting that differences relating to business matters were dealt with calmly. Brian and Peter Cavanagh strive for the same level of mutual respect in their current running of the Cavanagh Company. Brian speaks with equal warmth of the next generation of Cavanaghs to join the firm, noting that their input is especially helpful, as they "see things that others don't."

Brian and Peter Cavanagh extend a good deal of credit to all of their employees, who figure strongly in the firm's success. He characterizes Peter's son Dan, who joined the business five years ago, as "the perfect complement" to Peter in terms of research and development. Peter's other son Andy, who joined the company two years ago, will soon take over all in-house accounting. Andy also contributes to marketing and public relations efforts. Brian's daughter Kerri Cavanagh Frezza contributes her talents in the administrative offices. Brian notes that daily interactions with family members and staff regarding Cavanagh Company business matters, constitutes for him one of the firm's most enjoyable aspects.

Brian notes that as the company matures, the brothers are freed for charity work on a local and diocesan level—and not incidentally, for the golf course as well. Brian has served on the boards of several organizations, including Salve Regina University; the Mother of Life organization; the Harmony Hill School for disadvantaged youth in Chepachet; and Amos House living shelter and medical clinic in south Providence.

Brian says all of his and his brother Peter's efforts are geared toward making this generation of brothers "obsolete." Toward this end they have invested a lot of thought into plans for passing on the company to its newer members, and to the family as a whole. The brothers have implemented a stock-sharing plan involving one series of voting stock and another of non-voting stock to distribute assets evenly. As for the future, Brian says that the brothers are "keeping their eyes open," a sentiment that is easy to believe of this creative and dynamic family.

EVANS FINDINGS COMPANY

Evans Findings Company, located in East Providence has a rich history which has been gifted down from generation to generation. Four generations in all have carried on the tradition of creating high quality small metal parts for the medical, electronic, automotive, and lighting industries. The company also executes precision manufacturing for high pressure and vacuum furnaces, lab ware, fuel cells, batteries, and power supplies. But, the company had its humble beginnings in crafting jewelry findings over 75 years ago.

The heart and soul of the company was born in the mind and ingenuity of Thomas M. Evans in 1928. In the years prior to 1928, Thomas Evans worked for various metals manufacturers. One was the well-established Gorham Silver Company who specialized in silver services, cutlery, and elegant silver place settings. Evans learned the artistry of working with silver and other precious metals and decided he wanted to take his well-honed craft and begin a small, more specialized business in jewelry

Thomas M. Evans (second from left) and son Arthur (left) with some of the early employees in 1941.

Evans Findings' first commercial location on Canal Street.

findings. It was then he set out to start his own company from home.

"He just decided, one day, that he had a better idea on how to create jewelry findings. He set about using the knowledge he already had about casting, machine work, and tool work to build equipment to do just that," says Pete Evans, great grandson of Thomas Evans and now president of Evans Findings Company. "He had castings made which he machined out and put together in his basement." Thomas Evans then engineered a piece of equipment combining these parts which automated the process in producing precisely crafted jewelry findings. This new equipment was valued for its low cost to tool, easily interchangeable parts to form various sized findings, and its ability to perform high volume jobs with little manpower—an important consideration for a man in business for himself. What was this innovative piece of equipment called? The Evans Press, of course. There was only one problem with the Evans Press; it was loud.

Irate neighbors weren't as enthusiastic about Evans' new invention as he

was. In 1930 he was asked to move because of the noise it created. This challenge was a mere formality to Evans who picked up his small business and moved to a more accommodating location—Washington Street in Providence. The company expanded and remained there for the next 10 years. In 1940 it was a building inspector who insisted on a move. In addition to being noisy, the amount of equipment had grown and was now too heavy for the third floor space. Again, Evans took the move in stride. This time it was to 129 Canal Street, the first building ever owned by Evans Findings Company.

The Canal Street location saw much change and growth. It was there that the company became incorporated with six stockholders. These new partners were not new to the business. Five of them were Evans' children three of whom, Charles, James, and Arthur, helped run the company.

Evans Findings Company Incorporated now boasted close to 20

employees and was gearing up for new product needs outside the jewelry industry. Expansion was only natural. Evans had versatile equipment and when the demands for other small metal components for various industries became evident, Evans and his sons were ready to accommodate.

Diversification required more space. In 1950 the company constructed a new building at 55 Johnson Street. The 10,000-square-foot structure served the company well and Evans Findings Company gained a reputation for mass producing metal parts quickly and precisely. One of the first markets to benefit from its expertise was the hermetic sealing industry, which needed small tubing for transistor packages that concealed a miniaturization of electronics. In the mid-1950s, the need for these tiny tubes grew expeditiously. Evans, willing to accommodate, kept 10 presses running seven days a week just for this one part. "Our company probably produced billions of them," proudly states Pete Evans.

In 1983 a third generation member of the Evans family joined the company. Like his grandfather, Thomas E. Evans (Tim) had the drive and vision for creating new opportunity in the metal industry. In addition, he had an engineering degree from Brown University. He spent the beginning of his career at Texas Instruments where he developed his creativity and used his engineering skills. He ended his tenure there with over 20 patent applications credited to his name. Thomas Evans then brought his skills, along with some new ideas for business development, back home to the family business.

In 1984 the company moved to its present location, 33 Eastern Avenue in

The Evans Findings' family in 2004.

East Providence, a more modern building with room to grow. Evans Findings had evolved to include several fourth generation members including John and Dave, two of Thomas' sons. Evans further diversified in 1989 with the purchase of D-Mark, a metal stamping company located in nearby Attleboro, Massachusetts. Thomas' middle son, Pete, also a Brown University engineering graduate, was brought on board to manage this new division.

By 1995 Evans Findings had developed a separate technology-based business, manufacturing high-energy density capacitors. The Evans Capacitor Company was created to concentrate on this effort. Today, Pete Evans manages the operations while brother John heads up tool design; cousin Jim builds the tools and keeps them running; and Pete's wife, Lisa, designs and maintains the business software. Though retired, Tim stops in frequently to lend a hand and see old friends. Company sales are now international with customers in Puerto Rico, China, Europe, and South America.

Despite the steady incremental growth at Evans Findings Company, the family atmosphere still remains. "This is my second family," says Missy Golomb, an employee of the company for almost five years. "It's a great atmosphere here." It must be, consider-

ing that Geoff Feather has worked for the company for almost 40 years. His father joined the firm first, and Geoff followed in 1964. Later, Geoff recruited his two sons and nephew to be added to the team. As if that wasn't enough family togetherness, his sister-in-law, Cyndi Pires, came on board in 1975. "Geoff has more family here than I do!" quips Pete Evans. Not only do the employees have a generous health plan, they also have a 401K plan, a profit sharing plan, and a bonus plan in place. "Our employees share in the success of the business," says Pete Evans. This is a tradition he, no doubt, learned from his great grandfather.

The legacy that Thomas M. Evans built and passed down is strong. His philosophy transcends time. The "10 Demandments," a document Evans wrote in 1937, still hangs on the wall in Pete Evans' office. The list consists of "demandments" for his employees, present and future. Number four reads: "Give me more than I expect and I'll give you more than you expect." Number five: "Mind your own business and in time, you'll have a business of your own." Four generations of Evans' have heeded these simple rules and each has received what was promised.

FERGUSON PERFORATING COMPANY

When most people think of something "perforated" they probably picture paper with a perforated edge, but in fact many other examples are all around us. Perforated products, such as the ones manufactured by Ferguson Perforating Company, are hidden parts of the daily world in which we live. Public spaces such as airports and metro stations, production machinery, washers and dryers, jet engines, speakers, and office products all have perforated parts that make equipment run more smoothly, quietly, and efficiently, and often add an aesthetic quality to a product.

J. Cecil Ferguson, born in 1903, founded the company in 1927 to supply centrifugal liners and other products to the sugar industry. These liners were one of the earliest uses for perforated products. Ferguson had previously worked for both Western States Machine Company and American Tool and Machine Company in Massachusetts, the latter a manufacturer of centrifuges for both companies. Ferguson learned every aspect of the business and in his spare time studied engineering at the Massachusetts Institute of Technology. In 1924 Western States Machine Company ended its relationship with American Tool and

The original facility in 1937.

Founder, J. Cecil Ferguson.

brought Ferguson over to manage its New York office. In his new position Ferguson traveled throughout the United States, Central, and South America selling, installing, and servicing sugar equipment for the company. Through this experience, Ferguson acquired firsthand knowledge of what equipment the sugar companies needed, how to

build it, how to operate it, and who the decision-makers were. With this information in hand, Ferguson decided to step out on his own in 1927.

He moved to Providence and started the J.C. Ferguson Manufacturing Works at 55 Pine Street. He quickly built a loyal customer base, supplying top quality perforated products that were used by the sugar industry. He also developed an interest in the chocolate industry and created a wire mesh filter pad for cocoa presses, which was an advancement over the fabricated camel and human hair filters that had been widely used up until then. By 1935 Ferguson Manufacturing had outgrown its original space and moved to 87 Willard Street. Two years later the company grew too large for its space again and Ferguson purchased a plot of land at Ernest and Porter streets, where a 40 by 90-foot building was built. With the move the company was reincorporated as Ferguson Perforating and Wire Company. Incidentally, this Providence location is now known as the Manucenter and was the first industrial park in the United States.

One of the companies from which Ferguson purchased perforated screens was a firm in Prague, Czechoslovakia. The owner asked Ferguson to come and visit the plant. When he arrived, the Czech owners confided that they were concerned about Hitler's intentions and didn't feel they could be relied upon as a supplier for much longer. They suggested to Ferguson that he begin manufacturing his own perforated screens in Rhode Island and proceeded to give him all the technical advice and know-how he would need. Ferguson returned with this knowledge and put his Rhode Island toolmakers and mechanics to work. From that point on the company was manufacturing its own product from scratch, without any reliance on subcontractors.

During World War II metals such as brass and copper, integral to Ferguson's production, came into great demand for the war effort. Doing its part, the company continued to manufacture products for the sugar industry, as well as parts used for gas masks. The war department realized that the equipment Ferguson was making for the sugar industry was necessary for the war effort. Sugar was one of the most common natural preservatives, and with the need for food products that would last and support the troops and the country, the government afforded material allocations to Ferguson to produce the screens. Centrifuge screens almost identical to those used by the sugar industry were also supplied to the munitions manufacturers for use in the production of gunpowder.

Bruce Ferguson, president.

Perforating press, designed and built in Rhode Island, being installed in Pennsylvania plant.

Over the next few decades Ferguson Perforating continued to expand, and added to the original building a number of times. In 1965 Cecil Ferguson's son, Bruce, joined the company. Seven years later, Bruce became president of the family business. In 1978 the company purchased a new piece of land adjacent to its existing property. This allowed the firm to expand the physical plant to 66,000 square feet. By this time the business was manufacturing perforated parts for a vast array of products including, but not limited to, the centrifuge basket liners, washers and dryers, silencers for the power generation industry, HVAC installations, telecommunication enclosures, and home juicers. They also began manufacturing products such as perforated panels that were designed to absorb noise in public spaces.

In 1988 J. Cecil Ferguson passed away, transferring control of the company to his son, Bruce. Bruce Ferguson was now making perforated parts for the U.S. Navy's submarine fleet and the nacelles (liners) for jet engines, which helped quell the turbines inherently high noise levels. In 1995 Ferguson Perforating Company decided to build a new 60,000-square-foot plant in New Castle, Pennsylvania. This area was closer to many of the company's suppliers and customers. The Providence location continued to be the headquarters for the firm's administration, tool building, and capital equipment manufacturing divisions, as well as the center of production for the sugar and aerospace business. In 2001 Ferguson's Pennsylvania plant won the Governor's Environmental Excellence Award for its innovative approaches to running a cleaner facility and its creative ways of recycling. Governor Schweiker personally presented the award to Bruce Ferguson.

Today the Ferguson Perforating Company continues to follow the path to success laid out by its founder. Using such advanced equipment as computer numerical control (CNC) presses, the business can produce perforated products with great efficiency and precision. It offers its customers a complete machining, fabricating, welding, and tooling facility and has been certified for ISO 9001:2000. A large part of the company's success is based on the strong relationship Ferguson, like his father before him, shares with his employees. The friendly and professional work environment that the Fergusons have created over the company's 77 years of existence has helped shape the business. The fact that Ferguson Perforating Company employs multiple members and generations of several families is a rarity in today's world—a true testament to Cecil Ferguson's vision for the future.

Examples of perforated tubes that are used in filters and mufflers.

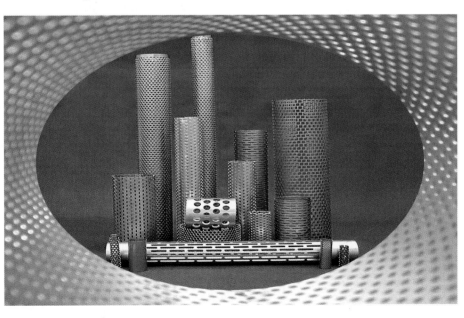

GENCORP INSURANCE GROUP

The waterfront town of East Greenwich that serves as home to Gencorp Insurance Group, Inc., has grown from a tiny seventeeth century Queen's colony that once housed Her Majesty's jail, to the most affluent town in Rhode Island. Gencorp has blossomed along with the community, now serving as one of the largest insurance and financial services agencies in the state. Robert (Bob) Padula, president and chief executive officer, whose office view is punctuated by sailboat masts on the cove, has come a long way from the Ph.D. candidate in history who was "talked into" the business by his brother, Fred. "Nobody had any money. All they had was energy and determination," Bob says as he describes the company's founders, who pursued their dream during the post-World War II boom in this tiny coastal town.

Having studied the insurance business via correspondence school while stationed abroad, Fred Padula, Bob's brother and a returning World War II veteran, teamed with businessman Stephen D'Attore after returning to the States. Fred's first client, the owner of an ice cream stand, paid a $7.50 premium to insure $500 worth of business assets. Fred went on to night school, studying business and finance while pursuing the insurance business during the day. The agency soon became a full-service insurance and financial services company.

Joseph Glover, a returning Navy veteran, signed on with D'Attore and Padula in 1948. In 1951 the agency incorporated and Padula and Glover

From left to right: John A. Padula, Robert G. Padula and Fred A. Padula.

became partners. The name changed to D'Attore, Glover and Padula, Inc. in 1955 and Glover and Padula bought out D'Attore in 1959. The firm moved to the Dean Building on Main Street a few years later and remained there for more than a decade. At the time of the move, premium volume for D'Attore, Glover and Padula had risen to $300,000.

In June 1969 Fred Padula bought out Joe Glover, becoming the sole owner of the agency. Bob Padula also joined the firm that year and a third brother, John, came on board as operations manager in 1970. Two more brothers, Ray and Tony, soon followed and contributed their talents to the firm's financial services and sales divisions.

In 1975 the firm moved to the old site of the Koch Pharmacy, again on Main Street in East Greenwich (where it remains today). Office hours from 7:00 a.m. to 7:00 p.m. helped foster Glover-Padula's expansive growth during the 1970s and 1980s. Fred Padula retired from the firm in 1987 after 40 years in business, leaving behind a tradition of service that kept their office open during a blizzard that closed down all of Main Street. With a plan to improve services to clients and establish the firm as a leader in the insurance profession, Bob and

John Padula partnered with local agent Thomas DiSanto Jr.'s Gallo/Thomas agency in 1992. Both Glover-Padula and Gallo/Thomas operated under the aegis of the Gencorp Insurance Group, continuing to offer a broad base of insurance carriers and personalized services to clients.

Gencorp's Main Street home office.

Main Street, East Greenwich, Rhode Island in early 1900s.

The rear of Gencorp's building from Marlboro Street.

In 2000 the firm added the Gencorp Insurance and Financial Services division to become the comprehensive financial service and insurance agency it is today. The new division specializes in the provision of services to individuals of high net worth on the retail side. On the wholesale side, Gencorp now offers "backroom" insurance and administrative services to a network of New England agencies, brokers and non-insurance professionals such as banks, investment advisors, lawyers, and certified public accountants. Affiliated Gencorp network agencies in Rhode Island and Massachusetts offer a full range of insurance and financial products, reinforcing the firm's commitment to local clients.

Gencorp also maintains "cluster agencies" in Portsmouth at the office of its affiliate the Portsmouth Agency, and in Cumberland at the Hanaway Agency. Its plans for the future include an expansion into the New York market. Although Bob Padula notes that the firm is "always looking" for new opportunities, he says Gencorp will remain a private company under his stewardship.

Throughout the years, Gencorp's client roster has included all types of businesses. One of the more colorful clients was a man who came in with his father to purchase a $250 policy, just as the organic food market was hitting its stride. A father couldn't have shown faith in his son at a more timely moment. Today Cornucopia Natural Foods hauls natural foods all across the country. Another success story is Del's Lemonade, which signed on with Gencorp when it was a small company. Del's now serves clients as far away as Venezuela and

was profiled in the PBS television series, *Small Business 2000.*

The Padula brothers' commitment to community also extends to professional organizations. Fred Padula, a "perennial member" of the East Greenwich Lion's Club, also served as Rhode Island's first insurance agent named to Travelers Insurance's National Advisory Council. Bob Padula, past president of the Independent Insurance Agents of Rhode Island and the Rhode Island Society of Chartered Property and Casualty Underwriters, currently serves on the advisory councils of several national insurance companies, and as chairman of Travelers Insurance Advisory Council.

Gencorp is now in its third generation and has a premium volume in excess of $80 million. Bob's son Joseph has joined the company, as well as his nephew Rick Padula who runs the Glover-Padula sales group. Gencorp employees who are not part of the Padula family also demonstrate remarkable loyalty to the company. Judy Briggs recently celebrated her 43rd anniversary with Gencorp, and many others are enjoying tenures of more than 25 years.

Bob Padula characterizes his brother Fred's encouragement as "serendipitous." The Rhode Island business community must be in agreement.

Some of Gencorp's 60-plus employees.

H B WELDING INC.

A relaxing drive through the scenic countryside of Rhode Island, and the neighboring states of Massachusetts and Connecticut, has a slightly different twist for the Bacon family from Pawtucket. They are likely to start talking about how many of their employees it took to build a passing bridge, school, or shopping center. Even a short drive to the airport has them pointing out structures that they helped construct. Their company, H B Welding, does iron and specialty stud work; two components that are vital to holding any building's steel supports steady so the structure won't shift. They also erect pre-cast buildings and do other miscellaneous iron work.

The business was started over the dining room table 19 years ago. Helen Bacon, owner and president of H B Welding, remembers the day her husband Leo came home and suggested they start their own business. He had been an ironworker for many years, a master in the grueling stud work that required him to work in a crouched position all day with a heavy, powered machine.

"Not many people specialize in stud welding," Helen says. So when Leo's boss suggested he start his own business, it was an appealing idea. When the couple looked into the logistics of starting a company however, they discovered a catch. Back in 1985 a person could not be a member of the ironworker's local union *and* own a construction company. Unfortunately, Leo had too much invested in the way of pension and health care benefits to risk leaving the union. That union rule has since been changed, but at the time Leo encouraged his wife to start the company.

From that inauspicious beginning, H B Welding has grown into a company with more than $5 million in revenues. One of its biggest contracts came in 2003 when the firm won a bid for a Stop N' Shop warehouse, an area about a million square feet, in Massachusetts. The project increased the number of ironworkers the company employed to about 60.

Leo and Helen Bacon, founders of H B Welding.

"There are very few people who thought I would still be afloat 19 years later," says Helen Bacon. "In construction, most of the smaller companies go out (of business) after five years. But then, I didn't know that." She admits that there were a lot of things she didn't know back in 1985 when she started the company. For the first few years, they bid only on jobs involving the stud work that Leo was familiar with, and Leo trained and worked alongside two or three other ironworkers. It wasn't enough to keep the company busy, however, so they began bidding on small construction jobs. With a ready source of labor through the Ironworkers Local 37, H B Welding needed contracts to put the men to work.

Helen ran the business out of her home to save money and wasn't able to pay herself a salary at times. She took classes and read books on construction

and went to seminars; anything to educate herself. Several years later Helen learned her company could qualify for minority status and thus be allowed to compete for certain state or school projects requiring minority participation. She obtained the Woman Business Enterprise (WBE) certification and has renewed it every year since 1988. "The WBE certification never guaranteed a contract," she adds. If her company wasn't competent for the job, and the bid wasn't competitive, they would not get the job. "It's a numbers game," says Helen.

However, the numbers extend far beyond a bid that is submitted for a contract. Insurance requirements on trucks and properties, worker's compensation payments, and general liability came as a "rude awakening" for Helen. Even now she says, "you can go insurance broke. It's one of my most expensive items, in addition to payroll and employee benefits." Massachusetts and Connecticut have different requirement than Rhode Island, and it's her responsibility to know all the details.

"It isn't easy to stay in business," Helen said. Every day presents its own set of problems. "When you work for someone else, your day is done when you go home. When you work for someone else and there is a problem, you can go to your boss. But when you own your own company, you are the boss and you have to find your way around."

H B Welding's current chief estimator for jobs, Dennis DeCorte, started giving Helen friendly advice back when he worked for another company. In the mid-1990s; when the company where he had been employed for 15 years folded, Helen hired him right away. "Dennis had valuable contacts and knew his way around in this male dominated industry," says Helen. "He was an immense asset to the company and he helped us grow."

Those contacts and know-how translated to contracts for steel work, including expansion work at TF Green Airport in Warwick (a.k.a. Providence Airport) and steel framework and pre-cast concrete sheathes for a 30-story Westin Hotel in Providence and the Bourne Middle School in Massachusetts. H B Welding employees have also built bridges, at times having to work off a barge at the edge of a river. Such projects have included placing long-span steel girders on a bridge at Route 2/32 in Connecticut; constructing two bridges in Barrington on Route 114; three approaches to the Jamestown Bridge; four small bridges in Woonsocket; repair jobs on Interstate 95 bridges; and many other undertakings.

Over the years Helen has found many personal rewards that have come from her foray into the business world. She takes pride in being able to employ

National Association of Women in Construction (NAWIC) brunch.

Stop N' Shop warehouse in Freetown, Massachusetts.

people and overcome problems. She also finds her own children—two boys and a girl—are proud of her efforts to start her own company.

To become part of the business, her son John went through the ironworker's union three-year apprenticeship program. Trained by Dennis DeCorte, John now works as an estimator, bidding on projects for his mother's company. Helen's daughter, Diane Laliberte, also went through the apprenticeship program, and is now Helen's right hand administrative secretary. Diane is familiar with union rules and all the paperwork associated with providing jobs. A 16-year-old grandson, Stephen, has also worked for the company on a limited basis. Husband Leo retired about seven years ago, but stops by often to run errands for the company.

Helen says it isn't easy being a woman in a man's business. "I am going to show them that I can do it. It's been a struggle, but then life isn't always easy and it can be a struggle. I had to prove it to myself that I could do it, so maybe I worked harder than anybody else." These days Helen can say quite proudly: "this bridge is good, we worked on it."

JOHN R. HESS & COMPANY, INC.

Nationally recognized for its commitment to public safety for the past 35 years, John R. Hess and Company, Inc. has helped lead the charge for responsible chemical handling and transportation. The Cranston-based company distributes both organic and inorganic chemicals to a wide range of industries and manufacturers. Most of its customers are located in the New England states, as well as eastern New York and northern New Jersey. Huntsman Chemical Company, BASF Corporation, Stepan Chemical Company, and Astaris are just a few of the dozens of suppliers the company represents. From amphoterics used in baby shampoo to ethylene glycol in paint products, the firm sells the raw materials to chemical businesses. They, in turn, use them to produce cosmetics; pharmaceuticals; industrial and institutional cleaners; specialty coatings for textiles, paper, and leather; and other applications.

The business originated in 1928 in Providence and was known at the time as Sessions-Gifford. Both owners, Henry Sessions and Delbert Gifford, died relatively young, leaving the business in the hands of Delbert Gifford, Jr. The younger Gifford merged the business with his own company, Giffordline Chemical Company, and moved all operations to Cranston.

When Delbert Jr. died at the age of 42, his widow ran the business for two years. John Hess and Delbert Jr. had been friends who enjoyed a mutual

T. Anthony (Tony) Thompson, executive vice president.

John R. Hess, chairman of the company.

respect as competitors since Hess worked at George Mann Company, one of Giffordline Chemical's rivals. Delbert's widow, Marie, offered to sell the company to Hess.

"I was the vice president and sales manager at George Mann at the time. I had been there for 22 years and on the road selling for 15 of those," recalls Hess. "But there was the appeal of having my own business. I was able to borrow the money, with the support of my family, and I took the offer."

The opportunity was a culmination of years of hard work for Hess. He was unsure of what direction life would take him when he graduated from Brown University in 1943, while World War II was in full swing. Hess immediately went into the service reaching the rank of Master Sergeant with 20 months of service in Europe and North Africa. On December 10, 1945 Hess was a free man again looking to start a career. Graduate school lost out to a sales position with George Mann and Company, Inc., a Rhode Island chemical distributor. Although he didn't realize it at the time, Hess had found his niche.

After assuming ownership of Giffordline Chemical in 1969, Hess gave the company a new name, John R. Hess and Sons, Inc. His eldest son Stephen joined the company in 1970, followed by his other son Peter in 1973. Stephen served as vice president for a time and remained with the family business

until 1986, when he left to pursue his own ventures.

With the departure of one of his sons, Hess changed the name of the business to John R. Hess and Company, Inc. In 1990 Stephen's son Kyle joined the company. A civil engineer by trade, today Kyle is responsible for the blending and manufacturing end of the business. A year before Kyle came on board, Peter became company president. This enabled John Hess to fulfill a calling that he had since the early 1960s—to be a Peace Corps volunteer.

"At the time I wasn't able to do it. I had a mortgage and three kids. But after the Berlin Wall came down, more Peace Corps opportunities opened up for business volunteers as advisors for liberated countries like Poland, Czech Republic, Slovakia, and Latvia," says Hess. Demonstrating that you are never

Peter Y. Hess, president.

too old to realize a dream, 72-year-old Hess joined the Peace Corps and spent the next two-and-a-half years working in the Czech Republic. He helped transform an historic building in the city of Pilsen into a U.S. business and cultural exchange center. The structure was renovated in time for the ceremony commemorating the 50th anniversary of the liberation of Pilsen by the U.S. Army in 1945.

Hess later worked as an environmental volunteer and joined the Occupational Safety Research Institute in Prague. Here he used his chemical

John R. Hess & Company, Inc.'s headquarters.

industry background to build an informational network whereby Czechs could be educated in such matters as safe chemical storage, truck placarding, and workers' right to know laws. "It was one of the best things I ever did in my life," Hess says of the experience.

When he returned in 1996, Hess continued his earlier efforts of the 1970s and 1980s to become a stronger advocate for chemical safety awareness in the United States. As a founding member of the Massachusetts Chemical Industry Council prior to entering the Peace Corps, Hess had encouraged educating companies and the public regarding proper transportation, storage, and disposal of chemicals. He had also lobbied Congress for effective regulations.

Prior to passage of the Clean Air Act in 1970, environmental legislation was virtually non-existent, giving chemical companies free rein in the manufacture, distribution, and use of their products. The Clean Air Act which went into effect in 1975 was the first step in

regulating the chemical industry. Deciding to take a proactive approach Hess, as president of the National Association of Chemical Distributors (NACD) for three years, opted for a policy to work with Congress and regulators to design legislation that would ensure public safety and be cost effective. Hess was instrumental in starting a responsible distribution program, an extension of the responsible care program initiated by the

Dawn Carter, director of administration.

Chemical Manufacturer's Association. He also served as the first president of the National Association of Chemical Distributors Educational Foundation. Today the foundation offers classes to emergency response personnel, chemical transporters, and the public about how to handle chemicals. It also offers "You Be The Chemist" programs for grade school students, starting with the third grade.

Hess believes in practicing what he preaches. His business is certified as an ISO 9002 company, meaning it conforms to the highest of industry standards. "I'm proud that we have done what we said we would do," says Hess. "We want to distribute raw materials safely, lawfully and to people who will use them wisely. We want to be straightforward and honest. I believe our company accomplishes those goals, and will continue to do so."

INTERNATIONAL INSIGNIA CORPORATION

In the middle of the 19th century, Samuel N. Meyer started a small haberdashery business in Washington, DC. He couldn't have foreseen then that his little shop would evolve into one of the the oldest manufacturers of custom-made military insignia in the United States. It has endured for more than 140 years and through five generations.

In what was then termed as a "horse and buggy" business, Meyer went from door to door peddling his talents to create clothing for the citizens of Washington, while his wife acted as seamstress for the fledgling company. At the time of the Civil War, Meyer saw the great need arising for uniforms for the military officers and enlisted men of the armed services. He seized upon the opportunity and his company, S.N. Meyer, became one of the first suppliers of uniforms to the military. In no time, more uniform and medal manufacturers quickly opened throughout the city, but Meyer was way ahead of them.

Samuel Meyer came to create articles of uniforms for some of our country's earliest and most notable military officers. One such officer was Rear Admiral Francis Higginson. Higginson fought in the Civil War, taking part in the blockade of Charleston. He was also

Samuel N. Meyer

Outside entrance to International Insignia Corporation's old location, circa 1960.

captain of the *U.S.S. Massachusetts*, one of the first battleships in the U.S. Navy, during the Spanish American War. For Higginson, Meyer designed and manufactured his dress hat, which was adorned with wide gold embroidered trim, as well as elegantly styled gold embroidered epaulettes.

In addition to the creation of military uniforms, Meyer also expanded his business to include embroidered cloth insignia patches for the military. By the latter part of the 19th century Meyer's business had grown tremendously and once again he expanded his business, this time into the area of metal design and manufacturing. Among the items Meyer created were ceremonial naval swords, which today are highly sought after by military aficionados. He also made metal insignia and buttons for military uniforms.

Realizing that New York City was quickly becoming the nation's hub for

the manufacturing industry, Meyer sent his son, Nathan Meyer, to New York to establish the family business in Manhattan. Upon Samuel Meyer's retirement, Nathan took over the business and it officially became N.S. Meyer.

By the beginning of the 20th century, N.S. Meyer began to focus its energies on being a supplier of embroidered badges and metal insignia, with most of the company's manufacturing being done by Swift and Fisher of Attleboro, Massachusetts. The company was responsible for creating a myriad of military insignias during World War I. By the 1920s N.S. Meyer began creating insignia for the Philippine Scouts, a component of the regular United States Army, including the 45th and 57th Infantry Regiments, the

24th Field Artillery Regiment, and the 92nd Coast Artillery Regiment.

In 1924 the United States Army Quartermaster Corps created regulations for the research, design, and development of distinctive unit insignia, shoulder sleeve insignia (patches), flags, medals, seals, coats of arms, and other heraldic items for the army. This created uniformity in military insignia design and greater governmental control over what was produced and by whom. Furthermore, it dictated what the insignias and various other military items looked like. From this point on, the U.S. Quartermaster Corps officially recognized N.S. Meyer as one of the major suppliers of military insignia for the armed forces.

International Insignia Corporation's new location in 2001, at 1280 Eddy Street.

Abner Raeburn on the left and grandson Robert K. Raeburn in 1962 at a Christmas party.

Nathan S. Meyer.

In 1926 Nathan Meyer's daughter, Marjorie, married Abner Raeburn. Shortly after, in the 1930s, the company came under Raeburn's leadership.

While many companies ceased to exist during the Depression Era, N.S. Meyer persevered through those difficult years, thanks to their years of experience in the field and professional ingenuity. In fact, the company continued to grow, expanding its sales and manufacturing forces, becoming the leader in its field.

In 1936 N.S. Meyer became the manufacturer of note for the distinctive Polar Bear Crest, used by the 31st Infantry Regiment, one of the first military units to receive a unit insignia.

Before the onset of World War II, N.S. Meyer found its services in great demand by the armed forces. The company is credited with manufacturing the highly collectible United States Army and Air Force World War II Service Pilot's Wings. They also produced United States Marine ribbon bars, and medals and insignia for the Oklahoma National Guard that participated in the war. Most notably, N.S. Meyer created and manufactured medals and awards, including Bronze Stars and Silver Stars for the nation's most decorated officers. Among them were U.S. Army General George S. Patton, the Four-Star General who fought in the European Theater, and U.S. Army General Douglas MacArthur, who fought in the Pacific War and one of the last U.S. Army Generals to be awarded Five Stars.

N.S. Meyer also manufactured medals and insignia for the military that fought in the Korean War, including the Chief Aircrew Wing for the United States Air Force. In addition, when the 31st Infantry Regiment was reactivated in Korea in 1946, Meyer manufactured a new Polar Bear Crest insignia, approved by the War Department in 1924. That insignia has been worn by the regiment and its successor battle groups and battalions ever since.

In the 1950s Robert A. Raeburn, Abner's son, began working at the company. N.S. Meyer again expanded, this time buying D & N Manufacturing from its owner, Howard Nelson. D & N Manufacturing, well known in the Rhode Island jewelry community, was also the company that had been doing most of the stamping and enamel work for Meyer. Raeburn invited Nelson to stay on and help run the now larger company, which Nelson gladly agreed to do.

In 1954 D & N Manufacturing became International Insignia and was incorporated as a Rhode Island company. At this time the firm opened a

Marjorie Meyer and Abner Raeburn about 1959.

manufacturing facility at 387 Charles Street in Providence, Rhode Island. The incorporation of International Insignia made N.S. Meyer the first wholesaler of military insignia with its own manufacturing facility. As a self-contained manufacturer, all aspects of the insignia process including the purchase of raw materials, stamping, soldering, enameling, and the sale of products, all happened within the company.

During the 1950s the Raeburn family also continued to grow. Robert's wife Joann gave birth to a son, Robert K. Raeburn.

Howard L. Nelson on the left and Robert A. Raeburn in 1955.

Raeburn's son, Robert K., developed an early interest in the family business. A student of business and economics who graduated with honors in 1977, Robert K. began interning at International Insignia, the family's manufacturing facility in Providence. He had always been mechanically inclined, and was excited about learning every detail of the family business from design to manufacturing. From his days as an intern through his later years as a company employee, Raeburn continued to be an avid student on the job, learning all aspects of the manufacturing business. He moved from department to department, gaining a wide understanding of the company, including the intricacies of insignia manufacturing from the employees who had been working for the company most of their lives.

Having accrued a vast amount of knowledge and hands-on experience in the company, Robert K. Raeburn was promoted to plant manager in 1984. In his new position, he applied his skills in production and salesmanship and began to make improvements in the areas of production and purchasing to enhance the productivity of the business. His innovations proved to be highly successful, cost efficient, and profitable. Under his guidance, the company grew to 75 employees and expanded its manufacturing space by 40 percent to 13,000 square feet.

During the 1980s and 1990s, the United States military began a drastic reduction of personnel. This was especially true in the Air Force and Army sectors of the military, two of International Insignia's largest clients. By the early 1990s Robert K. Raeburn was president and CEO of International Insignia and once again he set about making improvements that would set the company moving in an even more efficient and cost effective direction. Raeburn realized that new markets had to be located in order for the company to sustain its

Robert K. Raeburn in 1998 at the old location.

steady rate of growth. One of the ways he accomplished this was by downsizing the workforce and cross training its remaining employees. He also found more cost-effective ways of achieving the quality of manufacturing the company had enjoyed, utilizing state-of-the art equipment.

Through careful and in-depth research it became clear to him that the company's manufacturing segment was rapidly changing from what it once was. The benefits of being a self-contained company were quickly disappearing, and to continue using the methods that had proved so successful for many years could now be its death knell. Raeburn sought out smaller shops that could do specific tasks, thereby cutting manufacturing and employee costs that could bury a small company. He also expanded their sales market to include the highly lucrative business of promotional items for corporations. He joined and began to do business with members of the Advertising Specialties Institute, which also proved to be highly profitable. Once again, Raeburn's professional instincts proved to be uncannily on target.

In 2000 Raeburn acquired International Insignia from his father, and N.S. Meyer was sold to Vanguard Industries. In June of the same year Raeburn purchased a property at 1280 Eddy Street in Providence, containing 25,000 square feet, and by the day after Labor Day the company was operating out of its new facility. Raeburn gave his 55 employees the week of the move off, but most of them came in without pay to help the company set up its physical plant. Such loyalty is a reflection of how well Raeburn treats his employees.

Since Raeburn acquired the company, and with his excellent manufacturing and marketing instincts, business has grown by 50 percent. It also continues to enjoy the same strong association with the nation's military as it did back in the Civil War. Most recently, International Insignia was honored with the contract to develop two medals for the war on terrorism for the United States government: the Service Medal and the Expeditionary Medal.

Howard L. Nelson in 1989 just before his retirement from the company.

The company's enamel department, mid-1960.

LIN TELEVISION CORPORATION

In an industry where mergers and acquisitions take place on a daily basis, LIN Television Corporation has both survived and thrived to become a powerful presence across the airwaves of Providence and beyond. The organization ranks as one of the leading independent pure-play station group operators in the nation. LIN currently operates 24 stations in 14 markets, encompassing 7 percent of U.S. television households and all of the 1.2 million television households in Puerto Rico. Such success was achieved despite the sometimes harrowing episodes of hostile takeovers, company moves, and turbulent capital markets.

The company's predecessor, LIN Broadcasting Corporation, was established in the mid-1960s and headquartered on the corner of 56th Street and Sixth Avenue in New York City. LIN Broadcasting was involved in several arenas, including radio and television broadcasting, music publishing and record labels, direct market-

WPRI Channel 12/FOX Providence.

ing, and information and learning. LIN management made further acquisitions in broadcasting, owning seven television stations by 1983.

It expanded into paging and entered the cellular telephone business in the early 1980s. By 1985 the organization owned and managed cellular telephone licenses serving New York, Philadel-

Gary R. Chapman, chairman, president, and CEO of LIN Television Corporation.

phia, Los Angeles, Dallas, and Houston. The company sold its paging operations and six of its radio stations in 1986 to help finance the development of its cellular business.

Much of the organization's success over the past 15 years is due in part to the leadership and business acumen of Gary R. Chapman, who serves as chairman, president, and CEO of LIN Television Corporation. Chapman joined LIN Broadcasting as president of television operations in December, 1988.

The Iowa native's interest in the television business began at the tender age of seven. His uncle had been the station news director at WOC radio in Davenport. When the first television station signed on in the city, Chapman's uncle read the news for the station. Young Gary accompanied his uncle and watched the newscast with awe. "At Thanksgiving all of my family would meet at my grandmother's house. Uncle Bill took me with him to watch him do the news. Then we would go

Eyewitness News Team.

back to my grandmother's for dessert," remembers Chapman.

Chapman attended Southern Illinois University in Carbondale, where he studied radio and television communications. As part of the curriculum, he worked in a variety of crew positions, ranging from camera operator to technical director to anchor talent. Some of his earliest assignments involved covering local athletic events. "At first the teacher would send us with a tape recorder to cover high school games. The class would critique our play-by-play color commentary. After doing this for a season, we would do the real games," he says.

The general manager of the one AM radio station in town heard Chapman on the air and was impressed. He contacted the college, called Chapman, and offered him a job doing play-by-play for Carbondale High School games. Since Chapman wanted to get involved in sales, he persuaded the station to let him do some sales work in addition to the play-by-play analysis. He was paid $15 to $20 per game for providing play-by-play and 15 percent commission on sales. As part of his duties, Chapman also wrote and produced 60-second radio spots.

Following graduation in 1967, Chapman went to work in the sales department of NBC affiliate KSDK-TV

in St. Louis. Over the next decade he moved up the ranks to become the director of marketing and research for the station's owner, Pulitzer Television. In 1979 he transferred to WLNE-TV in Providence, which was also owned by the parent company Pulitzer Television. Chapman served as general manager there for five years. The station was sold in 1983 to Freedom Newspapers, Inc. out of Orange County, California. Chapman was promoted to director of broadcasting and, in 1987, he was named senior vice president of broadcasting for Freedom.

In late 1988 Chapman was ready for new challenges and joined LIN Broadcasting in New York City. At the time LIN was a public company with two major divisions—television and cellular telephones. Chapman headed up the television division. McCaw Cellular Communications took control of the company in March 1990, purchasing 52 percent of its shares. His new boss was more concerned with the cellular telephone branch of the company and invited Chapman to take the television business anywhere he desired. After two years in the Big Apple, Chapman wanted to return to Providence. He had been living in an apartment in New York City, and returning home to Bristol, Rhode Island on weekends to be with his wife and children.

In a bold move, Chapman took the television company out of New York City in December 1990 and transplanted it into the much smaller market of Providence. "I traded the Hudson River for Narragansett Bay," he says. The move proved to be brilliant for both the company and Chapman. In June 1994 he became CEO of television operations, and chairman six years later.

Paul Karpowicz is another major contributor and visionary in the broadcast company's success. For the past ten years he has held the position of vice president of television operations and has served as director since 1999. Karpowicz was the general manager of the LIN TV CBS network station WISH-TV in Indianapolis for five years before joining LIN in Providence.

AT&T acquired McCaw Cellular Communications in 1994. LIN Broadcasting's television operations were then spun off as a public company traded on the NASDAQ stock market with 45 percent of the shares owned by AT&T. The company was renamed LIN Television Corporation and was the owner or operator of 12 stations. LIN Television Corporation remained a public company until March 1998, when it was acquired by Hicks, Muse, Tate and

Receive satellite dishes at WPRI.

Furst, Inc. (HMTF), a private investment firm based in Dallas, Texas. At the time of the acquisition, LIN contributed its NBC affiliate in Dallas to a joint venture with the NBC affiliate in San Diego.

Under the ownership of HMTF, LIN has experienced significant growth through numerous acquisitions. In June 1999 LIN acquired WOOD-TV in Grand Rapids, Michigan, a station to which it had provided consulting services for several years. Two months later it created Banks Broadcasting, a minority-owned television broadcast company in which LIN holds a 50 percent interest. Currently Banks owns KWCV-TV, the WB affiliate in Wichita, Kansas and KNIN-TV, the UPN affiliate in Boise, Idaho. LIN extended its influence beyond the mainland United States in October of that same year when it purchased

WAPA-TV in San Juan, Puerto Rico. Two years later LIN became a multi-channel presence on the island when it purchased WJPX-TV and three satellite facilities.

Station acquisitions continued in 2000, when LIN bought WLFI-TV out of Lafayette, Indiana in exchange for 66 percent interest in its station WAND-TV in Decatur, Illinois. LIN still provides management oversight for WAND today. LIN also purchased WWLP-TV in Springfield, Massachusetts in 2000. The following year the company acquired WNLO-TV in Buffalo, New York.

In early 2002 LIN exercised and closed on options to buy three stations that it was already managing—WVBT-TV in Norfolk, Virginia; WOTV-TV out of Battle Creek, Michigan; and WCTX-TV in New Haven, Connecticut.

The company agreed to purchase seven stations in six markets from STC Broadcasting in February and completed the acquisition in May. LIN Television Corporation became a public company again that same year. It was renamed LIN TV Corp. and trades on the New York Stock Exchange under the symbol TVL.

In seven markets, LIN operates more than one station. In Providence, for example, LIN owns WPRI-TV; a CBS affiliate and WNAC-TV; a FOX station. These "duopolies" are part of the organization's marketing strategy to pair up leading news stations with emerging networks. "We provide a lot of news for the more mature demographics through CBS, NBC, and ABC, and

Eyewitness News Chopper 12.

reach a much younger target audience with WB, UPN, and FOX," explains Chapman. "This way we can provide a much larger audience reach."

In addition, LIN operates low power stations in Austin and Indianapolis which are affiliates of Univision or Telefutura. These stations serve the Hispanic market, thus further broadening the organization's audience and advertising base.

These corporate strategies have also proven to be highly successful for LIN in ways that cannot be measured in mere dollars and cents. When Chapman began his career with the organization in 1988, LIN employed 700 workers. Today the total number of employees exceeds 2,000. Through employee recognition programs like "The Circle of Excellence," LIN workers are rewarded for exemplary performance and made to feel appreciated.

Initiated in 1990 when McCaw Cellular owned the company, this program honors employees who are singled out by their peers for their excellent work record. The reward is a five-day cruise to such exotic places as the Bahamas, the Caribbean, or Alaska. Approximately 5 percent of the work force is chosen to go each year, excluding members of management who are not eligible. The trip is not counted as vacation time and is not taxable.

"LIN has a special culture that stems from the employees themselves," says Chapman. "These people are there because they exemplify LIN culture. They enjoy their work and they are helpful to their fellow employees. It's a great morale builder." A large segment of the workforce also owns stock in the company. Through various stock options, employees are "collectively owner/operators of the company," Chapman says.

Community service is another strongly encouraged facet of LIN culture. The organization, through WPRI-TV, is very active in "Meeting Street School," a program established in Providence in 1946 which provides educational and therapeutic services to children and their families. Each year Meeting Street assists 1,700 children and young adults, many of whom have disabilities and developmental delays. Last year LIN donated a day's work from 50 of its executives who came from around the country and Puerto Rico to help build and prepare games for a school fair. When it was over, they presented a $10,000 check to the Meeting Street School.

WPRI-TV, the CBS affiliate in Providence, is a sponsor of the Fourth of July parade in the city of Bristol. Hailed as the oldest and one of the longest parades in the nation, the annual event is attended by tens of thousands of spectators. LIN is actively involved in a myriad of programs throughout the nation including the Boys Club in Austin, Texas and Habitat for Humanity in Springfield, Massachusetts. It has also helped to fund the development of public parks in Ft. Worth and Indianapolis.

Chapman says LIN will continue to grow and add additional markets. Unlike other corporations in the communications industry, however, LIN has no designs on branching out into radio or related fields. We believe it is important to stick to what we know and remain focused on what we do best," says Chapman. "And television is what we do best."

MEETING STREET

• *The young father of a developmentally-challenged baby had withdrawn from his unresponsive child. That was until one evening when his wife was working on play exercises recommended by the Meeting Street staff. The baby smiled, made a sound, and waved. The father hesitated and then waved and smiled back, and a family that had been fragmented takes the first step on the path to wholeness.*

• *The parents of a young child with cerebral palsy did not know whether their daughter would ever walk, talk, or feed herself. In six years at Meeting Street, however, she grew into a confident, independent, young girl who makes friends easily, manages her motorized chair with precision, is adept on the computer, and attends her neighborhood public school.*

• *An 11-year-old with severe hearing loss practiced patiently in a state-of-the-art audiology booth at Meeting Street, until he learned to respond to a particular sound with a specific action. This seemingly simple act was a giant leap forward in his development.*

These are true stories of the challenges and triumphs of children and families enrolled in programs through Meeting Street. In 1946 Dr. Eric Denhoff and Margaret "Poggy" Langdon Kelly envisioned a community where individuals of all abilities were valued. Instead, what they saw was a world of limitations and isolation for individuals with

An elementary school student welcomes a friend at the beginning of a new school day.

Meeting Street was founded in 1946 by Dr. Eric Denhoff, a pediatrician (above left), and Margaret "Poggy" Langdon Kelly, an educator (above right).

disabilities. Dr. Denhoff (1913–1982) was born in Brooklyn, New York into a family that had fled the late 19th century persecutions of Jews in Russia. "Poggy," (1904–2001) as she was known from childhood, came from a family with roots deep in New England. It was perhaps an unlikely meeting, but they both loved and firmly believed in the unlimited potential of all children.

Denhoff had worked his way through the University of Vermont playing football, and it was his coach who told him he had been accepted to the medical school there. After obtaining his medical degree in 1938, Denhoff served a residency at the Bradley Home in East Providence, where he worked with children with cerebral palsy. Dr. Denhoff experimented with medicines and exercises to aid those children who suffered from severe spasms. During this time he published the first of many professional papers about his research.

Two months after the 1941 attack on Pearl Harbor, however, Denhoff was off to the South Pacific. He spent the next three years in military hospitals where he treated not only soldiers, but adults and children in New Caledonia. During this time he was made head of the medical laboratory. "He learned a lot about blood work and lab medicine," says his wife, Sylvia Denhoff. "This gave him a good background to become a wonderful diagnostician." Sylvia and

Eric Denhoff wrote each other constantly during his absence and were married right after his return to Providence in 1945. It was then and there that Dr. Denhoff set up his private pediatric practice.

The next year, the Easter Seal Society tapped Poggy to explore "unmet needs" for the handicapped in Rhode Island. While trying to decide what exactly those unmet needs were, Poggy spoke with Dr. Arthur Ruggles (then superintendent of Butler Hospital and a leading figure in the community) and Dr. Charles Bradley of the Bradley Hospital, where Denhoff had served his residency. Both doctors suggested that she see the young, new pediatrician in town, Dr. Denhoff.

Poggy liked to tell the story of how they first met. Upon her initial meeting with Dr. Denhoff, he immediately reached into his desk drawer and pulled out a fully developed plan for a facility he hoped to open one day. In his practice as a pediatrician, Dr. Denhoff saw children with cerebral palsy and other problems. He firmly believed that early diagnosis and therapy—integrated with education—were key for children to realize their potential and live a fulfilling life. Poggy was immediately taken with

A pre-schooler celebrates her achievements at Meeting Street's Bright Futures Early Learning Center.

A four-year-old boy and his classmate play together with a toy on the tray of her wheelchair.

the plan and agreed, at that time, that children with CP were most in need of help. In 1946 she mobilized fundraising and publicity campaigns to make their shared vision a reality.

The two were offered rent-free a tiny, two-story, two-room school in Providence. Located on Meeting Street, the historic building which dated to 1769, had housed the first free school in Providence and later Brown University, but had been abandoned for years. Excited volunteers repaired and painted, and in November 1947 Meeting Street School opened with two students.

Dr. Denhoff volunteered his services as unpaid medical director for the next 35 years, until his death in 1982. The last 20 years of his medical practice, he specialized in pediatric neurology, and pioneered drug treatment for ADHD or hyperactivity in children which prevented learning. He always said that drugs without therapy or counseling were useless.

Meeting Street rapidly grew to 15 students and six part-time staff members. Its early concentration on cerebral palsy quickly evolved into broader research and treatment programs. This was a result of the discovery that cerebral palsy

was only one of a number of related disorders of the nervous system.

As the school grew, it became known nationally and internationally for its firsts. It was the first to educate and treat children with multiple challenges and the first to create programs for infants with physical handicaps, children with learning disabilities, and all interested parents. Meeting Street also pioneered what is now known as early intervention and was instrumental in drafting state and federal legislation, creating early intervention as a mandated entitlement program.

Another important first was the philosophy of inclusion—once known as "mainstreaming." Simply put, inclusion means recognizing and involving individuals with disabilities as valued members of the community. At Meeting Street children and young adults with and without disabilities learn and explore together, and develop meaningful friendships along the way. Meeting Street pioneered this concept, recognizing the integral value of all children and helping them discover their talents and develop their skills. Every program was developed to help children lead fulfilling lives and to become contributing members of the community.

From its roots on Meeting Street,

the school expanded to space on the Butler Hospital campus in 1957. In 1975 it moved to the former Nicholson File Company building on Waterman Avenue in East Providence—just three miles over the river from its first home. In 1985 Meeting Street opened the Bright Futures Early Learning Center, the nationally accredited, fully-inclusive center which currently serves infants and young children. In 2006 Meeting Street will return to its roots when it opens its new National Center for Excellence in the heart of Providence. The organization is currently developing plans for a unique campus that will foster greater learning and inclusion opportunities for children and young adults of all abilities, and will serve as a focal point for research and training.

Today Meeting Street serves 1,700 children, young adults, and their families throughout Rhode Island and nearby Massachusetts and Connecticut. Its mission and philosophy remain the same: to help children and young adults, of all abilities, live full and meaningful lives. Meeting Street has been a vital part of Rhode Island for nearly six decades and continues to live up to its motto of "teaching skills, touching hearts, changing lives...believing in the possibilities."

A high school sports enthusiast scores a basket during adapted physical education class.

NATCO

Natco is an innovative and diversified, third generation family business with its main focus on home decor. A Rhode Island company with its headquarters in West Warwick, the 87-year-old company continues to expand both internally and through acquisitions. Throughout its history Natco has enjoyed healthy and productive relationships with its customers and employees. It stands out as a shining example as one of the more solid and successful family-owned businesses on the American landscape.

The beginnings of the company date back to 1917 when Arthur Galkin, the son of Russian immigrants, first started a waste paper business along with partner Meyer Levitt. The company was originally called the National Waste Paper Company. Galkin was the working partner of the two with Levitt, a Providence grocery store owner, the financier. The company quickly became profitable and bought its first facility on South Water Street in 1918. Sadly, in 1922 the building suffered a catastrophic fire and with no insurance the company began to lose customers to its competitors. But the young team of Galkin and Levitt were undeterred, and quickly got back on their feet. They purchased land at 92 Narragansett Street, building a 14,000-square-foot facility. When the building was complete, they expanded into a new business, City Coal

Arthur Galken 1894-1992, Founder.

Company, using their good credit to buy coal. Their unflagging spirit soon won back most of the National Waste Paper Company clientele, and the team thrived on both fronts.

Galkin not only excelled at business, but was also an ingenious systems designer. In order to get the coal processed and delivered in the most efficient manner, he designed a silo system. When coal was brought in by train it would be placed on a conveyor belt, transported to the top of the silo and then fed into trucks below by gravity. This system made the receiving and delivery of coal—

once a slow and messy business—quick and easy.

By 1925 the company began buying rubber waste from U.S. Rubber. Galkin, always striving to fill the needs of the public, again came up with an idea for a new product. Using the waste tile purchased from U.S. Rubber, Galkin conceived of a way to die cut the rubber tiles into strips and wire them together to make doormats. In 1927 the company introduced its revolutionary "Neo Link" doormat, which was a huge success. It was the first doormat to hit the U.S. market, originally selling for 60 cents.

As the company began to diversify its businesses and products more and more, it was decided that a new name was needed that would encompass all the existing and future businesses. In 1934 the business officially became Natco Products Corporation. The name was devised from combining the company names, National Waste Paper Company and City Coal.

An outgrowth of Natco's relationship with U.S. Rubber was the creation of a line of beach bags to complement swimsuits, and other beach items that U.S. Rubber was already manufacturing. In 1938 Natco agreed to create colorful fabric-covered, rubberized beach bags for the company. Of the 60 or so samples Natco would produce each year, U.S. Rubber would select approximately 40 designs, and Natco was then free to sell the remaining ones as their own product. It was the beginning of Natco's "Department S," one of the company's most successful and enduring product lines. There were over 200 employees solely dedicated to the manufacturing of the bags.

During World War II, when rubber for commercial use on the American market was non-existent, Arthur Galkin again came up with yet another innovative idea. He began buying waste from a Massachusetts company, Bird & Son, which was making a simulated rubber product called "Rubberlike." Galkin came up with a way to run the product over a hot pipe, giving it the

First factory in Providence, Rhode Island.

shape it needed to become a stair tread. The product became a major seller for Natco, selling to major store chains and hardware stores nationally.

In 1949 one of Arthur Galkin's two sons joined the company. Robert Galkin became Natco's leading Midwest salesman, building the company's mat sales division to nearly a half a million dollars. That same year Natco moved from Narragansett Street to its new 28,000-square-foot Dexter Street facility.

By 1952 sales had skyrocketed to well over a million dollars, with no signs of slowing down. The company broke ground for a 44,000-square-foot facility on 1400 Post Road in Warwick. The new site proved to be an unwelcome boondoggle for Natco. Under the advice of a well-known local architect, the company had built the modern facility on land that they would come to discover was a peat bog. Shortly after the company moved into the building, the structure began sinking several inches a week. Undaunted, Galkin led a team of engineers who developed an intricate

Robert, Warren and Arthur Galkin at hyrdo site, 1990.

system of support pilings to stop the sinking, After a period of trial and error the building was not only saved, but actually emerged stronger than it was when first erected.

Natco continued its upward spiral toward greater and greater success, and once again moved to meet the growing demands of the business. The company moved from the Post Road building and purchased the 140,000-square-foot Arctic Mill in West Warwick, Rhode Island.

Arthur's other son, Warren Galkin, joined the family business in 1957. Warren received his BS in Physics from Brown University and his MBA from Wharton, writing his masters thesis on product diversification for small companies. Warren was also a Navy veteran with a lot of experience in machinery, a talent that would become extremely useful in the years to come.

By the 1960s after their relationship with U.S. Rubber ended, Natco expanded their line to include travel bags and light luggage. It was at this time the company began to develop a relationship with Pan American Airways, producing the trademark "PanAm" bags for the airline. Within no time, Natco was manufacturing custom travel bags for more than 60 airlines around the world.

The company continued to market floor matting and stair treads which now included Koroseal Vinyl matting, treads and clear gripper matting from B.F. Goodrich. Natco was also focusing on building its merchandising, marketing, and design departments as the company continued to grow. They created a major sales and distribution network throughout the United States, and began to create a well thought-out merchandising strategy for their products in

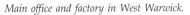

Main office and factory in West Warwick.

the retail markets. The plan included packaging, point of purchase displays, and also created a dealer incentive program to help drive traffic to their businesses. By the early 1970s Natco sales reached more than $6 million, and additional space was needed to meet the company's continuing growth. A 420,000-square-foot facility was purchased on Brookside Avenue in West Warwick.

In 1979 Mike Litner, Robert Galkin's son-in-law, joined Natco. Litner's arrival brought an infusion of new energy and ideas, which would once again broaden the company's horizons. His influence took Natco into new and exciting directions, especially into home improvement and home decor. Under his direction new highly-profitable markets opened up for the company, including the development, manufacture and sales of tapestries, printed carpets, play and game rugs for children and a multitude of other printed home decor items. Litner also expanded the company's sales reach to include the European, Canadian and Latin American markets. He was also instrumental in the hiring of some key personnel including Barry Brickman, John Mentuck

David Litner on game rug, 1994.

and Marc Zukowski. Brickman was well-seasoned in developing the home improvement market, while Mentuck and Zukowski were highly skilled in creating and maintaining relationships with domestic retailers.

In the late '70s Natco began to purchase carpet remnants, repackaging them into a popular new line. In 1985 Natco purchased the assets from Central Textile in Dalton, Georgia and started NPC South in a 20,000-square-foot facility. Under the leadership of Presidents Betty Kinnamon and then Roy Littman, the Georgia textile division grew exponentially. By the turn of the century it would expand into five buildings, covering more than 400,000 square feet.

In 1983 Natco diversified its holdings once again, this time founding Valley Hydro, a power generating plant along the Pawtuxet River. The facility operated within the historic 140,000-square-foot Arctic Mill, which was built in 1854. The company now sells its electricity to New England Power.

In 1993 Alan Ross was named as Chief Financial Officer. A year later Robert Galkin stepped down as the head of the company and named Mike Litner as Natco's new president. Robert Galkin now took on the position of chairman with Warren Galkin as vice chairman.

That same year Natco purchased Robertson Factories in Cordell, Oklahoma and Corona Curtain in Boston. Corona was a company with a great product, but because of management problems was rapidly losing its customer base. Litner took on the challenge eagerly and with the help of Alan Ross and Christine Bolton, he made the business profitable again. By 2003 Corona would become one of the major suppliers of window treatments and drapes with sales reaching more than $75 million.

In 1994 the company also made a major investment in the area of assisted-living facilities in the New England area. Natco went into partnership with Peter and Dianne Sangermano, first opening the Village at Waterman Lake in Rhode Island. The investment turned out to be a good one and now includes more than 10 properties in Rhode Island,

Mike and Jane Litner, 2003.

Massachusetts, and Connecticut, with over 1,500 rooms and 1,000 employees.

By the last decade of the 20th century, Natco made substantial inroads into the high-end textile market. The company was able to purchase Central Oriental, which sold imported rugs to the upscale department and carpet stores. Under Natco, Central developed new lines of both machine and hand-made rugs. Today Central Oriental is one of the leading importers of high quality rugs for the domestic market. Most recently in 2002 Natco purchased Flemish Weavers, which operates a state-of-the-art carpet weaving facility in Sanford, Maine. This new acquisition added domestically manufactured carpeting to its line of imported rugs.

Throughout all of its divisions Natco maintains high standards of quality control. A perfect example is its order picking. Each order is carefully inspected to meet the firm's stringent standards. The company takes quality control so seriously it built a new structure adjacent to its main Rhode Island plant, specifically to generate the best possible quality control. The company strongly adheres to a philosophy that their customers—who include major names such as Home Depot, Lowe's, Wal-Mart, Macy's, Sears, JC Penney, and dozens of others—should only expect the best from Natco.

To that end, Natco has created a "Six-Point Policy," which reflects the company's philosophy on every aspect of doing business.

Marketplace: Knowing and understanding the marketplace is a major key to the company's ability to thrive. It is not only important to know what is selling on the market, but also what is not selling. This knowledge guides the company to keep designing, manufacturing and marketing the best products that the market wants for the current and future retail marketplace.

Quality: To strive to provide the best quality products, with the highest standards in safety both in its products and for its employees. To create a quality workplace resulting in superior products.

Merchandising: Understanding the importance of innovative packaging, display, and advertising of its products.

Service: Providing prompt delivery of all products, the best in customer service, advanced quality control, and the utilization of state-of-the-art computer software to maintain expert delivery and account services.

Partnership: Treat all customers and employees as partners and work towards the success and profitability of all involved.

New York showroom during "Home Textile Market," 2003.

Flexibility: Be open to new ideas and concepts. Plan carefully to grow both internally and though acquisitions but allow for mistakes and learn from them.

This six-point policy continues to be Natco's key to success. The company's talented staff of international and domestic managers and design staff identify trends and develop profitable products. With its financial strength, impressive leadership, and strong market relations and knowledge, Natco continues to look for acquisitions to add to its exciting growth.

Today Natco companies utilize more than 1 million square feet of business property in four states. The company employs more than 1,600 employees and has group sales approaching $200 million. After 87 years Natco constantly strives to know its market, to design products for tomorrow and—as they have done so often in the past—get there first.

Stockholders meeting, 2002. Top row, left to right: Warren Galkin, Harris Kenner, Alan Ross, Wini and Bob Galkin. Bottom row, left to right: Ellen Kenner, Debra Krim, Mike and Jane Litner, and Martin Krim.

NRI COMMUNITY SERVICES, INC.

NRI Community Services, Inc. was founded in 1966, just as federal and state legislation and public policy was shifting mental health services from institutional to community settings. For its first 15 years NRI, like most community mental health centers, was a relatively small nonprofit agency. Professional staff served diverse child and adult mental health problems in an office setting. Founders Dr. Edward P. Nolan, Viola M. Berard, and Dr. Frank D.E. Jones focused on providing mental health services to those who were least able to pay.

In 1981 NRI's nonprofit board of directors hired Christian L. Stephens as its executive director. Stephens' approach was significantly different from the highly professionalized approaches of the past. Based on his work experience with low income youth and adults in community mental health and corrections programs in New York and Vermont, Stephens collaborated with the board of directors to redesign NRI's services.

An advocacy-oriented board of directors was elected and home and community-based services were prioritized. As part of the agency's new direction, a housing development subsidiary was formed, several job placement programs were initiated for clients, and an alternative school was started. Child and adult programs were refocused to concentrate more on the

NRI Community Services, Inc.'s Cummings Way office offers acute and long-term outpatient services in Woonsocket.

clients' goals rather than on their ailments. A more diverse workforce was also employed, which had a broader range and understanding of clients in all stages of recovery.

Through the efforts of an entrepreneurial-minded management team, funding and services were expanded. Alliances were made with a wide range of other organizations and arrangements for referrals were established. Involuntary hospitalizations were dramatically reduced as child and adult case management teams and a 24-hour crisis team intervened with clients. Substance abuse and violence intervention services were soon added as NRI merged other small nonprofit agencies into their organization. Finally, affiliated nonprofits were created to offer peer-provided services to families and people suffering from mental illness. The entire agency focused on individuals and groups in the community that were most "at-risk."

Today, nearly 40 years later, NRI Community Services (NRICS) is a significant small business in northern Rhode Island. It supports 265 jobs, pays $100,000 in

The Singleton House in Burrillville, a group home for people with mental illness.

property taxes, and has over a $12 million a year economic impact on the communities it serves. Along the way, it has garnered numerous awards and recognitions for housing, employment, crisis, volunteer, mental health, substance abuse, and rehabilitation programs. Stephens has also earned recognition, including the Piepenbrink Award from the National Council of Community Behavioral Healthcare, for his professional contributions to the field of mental health administration.

"Like any other nonprofit health or human services organization, our business succeeds because of the wealth of volunteer "stakeholders" that shepherd our resources and support our continuous efforts to improve our services," says Stephens. "Furthermore, our diverse staff understands the impact that poverty, bias, and community violence has had on the children and adults we serve. They listen to their 'customers' and partner with them in their recovery."

When Blackstone Valley Mental Health Realty Corporation was formed by NRICS in the 1980s, the Greater Woonsocket area was known for being home to several generations of refugee groups. This was due mostly to the availability of low cost rental housing. However, today Rhode Island has the fastest escalating housing prices in the United States—with one of the biggest gaps between income and housing costs. Rhode Island's small size and environmentally-protected areas, coupled with dense population, have also made it the state with the lowest rate of new housing development. To make the housing problem even more of a challenge, affluent commuters who work in the Greater Boston area occupy many units nearby, contributing to Rhode Island's very low vacancy rates.

NRI Community Services and Blackstone Valley Mental Health Realty Corporation

Christian L. Stephens, president and CEO.

have been a force in Rhode Island and created affordable housing for many of those most in need. In approximately 20 different locations in six cities and towns, nearly 140 housing units have been created for mental health and substance abuse clients. Group homes, supervised apartments, supported apartments, halfway houses, independent living apartments, sober houses, and a planned assisted living facility

provide specialized resources for people with HIV, those in recovery or who suffer from mental illness, and most often, people with some combination of aging, disability, and trauma that makes them at greater risk for relapse and homelessness. The efforts of these two organizations to tackle the state's housing crisis has established them as national leaders in the field of "supported housing."

Currently, federal policy pronouncements from the Center for Mental Health Services assert that the future of mental health and substance abuse services will be in "creating housing, employment, self-help, and peer support services that empower clients in their recovery." NRI Community Services is heeding this declaration, and working to provide the most progressive and effective programs possible. It is excelling at its mission because its clients, board, and staff have taken a common sense approach to improving community mental health services. The agency takes its responsibility to Rhode Islanders very seriously—an attitude that is highly-regarded throughout the state.

The Sadwin Apartments provide independent and supervised units in Woonsocket.

PALMER SPRING COMPANY

In an economy where small companies are routinely swallowed up by large corporations, it is no easy feat for a family-owned business to survive. The Palmer Spring Company of Providence has not only managed to endure, but has now thrived for more than 150 years.

Joseph Palmer, an Englishman and a blacksmith, founded Palmer Spring in 1849. When Palmer opened his blacksmith shop, the business specialized in forging tempered leaf springs for carriages, stagecoaches, and wagons. His customers came from near and far and included both businesses and private citizens. In a short time Palmer Spring also began to produce springs for steam fire trucks and railroad cars. Palmer built his business with the goal of upholding the highest standards when it came to craftsmanship and customer service. It is those enduring traits that have ensured the continuing success of the company.

One of the company's first products was the "easy riding" suspension system. Palmer manufactured and installed this system with great success in

Palmer Spring Company in Providence, at the corner of Dexter and Althea Streets in 1930.

automobiles that are now considered collectible treasures. Cars like Pierce Arrow, Nash, Stutz, and Packard, as well as emerging classics such as Buick, Cadillac, and Lincoln all benefited from the new system. Today the shop is known for its expert brake, front end, and suspension work, but the business still holds on to traditions and a style of workmanship that started when the company was first formed.

Over the 15 decades the firm has been in business, five generations of Palmers have played a major role in its operation. Through those years many changes have occurred in the manufacture of

automobiles and the parts they require, but there is still a need for springs. Douglas Palmer, the president of the company, sees the family as stewards of the business—just like the generations that came before them. A graduate of Tufts University with a master's degree in mechanical engineering, Douglas Palmer believes each aspect of the operation plays an essential part in its success.

The Palmer Spring blacksmith shop is still considered the heart of the company by its employees. What makes it unique is not only that they work on antique cars, but that in many cases they use the same tools that were used in the early days of the business. In fact, when stepping into the shop it looks much like it did 90 years ago.

Today the department is led by Ed Weidele, Jr. who started learning the craft more than 25 years ago. He is now a top suspension specialist. Springs for carriages, antique cars, and muscle cars—for which off-the-shelf parts are not available—are forged in the blacksmith shop. In more recent years the Palmer team of specialists has worked on vehicles such as a 1941 Packard One Fifty convertible coupe, once owned by General George S. Patton, Jr. and a 1932 Chrysler Imperial, once owned by actor Clark Gable. They are also the shop of choice for many car collectors in the New England area.

Palmer Spring Company's blacksmith shop as it appeared in 1930.

Another important division of Palmer Spring is its parts department. Where the blacksmith shop is the heart of the company, the parts department is what employees and management refer to as "the nerve center." It is here where you will usually find one of the other Palmer brothers, Reginald (Reggie), who also works with the machinery. Several thousand automotive parts make up the inventory at Palmer, which includes everything from wheel bearings, seals, brake components, suspension parts (including hundreds of leaf and coil springs), hoses, fittings, marker lamps, mirrors, and high-performance lubricants. The company believes their high success rate in fulfilling parts orders is no accident. It is due to its philosophy that it is better to have one of every part in stock, instead of a hundred of just one.

Palmer Spring Company understands the close connection between sales and service. Christopher, another fifth generation Palmer and one of the company's salesmen, shows how these two concepts go hand in hand on a regular basis. He visits customers at their garages, diagnoses the problem, specifies the necessary replacement parts, delivers the material, and can even advise them on installation techniques.

Today Palmer Spring has five locations in New England which includes two shops in Massachusetts, two in Rhode Island, and one in Maine. Couet

Spring, the New Bedford, Massachusetts shop, has been in business since the late 1800s and was once a carriage manufacturer. The carriages were offered in three different models and included the milk cart, buckboard, and two-seat surrey. At one point Couet held the honor of being the oldest blacksmith shop in New England, until it was forced to dismantle its coal-fired forge. Couet Spring now specializes in truck brake and suspension repairs. Jay Couet, Jr., the great-grandson of founder Emilio Couet, represents the fourth generation to now work for the company.

Palmer also has another division in Providence. The Ace Spring division manufactures brake shoes to the highest specifications, reconditioning cores and replacing brake lining blocks with like-new parts. Ace Spring produces brake shoes in a variety of sizes, as well as many types of lining materials for trucks. It also has an axle rebushing service.

Palmer Spring prides itself on treating customers and employees like family. Management has always held to a philosophy that its customers and employees come first. In the company newsletter, a large amount of space is devoted to Palmer Spring clients with in-depth articles about their businesses. Employees are rewarded for their good work and dedication, which is clearly

In this 1930 photo a mechanic is working on the undercarriage of a customer's truck. Watching in the pit is Al Ruerat, Palmer Spring manager and bookkeeper, who went on to become mayor of Warwick.

evident in how many of them have been with the company for 20 or more years. Recently, Russell Lamoureux received the company's coveted "Golden U-Bolt Award" for his 40-plus years of service and moments of "creative genius" at Palmer. The firm also stands firmly behind its older employees, recognizing the value, expertise, and experience of each senior staff member.

Over the years Palmer Spring has held on to its integrity and earned the devoted respect of its many long-time customers. In terms of the business, Douglas Palmer likens it to the life of a tree. When one waters and protects the tree it gives forth fruit and sustains life. However, when a person, or business, believes he is more important than the tree, it becomes tempting to kill the tree or sell it, leaving nothing left to grow. Palmer Spring has kept their "tree" alive through its dedication to its employees and customers and through the treasured art of blacksmithing, showing that it still holds a vital place in the automotive repair business. They have also proven that it is still possible to not only preserve a family business in a corporate era, but to thrive from generation to generation.

Palmer Spring listing in 1868 New Hampshire business directory.

PARK AVE. CEMENT BLOCK COMPANY, INC.

When Antonio Pezza arrived in the United States from his native town of Irti, Italy, he settled in the Knightsville section of Cranston, Rhode Island. A hard working self-reliant man, who wanted the best for his family, Pezza not only held down a steady day job, but began his own entrepreneurial operation—making concrete blocks in his backyard. In 1919 Pezza purchased his first piece of machinery from Sears and Roebuck for $60, a hand operated machine for making concrete blocks. Pezza set up his equipment and spent his free time making the blocks one at a time and selling them to people in Cranston for use in building garages and other structures.

Today, more than 85 years later, the Pezza family is still producing concrete blocks and a whole lot more at Park Ave. Cement Block Company, Inc. It has now become the largest producer of concrete masonry units in Rhode Island.

"In addition to manufacturing our concrete blocks, we also make other products as well," says Antonio Pezza, grandson of the company's founder. "For example, we make a concrete burial vault that we sell to the Catholic

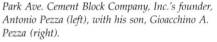

The first delivery trucks that didn't require workers to unload the concrete blocks by hand.

Diocese of Providence. Right now, we are also a building materials distributor and carry a complete line of landscape products."

Park Ave. Cement Block is one of two companies in Rhode Island that manufactures and sells concrete block and serves the needs of the building industry in southeastern New England. According to Pezza, it took many years for his family's company to achieve a prominent position in the world of concrete manufacturing. "Back when

Park Ave. Cement Block Company, Inc.'s founder, Antonio Pezza (left), with his son, Gioacchino A. Pezza (right).

my grandfather started the business, there were nine or ten different block companies in this area doing the same thing. It was a part-time thing that people did after hours. My grandfather went out on his own and started doing the business full-time," Pezza says. "In the late '20s or early '30s he moved from his backyard on Cranston Street to a corner lot on Park Avenue, which is near our current location at 30 Budlong Road."

In the 1950s Giacchino Pezza, Antonio's father, took over the business along with his two brothers. "When I was 10," Pezza recalls, "I remember our manufacturing facility had about half a dozen of these little block machines that made one block at a time. After World War II this industry started to grow. My father went to Kentucky and bought a used block machine. At about that time, they started putting the blocks into ovens and used steam to cure them rather than air drying. That was really the start of this company." Later, the Pezzas bought another automated machine from the Besser Company that made three blocks at a time. "Since that time, the three blocks machine has become an industry standard," Antonio

Pezza says. "It was around this time in 1960 that my father and his brothers moved the facility across the street to our present location.

Current president Antonio Pezza began working at his family's company at age 14, and learned the business from the ground up. "In the early days, they made concrete block out of cinders; cinders were the ashes or by-product from burning coal in the power plants. Our company was one of the first to make concrete block out of sand and stone and give it a new name, STONE-CRETE. Pezza was a real innovator, one of the leaders in our industry when it came to creating new products and trade names."

One of the advancements that the Pezzas introduced was the use of a flatbed delivery truck with rollers, which made the job of unloading trucks easier and quicker. "This is why my uncles and father were very successful. They were progressive. They were al-

ways the first ones to make improvements in the industry. My father and his two brothers took the business to the next plateau. They really came a long way from the '30s to the '60s. With a good business foundation, we've been able to build on their accomplishments."

Like his father and grandfather before him, Antonio Pezza continues to be an industry leader. The modern and efficient plant at his current location has two machines, which produce in excess of 3 million concrete blocks annually. With 25 employees and over an acre of covered storage attached to the manufacturing facility, Park Ave. Cement's physical plant is as impressive as its service record. The employees at Park Ave. take pride in the appearance of their physical plant and the ease with which clients can inspect the various products the company offers.

The Pezza family has long believed in supporting their industry. Park Ave. Cement Block was one of the charter

Park Ave. Cement Block Company, Inc. in 1953.

members of the National Concrete Masonry Association. "We always felt that we, as a company, should be active in organizations where we can learn from others in our industry," says Pezza. "We also believe in supporting agencies whose members purchase our product, like home-builders associations."

The company has been involved with most of the major construction projects in the area, including the Civic Center in downtown Providence in the 1970s, the Convention Center in the 1990s, and other major projects in Rhode Island and southeastern New England. "We are proud of our image, our quality, and our service," Pezza says. Three generations of the Pezza family have built a business, while they also helped build a region. For more than three quarters of a century, Park Ave. Cement has been a vital part of building Rhode Island—literally—from the ground up.

PORTSMOUTH ABBEY SCHOOL

In 1918 Father Leonard Sargent was searching for a property on which to build a Benedictine monastery. Dom Leonard had been a postulant at Downside Abbey, near Bath, England and returned to America with the intention of bringing the English Benedictine tradition of monasticism to his homeland. He had found a property on Narragansett Bay, Rhode Island, which Mrs. George Gardner Hall had put up for sale. As Dom Leonard drove onto the 70-acre plot of land, he knew in his heart he had found the place for the monastery. Following an old superstition, Dom Leonard dropped a medal of St. Benedict in the field, praying that his dreams would come to fruition for this piece of land. Today that property is the home of Portsmouth Abbey and the renowned Portsmouth Abbey School, continuing the 1,500-year-old tradition of Benedictine spiritual devotion and dedication to learning and enlightenment.

Father Hugh Diman founded Portsmouth Priory School (now Portsmouth Abbey School) in 1926. Dom Hugh, who had received his masters from Harvard, was no stranger to education. In 1896 he had opened the Diman School (now St. George's School) in Newport. Later in 1912 he also planned and founded

Benedictine monks in procession on a day of rogation (May, 1946).

the Diman Vocational School in Fall River. Dom Hugh saw his mission as creating a Catholic school that would foster its students' intellectual, spiritual, and physical growth, and by so doing would graduate ambitious, confident, and caring human beings.

To accommodate the needs of a school, renovations of existing buildings on the property and the construction of new ones commenced. The Manor House of Portsmouth Abbey became the first boys' dormitory and the old farmer's cottage became the chapel. A new schoolhouse was erected, and for the first time electricity was installed throughout the new campus. The school officially opened with 18 students on September 28, 1926. A dress code was established, which exists to this day, and all students were required to take part

in both indoor and outdoor sports which included riding "Duchess," a pony that had been given to the school by William Franklin Sands. The school day began with morning prayers at 6:30 a.m. in the chapel, followed by breakfast in the Manor House. Classes ran from 8:35 a.m. until 12:30 p.m. Students had the afternoons free until 4:30 p.m. when classes resumed. After night prayers and supper at 6:30 p.m., they had an hour-long study period and then went to bed.

By 1929 Dom Hugh was both headmaster of the school as well as prior of the monastery and school enrollment had grown to 40. Work began on the new St. Benet's House in 1931 and the school celebrated its first graduating class in June of that same year. Diplomas were awarded to Eugene Reid of New York who went on to Yale, and Richard Tobin of San Francisco who went on to Harvard. Senator David Walsh, the first Catholic governor of Massachusetts, gave the commencement address.

Throughout the school's many years of existence, none were more challenging than those during World War II. None were more reflective of the Abbey community's spirit toward fellow human beings either. Portsmouth Abbey became home to many students from England and the European continent, who might not have otherwise survived the wrath of Nazi Germany. The school also offered

Aerial view of campus from the west (circa 1950).

safe haven to many highly skilled faculty from abroad, and the promise of a more peaceful existence.

Portsmouth Abbey School takes pride in its notable alumni including statesmen such as Illinois Senator Peter Fitzgerald and former Assistant Attorney General William Ruckelshaus; authors John Gregory Dunne, Christopher Buckley, and E.J. Dionne; artists such as renowned abstract expressionist Alfonso Ossorio; and business leaders, Terry McGuirk and John Pepper.

In 1991 Portsmouth Abbey took action on a plan that it had been contemplating for 20 years, and became a coeducational campus for both boarding and day students. The move heralded a new direction for the school and brought many challenges. New houses had to be built to accommodate the female students, and the existing structures had to be converted as well. The school also had to develop new outreach channels to attract girls to the school. This new direction has proven an astounding success for the entire Portsmouth Abbey community.

Of the 27 buildings that reside on the 550-acre campus of Portsmouth Abbey and School, 16 of the structures have been designed by the world-renowned modernist architect Pietro Belluschi. Belluschi, who was part of the "Bauhaus" movement, the head of urban planning and architecture at the Massachusetts Institute of Technology (MIT) during the 1950s and the co-architect of the Pan Am Building in New York. He created on the campus what is considered the most important piece of conservative modernist architecture in Rhode Island: the Portsmouth Abbey Church of St. Gregory the Great. The campus church also contains some of the finest examples of liturgical arts anywhere in the United States. All of the buildings he designed on the campus were built between 1960 and 1991.

Belluschi's Saint Thomas More Library was dedicated in 1992 and serves the students, faculty, monastic and lay community at Portsmouth Abbey. The library contains more than

Students walking into the old classroom building as the bells toll (1965).

26,000 volumes of books, periodicals, non-print and online resources in the fields of math, science, literature, art history, theology, classics and history. The art seminar reading room holds more than 2,000 art books. The art book collection was established by Dom Hilary Martin and Dom Peter Sidler of the monastery. It is supplemented each year by donations from the Donald McGuire Book Fund. Among the library's collection are more than 200 titles authored by Portsmouth Abbey alumni.

The St. Thomas More Library also exhibits objects from the school's collection of art and antiquities from the 6th, 12th, and 14th centuries, as well as

The 18 "first boys" who were enrolled in Portsmouth Priory School (1926).

contemporary art. The school recently received a donation of 12,000 new classical music CDs and has a collection of 600 videos for both curriculum support and entertainment. The library offers a wireless computer network to its community, but students are required to learn how to do primary research using card catalogs and other basic research tools before relying on the Internet. Additionally, the library offers its students a place for quiet study.

The Abbey is also home to the Monastic Library, which is open to scholars by special permission and appointment. Designed by Belluschi as well, the

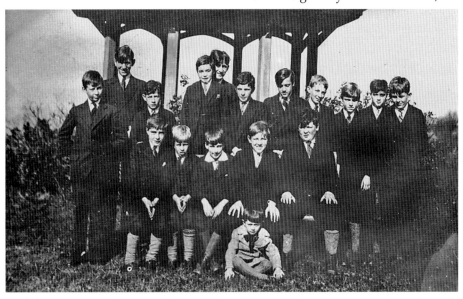

library contains more than 40,000 volumes. It houses some of the oldest texts in existence, including original writings from the 16th, 17th, and 18th centuries on subjects such as Christianity, religion, monasticism, and philosophy.

In 1998 the Portsmouth Abbey School recommitted itself to the "western intellectual tradition," which is grounded in the teachings that date back to ancient Greece and Rome up to the 21st century. Students concentrate on the learning of the classical languages, religion, literature, history and an integrated humanities program, as well as the arts and athletics.

Portsmouth Abbey School welcomed Dr. James De Vecchi as headmaster of the school in 2000. A graduate of the University of New Hampshire, Headmaster De Vecchi, has a Ph.D. in mathematics and has been a member of the faculty for over 30 years. His wife, Deb, is also a mathematics teacher at the school.

Aerial view of campus from the north (2002).

Portsmouth Abbey School places great importance on all students participating in both individual and team sports, a mandatory part of the school's curriculum. Under the 30-year leadership of the school's former Director of Athletics, Dom Bede Gorman, the athletics program has always allowed students to enhance their cognitive, spiritual, emotional, and social skills beyond the classroom. Sports such as lacrosse, soccer, football, basketball,

squash, golf, and sailing help students to develop practical skills of teamwork, strategy, and competition. To that end, the school has 21 varsity teams and 36 athletic teams competing in sports. On campus students have use of a state-of-the-art fitness center; two gymnasiums; a six-lane, all-weather track; nine tennis courts; eight squash courts; an indoor hockey rink; outdoor playing fields; and an 18-hole, Scottish links-style golf course.

Like athletics at the school, the visual arts and performing arts programs are of equal importance. In 2000 the school dedicated the Donald T. McGuire Fine Arts Center, named in honor of the late lay faculty member who was responsible for reviving the school's fine arts program. Designed after an old barn on the school campus, the building went on to win an award for architectural excellence. The Center contains an art gallery as well as art studios. Today the performing and visual arts programs offer students educational opportunities that are both classroom-oriented and extracurricular. A vast array of arts choices including theater, art history,

The Portsmouth Abbey School sailing team vies for position in a competitive race on Narragansett Bay.

Students meeting with a monk to discuss the day's assignment.

Modernist church designed by Pietro Belluschi in 1959, completed in 1960.

chamber orchestra, and photography are available to all students. The Abbey Players stage three dramatic performances each year and offer students the opportunity to grow both as artists and theater craftspeople. Another school group, the Abbey Singers, provides students with the ability to grow in their knowledge, understanding and appreciation of music. Students also take private music instruction in voice, piano, guitar and traditional orchestral instruments.

Portsmouth Abbey School is also home to a number of student clubs whose goal is to enhance the student's body of knowledge and the world at large. One of the newest groups to be formed on campus is the humanities discussion group. The group, which was formed, led, and run by students, is a place where they debate, Socratic style, on current events and cultural issues. Other groups on campus include Amnesty International; the Appalachian Service Project; the Creative Writing Workshop; *The Gregorian,* which is the school's yearbook; *The Raven*, the school's art and literary magazine; and *The Beacon*, the student newspaper.

Currently Portsmouth Abbey School, which instructs students in grades 9-12, has 340 enrolled students, of which over 200 reside on campus and the balance are day students. The male students

make up 55 percent of the student body and 45 percent are female. The students come from all nationalities and all religious backgrounds. The school was founded on the principle of students advancing to highly selective, secular colleges and universities, more than 20 percent of whom go on to Tier I universities and colleges. There are 60 teaching faculty, of whom three quarters are lay and one-quarter monastic. Tuition for boarding students is $30,000 per year and $20,000 for day students. The school offers merit scholarships for students with high personal potential as well as various financial aid programs. In affirming the school's philosophy of teaching students from all walks of life, the atmosphere of Portsmouth Abbey is more spiritual than religious. It is an environment that is vibrant, challenging and values the whole person.

While the Portsmouth Abbey School promotes a broad world view, the

Newly renovated McGuire Fine Arts Center at dusk (2002).

institution owes its existence to the Benedictine tradition. The English Benedictine congregation is the oldest of the 21 Benedictine congregations in the world. The present day English congregation is a direct descendant of the congregation, which began in the 13th century by the Holy See and can be found in England, Wales, the United States, Peru and Zimbabwe. The lives of the monks consist of prayer and work. Many are engaged in the running of schools and small parishes and mass centers near monasteries. Today Portsmouth Abbey is under the guidance of the Right Rev. Mark Serna, O.S.B., who is the Abbot. The institution continues to flourish as one of the nation's most prominent secondary schools, dedicated to its roots and the mission of helping young men and women grow in knowledge and grace.

THE PUBLIC ARCHAEOLOGY LABORATORY, INC.

The Public Archaeology Laboratory, Inc. has been uncovering the past—to make way for the future—since 1982. The nonprofit organization, located in Pawtucket, is a full-service cultural resource management firm with extensive experience in all phases of historic property investigation.

The organization's areas of expertise include urban and rural historic archaeology, pre-historic sites, burials, submerged cultural resources, military facilities, transportation structures, and industrial complexes. The staff maintains excellent working relationships with all state review agencies, and has a thorough knowledge of all local, state, and federal cultural resource regulatory requirements. All technical staff meet the professional criteria for their respective disciplines, which are established by the National Park Service.

The Providence skyline forms a backdrop for the first Rhode Island state prison (1842–1895) ruins.

of anthropology at Brown University. At that time the University created a cultural resource laboratory to study a stretch of land designated to become a right of way for Massachusetts' Interstate 495. During that survey, 28 pre-historic sites and 20 additional historic sites were discovered.

By 1982 it was no longer feasible for Brown University to operate its cultural resource laboratory. Five of the professionals on staff recognized the continuing need to serve the preservation demands of the community and incorporated an independent, private, not-for-profit entity. The Public Archaeology Laboratory, Inc. was established on July 21, 1982 and the five incorporators opened an office on the east side of Providence.

The lab moved to 210 Lonsdale Avenue in Pawtucket in 1985, where it remains today. The offices, technical reference and map libraries, production

department, and fully-equipped laboratory are housed in a three-story, 9,000-square-foot, state-of-the-art facility.

Today PAL is the largest cultural resource management firm in New England. The company's service area is primarily the six New England states and New York. However, it has conducted work in other areas of the country including North Dakota, Minnesota, Kansas, Arkansas, and Florida. PAL staff also surveyed several historic neighborhoods in the San Juan metropolitan area as part of the environmental studies for Tren Urbano, Puerto Rico's new light

This 1956 continuous truss-type bridge, spanning the Sakonnet River from Portsmouth to Tiverton, was recorded for the Rhode Island Historic Resource Archive by PAL's industrial historian.

A circa 1890 Queen Anne style home in Providence is part of the Wayland Square Historic District, recorded by PAL architectural historians.

Although The Public Archaeology Laboratory, Inc., or PAL, is little more than two decades old—a mere blip on the screen compared to the age of the many artifacts it has discovered—it has a rich history. The organization's roots go back to 1977 and the department

In Johnston, Rhode Island an archaeological crew begins excavation in preparation to move the remains found at an historic cemetery dating from 1823 to 1936.

rail. As the area's leading authority in cultural resource management, historic preservation planning, and regulatory consultation and compliance, clients seeking the lab's services include federal, state, and local agencies; nonprofit institutions; and private developers.

The company has completed more than 1,600 projects including the unearthing of Rhode Island's first prison (which dates back to the 19th century) at a future shopping mall site and the discovery of archaic period, Native American artifacts along the charted path for a natural gas pipeline. These amazing finds were made by the more than 40 trained professionals who use their talents, knowledge, and painstaking and time-consuming methods to link our modern world to the past.

PAL is currently led by one of the original founders from the Brown University lab, Deborah C. Cox, RPA. Cox, who holds a bachelor's degree from Rhode Island College in history and anthropology and a master's in anthropology from Brown, has served as president of the organization since its incorporation. Her passion for uncovering mysteries of the past and preserving history is imbedded in the lab's success.

Cox reinforces the company's mission to supply clients with the highest level of service available in the cultural resources management industry. She and her staff believe in the integrity of their profession, as well as meeting the client's needs on time and on budget. A multi-disciplinary approach to the work, combined with the talents of historic, pre-historic and marine archaeologists, architectural and industrial historians, preservation planners, historians and conservators, and technical support staff ensure excellent service and products.

The team is capable of handling cultural resource projects of any size and scope in the general fields of terrestrial and marine archaeology, architectural history, historical research, and preservation planning. Clients rely on the firm's ability to rapidly mobilize staff and resources to conduct historical and archaeological surveys, preservation planning studies, eligibility determinations, environmental impact assessments, regulatory compliance, and consultation.

Cox and PAL have been honored for tireless dedication and exceptional service in the field of cultural resources management. The lab received a Merit Award in the 2000 Design for Transportation National Awards, presented by the U.S. Department of Transportation, for its work on the Whitman Roundhouse Park in Massachusetts. It has also received the Rhode Island Historic Preservation and Heritage Commission's Frederick C. Williamson Professional Service Award.

PAL strives to educate the public about historic preservation and the conservation of archaeological and historical resources. It does this by producing videos, developing curriculum materials, hosting lecture series, and conducting workshops for the general public. Through its many educational programs staff members work with local museums, nature preserves, historical societies, public and private schools, local libraries, and Native American tribes. As a result of PAL's outreach efforts, communities learn valuable information about the history of their area and how to preserve its legacy.

With tiny brushes and trowels, cameras and computers, patience and passion, PAL staff sift through and record the past on a daily basis. They work hard to make a connection to the present and prepare for growth in the future. By preserving history and bringing to life the ways of centuries gone by, PAL's efforts allow us to look toward the future with a better understanding of who we are.

PAL archaeologists excavate a 7,000-year-old Native American site in Carver, Massachusetts.

RHODE ISLAND COLLEGE

The year was 1854—the middle of the 19th century—and with it came the recognition that the nation, then in transition from an agrarian to a more industrialized economy, would require a better-educated and more highly-skilled work force. A few visionaries believed that the key to improving education was by elevating teaching to the status of a profession, and that this might be best accomplished by educating a new cadre of teachers and educational leaders within a post-secondary setting.

From this thinking was born what is now known as Rhode Island College.

Rhode Island College is the oldest public institution of higher education in the state. The College offers undergraduate programs in the liberal arts and sciences, including programs in the fine and performing arts, and in a variety of professional fields such as teaching, social work, nursing, management, and accounting. It also offers a select range of graduate programs, predominantly in the fields of education, counseling, and social work.

Established as the Rhode Island State Normal School by an 1854 act of the General Assembly, the institution was created to address the increasing demand for formally educated teachers, particularly in the rapidly growing urban school districts. First classes were held at the Second Universalist Church at the corner of Weybosset and Eddy Streets in Providence. Facing financial pressures, the Normal School

A classroom in the Rhode Island Normal School at the turn of the century.

Rhode Island Normal School in Providence, the home of the Rhode Island Normal School from 1898 to 1920, when the name was changed to Rhode Island College of Education, (RICE). In 1958 RICE moved to a new campus in the Mount Pleasant section of the city. In 1997 the building above was torn down to make way for the Providence Place Mall.

moved to Bristol in 1857, where the town offered free accommodations at the former Congregational meeting house on Bradford Street.

Normal School operations were suspended in 1865, but the school re-opened in 1871 in a building near Hoyle Square in Providence. In 1879 larger quarters were secured with a move to a building formerly occupied by the Providence High School, bounded by Waterman, Angell, and Benefit Streets. In 1893 the first Observation and Training School was opened in a former grammar school on the corner of Benefit and Halsey Streets.

Later that year, the General Assembly passed a resolution committing the state to constructing a new building *"...at an expense not to exceed the sum of two hundred thousand dollars."* The state turned over the old prison property at Gaspee and Promenade streets to the Normal School Building Commission the following year, with additional land acquisitions subsequently enlarging the campus to a total of about five acres.

This newer and much grander facility was opened on Capitol Hill in 1898. The first floor of this structure was occupied by the Observation and Training School, which was named in honor of noted education advocate Henry Barnard in 1920. In that same year the Normal School was re-chartered by the General Assembly as the Rhode Island College of Education (RICE), giving it the power to grant baccalaureate degrees

and earning it the distinction as the first normal school in New England to become a college of education.

In 1925 the College offered its first graduate degree program, leading to the master of education. Increased growth at the College led to the construction of a separate Henry Barnard School, which opened in 1928 on the same campus.

In 1939 the College's curriculum was revised to include programs specifically designed to prepare teachers for secondary schools, and in 1943 the College was accredited by the American

A leading school of teacher preparation, Rhode Island College of Education was the official name of the College until 1960 when the name was changed to RIC, as it became a liberal arts school.

Association of Teachers Colleges. In that era, RICE could boast of being one of the few accredited institutions of teacher education in the country. In 1945 facing the return of members of the armed forces, it was clear that the College would need to expand its physical plant and began to press for additional space. This was accomplished in 1958 with the move to a newly-constructed campus in the Mount Pleasant section of Providence. A year later, the General Assembly assigned the institution a new mission: in addition to its teacher education programs, the College was to offer a comprehensive curriculum in the arts and sciences and add a program in the industrial arts. To reflect this new mission, the institution's name was changed to Rhode Island College in 1960.

In its new role as a comprehensive institution of higher education, the College entered a period of rapid expansion. From an enrollment of under 1,000 during the 1959–60 academic year, the student body grew to over 6,000 by 1970 and reached over 9,000 by 1980. From the opening of the Mount Pleasant Campus to the present day, the College has grown from six buildings on 48 acres to 42 buildings on 180 acres.

Students congregate for athletic competitions at the campus on the corners of Gaspee and Promenade Streets in 1930. Note the primarily female student population of the day.

During its long history, the school has had two of its alumni serve as College president. In 1973, Charles B. Willard ('34) was named as the institution's fifth

Rhode Island College entrance on Mount Pleasant Avenue, which was redesigned in 2001.

president, and in 1990, native Rhode Islander John Nazarian ('54) was named as its eighth president. In 2004 President Nazarian celebrates his 50th anniversary with the College, having served as professor, administrator, vice president, and president.

Under the leadership of 16 principals or presidents, the institution has been known by three different names and seen its mission significantly increased throughout the years. Even so, the vision of its early proponents has continued without change: to provide an education of quality at a cost that is affordable, thereby strengthening the social and economic fabric of Rhode Island.

Rhode Island College—150 years and still growing.

THE ROBINSON GREEN BERETTA CORPORATION

For more than half a century, the Robinson Green Beretta Corporation, an architectural engineering and interior design firm, has been building a foundation of quality, service, and customer satisfaction in Rhode Island.

The company's history began with the 1946 formation of the firm Cull & Robinson, located in Providence's Industrial Bank Building. That same year Joseph A. Beretta, an enterprising young architect and civil engineer joined the firm.

The partnership grew rapidly and the company secured such projects as downtown Providence's First Federal Savings Bank, Fox Point Elementary School and the University of Rhode Island's main library at the school's Kingston campus. It was during these early years that the goal of putting the customer's needs first became paramount to each project.

In 1958 Beretta partnered with Knight D. Robinson, one of Cull & Robinson's founders, and Conrad E. Green to form Robinson, Green & Beretta (RGB). The firm remained in the historic Thomas F. Hoppin House, where Cull & Robinson had begun operations. The building, also known as Hoppin Villa, provided a fitting location for the firm's first years, as it is one of the area's most stately and beautiful homes built in the mid-19th century.

Courtyard by Marriott in Providence, Rhode Island.

Into the 1960s the firm continued pursuing large commercial jobs with great success. They maintained their focus on schools, office buildings and projects for the United States Navy. In 1969 the partners incorporated the firm and Beretta was named president and chairman of the board. Although the structure of the company changed, the mission was the same—to build quality structures that resulted in the highest customer satisfaction possible.

The 1970s brought new growth and positive change to RGB, both in projects and staff. In 1973 Beretta's son, Joseph R. Beretta, joined the business. A graduate of Norwich University with a degree in business administration, the young Beretta filled the role of accountant and assisted the controller. He continued to hone his skills and soon earned a master's of business administration from Bryant College.

The firm's project list expanded to include the Rhode Island Veteran's Home in Bristol; dormitories for Providence College, University of Rhode Island and Brown University; the Frank Licht Judicial Complex; libraries for Salve Regina University and Roger William University; and the Narragansett Electric re-powering station.

In the mid-1980s the company realized an opportunity for growth and expansion. A second office was established in Tampa, Florida and RGB introduced its work to the southeastern region of the country.

By 1988 Robinson Green Beretta had outgrown its original home at Hoppin Villa and needed a new facility to accommodate its expanding staff and workload. The company relocated its headquarters to the 20,000-square-foot location in the Foundary Complex, a large multi-use facility, at 50 Holden Street in Providence.

After serving the company for nearly 25 years, Joseph R. Beretta was named president in 1997. Sadly four years later marked the passing of his father, the last founding member of Robinson Green Beretta.

The company's services have evolved over the past 58 years to include feasibility studies, planning and analysis, design and construction administration. Areas of expertise include planning, architecture, historic preservation, civil and site engineering, structural engineering, interior design, interior space planning, plumbing design, facilities evaluation and planning, construction, and monitoring.

Children's seating area at Casey Family Services in Providence which won Rhode Island Monthly's 2003 Design Awards, for commercial interior design.

Green Hall after renovation at the University of Rhode Island.

Today's RGB Corporation is not far removed from its beginnings. The corporate officers have ensured that the integrity of the company's goals survived the decades and play a vital role in moving forward.

In 2003 the company made a strategic shift to reinforce the values created so many years ago. RGB continued on its path of growth, introducing many young and talented members to its leadership team. Therefore, the executive staff saw the importance of creating a new mission statement:

"…to pursue, effectively manage and successfully execute rewarding projects. By focusing on its clients goals through quality design and excellent service, RGB will improve and expand its position in the community."

These words put into print the company's actions and motivations of many years past.

During this time of vital change, Beretta reflected on the situation: "My father had a love for architecture and a vision to build a company that would sustain the test of time through quality designs and a solid, successful reputation," he said. "I have done my best to continue to build upon that vision and have every confidence that these young men and women have the determination and talent to continue on this path."

Among the company's many goals, an emphasis is placed on responding to the specific needs of every client. RGB believes it must be professionally and financially competitive, its projects must be actively managed (an accountable project manager oversees every job) and that success can be measured only by achieving customer satisfaction. Quality control is a standard for the firm. Reviews are performed at the critical stages of all projects and effective cost-control methods are always implemented.

As validation of the firm's desire to provide quality services, RGB has been honored with many awards including: The *Rhode Island Monthly* 2003 Design Awards, Commercial Interior Design for the Casey Family Services facility; the *Masonry Construction* magazine's "Top Projects 2003" honor for the $20 million Rhode Island Public Transit Authority maintenance facility; and the 2002 IMI Golden Trowel Award for the Providence Courtyard by Marriott—Union Station Plaza.

The company has found success in its pursuit of providing the best services possible to its clients. In fact, two out of every three jobs are currently commissioned by repeat customers—a true testament to a company that follows its mission statement.

As the leaders of The Robinson Green Beretta Corporation consider the future, they realize that the key to further success is in their history. Since 1946 RGB has been the architect of award-winning structures and the provider of superior customer satisfaction—a legacy that will continue for many years to come.

Harborside Recreational Center, Johnson & Wales University, Rhode Island.

SPEIDEL

Fredrich Speidel founded the world renowned Speidel Company in 1867; known today as Speidel, Inc. With an initial investment equivalent to $10 Speidel started making gold and silver chains with his wife from the basement of his home in Pforzheim, Germany. He has been credited with developing the gold-over-metal method of manufacturing called "bi-metal," which has proved tremendously successful. In 1896 he built the company's first factory and installed state-of-the-art machines that automated the production of gold chain, previously manufactured entirely by hand.

Shortly before World War I Fredrich Speidel sent his three sons Albert, Edwin and Eugene to America, to establish a branch of the family's jewelry chain manufacturing business. The Speidel Chain Company was officially founded in the United States in 1911. By 1912 the Speidel brothers hired the architectural firm Monks & Johnson to design the company's first headquarters at 70 Ship Street; an area that later became known as the jewelry capital of the world. The five-story building, with its European-style front, was originally called the Doran-Speidel Building. In 1912 Edwin Speidel went on to found the Automatic Chain Company which produced neckchain, chain-by-the-foot, and watch bracelets, most of their output being sold to watch manufacturers such as Bulova.

At first, only chain was made in the new facilities. During the 1920s, costume jewelry and watchbands were added to the line. Men's watchbands surged in popularity due to their introduction and use in the military during World War I. In the early 1920s Albert Speidel formed "Speidel Brothers," producing watch bracelets that were manufactured and sold primarily to wholesalers. In 1928 the Speidel Family in Germany and the brothers who lived in the United States, decided to merge all of these businesses into the Speidel Corporation in order to strengthen their position. The first president of Speidel Corporation was Albert Speidel, one of

Fredrich Speidel Sr. (seated) with his three sons and other family members, circa 1910.

the Speidel brothers living in Providence, Rhode Island. In 1934 Paul Levinger was hired by Speidel Corporation as an assistant.

In 1937 Albert Speidel died at an early age from pneumonia. His brother Edwin, the founder of the Automatic Chain Company who had not been active in Speidel Corporation up to this time, became president of Speidel Corporation and Paul Levinger was made vice president. At that time the majority control of the business was held by the German family. However in 1939 all of the shares held by the German stockholders were purchased by Edwin Speidel and Paul Levinger.

Watchband production was cut back during World War II when Speidel converted most of its facilities and started manufacturing cathode ray tubes for radar and other electronic applications. However Speidel came back strong in watchbands as soon as peace returned. In 1947 Speidel brought out its first modernized version of the

scissor-type expansion band called the Golden Knight. It proved to be a tremendous success in the men's watch bracelet field. The company also introduced elaborate packaging for its line of watch bracelets.

A planned reduction of its costume jewelry production was soon instituted, leading to the discontinuation of costume jewelry in the early '50s. National advertising for watch bracelets under the name Speidel and the building of a brand name began after the end of World War II, first in magazines and then in radio with a program called "Stop the Music." This proved to be an outstanding success and helped to make the name of Speidel nationally known. In 1949 Speidel changed with the times and discontinued radio advertising. Instead it concentrated its advertising budget in television, purchasing a number of fully sponsored programs and making Speidel one of the earliest television advertisers in the United States.

In 1951 with the advent of the Korean War, Speidel began manufacturing identification bracelets. The first product in this category was the Photo

Ident, a combination ident bracelet with photo and an expandable wristband, which was advertised on television. It was an immediate success—of major proportions.

In 1956 Speidel started manufacturing men's jewelry. The goal was to diversify its inventory and combat the increasingly heavy competition in metal watch bracelets from Japanese imports. Heavy opposition to this move by other manufacturers made it necessary for Speidel to change its method of distribution from general jobbers to sole distributors. Over the next three years a number of such sole distributorships were established in strategic geographic locations. Its sales force was also built up to provide adequate coverage to all areas of the United States, something which had been rather difficult to achieve through the distribution by general jobbers. The introduction of the men's jewelry line did not prove to be successful and in 1959 Speidel discontinued it.

In the meantime, heavy investments had been made in the development of automatic equipment to produce a brace-

let similar to the German Fixo-Flex. A few years earlier a German manufacturer had sent the first version of the Fixo-Flex bracelet to Paul Levinger who had worked out a license contract with the inventor, Karl E. Stiegele. In 1956 the first automatically produced bracelet under this patent was introduced as a test under the name of Kingsway. By 1959 the company officially introduced the new watchband as the "Twist-O-Flex," which still exists today. The Twist-O-Flex, considered light years ahead of any other watchband products, was a sales phenomenon and was "the" fashion statement of its time. The company's independent distributorships, such as Gluck, GKG, Gerwe Brown, and Simon Golub became enormously profitable due in no small part to the Speidel Twist-O-Flex watchbands. Speidel went on to introduce two other highly popular

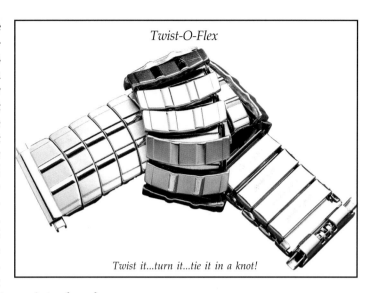

Twist-O-Flex

Twist it...turn it...tie it in a knot!

Speidel's Twist-O-Flex revolutionized metal watchbands forever.

versions of the Twist-O-Flex: the Ladies Twist-O-Flex introduced in 1961 and the Youth Twist-O-Flex in 1963.

In 1959 Speidel introduced a line of chain I.D. bracelets called Big Boy/Best Girl as an attempt to diversify its jewelry line. This line has enjoyed steady and increased sales over the years and remains one of the most popular bracelets sold in the industry.

By 1964 the company, now owned by Paul Levinger, had grown significantly both in size and importance to the jewelry industry. Levinger sold the company to Textron, Inc. in May of that year. By 1966 Speidel had expanded its distribution capacity and entered the men's toiletries market, with the introduction of a men's fragrance, British Sterling. The company aggressively marketed the product with such enduring phrases as, "Make him a legend in his own time," which helped to create a market success without parallel. Speidel became one of Textron's top local divisions in sales volume and performance.

Factory workers fabricationg watchbands in the Ship Street facility, circa 1950.

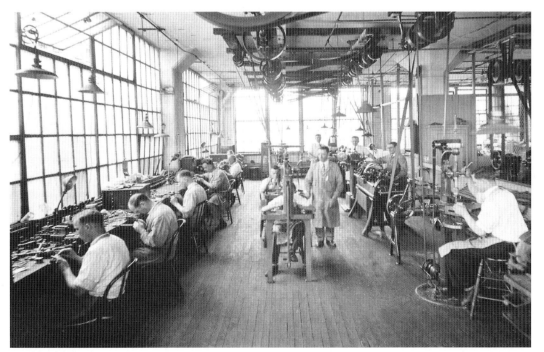

The company began to expand its marketing reach internationally in the 1970s, beginning with Canada in 1971. The company furthered its sales market by branching out to Australia and New Zealand in 1972; Great Britain and Ireland in 1973; and Germany, Switzerland, Norway, Sweden, Denmark, and Finland in 1974.

In the midst of the their international sales expansion, Speidel started OEM (Original Equipment Manufacturing) Business Supplies in 1972. OEM manufactured metal watchbands directly for watch companies such as Seiko, which at the time had just introduced the "quartz" watch, the first totally machine assembled timepiece, which dramatically reduced watch prices. That same year Speidel began its watchband replacement program for mass merchandisers, making it much easier for consumers to find the appropriately-sized watchband replacement at their local store.

Speidel introduced its newest version of the highly successful Twist-O-Flex in 1988, called the Euro-Flex watchband. The new watchband incorporated heavier metals and contemporary European styling.

Speidel's rich leather calfskin watchband with contrast stitching.

Speidel's headquarters in East Providence, Rhode Island.

Speidel continued to expand its line of products with the introduction of the "Signet" watch line in 1994; a patented plastic top shell watchband in 1995; and the first watchband with rubberized coating in 1996.

In 1997 Textron sold Speidel to the Austrian-based Hirsch Armbaender AG, the leading manufacturer of leather watchbands in Europe. The new company was named Hirsch-Speidel Inc. Two years later, as part of a global manufacturing consolidation strategy, Hirsch closed Speidel's original Ship Street property and relocated its headquarters to East Providence. In coordination with the move, Speidel closed down its manufacturing operations and outsourced its workload. A portion of the production continued in Rhode Island with local manufacturing companies, and the balance moved overseas.

Jeffrey Massotti, who became the divisional president after Hirsch's acquisition of the company, purchased Speidel back from Hirsch in 2002. The company's ownership had once again returned to the United States. Massotti had joined the company in 1992, following an internship at Speidel while attending college. In his short time with the company, he worked in almost every department before being named divisional president in 1999. Massotti purchased the nearly 100-year-old business from Hirsch, under the name JRM Holding, Inc. in December 2002. The company still enjoys a strategic relationship with Hirsch under Massotti's ownership. JRM Holding, Inc is also the owner of the Providence Watch Hospital, a 65-year-old company which offers expert watch repair and warranty services for many well-known watch brands to consumers and retail jewelers across the country.

Under Massotti's management, the company is reinventing itself with a focus on sales and distribution services. In 2002 Speidel introduced a highly successful line of Speidel watches to add to its brand name products. In addition to Speidel's well-known watchbands and watch attachments, it also markets a wide variety of jewelry items including ID bracelets, children's jewelry, 14-karat gold earrings and neck chains, pearl jewelry, and men's jewelry accessories.

The company, and its 150 employees, will celebrate its 100th anniversary in 2004. President & CEO Massotti firmly believes that Speidel is only "as good as the people it employs." In Massotti's own words, "Our employees are enthusiastic. They want to be part of a team that is known for a quality product and to help ensure that Speidel remains the #1 recognized brand in the world for watchbands. Even today, there is no other branded watchband company that attaches more watches to your wrist than Speidel, which is a source of great pride."

A nanny watches children playing in the sand at Narragansett Pier, circa 1905. Courtesy, Louis H. McGowan Rhode Island postcard collection

TACO

Elwood White was born in Lafayette, Indiana in 1881, son of the Right Reverend John Hazen White who was the area's first Episcopal Bishop. An entrepreneurial type, Elwood graduated from Purdue University with a degree in engineering and married Luella Perrin in 1910. They named their son, born in 1913, John Hazen White after his grandfather.

Elwood White moved around with his job as star salesman for the American Radiator Company (now American Standard), at that time one of the largest companies in the emerging indoor heating industry. The family soon moved to Massachusetts, near Boston. Elwood and Luella were modest people whose idea of a good time was a simple meal at a hotel in Boston, but Elwood dreamed of owning his own company.

In 1920 when Elwood discovered the Thermal Appliance Company (TACO) in Bayonne, New Jersey, it had three employees, one product, and

no customers. Thermal had Robert Blanding, however, who Elwood considered an engineering genius. Since Blanding lived in Providence, Rhode Island, Elwood relocated the company. Blanding soon produced a tankless water heater and a tempering valve that mixed hot and cold water together. The combination of sales and inventive

John Hazen White Sr. (1913–2001) built Taco into a world class manufacturer. He was a man of high integrity who believed that business had an obligation to the community.

talent propelled the company to the forefront of the industry.

Elwood's son John graduated from Yale University in 1937 with a degree in English and a lifelong love of sailing. That year he decided to marry Mary Tefft Schwarz (a.k.a. Happy), a Philadelphia debutant. The family story is that John asked his father for a job, Elwood asked his son what he wanted to do and John replied, "I don't know, what do you do in this company?"

Elwood put John in the sales office in New York City, serving as company treasurer and doing advertising. That's where John was when World War II began and metal was diverted to the war effort. Elwood thought the company could survive if he could produce a gun mount, about the size of a deck of cards, that could withstand the stress of battle. While in Washington in 1942 Elwood got a Navy contract, then developed pancreatitis, and died—at age 56.

At age 29 John abruptly found himself responsible not only for his own family, but also for the company's 100 employees. He knew nothing about the manufacturing side of the business,

Taco developed a self-lubricating pump from a European design that became its famous "00" series of pumps.

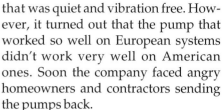

but he quickly went to Washington to assure the Navy that the company could fulfill its contract.

Trying to learn as much as possible in the shortest time, John asked one of his sailing acquaintances if he could meet with his father, Lester Abberley, a successful New York attorney. Unbeknownst to John, Abberley was a friend and business partner of Nelson Rockerfeller and one of New York's most influential businessmen. For the next five years Abberley advised John and took pride in his successes, as John obtained other Navy contracts throughout the war amounting to some $3 million.

After the war Robert Blanding retired but his inventions for radiator fittings and circulator pumps propelled the company into the booming 1950s. In 1954 the company moved its 125 employees from Providence to an abandoned trolley barn in Cranston, hoping to grow the business into the larger space. John also moved his growing family from Old Greenwich, Connecticut, to Barrington, Rhode Island. The next

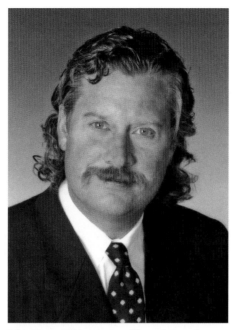

John Hazen White, Jr., president of Taco, Inc.

Taco products are universally known for their quality, durability, and ease of installation and maintenance.

few decades would bring some hard business lessons.

While traveling in Europe, John discovered what seemed like the pump of his dreams in Switzerland, so he quickly bought exclusive rights to manufacture and sell it in the United States and Canada. The pump was the Perfecta, a small, self-lubricating circulator

that was quiet and vibration free. However, it turned out that the pump that worked so well on European systems didn't work very well on American ones. Soon the company faced angry homeowners and contractors sending the pumps back.

John decided the firm would stand by their product and replaced every single one. They went through eight revisions of the pump before they found a design solution years later. The financial fiasco did two things: it increased the company's reputation for ethics and reliability, and taught the company to do its own field trial product testing so problems could be corrected before distribution.

The business was barely out of that crisis when the machinists union called a strike in 1976 that lasted for 14 months. Despite John having personally helped some of the employees in the past, a number of his workers supported the union. During this time John and every member of his family, plus all the management, stepped in to keep production going. However, some of the working conditions surprised them, and changes were made to make things better. John's wife, Happy, cleaned the workspace and bathrooms and made curtains for the ladies room in an attempt to make the place more cheery. When the head engineer commented on what a miserable job it was to work on the production floor, Happy said, "Now you know what the people have to work with. So why don't we figure out something better." After the union was defeated and the strike ended, John immediately hired back anyone who hadn't been destructive toward the company and started asking them how things could be improved.

In the 1980s and 1990s Taco expanded operations with larger commercial pumps and overseas contracts. However, profits throughout the manufacturing industry were down and new regulations combined with a recession made running the business increasingly difficult. John debated retiring and closing the plant, or selling the company.

Taco employees learn about new products at the Taco Learning Center.

John Jr., his youngest child, had other plans though. He asked his father to give him six months to turn things around, or at least point them in the right direction. A graduate of the College of Wooster in Ohio and an English major, John Jr. had nonetheless worked at the company on and off for years and had his own ideas for how the company should be structured and managed. The 1990s were an especially pivotal decade for the company. Manufacturing plants were closing and workers were dismissed as companies moved production out of the country to cut costs. The Whites watched the trend, but remained committed to keeping their core business in Rhode Island.

It was clear though that something had to change if the company was to remain competitive. So the Whites called in a business consultant who advised them, over several years, about streamlining the manufacturing process and modernizing equipment. The Whites were in agreement that they did not want their valued workers laid off as a result of new technology, but they faced a conundrum. Few workers knew how to operate the new equipment. The solution was to train the labor force—the people they had called friends for years.

The father and son team worked side-by-side with a manufacturing veteran, a Mr. Fix-it consultant, who guided them through the next few years of major capital expenditures in new machinery and investments in the firm's employees. They built a learning center on-site

because John Sr. felt it made people better citizens and gave them a better way of life.

"We had 500 employees when we were doing $40 million of business in 1992, and we had 500 employees in 2003 when we did $130 million. And with less than one-half percent employee turnover," John Jr. says. An admitted people-person, he is frequently found on the manufacturing floor and knows every employee by first name. Among his first acts when he became president in 1996 was to remove layers of middle management.

"Management historically has been built on fear and a sort of superiority," White Jr. says. "You advance in the company because you earned some status as better than anyone else. And it's all wrong to me. The people who deserve to be promoted know how to work with people. What we have tried to do is to level out the layers. From me to the hourly guy, there's one layer—two if you include a foreman. It does me no good

Instruction in a variety of subjects and degree programs is free to Taco employees.

Taco produces efficiently using a cellular approach to manufacturing.

to have four people between me and them, because everyone puts their own spin on it."

John firmly believes in listening to his employees and implementing their ideas. He recalls a prime example when manufacturing output doubled and a product line grew by 400 percent when he took the advice of his manufacturing staff. "This is how we beat our competitors. We don't have the resources to operate like a large corporation and chase cheap labor around the globe," he says. "Our way to survive, grow, and develop is through our people."

Now called Taco, Inc, with its headquarters in Cranston, the company has remained family-owned through three generations. They came close to closing their doors more than once, but they currently enjoy a national and international reputation for innovative and reliable products in the highly specialized heating and cooling industry. The firm is a leading manufacturer of components used in residential, commercial, industrial, and institutional hydronic systems.

The company has manufacturing, distribution, and sales facilities in Cranston, Fall River, Massachusetts, and Ontario, Canada. Its products are sold throughout North America and in Mexico, Central and Latin America, the Middle East, and Asia.

Taco is proud to be known for constant innovation, quality, and service. The reason, according to John Hazen White Jr., is its employees. Through jobsite training and free educational programs for employees, the company has empowered its workers to be partners in the firm's success. "These people have forgotten more than I will ever know, so let them do what they do best," says White Jr., who began working on the company's manufacturing floor while he was still in high school in 1976.

The firm founded the Taco Learning Center in 1992. John estimates that the company's workforce is 30 to 40 percent Asian or Hispanic, so the center developed classes in English as a second language and citizenship training. It has an accredited G.E.D. program and a branch of Johnson & Wales University

(White serves as a visiting professor at the school's main campus). Last year the center graduated its first MBA students. In the summer it runs art and music camps for the children of employees, and an oceanography program with the University of Rhode Island. Classes are open to any employee at no cost. "We have tried to instill a sense of community and partnership," White says. "Success is so dependent on people being able to contribute, not just getting paid for what they do."

He says his father "instilled all these beliefs in me," although the two of them differed in many areas. The family has a legacy of hard work, faith, loyalty, and stubbornness, along with a sense of discovery and a spirit of fun that has led each generation forward.

John Sr. spent a good portion of his later life taking out large *Red Alert* ads in the *Providence Journal* newspaper, pointing out corruption in government and unfavorable business practices that he thought hurt everyone in Rhode Island. When asked why he did it, White Sr. said it was civic duty. "No company should be just a money machine. They have social responsibilities." He was also a major philanthropist, and gave away millions to local universities and a variety of worthy causes.

John Jr. now oversees the day-to-day business of producing world-class Taco pumps, valves, and heat exchangers that most people take for granted— unseen in boiler rooms and basements, unnoticed until they don't work. Until the day John Hazen White Sr. died in March 2001, young John and his father continued to joke that he was still in his first six months of "turning things around."

A TIMELINE OF RHODE ISLAND'S HISTORY

Circa 10,000 BC Paleo-Indians came to New England.

Circa 6,000 BC Atlantic Ocean levels rose to create present coastlines and Narragansett Bay.

1524
Giovanni da Verrazano explored the New England coast on behalf of France, named an island "Luisa," and landed on Aquidneck Island.

1614
Adriaen Block, a Dutch explorer, renamed the island of Luisa for himself and built a trading post, later called Ninigret's Fort, in present-day Charlestown.

1616–19
A disease (probably chicken pox) swept Cape Cod, eastern Massachusetts and the east side of Narragansett Bay, causing many Native Americans to die, substantially reducing the number of Wampanoags which allowed the unscathed Narragansetts to seize Aquidneck, Prudence, and Patience Islands, and the Providence area.

1620
The Plymouth Colony was founded.

1628
The Pequots defeated the Narragansetts in battle and seized the Westerly-Stonington area.

1630
Massachusetts Bay colony was founded.

1631
Roger Williams came to Massachusetts.

1633
The Pequots were struck by smallpox and lost 82 percent of their population.

1635
Roger Williams was convicted of sedition and heresy and sentenced to banishment from Massachusetts Bay.

1636
Roger Williams fled from Salem and founded Providence, the first town in Rhode Island, on land given to him by Miantonami and Canonicus, chief sachems of the Narragansetts. The Massachusetts trader John Oldham was killed by Native Americans on Block Island, and his death became one of the precipitating causes of the Pequot War.

1637
Roger Williams served as a go-between for Massachusetts Bay and the Narragansetts, convincing the Narragansetts not to ally themselves with the Pequots. In the subsequent Pequot War, the Narragansetts sided with the Puritans in crushing the Pequots. Ann Hutchinson and the Antinomians were disarmed, disenfranchised, and ordered into exile by Massachusetts Bay.

1638
In March the Antinomians founded Pocasset, renamed Portsmouth in 1643, the second town in Rhode Island. Roger Williams founded the first Baptist church in America. Twelve of the first settlers insisted that Roger Williams' grant from the Narragansetts be shared with them and persuaded him to include them as "proprietors" on the original Indian deed. They then granted themselves additional land south of the Pawtuxet River.

1639
The third town, Newport, was founded by the secession of William Coddington, John Clarke, and others from Portsmouth.

1641
A public school opened in Newport.

1642
Samuel Gorton, another religious refugee from Massachusetts, started a settlement at Shawomet, renamed Warwick in 1646. William Arnold, William Harris, and some other "original proprietors" who had gotten tracts of land south of the Pawtuxet, pledged allegiance to Massachusetts and registered deeds to their land there, giving Massachusetts a claim to annex that area.

1643
Massachusetts, Plymouth, and Connecticut formed the United Colonies, a military alliance, which excluded and threatened Rhode Island. In the fall Roger Williams sailed to England to get a charter. Soldiers from Massachusetts arrested Samuel Gorton at his settlement in Shawomet for "trespassing on Massachusetts land" and imprisoned him. In the war that broke out between the Mohegans and the Narragansetts, Miantonami was captured and murdered.

1644
Roger Williams obtained a charter for the "Province of Providence Plantations in Narragansett in New England." He also published *The Bloudy Tenent of Persecution*, the great defense of freedom of religion and separation of church and state, and *A Key into the Language of America*, the first English dictionary of a Native American language. John Clarke founded the First Baptist Church of Newport.

1647
Canonicus died.

1650
William Coddington returned to England and obtained a patent making him "Governor for Life" over Newport and Portsmouth.

1651
Three Baptists, including John Clarke from Newport, were arrested in Lynn, Massachusetts, and Puritan Obadiah

Steamships docked at the wharves on the Providence River, 1907. Courtesy, Louis H. McGowan Rhode Island postcard collection

Holmes was publicly whipped with 30 lashes "well laid on." Roger Williams and John Clarke returned to England to get Coddington's patent revoked, which was accomplished in 1652. Williams returned to Rhode Island in 1654 and Clarke remained as colonial agent until 1664.

1652

Providence Plantations passed a law to prevent slavery in Rhode Island. John Clarke published *Ill News from New England*, his account of the arrest and treatment of the Baptists in Massachusetts. Clarke was the only Rhode Islander besides Roger Williams to publish a book in the 17th century.

1654

The four towns were finally united under a single government, and Roger Williams was elected president.

1656

A split in John Clarke's church resulted in the Second Baptist Church of Newport, a General Six-Principle Baptist church.

1657

The first Quakers settled in Newport; Rhode Island rejected Plymouth Colony's request to exclude Quakers.

1658

The first Jews settled in New England at Newport. Massachusetts enacted a law to execute Quakers. Contrary to Rhode Island law, the Boston-based Narragansett Proprietors (Atherton Syndicate) purchased land from the Narragansetts, beginning a land squabble that would not be settled until 1711.

1659–60

Massachusetts hung four Quakers, including Mary Dyer of Newport.

1659

War broke out between the Narragansetts and the Mohegans. The United Colonies intervened on the side of the Mohegans and overawed the Narragansetts.

1660

The United Colonies imposed a humiliating treaty on the Narragansetts, fined them 2,000 fathoms of wampum, and gave them four months to pay the fine. Unable to meet the deadline, the Narragansetts mortgaged their land to the

The Ocean House at Watch Hill in Westerly was a grand seaside resort (postcard circa 1907–1910). Courtesy, Louis H. McGowan Rhode Island postcard collection

Narragansett Proprietors. Rhode Island refused to recognize these actions. The monarchy was restored in England and all actions taken by Parliament during the Interregnum were voided, including Roger Williams' charter for Providence Plantations.

1662

The Narragansett Proprietors foreclosed the mortgage and claimed all of the Narragansett lands. Rhode Island declared the whole deal to be invalid.

1663

John Clarke obtained the charter for "The English Colony of Rhode Island and Providence Plantations in New England in America," which guaranteed the "lively experiment" in religious freedom.

1671

The first Seventh-Day Baptist Church in America was created by a split in John Clarke's church in Newport.

1675–1678

King Philip's War.

1675

King Philip's War began in June with Indians plundering homes on Pokanokut Neck in present-day Bristol, after the settlers fled to their church meetinghouse in Swansea, Massachusetts. In December an army of the United Colonies destroyed the fortress of the Narragansetts in the Great Swamp Fight in present-day South Kingstown. Connecticut subsequently claimed all of southern Rhode

Island by "right of conquest."

1676

In March the Indians burned Providence, and all white settlements on the west side of Narragansett Bay were destroyed. Subsequently, the Native Americans in southern New England were defeated. King Philip was killed near Mount Hope in August by an Indian warrior serving under Colonel Benjamin Church.

1678

The Peace of Casco with the Abenaki in Maine ended King Philip's War.

1684

Rhode Island passed a law protecting freedom of conscience for Jews. This exempted them from prosecution under the British Navigation Acts that prohibited them from being merchants.

1686

The first Huguenots arrive in New England, and 45 of these families settled in present-day East Greenwich in a place called "Frenchtown." One of them, Gabriel Bernon, was the force behind the creation of the King's (later St. John's) Church in Providence in 1722, the third Anglican church in Rhode Island.

1686–1689

The Dominion of New England reduced Rhode Island to a county in the larger entity. The Charter of 1663 was hidden during this time.

1689

Rhode Island reemerged as a separate colony.

1689–97

King William's War: Block Island was attacked three times by the French.

1694

Rhode Island commissioned its first privateers.

1696

The Rhode Island General Assembly became a bicameral body. A Boston-owned ship, the *Seaflower*, sold African slaves in Newport for the first time.

1697–1701

The Charter of 1663 was threatened with revocation by the British.

1697–1727

Samuel Cranston served as governor of Rhode Island.

1700

First church meetinghouse built in Providence. The first recorded slave trade ships departed from Newport, launching Rhode Island into the African slave trade.

1701

Trinity Church founded in Newport, the first Anglican parish in Rhode Island.

1703-13

Queen Anne's War: Rhode Island grudgingly supplied soldiers, but commissioned more privateers.

1709

Ninigret, the Narragansett "king," deeded all vacant Indian land to the colony, except 64 square miles which became known as the "reservation."

1713

Newport established the first poor house in Rhode Island.

1719

When Rhode Island codified its laws, a provision barring Roman Catholics from citizenship was inserted.

1723

Twenty-six pirates were hanged in Newport as Rhode Island sought to change its reputation as a pirate haven.

1726

Trinity Church (Anglican), designed by Richard Munday, was built in Newport.

The "Independent Man" stands on top of Rhode Island's capitol. Sculpted by George T. Brewster and cast by Gorham, the statue was raised to its place on December 18, 1899. Courtesy, Rhode Island Department of Transportation/Earl H. Goodison photo

1728

The western border of Rhode Island with Connecticut was settled.

1731

The Old State House in Providence was completed, to be the co-capital of Rhode Island along with Newport.

1732

James Franklin founded Rhode Island's first newspaper in Newport.

1736

The first slave trade ship sailed from Providence.

1739

The Old Colony House, designed by Richard Munday, was built in Newport.

1739–1748

King George's War: privateering commissions were issued to 35 Newport merchants.

1743

A religious revival among the Narragansetts resulted in most of them converting to Christianity.

1746

The eastern border with Massachusetts, determined by a royal commission in

1727, was finally enforced, bringing Bristol, Warren, Barrington, Little Compton, and Tiverton into Rhode Island.

1748

The Redwood Library, designed by Peter Harrison, was erected in Newport.

1750

The Narragansett Indian Church was built in Charlestown

1754–63

French and Indian War: Rhode Island merchants lost at least 215 ships.

1759

Designed by Peter Harrison, Touro Synagogue was erected in Newport.

1762

Providence had its first printing press, and the *Providence Gazette and Country Journal* was started by John Goddard.

1764

A college was chartered, which took the name of Brown University in 1804. The General Assembly adopted the *Rhode Island Remonstrance* against Britain's new Sugar Act of 1763. In July Newporters stoned a British press-gang and fired 10 cannon rounds at the *H.M.S. St. John* in the harbor.

1765

Newporters burned a tender to *H.M.S. Maidstone* because of press-gang activities. *The Rights of the Colonies Examined* by Stephen Hopkins denounced the Stamp Act, saying that Parliament had no right to levy taxes on the colonies not represented in Parliament. In August there was a Stamp Act riot in Newport and effigy burning in Providence.

1768

The "Newport Massacre" occurred when colonists threatened British soldiers who fired upon them, killing one.

1769

A Newport mob scuttled the British sloop *Liberty* in the harbor, and the British customs officer in Providence was tarred and feathered.

1770

Rhode Island College (later called Brown University) relocated to Providence.

1771

The British collector of customs in Newport was beaten and dragged through the streets.

A nanny watches children playing in the sand at Narragansett Pier, circa 1905. Courtesy, Louis H. McGowan Rhode Island postcard collection

1772

Eight boatloads of men from Providence burned the revenue cutter *H.M.S. Gaspee* after it became stuck on a sandbar near Pawtuxet.

1774

Stephen Hopkins and Samuel Ward were elected delegates to the First Continental Congress; Rhode Island was the first colony to take this action. Rhode Island banned the importation of slaves.

1774–75

The meetinghouse for the First Baptist Church in Providence was constructed, the largest building project in New England at the time.

1775

English tea was burned in Market Square in Providence. In the first naval action of the Revolution, the Rhode Island sloop *Katy* captured the British sloop *Diana* near Prudence Island. Esek Hopkins was appointed by Congress to be Commodore of the American Navy.

1776

The General Assembly repealed the test oath of allegiance to the king for all colonial officers. The Assembly ratified the Declaration of Independence. The British occupied Newport.

1778

Rhode Island easily ratified the Articles of Confederation. In July General Richard Prescott, the British commander of the forces at Newport, was abducted in a daring raid in Portsmouth and later exchanged for the captured American general, Charles Lee. Rhode Island recruited a regiment of African American soldiers who first fought in the Battle of Rhode Island, a rear-guard action, as colonial troops withdrew from Aquidneck after an aborted attack on Newport.

1779

The British evacuated Newport.

1780

Count Rochambeau and 6,000 French soldiers landed at Newport; General Nathanael Greene was given command of the southern forces of the Continental Army. The African Union Society was founded in Newport.

1781

Nathanael Greene's tactics forced the British out of the Carolinas and back to Yorktown, Virginia.

1783

The General Assembly removed the anti-Catholic provision in the laws dating from 1719.

1784

The General Assembly passed a gradual emancipation law to end slavery.

1785

The first July 4th parade held in Bristol.

1786–1790

The Country party dominated the General Assembly.

1787

Rhode Island barred its citizens from engaging in the African slave trade; John Brown of Providence dispatched the *General Washington* to China, the second ship from New England to enter the China trade. Rhode Island refused to send delegates to the constitutional convention in Philadelphia.

1788–89

Rhode Island repeatedly rejected the ratification of the U.S. Constitution.

1788

Moses Brown and Stephen Hopkins convinced Massachusetts and Connecticut to outlaw the African slave trade.

1789

Moses Brown organized the Providence Society for Promoting the Abolition of Slavery.

1790

Rhode Island joined the Union by ratifying the Constitution. Slater Mill successfully spun cotton yarn with water-powered machinery, launching America's industrial revolution.

1791

John Brown founded Providence Bank.

In 1869 the State of Rhode Island purchased land in Cranston and subsequently located most of its institutions there. The old prison on Cove Street in Providence was abandoned and the prisoners moved to this new facility, the Adult Correctional Institution, in 1878. Courtesy, Providence Public Library

1799

Brown & Ives founded the Providence Insurance Company.

1800

The General Assembly passed a law requiring every town to establish a public school; only Providence and Smithfield complied and the law was subsequently repealed. Richard Jackson founded the Washington Insurance Company.

1804

Nicholas Brown, the younger, endowed the college in Providence, which was named Brown University in his honor.

1806

The Brown & Ives China trade ship *Ann & Hope* sank near Block Island with a cargo valued at $500,000.

1808

Brown & Ives created the Blackstone Manufacturing Company, shifting from oceanic commerce to industry.

1813

Oliver Hazard Perry, commanding American forces, defeated the British in the Battle of Lake Erie.

1815

The "Great Gale" struck Rhode Island causing extensive damage to Newport and Providence.

1819

The African Union Meeting House and School was founded in Providence, later becoming the Meeting Street Baptist Church in 1840 and renamed the Congdon Street Baptist Church in 1871.

1820

The Providence Washington Insurance Company was formed by the merger of the Providence and Washington Insurance companies.

1821

Providence installed its first gaslights on some streets.

1822

The General Assembly voted to disenfranchise black voters.

1823

The first U.S. textile strike occurred in Pawtucket when workers struck against Slater Mill.

1824

Rioters tore down the homes of blacks during Providence's Hard Scrabble Riot.

1828

The Blackstone Canal, running from Providence to Worcester, was opened. Rhode Island granted the first railroad charter to build a line from Boston to Providence. The first Roman Catholic parish in Rhode Island was established in Newport. The state passed an act once again requiring all towns to create public schools.

1831

Jabez Gorham began producing silverware, laying the foundation for what

later became the Gorham Manufacturing Company, the largest silverware maker in the world. The Olney Lane Riot against black residents ended with the killing of four rioters by the Rhode Island Light Infantry. In order to cope with urban growth and disorder, the General Assembly adopted an act to incorporate the city of Providence.

1832

The incorporation of Providence went into effect and a mayor and city council were elected.

1833

Providence saw its first public antislavery meeting.

1835

The Boston & Providence Railroad opened. Zachariah Allen founded the Manufacturers' Mutual Fire Insurance Company, the first of its kind in the U.S.

1835–1840

A split from the African Union Meeting House produced the Second Freewill Baptist Church (now called the Pond Street Baptist Church).

1836

A. & W. Sprague Manufacturing Company established.

1837

The Stonington Railroad reached Providence. Another split from the African Union Meeting House created a Wesleyan Methodist Church (A.M.E. Zion)

1838

A third break from the African Union

Meeting House produced the Bethel A.M.E. Church.

1839
George Noble Jones of Georgia built "Kingscote," the first of the Bellevue Avenue mansions in Newport.

1841
The China trade ended for Providence with the arrival of the *Lion*. Because the General Assembly would not reform the malapportionment of the legislature or disenfranchisement of most Rhode Island men, the People's Convention wrote a state constitution and saw it overwhelmingly ratified in a referendum in December.

1842
Thomas Dorr was elected governor under the People's Constitution. The legal state government refused to cede power and the "Dorr War" ensued, leading to Dorr's defeat. The legal government wrote a new constitution, which reformed the government and reenfranchised African Americans. The first African American church in Newport was the Colored Union Church.

1845–1849
Henry Barnard served as Rhode Island's first commissioner of education and drafted the School Law of 1845.

1846
The Providence & Worcester Railroad was completed.

1847
Butler Hospital for the Insane was founded in Providence. Rocky Point Park opened in Warwick.

1848
The Union Passenger Depot, designed by Thomas Tefft, was built and was the largest railroad station in the nation at that time.

1849
The American Screw Company invented a machine to make pointed screws, helping it to become the largest screw manufacturer in the world.

1852
As a consequence of the mistaken execution of John Gordon, Rhode Island abolished capital punishment. The B.B. & R. Knight Company was founded and produced textile goods under the trademark of "Fruit of the Loom."

1853
Brown & Sharpe Manufacturing Company was founded and later became the world's largest maker of precision industrial tools.

1853–1854
Matthew C. Perry negotiated the opening of Japan.

1854
Rhode Island began a teacher training institute which evolved into Rhode Island College in 1957.

1854–1855
The Know-Nothing party won the state offices and legislature.

1856
The new Republican party won the governorship for the first time.

1857–1858
The last great antebellum religious revival swept Providence.

1857
George Corliss established the Corliss Steam Engine Company, later to become the largest steam engine manufacturer in the world.

1861–1865
The Civil War: Rhode Island exceeded its quota of soldiers and its industries produced nearly everything needed to equip and supply an army. Battle deaths and disease claimed 1,685 men.

1861
The Rhode Island 1st Regiment was the first fully-equipped unit to arrive in Washington, D.C. After the Battle of Bull Run, this three-month regiment was discharged. The U.S. Naval Academy moved from Annapolis, Maryland to Newport for the duration of the war.

1862
The final boundary adjustment with Massachusetts brought the eastern part of Pawtucket and East Providence into the state, in exchange for a section that became part of Fall River, Massachusetts. The Corliss Steam Engine Company milled the ring washer and bearings for the revolutionary iron ship, *U.S.S. Monitor*. General Ambrose E. Burnside was appointed commander of the Army of the Potomac, but led it to disaster at Fredericksburg, Virginia.

1863
A black regiment, the Rhode Island 14th Heavy Artillery, was recruited and sent to war. The first streetcar line, running from Providence to Pawtucket, was built. Bryant & Stratton Business College opened in Providence, developing into an accredited four-year college in 1964.

1864
William Nicholson invented machinery to mass produce files, helping his company Nicholson File Company to become the largest of its kind in the world.

1866
Rhode Island outlawed racial segregation in schools. Joseph Manton built a steam-powered automobile that went from Providence to Warwick.

1868
Rhode Island Hospital opened.

1869
U.S. Torpedo Station was established on Goat Island at Newport; a major hurricane hit Rhode Island.

1870
The state insane asylum opened at Howard in Cranston.

1872
George B. Brayton of East Greenwich invented and patented an internal combustion engine.

1873
The state workhouse and house of corrections opened at Howard in Cranston.

1874
The state almshouse opened at Howard in Cranston.

1876
Polo was introduced to the United States in Newport.

1877
The Rhode Island School of Design was founded.

1878
Providence dedicated its new City Hall. The Providence County Jail and State Prison were relocated to Cranston.

1879
The Providence Grays won the National League baseball pennant. The Newport Casino, designed by McKim, Mead & White, was built.

1880
The state purchased the remainder of

the Narragansett Indian Reservation and detribalized the Narragansetts. The first national meet of bicyclists took place in Newport and formed the League of American Wheelmen.

1881

The United States Lawn Tennis Association held its first championship tournament at the Newport Casino. Nelson Aldrich became a U.S. Senator, serving until 1911 during which time he came to be called the "General Manager of the United States." The State Reform School for girls opened in Oaklawn.

1883

The U.S. Naval Training Station was established in Newport. The State Reform School for boys opened in Sockanosset

1884

The Naval War College was established in Newport. The Providence Grays won the National League pennant and the world baseball championship.

1886

Crescent Park, "the Coney Island of New England" opened in Riverside. John Roberts raced his steam-powered automobile at Narragansett Trotting Park in Cranston at 20 m.p.h. Rhode Island adopted an amendment to its state constitution prohibiting the sale of liquor.

1887

The Cathedral of Saints Peter & Paul was consecrated.

1888

The "Bourn Amendment" to the state constitution granted equal voting rights to foreign-born citizens in general elections.

1889

Rhode Island repealed its constitutional prohibition of the sale of liquor.

1890

The Providence Symphony Orchestra was established.

1892

Rhode Island College of Agriculture and Mechanic Arts, a land-grant college, was founded (renamed the University of Rhode Island in 1951). The first electric streetcars began running in Providence on Broad Street. "Marble House," designed by Richard Morris Hunt, was built in Newport for William K. Vanderbilt.

The principal buildings of the American Screw Company stood empty from the time the company left the state in 1946 until arsonists destroyed them in a fire in 1971. Courtesy, The Providence Journal

1893–1895

"The Breakers," designed by Richard Morris Hunt, was erected in Newport for Cornelius Vanderbilt.

1894

The United States Golf Association held is first championship tournament in Newport. Charles I.D. Looff took over Crescent Park and built a showcase carousel the following year.

1896

The cornerstone was laid for a new state capitol, designed by McKim, Mead & White. The first automobile track race in America took place at Narragansett Park in Cranston.

1900

Providence became the sole capital of Rhode Island and the new State House was occupied. The first legislative session occurred the following year. The Corliss Steam Engine Company was sold to the International Power Company, ending one of Providence's "Five Industrial Wonders of the World."

1902

Great Streetcar Strike in Providence.

1905

The Rhode Island census revealed the state to have a Roman Catholic majority. Muckraking journalist Lincoln Steffans described Rhode Island as "A State for Sale."

1906

James H. Higgins was the first Roman Catholic to be elected governor of Rhode Island.

1907

The steamer *Larchmont*, sailing from Providence, sank near Block Island losing 111 lives. Vanity Fair amusement park opened in Riverside.

1908–1913

The American Locomotive Company manufactured the ALCO, America's finest automobile, in the old Corliss Steam Engine plant.

1908

Aram J. Pothier was the first French-Canadian to be elected governor of Rhode Island. Rhode Island adopted its first speed limits for automobiles.

1914

Johnson & Wales School of Business opened in Providence, evolving into Johnson & Wales University by 1988.

1915

Work began on the Scituate Reservoir, Rhode Island's principal water supply which became fully operational in 1928.

1919

Providence College was opened by the Dominicans. Women's suffrage was granted in Rhode Island.

1920

Rhode Island's textile giant, the B.B. & R. Knight Company, was sold to the Consolidated Textile Company of New York.

1922

Isabelle Ahearn O'Neill was the first woman elected to the Rhode Island General Assembly. A major textile strike resulted in the death of one worker.

1924

A bromide bomb exploded in the Senate chambers, ending a Democratic filibuster. Republican senators fled across state lines, preventing the Senate from having a quorum and paralyzing the state government.

1926

The Rhode Island Reds, a professional hockey team, began operations.

1928

Pope Pius XI excommunicated 63 petitioners of the French-Canadian "Sentinellist" protest. The Industrial Bank Building was completed.

1929

Opening of the Mt. Hope Bridge.

1930

The New York Yacht Club moved the America's Cup races to Rhode Island, where they remained until the Cup was lost in 1983.

1931

The nation's first state-owned airport was opened at Hillsgrove (later named T. F. Green Airport).

1934

Violent textile strike was ended by Rhode Island National Guard troops, resulting in the death of two strikers, with scores wounded. The Narragansetts reorganized and became incorporated. Voters approved a statue legalizing pari-mutuel betting on horse races, within 74 days Walter O'Hara opened Narragansett Park in Pawtucket.

1935

The Democrats gain control of Rhode Island government in the "Bloodless Revolution."

1936

Rhode Island was the first state to use voting machines in all districts.

1937

The "Race Track War:" Governor Robert Quinn declared martial law around Narragansett Park in Pawtucket, as part of the Quinn-O'Hara-McCoy "War of the Wild Irish Roses" for con-

Welders from Electric Boat, a division of General Dynamics, are fabricating pieces at Quonset Point for nuclear-powered submarine hulls in 1974. When the Navy withdrew from the state, Electric Boat was the first industrial tenant to occupy former aircraft hangers and other facilities. Courtesy, The Providence Journal

trol of the state's Democratic party.

1938

The Hurricane of 1938 killed 311 Rhode Islanders and caused over $100 million in damage.

1940

The Jamestown Bridge connected Narragansett and Jamestown.

1941

The Quonset Naval Air Station was commissioned.

1943

The Textron conglomerate corporation was formed.

1943–1945

A workforce that reached 21,000 built more than 60 liberty ships and armed cargo carriers at the Walsh-Kaiser shipyard in Providence.

1945

The *Black Point*, the last ship sunk by a German U-Boat, was torpedoed off of Point Judith. Germany surrendered the next day, but the U-853 was destroyed in Block Island Sound. John O. Pastore was the first Italian-American

governor of the state. Nearly all textile mills were closed by post-war strikes. The Preservation Society of Newport County was formed to save threatened historic houses.

1946

The American Screw Company relocated to Connecticut, marking the end of the second of Providence's "Five Industrial Wonders of the World."

1947

Rhode Island instituted its first sales tax.

1948

The state held its first primary election.

1949

WJAR-TV was Rhode Island's first television station.

1950

John O. Pastore was the first Italian-American to become a U.S. Senator.

1951

Textile workers struck at 16 mills in the state. The Rhode Island Development Council was established, which was renamed the Department of Economic Development in 1974.

1954 Hurricane Carol inundated Providence and 19 people died, Hurricane Edna followed two weeks later. The Nicholson File Company left Rhode Island after a five-month strike, ending the third of Providence's "Five Industrial Wonders of the World." The first Newport Jazz Festival was staged.

1955

Hurricane Diane brought the worst flooding in the history of the state, leading to 1961's construction of a hurricane barrier in Providence. Construction on Interstate 95 began.

1956

The threatened bulldozing of Benefit Street by urban renewal and Brown University's destruction of blocks of historic houses caused the organization of the Providence Preservation Society.

1964

The Brown & Sharpe Manufacturing Company moved from Providence to North Kingstown. The state decided to create Rhode Island Junior College, which was renamed the Community

College of Rhode Island in 1980.

1965

The Roger Williams National Memorial gained authorization. Governor John Chafee signed Rhode Island's first fair housing law.

1966

The last New England mill associated with "Fruit of the Loom" was closed. The construction of Interstate 95 was finished in Rhode Island. The Fox Point Hurricane Barrier was completed.

1968

Doris Duke founded the Newport Restoration Foundation to rescue threatened colonial homes. Midland Mall (now Rhode Island Mall) opened as the first suburban mall in the state.

1969

The Newport Bridge was opened (later renamed the Pell Bridge in honor of Senator Claiborne Pell). The Newport Music Festival was established, becoming one of the "Top 100 Events in North America" by the 1990s. The old Rhode Island Department of Agriculture and Conservation was reorganized as the Department of Natural Resources. In 1977 it was renamed the Department of Environmental Management.

1970

The Pawtucket Red Sox became the AAA farm team for the Boston Red Sox.

1971

Most of the American Screw Company's old factories were destroyed by a massive arson fire. Rhode Island adopted its first permanent personal income tax law. The Newport Jazz Festival ended after gate crashers rushed the stage and wrecked the scene. Bryant College moved to a new campus in Smithfield.

1972

The first campus of the new Rhode Island Junior College opened in Warwick. Warwick Mall was completed.

1973

The Cruiser-Destroyer Force of the U.S. Navy Atlantic Fleet was relocated from Rhode Island. Save the Bay was organized to stop pollution and clean up Narragansett Bay. Johnson & Wales College opened its culinary arts division, which became one of the nation's

leading culinary schools. The Providence Civic Center (now Dunkin' Donuts Center) was dedicated. The state ban on lotteries was repealed.

1974

The Rhode Island Lottery was established. Quonset Point Naval Air Station was decommissioned. Rhode Island Hospital Trust Tower was dedicated.

1975

Vincent Cianci became mayor of Providence, the first Republican mayor in 34 years. Lincoln Mall opened.

1976

John H. Chafee won a U.S. Senate seat, the first Republican since 1930 to win a Senate election in Rhode Island.

1976–1977

The Narragansett Bay Park system was formed. The first Parade of Tall Ships at Newport took place.

1977

The Rhode Island Reds finished last in the American Hockey League and were sold to Binghamton, New York.

1978

The worst blizzard on record in the state's history dumped three to five feet of snow and paralyzed the state for a week.

1979

The Narragansetts were officially restored as a tribe and awarded 1,800 acres of land in Charlestown, and a congressional appropriation in excess of $2.1 million for land purchases. Florence Kerins Murray became the first female member of the Rhode Island State Supreme Court.

1980

Claudine Schneider was the first woman elected to Congress from Rhode Island and the first Republican to win a congressional seat in the state since 1938. The relocation of the railroad tracks and the building of a new station began in downtown Providence.

1981

The longest game in the history of organized baseball ended with Pawtucket winning in the bottom of the 33rd inning.

1982

Susan Farmer was elected secretary of state, becoming Rhode Island's first female general officer. The "blue laws"

prohibiting Sunday sales was repealed.

1983

Providence Mayor Vincent Cianci was indicted for assault and extortion.

1984

Mayor Cianci was forced to resign as a result of his conviction on assault and extortion charges. Arlene Violet became Rhode Island and the nation's first female state attorney general. "First Night" came to Providence.

1985

Roger Williams National Memorial opened to the public. Hurricane Gloria struck Rhode Island; one person died. Joseph Bevilacqua, chief justice of the Rhode Island State Supreme Court, resigned in the midst of an impeachment inquiry into charges of corruption. Corruption was uncovered in the Rhode Island Housing Mortgage and Finance Corporation.

1987

The new railroad station in Providence was opened. Rhode Island's new constitution went into effect. Gorham Manufacturing Company moved from Providence to Smithfield.

1988

Construction began on Waterplace Park and the relocation of the downtown rivers in Providence.

1989

An oil tanker, *World Prodigy*, went aground, spilling millions of gallons of oil into Narragansett Bay.

1990

Bruce Sundlun was the first Jewish person to be elected governor of Rhode Island. The Citizens Bank Tower was completed. Raymond J. "Junior" Patriarca and most of his top Mafia lieutenants were arrested. The owner of Gorham Manufacturing Company, Dansk International, moved the headquarters to New York.

1991

The state-wide credit union crisis led to the closing of 45 credit unions and banks in Rhode Island. The renovation of Exchange Place was completed. Vincent Cianci became mayor of Providence again. Raymond J. "Junior" Patriarca pleaded guilty to racketeering, and he and his associates were imprisoned.

1992

The new Jamestown-Verrazzano Bridge opened. RIght Now! and Operation Clean Government, statewide reform coalitions founded by the religious community, pressured the General Assembly to reform state government. A bill was passed that ended the abuse of the state pension system by legislators. Another bill was enacted to end the "revolving door" for ex-state legislators' getting state jobs. The voters approved four-year terms for general officers, but rejected a pay raise for the legislature. Professional hockey returned with the Providence Bruins, a minor league affiliate of the Boston Bruins. The Newport Jazz Festival returned.

1993

Thomas Fay, Chief Justice of the Rhode Island State Supreme Court, was forced to resign in the face of impeachment proceedings because of corruption. Ex-Justice Fay and Court Administrator Matthew Smith both were indicted for using state money for personal use. Rhode Island's first law school opened at Roger Williams University. The new Rhode Island Convention Center was dedicated. Waterplace Park opened.

1994

Rhode Island State Auditor General Anthony Piccirilli was forced to resign as a result of a wide-ranging court scandal. Thomas Fay and Matthew Smith pleaded guilty to charges. Rhode Islanders voted to reduce the size of the General Assembly, effective in 2003, and state legislators had to choose whether to receive a salary of $10,000 or a future state pension. The new Westin Hotel opened. Artist Barnaby Evans created "WaterFire" on the rivers in downtown Providence. The last Navy ship to call Newport homeport departed.

1996

Reverend Geralyn Wolf was elected Bishop of the Episcopal Diocese of Rhode Island, only the second woman in the United States to head an Episcopal diocese. An earthquake, measuring 3.5 on the Richter scale, shook southern New England. Former Governor Edward DiPrete was indicted for racketeering,

This view of Garden City in Cranston dates from 1953. Established in 1947, Garden City was a 233-acre development that included single-family homes, apartment buildings, a school, and the state's first suburban shopping center. While the shopping center has since been eclipsed by newer and larger malls, such as Midland, Warwick, and Lincoln malls, it remains Rhode Island's only planned suburban shopping community. From the Rhode Island Development Council. Courtesy, Providence Public Library

extortion, and bribery. The *Providence Journal* was sold to the A.H. Belo Company of Dallas, Texas. The *North Cape* oil barge split open and spilled 800,000 gallons of oil onto Moonstone Beach.

1998

The Fleet Skating Center opened in downtown Providence. Former Governor Edward DiPrete pleaded guilty to 18 counts of racketeering, bribery, and extortion and was sentenced to one year in the Adult Correctional Institution.

1999

Providence Place Mall officially opened. Fleet Financial Group merged with BankBoston and moved its headquarters from Providence to Boston. Fleet was then bought by Bank of America for $47 billion in 2004.

2001

All of Brown & Sharpe, with the exception of a software unit, was bought by Hexagon AB of Sweden. The remaining division was sold in 2002. Federal "Plunder Dome" indictments and convictions for corruption in Providence city government were handed down. Mayor Vincent Cianci was indicted.

2002

Mayor Cianci and others were convicted of city hall corruption. The mayor was sentenced to five years in federal prison. The last elements of Gorham were transferred from the state.

2003

David Cicilline, an openly gay man, became mayor of Providence, promising reform and an end to corruption in municipal government. The two most expensive public works in the state's history, the relocation of I-195 in Providence and the sewage overflow project, began. An inferno at The Station in West Warwick killed 100 persons, the fourth worst nightclub fire in U.S. history. The state police raided the Narragansett Smoke Shop in Charlestown for selling untaxed cigarettes. A fire consumed the derelict Greenhalgh Mill and damaged or destroyed nearly 20 houses in Pawtucket.

2004

Senate President William Irons and Senator John Celona were forced to resign for ethics violations. An effort to expand T. F. Green Airport was initiated.

BIBLIOGRAPHY

State and local history, as it has been written, helps to shape a state's self-image and to mold perspectives on contemporary life. For the scholar such writings of the past are invaluable even when they are incomplete, unbalanced, and even fanciful. Rhode Island's written history is heavily concentrated on the colonial and early 19th century, leaving huge gaps for the post-Civil War era and the 20th century. We have attempted to fill the information voids by conducting much original research in archives, newspapers, government publications, and unpublished works. The following have been invaluable to our research: Rhode Island Historical Society's library, graphic, and manuscript divisions and its journal *Rhode Island History*; Newport Historical Society; the John Hay Library at Brown University; Rhode Island College's Special Collections which houses many of the older state histories and volumes of business biographies; Providence Public Library's Rhode Island Index and its R.I. Collection; Rhode Island State Archives; and the Rhode Island Jewish Historical Society and its journal *Rhode Island Jewish Historical Notes*. A valuable reference tool was the annual volumes of the *Providence Journal Bulletin Almanac* (1887–1998). Extremely helpful for economic developments and many other trends was the *Board of Trade Journal*, also known as the *Journal of Commerce* and as the *Providence Magazine*, which ran to 45 volumes (Providence: Providence Board of Trade [later Greater Providence Chamber of Commerce], 1889–1935). Also helpful were the published surveys of towns and historical districts conducted by the Rhode Island Historical Preservation Commission, and the periodic economic development surveys and reports issued by the Rhode Island Economic Development Corporation. Of course, we mined several newspapers, most important among them being, *The Providence Evening Bulletin, The Providence Journal, Woonsocket Call,* and the *Pawtucket Times*. What follows is a partial list of mostly secondary sources which shaped both our content and our interpretation.

Adler, Emily Stier and J. Stanley Lemons. *The Elect: Rhode Island's Women Legislators, 1922–1990*. Providence: The League of Rhode Island Historical Societies, 1990.

———. "The Independent Woman: Rhode Island's First Woman Legislator," *Rhode Island History,* 49 (February, 1991), 3–11.

Baldwin, Peter. "Becoming a City of Homes: The Suburbanization of Cranston, 1850–1910," *Rhode Island History,* 51 (February 1993), 3–21.

Barker, Harold C. *History of the Rhode Island Combat Units in the Civil War.* n.p., 1964.

Beck, Sam. *Manny Almeida's Ringside Lounge: The Cape Verdeans' Struggle for their Neighborhood.* Providence: Brown University Press, 1992.

Bourne, Russell. *The Red King's Rebellion: Racial Politics in New England, 1675–1678.* New York: Athenaeum, 1990.

Brett, Roger. *Temples of Illusion: The Golden Age of Theaters in an American City* [Providence]. Bristol, Rhode Island: Brett Theatricals, 1976.

Bridenbaugh, Carl. "Colonial Newport as a Summer Resort," *Rhode Island Historical Society Collections,* 26 (January 1933), 1–23.

———. *Fat Mutton and Liberty of Conscience: Society in Rhode Island, 1636–1690.* Providence: Brown University Press, 1974.

Buenker, John D. "Urban Liberalism in Rhode Island, 1909–1919," *Rhode Island History.* 30 (May 1971), 35–51.

Cady, John Hutchins. *The Civic and Architectural Development of Providence.* Providence: Ackerman Standard Press, 1957.

Carroll, Charles. *Rhode Island: Three Centuries of Democracy.* 4 volumes. New York: Lewis Historical Publishing Company, 1932.

Cassedy, James H. *Charles V. Chapin and the Public Health Movement.* Cambridge: Harvard University Press, 1962.

Cave, Alfred A. *The Pequot War.* Amherst: University of Massachusetts Press, 1996.

Chudacoff, Nancy. "The Revolution and the Town: Providence 1775–1783," *Rhode Island History,* 35 (August 1976), 71–89.

Chyet, Stanley. *Lopez of Newport: Colonial American Merchant Prince.* Detroit: Wayne State University Press, 1970.

Coleman, Peter. *The Transformation of Rhode Island, 1790–1860.* Providence: Brown University Press, 1963.

Collier, Theodore. "Providence in Civil War Days," *Rhode Island Historical Society Collections,* 27 (July 1934), 66–84.

Conforti, Joseph. *Our Heritage: A History of East Providence.* White Plains, New York: Monarch, 1976.

Conley, Patrick. *Democracy in Decline: Rhode Island's Constitutional Development, 1775–1841.* Providence: Rhode Island Historical Society, 1977.

Cottrol, Robert J. *The Afro-Yankees: Providence's Black Community in the Antebellum Era.* Westport, Connecticut: Greenwood Press, 1982.

Coughtry, Jay. *The Notorious Triangle: Rhode Island and the African Slave Trade, 1700–1807.* Philadelphia: Temple University Press, 1981.

Crane, Elaine Forman. *A Dependent People: Newport, Rhode Island in the Revolutionary Era.* New York: Fordham University Press, 1985.

Cronon, William. *Changes in the Land: Indians, Colonists and the Ecology of New England.* New York: Hill & Wang, 1983.

Daniels, Bruce C. *Dissent and Conformity on Narragansett Bay: The Colonial Rhode Island Town.* Scranton, Pennsylvania: Wesleyan University Press, 1983.

Dennison, George M. *The Dorr War: Republicanism on Trial, 1831–1861.* Lexington: University of Kentucky Press, 1976.

Downing, Antoinette E. and Vincent J. Scully, Jr., *The Architectural Heritage of Newport, Rhode Island, 1640–1915.* 2nd edition. New York: American Legacy Press, 1977.

Downs, Jacques M. *The Golden Ghetto: The American Commercial Community at Canton and the Shaping of American Foreign Policy, 1784–1844.* Bethlehem: Lehigh University Press, 1997.

Drake, James D. *King Philip's War: Civil War in New England, 1675–1676.* Amherst: University of Massachusetts Press, 1999.

Edwards, Knight. "Burnside: Rhode Island Hero," *Rhode Island History,* 16 (January 1957), 1–22.

Field, Edward. (ed.) *State of Rhode Island and Providence Plantations at the End of the Century: A History.* 3 volumes. Boston: Mason Publishing Co., 1902.

Findlay, James F. "The Great Textile Strike of 1934: Illuminating Rhode Island's History in the Thirties," *Rhode Island History,* 42 (February 1983), 17–29.

Fitts, Robert K. *Inventing New England's Slave Paradise: Master/Slave Relations in Eighteenth Century Narragansett, Rhode Island.* New York: Garland Publishing Co., 1998.

Fortin, Marcel (ed.). *Woonsocket, Rhode Island: A Centennial History, 1888–1988.* Woonsocket, Rhode Island: The Woonsocket Centennial Committee, 1988.

Gaustad. Edwin. *Liberty of Conscience: Roger Williams in America.* Valley Forge, Pennsylvania: Judson Press, 1999.

Gerstle, Gary. *Working Class Americanism: The Politics of Labor in a Textile City, 1914–1960.* Cambridge, England: Cambridge University Press, 1989.

Gersuny, Carl. "Seth Luther: The Road from Chepachet," *Rhode Island History,* 33 (May, 1974), 47–55.

Gettleman, Marvin. *The Dorr War: A Study in American Radicalism, 1833–1849.* New York: Random House, 1973.

Gilbane, Brendan F., "Pawtucket Village Mechanics: Iron, Ingenuity and the Cotton Revolution," *Rhode Island History,* 34 (Fall 1975), 3–11.

Gilkeson, John S. *Middle-Class Providence, 1820–1940.* Princeton: Princeton University Press, 1986.

Goldstein, Sidney. *The Greater Providence Jewish Community: A Population Survey.* Providence: Jewish Committee of Providence, 1964.

Goodman, Jay. *Democrats and Labor in Rhode Island, 1952–1962: Changes in the Old Alliance.* Providence: Brown University Press, 1967.

Greene, Welcome Arnold. *The Providence Plantations for Two Hundred and Fifty Years: An Historical Review of the Foundation, Rise and Progress of the City of Providence.* Providence: J.A. & R.A. Reid, 1886.

Hall, Joseph D. (ed.) *Biographical History of the Manufacturers and Businessmen of Rhode Island.* Providence: J. D. Hall, 1901.

Hartz, Louis. "Seth Luther: Working Class Rebel," *New England Quarterly,* 13 (September, 1940), 401–418.

Hayman, Robert. *Catholicism in Rhode Island, the Diocese of Providence, 1780–1886.* Providence: The Diocese of Providence, 1982.

————. *The Diocese of Providence, Rhode Island: A Short History, 1780–2000.* Strasbourg, France: Editions du Signe, 2000.

Hedges, James B. *The Browns of Providence Plantations.* 2 volumes. Providence: Brown University Press, 1952, 1968.

Herndon, Ruth Wallis. *Unwelcome Americans: Living on the Margin in Early New England.* Philadelphia: University of Pennsylvania Press, 2001.

Hoffman, Charles and Tess. *Brotherly Love: Murder and the Politics of Prejudice in Nineteenth Century Rhode Island.* Amherst: University of Massachusetts Press, 1993.

————. *North by South: The Two Lives of Richard James Arnold.* Athens: University of Georgia Press, 1988.

Ihlder, John. *The Houses of Providence: A Study of Present Conditions and Tendencies.* Providence, 1916.

James, Sydney V. *Colonial Rhode Island: A History.* New York: Scribner, 1975.

————. *John Clarke and His Legacies: Religion and Law in Colonial Rhode Island, 1638–1750.* Edited by Theodore Dwight Bozeman. University Park. Pennsylvania: Pennsylvania State University Press, 1999.

————. *The Colonial Metamorphoses in Rhode Island: A Study of Institutions in Change.* Edited by Sheila Skemp and Bruce C. Daniels. Hanover, New Hampshire: University Press of New England, 2000.

Jones, Daniel P. *The Economic and Social Transformation of Rural Rhode Island, 1780–1850.* Boston: Northeastern University Press, 1992.

Kellner, George H. and J. Stanley Lemons. *Rhode Island: The Independent State.* Woodland Hills, California: Windsor Publications, Inc., 1982.

————. "Providence: A Century of Greatness, 1832–1932, *Rhode Island History,* 41 (February, 1982), 3–18.

Kert, Bernice. *Abby Nelson Rockefeller: The Woman in the Family.* New York: Random House, 1993.

LaFantasie, Glenn W. "Act for All Reasons: Revolutionary Politics and May 4, 1776," *Rhode Island History,* 35 (1976), 39–47.

Lancaster, Jane. *Inquire Within: A Social History of the Providence Athenaeum since 1753.* Providence: The Providence Athenaeum, 2003.

Leach, Douglas Edward. *Flintlock and Tomahawk: New England in King Philip's War.* New York: W. W. Norton, 1966.

Lemons, J. Stanley and Michael McKenna, "The Re-enfranchisement of Rhode Island Negroes," *Rhode Island History,* 30 (February, 1971), 3–13.

Lemons, J. Stanley, and Diane Lambert. "John Carter Minkins: Pioneering African American Newspaperman," *New England Quarterly,* 76 (September, 2003), 413–438.

Lemons, J. Stanley. "Rhode Island and the Slave Trade," *Rhode Island History,* 60 (Fall 2002), 95–104.

————. "Rhode Island's Ten Turning Points: A Second Appraisal, "*Rhode Island History,* 45 (May 1986), 57–70.

————. "The Automobile Comes to Rhode Island," *Rhode Island History,"* 52 (August, 1994), 71–93.

————. *FIRST: The First Baptist Church in America.* Providence: Charitable Baptist Society, 2001.

Lepore, Jill. *The Name of War: King Philip's War and the Origins of American Identity.* New York: Knopf, 1998.

Levine, Erwin L. *Theodore Francis Green.* 2 volumes. Providence: Brown University Press, 1963, 1971.

Lovejoy, David S. *Rhode Island Politics and the American Revolution, 1760–1776.* Providence: Brown University Press, 1958.

Mayer, Kurt B. *Economic Development and Population Growth in Rhode Island.* Providence: Brown University Press, 1953.

McLoughlin, William. *Rhode Island: A Bicentennial History.* New York: W.W. Norton, 1978.

————. "Rhode Island's Ten Turning Points," *Rhode Island History,* 45 (May, 1986), 41–54.

Melish, Joanne Pope. *Disowning Slavery: Gradual Emancipation and "Race" in New England, 1780–1860.* Ithaca: Cornell University Press, 1998.

Mohr, Ralph S. *Governors for Three Hundred Years, 1638–1954, Rhode Island and Providence Plantations.* Providence: State of Rhode Island Graves Registration Committee, 1954.

Molloy, Scott. *Trolley Wars: Streetcar Workers on the Line.* Washington, DC: Smithsonian Institution, 1996.

————. *No Philanthropy at the Point of Production: A Knight of St. Gregory against the Knights of Labor, the 1885 Strike at the Woonsocket Rubber Company.* Kingston, Rhode Island: Rhode Island Labor History Society, 2003.

Morganthau, Ruth S. *Pride Without Prejudice: The Life of John O. Pastore.* Providence: Rhode Island Historical Society, 1989.

Polishook, Irwin H. *Rhode Island and the Union, 1774–1795.* Evanston, Illinois: Northwestern University Press, 1969.

Raub, Patricia. "Another Pattern of Urban Living: Multifamily Housing in Providence, 1890-1930," *Rhode Island History,* 48 (February 1990), 3–19.

Richardson, E. *History of Woonsocket.* Woonsocket: S.S. Foss, printer, 1876.

Rivard, Paul E. "Textile Experiments in Rhode Island, 1788–1789," *Rhode Island History,* 33 (May 1974), 35–45.

Schroder, Walter K. *Defense of Narragansett Bay in World War II.* Providence: Rhode Island Bicentennial Foundation, 1980.

Skemp, Sheila. "A Social and Cultural History of Newport, Rhode Island, 1720–1765." Unpublished Ph.D. thesis, University of Iowa, 1974. Ann Arbor University Microfilms.

Smith, Judith. *Family Connections: A History of Italian and Jewish Immigrant Lives in Providence, RI, 1900–1940.* Albany: State University of New York Press, 1985.

Smith, Matthew J. "The Real McCoy and the Bloodless Revolution of 1935," *Rhode Island History,* 32 (August 1973), 67–85.

Smith, Norman. "The Ku Klux Klan in Rhode Island," *Rhode Island History,* 37 (May 1978), 35–45.

Sorrell, Richard S. "Sentinelle Affair: Religion and Militant Survivance in Woonsocket, Rhode Island," *Rhode Island History,* 36 (August, 1977), 66–79.

Stanton, Mike. *The Prince of Providence: The True Story of Buddy Cianci, America's Most Notorious Mayor, Some Wiseguys, and the Feds.* New York: Random House, 2003.

Steffans, Lincoln. "Rhode Island: A State for Sale," *McClure's Magazine,* 24 (February, 1905), 337–353.

Sterns, Evelyn Savidge. *Ballots and Bibles: Ethnic Politics and the Catholic Church in Providence.* Ithaca: Cornell University Press, 2004.

Stokes, Howard K. *The Finances and Administration of Providence.* Baltimore: Johns Hopkins University Press, 1903.

Sullivan, Joseph. *Marxists, Militants & Macaroni: The I.W.W. in Providence's Little Italy.* Kingston, Rhode Island: Rhode Island Labor History Society, 2000.

Sweet, John Wood. *Bodies Politic: Negotiating Race in the American North, 1730–1830.* Baltimore: Johns Hopkins University Press, 2003.

Thomas, A. P. *Woonsocket: Highlights of History, 1800–1976: a Bicentennial Project for the City of Woonsocket.* East Providence: Woonsocket Opera House Society, 1976.

Thompson, Mack. *Moses Brown: Reluctant Reformer.* Chapel Hill: University of North Carolina Press, 1962.

Van Broekhoven, Deborah B. *The Devotion of These Women: Rhode Island in the Anti-slavery Network.* Amherst: University of Massachusetts Press, 2002.

What A Difference a Bay Makes. Providence: Rhode Island Historical Society and the Rhode Island Department of State Library Services, 1993.

Wheeler, Robert A. "Fifth Ward Irish: Immigrant Mobility in Providence, 1850–1870," *Rhode Island History,* 32 (May 1973), 52–61.

Williams, Roger. "Copy of a Letter of Roger Williams: Telling of the Burning of Providence and of his Conference with the Indians during King Philip's in 1676." Transcribed with introduction and notes by Bradford Swan. Providence: Rhode Island Historical Society, 1971.

Winslow, Ola E. *Master Roger Williams: A Biography.* New York: Macmillan, 1957.

Withey, Lynn. *Urban Growth in Colonial Rhode Island: Newport and Providence in the 18th Century.* Albany: State University Press of New York, 1984.

Woodward, William McKenzie, and Edward F. Sanderson. *Providence: A Citywide Survey of Historic Resources.* Providence: Rhode Island Historical Preservation Commission, 1986.

Wright, Marion and Robert J. Sullivan. *The Rhode Island Atlas.* Providence: Rhode Island Publications Society, 1982.

INDEX